De Facto States in Eurasia

This book explores the phenomenon of de facto states in Eurasia: states such as Abkhazia, Nagorno-Karabakh, and the Transnistrian Moldovan Republic. It examines how they are formed, what sustains them, and how their differing development trajectories have unfolded. It argues that most of these de facto states have been formed with either direct or indirect support from Russia, but they all have their own internal logic and are not simply puppets in the hands of a powerful patron. The book provides detailed case studies and draws out general patterns, and compares present-day de facto states with de facto states which existed in the past.

Tomáš Hoch and Vincenc Kopeček are Assistant Professors in the Department of Human Geography and Regional Development at Ostrava University, Czechia.

Routledge Contemporary Russia and Eastern Europe Series

83 **The City in Russian Culture**
Edited by Pavel Lyssakov and Stephen M. Norris

84 **The Russian Economy under Putin**
Edited by Torbjörn Becker and Susanne Oxenstierna

85 **New Conservatives in Russia and East Central Europe**
Edited by Katharina Bluhm and Mihai Varga

86 **Civil Society, Social Change, and a New Popular Education in Russia**
W. John Morgan, Irina N. Trofimova, and Grigori A. Kliucharev

87 **The Russian Economic Grip on Central and Eastern Europe**
Edited by Ognian Shentov, Ruslan Stefanov and Martin Vladimirov

88 **Law and Power in Russia**
Making Sense of Quasi-Legal Practices
Håvard Bækken

89 **Putin's Third Term as Russia's President, 2012–18**
J L Black

90 **Soviet and Post-Soviet Sexualities**
Edited by Richard C. M. Mole

91 **De Facto States in Eurasia**
Edited by Tomáš Hoch and Vincenc Kopeček

Seriesurl:https://www.routledge.com/Routledge-Contemporary-Russia-and-Eastern-Europe-Series/book-series/SE0766

De Facto States in Eurasia

Edited by
Tomáš Hoch and Vincenc Kopeček

LONDON AND NEW YORK

First published 2020
by Routledge
2 Park Square, Milton Park, Abingdon, Oxon OX14 4RN

and by Routledge
52 Vanderbilt Avenue, New York, NY 10017

Routledge is an imprint of the Taylor & Francis Group, an informa business

© 2020 selection and editorial matter, Tomáš Hoch and Vincenc Kopeček; individual chapters, the contributors

The right of Tomáš Hoch and Vincenc Kopeček to be identified as the authors of the editorial material, and of the authors for their individual chapters, has been asserted in accordance with sections 77 and 78 of the Copyright, Designs and Patents Act 1988.

All rights reserved. No part of this book may be reprinted or reproduced or utilised in any form or by any electronic, mechanical, or other means, now known or hereafter invented, including photocopying and recording, or in any information storage or retrieval system, without permission in writing from the publishers.

Trademark notice: Product or corporate names may be trademarks or registered trademarks, and are used only for identification and explanation without intent to infringe.

British Library Cataloguing-in-Publication Data
A catalogue record for this book is available from the British Library

Library of Congress Cataloging-in-Publication Data
Names: Hoch, Tomáš, 1980– editor. | Kopeček, Vincenc, 1980– editor.
Title: De facto states in Eurasia / edited by Tomáš Hoch and Vincenc Kopeček.
Description: Abingdon, Oxon ; New York, NY : Routledge, 2019. | Series: Routledge contemporary Russia and Eastern Europe series ; 91 | Includes bibliographical references and index.
Identifiers: LCCN 2019016166 (print) | LCCN 2019019526 (ebook) | ISBN 9780429244049 (eBook) | ISBN 9780429520785 (Adobe Reader) | ISBN 9780429548956 (Mobipocket) | ISBN 9780429534256 (ePub3) | ISBN 9780367199128 (hardback) | ISBN 9780429244049 (ebk)
Subjects: LCSH: Former Soviet republics—Politics and government. | Self-determination, National—Former Soviet republics. | Former Soviet republics—History—Autonomy and independence movements. | Former Soviet republics—Administrative and political divisions. | Former Soviet republics—Foreign relations—Russia (Federation) | Russia (Federation)—Foreign relations—Former Soviet republics.
Classification: LCC DK295 (ebook) | LCC DK295 .D4 2019 (print) | DDC 947.08—dc23
LC record available at https://lccn.loc.gov/2019016166

ISBN: 978-0-367-19912-8 (hbk)
ISBN: 978-0-429-24404-9 (ebk)

Typeset in Times New Roman
by codeMantra

Printed in the United Kingdom
by Henry Ling Limited

Contents

List of maps	ix
List of tables	xi
Notes on contributors	xiii
Note on the transcription and usage of geographical names	xvii
Acknowledgement	xix
Abbreviations	xxi

Introduction   1
VINCENC KOPEČEK AND TOMÁŠ HOCH

SECTION 1
De facto statehood: understanding the concept   9

1.1 Terminology   11
EMIL ASLAN SOULEIMANOV

1.2 De facto statehood: overview of the research   16
TOMÁŠ HOCH

1.3 De facto states and other unrecognized entities in Eurasia   27
VINCENC KOPEČEK

SECTION 2
Russian territorial expansion and de facto states in the first half of 20th century   41

2.1 Introduction to Russian and Soviet territorial expansion   43
VLADIMÍR BAAR AND SLAVOMÍR HORÁK

vi *Contents*

2.2 Bukharan People's Soviet Republic: from protectorate to SSR 46
SLAVOMÍR HORÁK

2.3 Tuva and Mongolia: between annexation and independence 63
VLADIMÍR BAAR, BARBARA BAAROVÁ AND
JAROSLAV KURFÜRST

SECTION 3
The emergence of de facto states 79

3.1 Factors of de facto states' formation in the post-Soviet area 81
TOMÁŠ HOCH

3.2 Formation of de facto states in Abkhazia and South Ossetia 86
TOMÁŠ HOCH AND EMIL ASLAN SOULEIMANOV

3.3 Nagorno-Karabakh and Javakheti: two different trajectories of
Armenian separatist movements 109
VINCENC KOPEČEK

3.4 Unfinished story of the Donetsk and Luhansk People's
Republics: towards a de facto state? 136
ALEXANDRA ŠMÍDOVÁ AND TOMÁŠ ŠMÍD

SECTION 4
How de facto states are sustained and instrumentalized 157

4.1 Factors of de facto states' sustainability 159
VINCENC KOPEČEK

4.2 Unrecognized states as a means of Russia's coercive diplomacy?
An empirical analysis 168
EDUARD ABRAHAMYAN

4.3 The patron-client relationship between Russia and Transnistria 183
MARCIN KOSIENKOWSKI

4.4 The Nagorno-Karabakh Republic and the Republic
of Armenia: who instrumentalizes whom? 208
VINCENC KOPEČEK

Contents vii

4.5 Inside a de facto state: forming and sustaining the Abkhazian and Nagorno-Karabakh Republic polities 225
VINCENC KOPEČEK

SECTION 5
Why de facto states fail 247

5.1 Possible ends of de facto states 249
VINCENC KOPEČEK

5.2 Explaining de facto states' failure 252
HUSEYN ALIYEV

5.3 Why de facto states fail. Lessons from the Chechen Republic of Ichkeria 262
EMIL ASLAN SOULEIMANOV

5.4 The emergence and failure of the Gagauz Republic (1989–1995) 274
SLAVOMÍR HORÁK

Conclusion 296
VINCENC KOPEČEK AND TOMÁŠ HOCH

Index 299

List of maps

1	Post-Soviet de facto states (including borderline cases and occupied territories)	2
2	Bukharan People's Soviet Republic (1920–1924)	47
3	Tuva and Mongolia between the First World War and the Second World War	64
4	South Ossetia	87
5	Abkhazia	89
6	Nagorno-Karabakh and Javakheti	110
7	Donetsk and Luhansk People's Republics	137
8	Chechnya	263
9	Gagauzia and Transnistria	275

List of tables

1   Post-Soviet de facto states (including borderline cases)   35

Notes on contributors

Eduard Abrahamyan is a doctoral research fellow at the University of Leicester, School of History, Politics & International Relations. His main area of expertise is the evolution of NATO's security and partnership policies in the Black Sea, Caucasus, and Central Asia. He is a regular contributor to the *Jane's Security: Military Capabilities Module, Jamestown Foundation, National Interest,* and *CACI Analyst.* Besides analytical texts, he has also published in the *Journal of Southeast European and Black Sea Studies.*

Huseyn Aliyev holds a PhD in Political Science from the University of Otago in Dunedin, New Zealand, and works as an Assistant Professor at the Central & East European Studies Centre, School of Social and Political Sciences, University of Glasgow, United Kingdom. His research interests include civil wars, non-state armed groups, informal politics, and institutions in the former Soviet Union and beyond. Huseyn is the author of over twenty articles in prestigious international journals, including *International Security, Journal of Strategic Studies, Security Dialogue, Political Violence and Terrorism, Europe-Asia Studies, Problems of Post-Communism, Third World Quarterly,* and *Journal of Southeast European and Black Sea Studies.* He also authored several monographs, including *When Informal Institutions Change. Institutional Reforms and Informal Practices in the former Soviet Union* (University of Michigan Press, 2017), *Post-Communist Civil Society and the Soviet Legacy: Challenges of Democratisation and Reform in the Caucasus* (Palgrave Macmillan, 2015), *Individual Disengagement of Avengers, Nationalists and Jihadists: Why Ex-Militants Choose to Abandon Violence in the North Caucasus* (with Emil Aslan Souleimanov, Palgrave Macmillan, 2014), and *How Socio-Cultural Codes Shaped Violent Mobilization and Pro-Insurgent Support in the Chechen Wars* (with Emil Aslan Souleimanov, Palgrave Macmillan, 2017).

Vladimír Baar is a Professor and the Head of the Department of Human Geography and Regional Development, Faculty of Science, University of Ostrava, Czechia. His research covers political and economic

xiv *Notes on contributors*

transformation in the post-Soviet area as well as historical geography of the same region. Vladimir has published more than fifty academic articles in Czech and international journals, including *Europe-Asia Studies, Problems of Post-Communism, Bulletin of Geography, Journal of Nationalism Memory and Language Politics,* etc. He has authored several Czech language monographs and university textbooks.

Barbara Baarová is an Assistant Professor at the Department of Human Geography and Regional Development, University of Ostrava, Czechia. Her research interests focus on issues of nationalism and religious and linguistic issues in geographic education, in particular in the post-Communist area. Barbara has published several articles and book chapters in Czech, Polish, and English, and is an author of four textbooks.

Tomáš Hoch studied political and cultural geography at the Department of Human Geography and Regional Development, University of Ostrava, Czechia, where he is currently working as an Assistant Professor. His research focusses on the nationalism, separatism, conflict transformation, state-building, and nation-building processes inside of the post-Soviet de facto states. His recent publications include articles in *Europe-Asia Studies, Problems of Post-Communism, Iran and the Caucasus,* and *Bulletin of Geography.*

Slavomír Horák is an Assistant Professor at the Department of Russian and East European Studies, Institute of International Studies, Faculty of Social Sciences, Charles University in Prague, Czechia. His research covers political, social, and economic issues in the former USSR, with a focus on Central Asia, particularly on Turkmenistan's domestic issues, informal politics, and state- and nation-building. He is the author of numerous articles published in respected international journals (*Problems of Post-Communism, Central Asian Survey, Nationalities Papers, The China and Eurasia Forum Quarterly, Central Asian Affairs, Demokratizatsiya,* etc.), of several book chapters, and of five Czech language monographs.

Vincenc Kopeček holds a PhD in Political and Cultural Geography and works as an Assistant Professor at the Department of Human Geography, University of Ostrava, Czechia. In his research, he focusses on ethnic minorities, de facto states, and informal politics in the South Caucasus. He has published in *Europe-Asia Studies, Problems of Post-Communism, Caucasus Survey,* the *Annual of Language & Politics and Politics of Identity* (renamed *Journal of Nationalism, Memory and Language Politics*), and *Bulletin of Geography.*

Marcin Kosienkowski holds a PhD in Political Science from Maria Curie-Skłodowska University in Lublin, Poland. He works as an Assistant Professor at the Department of International Relations, Institute of Political Science and International Affairs, Faculty of Social Sciences, The John Paul II Catholic University of Lublin, Poland. Marcin's area of expertise

Notes on contributors xv

is separatism, nation-building, conflict transformation, digital diplomacy, and economic transformation in the post-Soviet area, in particular in Moldova, Transnistria, and Gagauzia. He has published numerous articles in Polish and English language journals, including the *Soviet and Post-Soviet Review*, and several books and book chapters in respected Polish and international publishing houses (Manchester University Press, Lexington Books, Catholic University of Lublin Publishing House).

Jaroslav Kurfürst holds a PhD in Political and Cultural Geography from the University of Ostrava, Czechia, and works at the Ministry of Foreign Affairs of the Czech Republic. He held a number of high-ranked diplomatic positions in Czech embassies in Russia, the United States, and Belgium. He was also the Director of the Security Policy Department, the Director of the EU Common Foreign and Security Policy Department, and the Chief Director of the European Section at the Ministry of Foreign Affairs of the Czech Republic. His academic area of interest is Russian geopolitics in both regional and global contexts. Jaroslav has published in several Czech and English language journals, including *East European Thought* and *Czech Journal of International Relations*, and he is also an author of a Czech language monograph on Russian geopolitics.

Tomáš Šmíd holds a PhD in Political Science from the Masaryk University in Brno, Czechia, where he works as an Assistant Professor at the Department of Political Science, Faculty of Social Science. His area of expertise includes asymmetric security threats (organized crime, ethnic conflicts, terrorism) and conflict research in the post-Soviet area, the Caucasus in particular. Tomáš is the author of more than thirty academic papers, including articles in *Journal of Strategic Studies, European Journal of Criminology, Czech Journal of Political Science*, etc., and five Czech language monographs.

Alexandra Šmídová is a PhD student at the Department of Political Science, Masaryk University, in Brno, Czechia. Her research interest is focussed on the issues of nationalism, ethnic conflicts, and security in the post-Soviet area, Ukraine in particular.

Emil Aslan Souleimanov is an Associate Professor at the Department of Security Studies, Institute of Political Studies, Faculty of Social Sciences, Charles University, in Prague, Czechia. His area of expertise is irregular war, civil war, asymmetric conflict, ethnic conflict, insurgency, counterinsurgency, nationalism, historiography, and politics of memory in the Caucasus and the adjacent areas of Russia, Turkey, and Iran. Emil has authored around thirty articles in high-ranked international journals and several English-language monographs, including *How Socio-Cultural Codes Shaped Violent Mobilization and Pro-Insurgent Support in the Chechen Wars* (co-author Huseyn Aliyev, Palgrave Macmillan, 2017), *Individual Disengagement of Avengers, Nationalists and Jihadists:*

xvi *Notes on contributors*

Why Ex-Militants Choose to Abandon Violence in the North Caucasus (co-author Huseyn Aliyev, Basingstoke: Palgrave Macmillan, 2014), and *Understanding Ethnopolitical Conflict: Karabakh, Abkhazia, and South Ossetia Wars Reconsidered* (Basingstoke: Palgrave Macmillan, 2013).

Note on the transcription and usage of geographical names

Although this edited volume deals with the post-Soviet/Eurasian region, we do not regard it as a territorial study, and we do not expect the readers to know local languages, writing systems, and the peculiarities of their Romanization. Moreover, names and terms from at least 15 languages (Russian, Ukrainian, Georgian, Armenian, Azerbaijani, Moldovan, Abkhazian, Ossetian, Chechen, Gagauz, Uzbek, Tajik, Tuvan, Mongolian, and Chinese) appear in this volume; the usage of 15 different language-specific transliteration/transcription systems would only make the book less accessible. Thus, we have decided to keep the transcription into English as simple as possible, and we always use a transcription system with intuitive pronunciation for English-speakers.

The transcription of names from languages using non-Latin alphabets is mostly based on the BGN/PCGN (United States Board on Geographic Names/ Permanent Committee on Geographical Names for British Official Use) Romanization system. In order to make the text even more legible, we transcribe several letters of the Russian and Ukrainian alphabets differently from the BGN/PCGN system. Whereas the BGN/PCGN transcribes Russian and Ukrainian "й" as "y", we write, in accordance with the Post-Soviet Affairs journal, "i". We also do not transcribe "ь" and "ъ" (soft and hard signs), only in cases when the omission of the sign would substantially change the pronunciation. We write "y" instead of the hard sign (e.g. we write *syezd*, not *s"ezd*, as would be the BGN/PCGN transcription, or *sezd*, the transcription which would completely omit the hard sign) or "i" instead of the soft sign (e.g. we write *Pridnestrovie*, not *Pridnestrov'e* or *Pridnestrove*). Unlike the BGN/PCGN transliteration system, which transcribes Russian "ё" as "ë", which rather implies the French pronunciation of the sign, we transcribe it as "yo". Exceptions are made for the names of well-known people where a different spelling has become conventional, such as Gorbachev, not Gorbachyov. Transcriptions of lesser known names from Chechen, Abkhazian, Ossetian, Tajik, Mongolian, and Tuvan, which also use Cyrillic, follow the pattern used for Russian and Ukrainian.

Names from other languages which use non-Latin alphabets, specifically Georgian and Armenian, are also mostly transcribed according to the BGN/PCGN Romanization system – with several differences, which are designed to make the text more understandable for English-speakers. For example, we do not differentiate between the aspired and non-aspired consonants, such as the Georgian "ვ" and "ქ", which we both transcribe as "k",

xviii *Note on the transcription and usage of geographical names*

or glottalized and non-glottalized consonants, such as the Georgian "ც" and "წ", which we both transcribe as "ts".

In the case of Moldovan, Uzbek, Gagauz, and Azerbaijani, which have switched from Cyrillic to Latin alphabets, we use the Latin-based versions of the names. We avoid the usage of specific graphemes or diacritics which are pronounced differently from English and would not be easily understood by English readers. We have transcribed these analogously to the BGN/PCGN Romanization of Russian. For example, when transcribing Azerbaijani or Uzbek names, instead of "ş" we write "sh", instead of "ı" we write "y", instead of "x" we write "kh", and instead of "c" we write "j", and we also use a simple "o" instead of "o'/ў" (e.g. Khojayev instead of Xo'jaev). In the case of Gagauz we omit "ä" and use "ya", we also write "ch" instead of "ç", "ts" instead of "ţ", a simple "e" instead of a hard "ê", as well as "sh" instead of "ş". We use "gh" in order to transcribe Georgian "ღ", Azerbaijani "ğ", or Uzbek "g", which sound similar to the French "r". In the case of Moldovan, we omit the diacritics. For Chinese, we use both Pinyin and Wade-Giles transcriptions (Wade-Giles in brackets).

For place names, we use the English exonyms where possible. Historical names, including geographical names, are used in an appropriate historical form and transcribed into English: for example, in the context of the 19th century we write Tiflis and not Tbilisi, or, if the person living in the 19th century was known under the Russian version of his/her name, we use the Russian version, even if there is a modern Uzbek, Azerbaijani, Armenian, etc. version of the same name.

A particularly problematic and sensitive issue is how to write place names from contested regions. To avoid confusion, we use the version which was in official use before the conflict had started. This is why we write, for example, Sukhumi (instead of Sukhum), Tskhinvali (instead of Tskhinval), Bendery (instead of Tighina), Stepanakert (instead of Khankendy), or Lachin (instead of Berdzor). When necessary, the less clear cases are explained in the footnotes.

There is also a question when denoting administrative units, whether to use the original terms (Russian, Ukrainian, Georgian, etc.) or their English equivalents. In order to make the book more intelligible for those whose field of study is not primarily the post-Soviet area, we have chosen the second option. Thus, we avoid the usage of the Russian (and Ukrainian) terms *krai* and *oblast*, which we translate into English by a single word: "region".[1] The Russian-language term *raion*, which is also used by other languages from the post-Soviet area, we translate as district. We use the same logic in reference to other languages – for example, we use the English term province instead of the Georgian *mkhare*, etc. In each chapter, however, the original term denoting the administrative unit or administrative position is given in brackets when first used.

Note

1 In tsarist Russia, *oblast* was an ordinary administrative unit, whereas *krai* was understood as a border region (literary *krai* means a "periphery"). In the Soviet Union, some of the oblasts had an autonomous status, a lower one than the autonomous republics. In the Russian Federation, *oblasts* and *krais* still exist as subjects of federation; however, their competences are the same.

Acknowledgement

This book has been prepared as a part of the project "De Facto States in Northern Eurasia in the Context of Russian Foreign Policy" (GACR 15-09249S), financed by the Czech Science Foundation.

Parts of Chapters 1.1 and 4.2 have been previously published in the *Journal of Southeast European and Black Sea Studies* in the article "Emil Aslan Souleimanov, Eduard Abrahamyan & Huseyn Aliyev (2018): Unrecognized states as a means of coercive diplomacy? Assessing the role of Abkhazia and South Ossetia in Russia's foreign policy in the South Caucasus, Southeast European and Black Sea Studies, 18 (1): 73–86". And parts of Chapters 5.2 and 5.3 have been previously published in the *Problems of Post-Communism* article "Huseyn Aliyev & Emil Aslan Souleimanov (2017): Why Do De Facto States Fail? Lessons from the Chechen Republic of Ichkeria, published online 11 Dec 2017". We would like to express our gratitude to these journals and their publisher, Taylor and Francis, for granting us the permission to use this material.

We would also like to thank our colleague Luděk Krtička, who created all maps for this monograph, for his help with the project.

Other people who deserve our sincere thanks are Christopher James Hopkinson and Richard Grenville Connor for their diligent proofreading of the manuscript. Finally, thanks to Peter Sowden at Routledge, and to the anonymous reviewers, for believing in this monograph and for their many useful suggestions which have turned this into a much better book. Any errors of fact or interpretation are, of course, our own responsibility.

Tomáš Hoch and Vincenc Kopeček

Abbreviations

A2/AD	Anti-Access/Area Denial
ASSR	Autonomous Soviet Socialist Republic
ATO	Anti-terrorist operation
BGN/PCGN	United States Board on Geographic Names/ Permanent Committee on Geographical Names for British Official Use
CIS	Commonwealth of Independent States
CSTO	Collective Security Treaty Organization
DCFTA	Deep and Comprehensive Free Trade Area
DKSR	Donetsk-Krivoy Rog Soviet Republic
DPR	Donetsk People's Republic
DRC	Democratic Republic of Congo
EAEU	Eurasian Economic Union
EU	European Union
FER	Far Eastern Republic
FSB	Russian Federal Security Service
GDP	Gross domestic product
IDPs	Internally displaced persons
JPKF	Joint Peacekeeping Force
LPR	Luhansk People's Republic
MP	Member of Parliament
MILF	Moro Islamic Liberation Front
MNLF	Moro National Liberation Front
NATO	North Atlantic Treaty Organization
NGO	Non-governmental organization
NKAR	Nagorno-Karabakh Autonomous Region
NKR	Nagorno-Karabakh Republic
NKVD	People's Commissariat for Internal Affairs
OGRF	Operational Group of Russian Forces
OSCE	Organization for Security and Co-operation in Europe
PSR	People's Soviet Republic
R2P	Responsibility to Protect
RSFSR	Russian Soviet Federative Socialist Republic

xxii   *Abbreviations*

RSR	Russian Soviet Republic
SBU	Ukrainian security service
SFSR	Soviet Federative Socialist Republic
SPLA	Sudan People's Liberation Army
SSR	Soviet Socialist Republic
TPR	Tuvan People's Republic
UN	United Nations
UNOMIG	United Nations Observer Mission in Georgia
UNRS	Ukrainian People's Republic of Soviets
USA	United States of America
USR	Ukrainian Soviet Republic
USSR	Union of Soviet Socialist Republics

Introduction

Vincenc Kopeček and Tomáš Hoch

Since the beginning of the 20th century, Eurasia[1] has witnessed two waves of political-territorial restructuring. The first wave took place in 1917–1925. It started with the collapse of the tsarist government and the Bolshevik coup d'état, and ended after the victory of the Bolshevik forces in the civil war and with the consolidation of the newly formed Soviet Union in early 1920s. The second wave has started in late 1980s, in the liberalization period of the late Soviet Union, when first nationalist movements began to formulate demands on changing status of their autonomous units – and seems that it has not come to its end so far. The events which followed after the 2014 Maidan Protests in Ukraine led to nothing else than to another political-territorial restructuring. Each of these two waves of political-territorial restructuring led not only to regime changes and the formation of newly independent and internationally recognized states but also to the formation of a number of internationally unrecognized and in most cases temporary political entities. Some of them, however, lasted for a longer period (several years or even decades), successfully governed their claimed territories, and were perceived as legitimate entities by substantial parts of their populations; but despite their factual existence they were recognized by only a handful of states or not at all. These entities are called de facto states[2] and this edited volume is dedicated to them.

In past decades, dozens of de facto states have appeared in almost all continents and macro regions – in Europe (e.g. Serbian Krajina, Republika Srpska, Northern Cyprus), Asia (e.g. Tamil Eelam, East Timor), Africa (e.g. Biafra, Katanga, Somaliland), Oceania (Bougainville), or the Caribbean (Anguilla). However, it is Eurasia, which is a home of most of the present-day de facto states (Map 1).

The book mostly deals with the five de facto states which emerged after the dissolution of the Soviet Union, that is, the Transnistrian Moldovan Republic, the Republic of Abkhazia, the Republic of South Ossetia, the Nagorno-Karabakh Republic, and the Chechen Republic of Ichkeria,[3] and three borderline cases from the same period, that is, the Gagauz Republic, the Donetsk People's Republic, and the Luhansk People's Republic.[4] In early 1990s, the post-Soviet area became a scene of numerous conflicts,

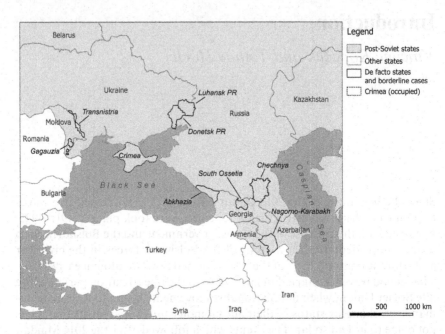

Map 1 Post-Soviet de facto states (including borderline cases and occupied territories).
Source: Authors.

and in most of them ethnicity played important if not crucial role. In some cases ethnic mobilization escalated into a violent conflict[5] and de facto separation of the self-declared entity. These entities, which we call de facto states, differed in their geographical location, internal political development, administrative structure, demographic homogeneity, economic characteristics, relations with the outside world, and also with their parent state (i.e. the state from which they attempted to break away). Some of these de facto states existed only for a short period before being re-absorbed by their parent states. The most visible examples of these short-lived entities are Gagauzia and the Chechen Republic of Ichkeria; both of them had been re-incorporated into their parent state (Moldova and Russia, respectively) relatively quickly. But in the cases of Abkhazia, South Ossetia, Nagorno-Karabakh, and Transnistria, the breakaway entities have not been re-incorporated into their parent state so far. These four de facto states all emerged as a consequence of armed conflicts in the early 1990s. On the one hand, their governments gained control over most of the territory they claimed and were relatively successful in the process of nation-building; on the other hand, they were either unable or unwilling to reach an agreement on their political status with the governments of their parent states. Although these conflicts are sometimes labelled as "frozen", the opposite

Introduction 3

is true. These conflicts can be labelled by many different names, but they are certainly not lacking dynamics. By 1994 the armed phases of the conflicts in Abkhazia, South Ossetia, Nagorno-Karabakh, and Transnistria have ended up in signing a ceasefire; however, all of them (except Transnistria) have continued to be the scenes of periodic escalations of violence (e.g. Abkhazia in 1998 and 2008; South Ossetia in 2004 and 2008; Nagorno-Karabakh in 2008, 2015, and 2016). Periodically recurring escalation of violence is only the most visible tip of the iceberg in the conflict dynamic, while these changes have also been accompanied by many significant transformations inside of respective societies.

The authors of the book claim that the emergence of de facto entities is nothing new in Eurasia and that there is a number of parallels which can be drawn between present de facto states and similar entities which existed in the past. Thus, the Bukharan People's Soviet Republic, the Tuvan People's Republic, and the Mongolian People's Republic are also analysed in this book. It seems that those de facto states, which have formed in Eurasia during both waves of political-territorial restructuring, have more things in common, and that there are similar factors behind their formation, sustainability, and also behind their potential demise. We argue that the formation of a number of de facto states in this region is not coincidental, and that substantial number of these de facto states have been used as specific tools in the frame of Russian/Soviet foreign policy in general and territorial expansion in particular. Further we claim, however, that to see these entities only as puppets in the hands of their powerful patrons would be an unacceptable simplification. All these de facto entities have their own inner logic and their performance is a result of a complex interplay of internal and external factors.

The book is structured into five sections which follow the logic of the life cycle of de facto state – from its formation (Section 3) through sustainability (Section 4) to possible failure and demise (Section 5). The book does not provide historical narratives of all de facto states in Eurasia, but on selected cases it provides an empirical analysis of formation, sustainability, and possible failure and demise of a de facto state. Each section begins with a brief theoretical overview of a particular problem followed by three to four case studies. Sections 1 and 2 are, however, somewhat different. In Section 1 the concept of de facto state is introduced (Chapter 1.1), followed by an overview of research on de facto states (Chapter 1.2) and an overview of de facto states and other unrecognized political entities from both waves of political-territorial restructuring in Eurasia (Chapter 1.3). Section 2 focusses on the first wave of political-territorial restructuring (1917–1925) and its aim is to draw parallels between the historical cases of Eurasia's de facto states and present-day de facto states. We argue that despite different geopolitical and historical contexts, the nature of de facto states is basically the same – and that this very fact enables us to learn from concluded life cycles of past de facto states. Chapter 2.1 deals with the logic of Russian territorial

4   Vincenc Kopeček and Tomáš Hoch

expansion which ultimately led to a formation of several de facto states in Russia's Far East. Chapter 2.2 is a historical narrative of the Bukharan People's Soviet Republic, which was formed from the Khanate of Bukhara (Russian protectorate), and ended up as a part of the Soviet Union in 1925. The main argument of the chapter is that although the Bukharan People's Soviet Republic was annexed by its patron state, in fact it continued to exist in a form of the Uzbek SSR, which eventually became an independent state in 1991. Chapter 2.3 is a comparative study of two Far Eastern de facto states – Mongolia and Tuva. Whereas both entities had similar origins and were perceived as Soviet puppet states before the Second World War, their fates were quite different. Whereas Tuva became voluntarily part of the USSR in 1944, Mongolia was finally recognized by the international community and admitted to the UN in 1961.

Section 3 focusses on the emergence of de facto states. Whereas in Chapter 3.1 main theoretical arguments on the emergence of de facto state are formulated, Chapter 3.2 is a comparative study of two de facto states which formed in the territory of Georgia in early 1990s – Abkhazia and South Ossetia. Chapter 3.3 is also a comparative study but focusses on two cases of ethnic Armenian separatism – Nagorno-Karabakh and Javakheti. It aims at identifying reasons why Nagorno-Karabakh did separate as a de facto state and why Javakheti did not. Chapter 3.4 is again a comparative study analysing the formation of the Donetsk and Luhansk People's Republics and answers a question to what extent these two newly born entities can be considered de facto states.

Section 4 aims at how de facto states are internally sustained or externally instrumentalized. In Chapter 4.1 basic theoretical arguments are formulated; the argument here is that besides the fact that at least Russia (mis-)uses several post-Soviet de facto states in order to follow its own strategic goals, de facto states are not mere puppets in the hands of their powerful neighbours and their viability is caused also by their internal cohesion and endeavour to behave as a state. Chapter 4.2 focusses on patron state's influence on the example of Russia and three South Caucasus de facto states – Abkhazia, South Ossetia, and Nagorno-Karabakh; it aims to unveil how Russia uses these de facto states as coercive policy tools against Georgia, Armenia, and Azerbaijan. In Chapter 4.3 the patron-client relationship is discussed in more detail on the example of Russia and Transnistria. Chapter 4.4 provides rather a different view of relations between de facto state and its patron. It aims at analysing the complex relations between the Nagorno-Karabakh Republic and the Republic of Armenia, which is not only Nagorno-Karabakh's patron state but also its kin-state. The main argument of the chapter is that unlike the relations between Russia and its client de facto states, Armenian-Karabakhi relations are more equal and also complex and that it is not only Armenia, which has influence in Karabakh, but that it is also Karabakh, which is capable to influence the decision-making processes in Armenia mostly by informal means. Chapter 4.5 provides an insight to

Introduction 5

the internal development in de facto states. It brings an empirical analysis of internal politics of Abkhazia and Nagorno-Karabakh, with a particular focus on development of political institutions.

Section 5 deals with the possible failure of de facto states. Whereas Chapter 5.1 discusses possible ends of de facto states – internal failure followed by a likely demise being one of them – the following chapters focus exclusively on an understudied phenomenon of de facto state's failure. Chapter 5.2 draws from the general literature on state failure and offers several concepts which in the opinion of the author play a role in de facto state's failure. Chapter 5.3 thoroughly applies these concepts on the case of Chechnya. The main argument here is that the internal failure of the Chechen Republic of Ichkeria in fact made it easier for Russia to reintegrate this breakaway entity. Chapter 5.4 focusses on the case of Gagauzia, which is a borderline case of de facto state and which lasted only for about three years. Although it aims at Gagauzia's failure and draws from the theoretical arguments made in Chapter 5.2, the author also shows how the process of Gagauzia's formation contained from its very beginnings germs of its own failure, which resulted into a peaceful reintegration into its parent state.

The inner logic of this book is thus to focus on the life cycle of post-Soviet de facto states and answer three main research questions: (1) Why de facto states emerge, (2) how they are sustained, and (3) which factors contribute to their demise. We do believe that the phenomenon of a de facto state in Eurasia is endemic, and if we want to understand currently existing post-Soviet de facto states, it is useful to turn our attention also to similar entities that existed in the period of formation of the Soviet Union.

Notes

1 The geographical name Eurasia has two different meanings. In political geography or geopolitics, it is often used for a territory of the former Soviet Union and some adjacent regions. However, in physical geography, the term Eurasia refers to the landmass of Europe and Asia, which is much larger than Eurasia in political geographical or geopolitical sense. Because we want to avoid the stereotype of approaching the region as primarily post-Soviet (i.e. we also analyse the pre-Soviet period), we decided to employ rather a neutral term Eurasia in its geopolitical sense.

2 During the past twenty years, several competing terms appeared in the scholarly literature, for example, unrecognized states, quasi states, contested states, or pseudo states. However, we consider the term "de facto state" as the most appropriate, neutral, and widely used, so it became our clear choice. From our point of view, a great number of seemingly synonymous terms (some of them also imbued with semantic nuances) have somewhat unnecessarily obscured the research field. For the discussion about the terminological profusion and different conceptualizations see Chapter 1.1.

3 In order to make the text more legible, we strive to avoid the usage of political names of de facto states where possible and prefer to use their geographical names. Thus, we mostly write Transnistria, Abkhazia, South Ossetia, Chechnya, Nagorno-Karabakh, Mongolia, Bukhara, or Tuva; political names are used

6 Vincenc Kopeček and Tomáš Hoch

only when it is necessary for understanding of the text (e.g. Nagorno-Karabakh can refer to the former autonomous region or the present-day de facto republic, which differ not only in their legal and political status but also in territory; or Bukhara can refer to the Khanate of Bukhara as well as to the Bukharan People's Soviet Republic). There are, however, de facto states which do not have any commonly used geographical names – and in these cases we always use their political names: Donetsk People's Republic (*Donetskaya narodnaya respublika*) and Luhansk People's Republic (*Luganskaya narodnaya respublika*). In some cases, the political names are somewhat problematic. The official name of the Chechen de facto state was the Chechen Republic of Ichkeria (*Nokhchin Pachkhalkkh Ichkeri*). The name Ichkeria was added in order to differentiate the entity from the Chechen Republic, which covers the same territory but is a subject of the Russian Federation. Ichkeria itself is a large region in southern Chechnya, "traditionally associated with the birth of the Chechen nation" (*Jaimoukha 2005, 22). The original political name of the de facto state in Nagorno-Karabakh was the Nagorno-Karabakh Republic (*Lernayin Gharabaghi Hanrapetutyun*); however, the political name Artsakh Republic (*Artsakhi Hanrapetutyun*) was used simultaneously. The new constitution which was approved by the referendum in 2017, however, introduced the Artsakh Republic as the political name of the entity; the Nagorno-Karabakh Republic can be also used and is understood as being identical with the Artsakh Republic (*NKR President 2017). The shift from Nagorno-Karabakh to Artsakh is motivated politically. The term Artsakh is perceived as a traditional Armenian name (allegedly from the ancient Urartian province of Urtekhe), whereas the term Karabakh is perceived as brought by the non-Armenian conquerors of Artsakh; "kara" is from Turkish word for black, "bakh" from Persian word "garden". In fact, Karabakh thus means the "Black Garden" and denotes a larger territory than Artsakh. The prefix "nagorno" is from Russian and means "upland" (often mistakenly translated as "mountainous") (*Chorbajian, Donabedian, and Mutafian 1994, 51–52). The Nagorno-Karabakh Republic in fact controls the upland part of historical Karabakh, the lowland is controlled by Azerbaijan and is not claimed by the Nagorno-Karabakh Republic. In the text of the book, we prefer to use the political name Nagorno-Karabakh Republic and geographical name Nagorno-Karabakh because it is better known in the English-speaking world than Artsakh. Like the Chechen Republic of Ichkeria, even the de facto state in South Ossetia added another toponym to its political name. Since the 2017 referendum the official name of the entity has been the Republic of South Ossetia – the State of Alania (*Respublikæ Khussar Iryston – Paddzakaad Allonston*). Alania refers to the ancient tribe of Alans, who are considered ancestors of modern Ossetians. Moreover, the toponym Alania also appears in the political name of the Republic of North Ossetia – Alania, South Ossetia's kin-state and subject of the Russian Federation (*Fuller 2017).

4 Because de facto states have not received international recognition or were recognized only by a handful of states, the qualifier "de facto" should precede references to the breakaway entity or its political bodies – for example, de facto Republic of Abkhazia, de facto President, de facto Prime Minister, or de facto Parliament. However, in this book we omit this qualifier when referring to the very existence of de facto states and their political institutions. This does not reflect the authors' political preferences in any way; the purpose is merely to maximize the readability and simplicity of the text.

5 The only exception is Gagauzia, which is often given as an example of a non-violent conflict. Nevertheless, even in the case of Gagauzia, the conflict escalated into a brief violence claiming several lives. See Chapter 5.4 for details.

Literature

Chorbajian, Levon, Patrick Donabedian, and Claude Mutafian. 1994. *The Caucasian Knot. The History and Geo-Politics of Nagorno-Karabagh*. London and New Jersey: Zed Books.

Fuller, Liz. 2017. "South Ossetia Referendum on Name Change Steers Clear of Thornier Unification Issue." *Radio Free Europe/Radio Liberty*, February 8. www.rferl.org/a/caucasus-report-south-ossetia-referendum-name-change/28298590.html.

Jaimoukha, Amjad. 2005. *The Chechens: A Handbook*. London and New York: Routledge.

NKR President. 2017. "Constitution of the Republic of Artsakh, non-official translation." *Official Website of the President of the Artsakh Republic*. www.president.nkr.am/en/constitution/fullText/.

Section 1

De facto statehood

Understanding the concept

1.1 Terminology

Emil Aslan Souleimanov

In a recent article, Galina Yemelianova reminds us of the post-Second World War roots of the idea of the de facto state. This idea appeared in the field of political science in the 1980s in response to the "new sovereignty game", reflecting the process of decolonization in Africa and Asia that saw the emergence of dozens of "factual" states (Yemelianova 2015). Back then, many newly emerging states possessed the formal attributes of independence, including formal external international recognition while lacking the basic capabilities to police their own territories. These states were termed quasi-states, a term coined by Robert Jackson as early as 1990. According to Jackson (1990), quasi-states, typically found on the African continent, were products of decolonization, and therefore lacked the "natural" and protracted process of evolutionary state-building. A second group of states, those marked by the capacity to govern themselves even while lacking formal international recognition, were branded secessionist, de facto, or unrecognized states.

Reflecting on these tumultuous developments, a great number of seemingly synonymous terms have been used interchangeably with de facto state, which appears to be the dominant and most frequently used concept as of today (e.g., Berg and Mölder 2012; Caspersen 2008a; O'Loughlin, Kolossov, and Toal 2011). As Laurence Broers et al. have noted, this has resulted in a profusion of terminology surrounding de facto states. Various other qualifiers or adjectives have been used to designate them: quasi-, para-, pseudo-, shadow-, phantom-, self-proclaimed, etc. (Broers, Iskandaryan, and Minasyan 2015). In fact, the use of these various terms, each of which is imbued with semantic nuances, has somewhat obscured the research field. As Harvey and Stansfield (2011) have pointed out, much confusion is due to the *ad hoc,* case-study-dominated literature on de facto states. Terminological consensus aiming at filtering (and standardizing) the widely swinging meanings and nuanced usages which were emerging in the literature were missing.

We shall review several key concepts and their attributes and definitions. For instance, Kolossov and O'Loughlin have used the term "pseudo-state", which they define as "islands of 'transitional' or 'incomplete' statehood".

12   *Emil Aslan Souleimanov*

Both authors locate pseudo-states in what they term the "zones of contact between empires and civilisations" from the Balkans to Afghanistan (Kolossov and O'Loughlin 1999, 155). These authors also offer a different definition of quasi-states, which they – unlike Jackson – regard as a certain form of criminal entity, a sort of parallel universe, run, in some instances, by drug barons, as may appear in urban ghettos as well. In contrast to quasi-states, pseudo-states are institutionalized entities with more or less established governments, significant control over their territory, and the attributes of states except for formal recognition (Kolossov and O'Loughlin 1999, 152–155).

For his part, Kolstø speaks of quasi-states, which he defines differently than Jackson. Jackson spoke of quasi-states as entities that "appear to be juridical more than empirical entities", emphasizing that they are "creatures of non-competitive international norms" (Jackson 1990, 26). In his understanding, quasi-states possess juridical sovereignty, but such weak states are not in a position to provide for their populations and are ineffective in terms of their institutions and authoritative domestic power. Inquiring into the different empirical context of the post-bipolar world, Kolstø refers to quasi-states as lacking external sovereignty, while he does not question their ability to police their own territory or provide for their populations (Kolstø 2006). Kolstø uses various terms – de facto states, para-states, unrecognized states, pseudo-states – interchangeably, but he prefers the term quasi-states. At the same time, in an attempt to eliminate this terminological jungle, Kolstø points to the Jacksonian concept of quasi-states as matching the recently coined concept of failed states, while the term quasi-states is reserved for unrecognized states only (Kolstø 2006, 723).[1] Taking on the phenomenon of de facto states as contested entities with separatist pasts, Deon Geldenhuys (2009, 7) utilizes the concept of contested states, which he defines by the "internationally disputed nature of their purported statehood, manifested in their lack of *de jure* recognition".

However, it was not until Scott Pegg's (1998) international law-focussed study of unrecognized states – in fact, the first book-long monograph ever to have been published about the matter – that the term de facto state itself was coined in the late 1990s. According to him,

> [t]he de facto state is a secessionist entity that receives popular support and has achieved sufficient capacity to provide governmental services to a given population in a defined territorial area, over which it maintains effective control for an extended period of time.
>
> (Pegg 1998, 26)

Pegg suggested six key criteria that a de facto state should fulfil. First and foremost, de facto states are marked by an "organized political leadership which has risen to power through some degree of indigenous capability" (Pegg 1998, 26). The notion of "organized political leadership" implies a condition that is weaker than an established government, as Pegg admits, pointing to the two out of four case studies from which he draws – Tamil Eelam and Somaliland – in addition to the Turkish Republic of Northern Cyprus and Eritrea, which have come to possess standard governments. While he emphasizes that de facto states are a product of the local population and enjoy its support, this definition would exclude puppet states. Pegg stresses the organized political leadership's basic ability to police its territory and provide government services to the local population, which are duties embedded in the crucial Montevideo Convention on the Rights and Duties of States (1933). Pegg's fourth key criterion is the capability of states to enter into relations with other states, as mentioned in the Montevideo Convention, which he treats rather lightly, since he believes that de facto states perceive that they have this capability, even though their perception is not shared by the international community. Pegg introduces a temporal threshold of existence of two years in order for political entities to be regarded as de facto states, along with a criterion of widespread international recognition, which de facto states usually lack (Pegg 1998).

This definition has been criticized on the grounds of being somewhat vague. In an attempt to better delineate what accounts for de facto states, in an edited volume devoted to this increasingly salient phenomenon, Caspersen and Stansfield (2011) work out three fundamental criteria: (a) *de facto* independence, including territorial control, for a period of at least two years. (De facto states are in control of most of the territory they claim, including its capital city and key regions, although this does not prevent them from claiming more territory.); (b) de facto states do not enjoy full international recognition. (Although some of them may enjoy partial recognition, they are not regarded as members of the international system of sovereign states.); and (c) de facto states show an aspiration for full, *de jure*, independence, either by means of a formal declaration of independence, the holding of a national referendum on independence, or other means that explicitly illustrate the secessionist entity's desire for separate statehood.

Although different definitions and names are used for these entities, Pegg (2008) claims that there is a fairly widespread consensus surrounding the basic elements of how to define a de facto state. In his words, disagreements come only around the edges of the definition while not disputing the basic elements of it (Pegg 2008, 1). Thus following Pegg (1998), Kolstø (2006), Caspersen and Stansfield (2011), and with regard to the Montevideo Convention on the Rights and Duties of States (1933), we consider de facto states to be regions that have a defined state territory, permanent population and their governments are in control of the entire territory they claim, or at least most of it. Their state authorities perform state administration, they have the capacity to enter into relations with other states, they have been seeking independence for at least two years while failing to gain international recognition of their independence (or they have been recognized by only a few countries). Based on this conceptualization, six present-day entities

14 *Emil Aslan Souleimanov*

(as of 2018) are commonly considered as de facto states: Abkhazia, South Ossetia, Nagorno-Karabakh, Transnistria, Northern Cyprus, and Somaliland (e.g., Kolstø 2006; Caspersen 2008b; Berg and Toomla 2009; Pegg 2017).

Note

1 It should be, however noted that Kolstø himself uses the term de facto states in his texts from 2010 onwards (see Blakkisrud and Kolstø 2012 or Pegg and Kolstø 2016).

Literature

Berg, Eiki, and Martin Mölder. 2012. "Who Is Entitled to 'Earn Sovereignty'? Legitimacy and Regime Support in Abkhazia and Nagorno-Karabakh." *Nations and Nationalism* 18 (3): 527–545.

Berg, Eiki, and Raul Toomla. 2009. "Forms of Normalisation in the Quest for De Facto Statehood." *The International Spectator* 44 (4): 27–45.

Blakkisrud, Helge, and Pål Kolstø. 2012. "Dynamics of De Facto Statehood: The South Caucasian De Facto States between Secession and Sovereignty." *Southeast European and Black Sea Studies* 12 (2): 281–298.

Broers, Laurence, Alexander Iskandaryan, and Sergey Minasyan. 2015. "Introduction: The Unrecognized Politics of De Facto States in the Post-Soviet Space." *Caucasus Survey* 3 (3): 187–194.

Caspersen, Nina. 2008a. "Separatism and the Democracy in the Caucasus." *Survival* 50 (4): 113–136.

Caspersen, Nina. 2008b. "From Kosovo to Karabakh: International Responses to De Facto States." *Südosteuropa* 56 (1): 58–83.

Caspersen, Nina, and Gareth Stansfield. 2011. *Unrecognized States in the International System*. London: Routledge.

Geldenhuys, Deon. 2009. *Contested States in World Politics*. London: Palgrave Macmillan.

Harvey, James, and Gareth Stansfield. 2011. "Theorizing Unrecognized States: Sovereignty, Secessionism, and Political Economy." In *Unrecognized States in the International System*, edited by Nina Caspersen and Gareth Stansfield, 11–26. London: Routledge.

Jackson, Robert H. 1990. *Quasi-states: Sovereignty, International Relations and the Third World*. Cambridge: Cambridge University Press.

Kolossov, Vladimir and John O'Loughlin. 1999. Pseudo-States as Harbingers of a New Geopolitics: The Example of the Transdniestr Moldovan Republic (TMR). In *Boundaries, Territory and Post-modernity*, edited by David Newman, 151–176. London: Frank Cass.

Kolstø, Pål. 2006. "The Sustainability and Future of Unrecognized Quasi-States." *Journal of Peace Research* 43 (6): 723–740.

O'Loughlin, John, Vladimir Kolossov, and Gerard Toal. 2011. "Inside Abkhazia: Survey of Attitudes in a De Facto State." *Post-Soviet Affairs* 27 (1): 1–36.

Pegg, Scott. 1998. *International Society and the De Facto State*. Aldershot: Ashgate.

Pegg, Scott. 2008. "The Impact of De Facto States on International Law and the International Community." Conference Paper. Opening the World Order to De

Facto States – Limits and Potentialities for De Facto States in the International Order. Brussels: European Parliament. http://unpo.org/images/professor%20scott%20pegg.pdf.

Pegg, Scott. 2017. "Twenty Years of De Facto State Studies: Progress, Problems, and Prospects." In *The Oxford Encyclopedia of Empirical International Relations Theory*, edited by W. R. Thompson et al. Oxford: Oxford University Press. http://politics.oxfordre.com/view/10.1093/acrefore/9780190228637.001.0001/acrefore-9780190228637-e-516.

Pegg, Scott, and Pål Kolstø 2016. "Lost and Found: The WikiLeaks of De Facto State–great Power Relations." *International Studies Perspectives* 17 (3): 267–286.

Yemelianova, Galina. 2015. "Western Academic Discourse on the Post-Soviet De Facto State Phenomenon." *Caucasus Survey* 3 (3): 219–238.

1.2 De facto statehood

Overview of the research

Tomáš Hoch

Academic studies on de facto states have, quite logically, mostly focussed on the post-Soviet space, where most of the contemporary de facto states are located. Though the post-Soviet de facto states are relatively small in terms of both population and area (discussed in more detail in Chapter 1.3), their existence has numerous consequences. The failure to find a solution to these prolonged conflicts represents a problem not only in the economic and political sphere but also for social development and international security. It is therefore unsurprising that during the past quarter of a century, de facto statehood has been an important area of research among political scientists, geographers, and experts in security studies, international relations, and area studies.

There have basically been three periods of research on de facto states. In the first period, which roughly took place between 1998 and 2004, scholarly texts tended to mainly present case studies exploring the roots of separatist conflicts and the possibilities for conflict resolution. One of the first authors who attempted to present a systematic theoretical account of the existence of de facto states in the international environment was Scott Pegg. His monograph International Society and the De facto State (1998) structurally focussed on issues related to the contested status of these entities. The great value of this breakthrough monograph is the in-depth theoretical insight into the topic of how de facto states emerge and are sustained, which was applied into specific case studies. In the author's own words, he tried to emphasize that de facto states are "a distinct type of actor in international relations that merited comparative academic study and not just ritualistic condemnation of their illegality in a world dominated by widely recognized sovereign states" (Pegg 2017, 2).[1] In this period of research at the turn of the millennium, the image of de facto states in academic literature was quite negative. Kolossov and O'Loughlin (1998) claimed that in the post-Soviet space the elites within de facto states had a strong criminal background and specialized in the illegal trade of weapons, drugs, and money laundering. Lynch (2004) characterized de facto states as highly criminal environments in which local politicians were puppets in the hands of external actors. In the case of Georgia's breakaway regions and in Transnistria, Russia was seen as the key actor controlling the "puppet governments", in the case

Overview of the research 17

of Nagorno-Karabakh it was Armenia. The same author speaks about Abkhazia and Nagorno-Karabakh as entities that have the institutional features of statehood, but are unable to fill it with content (Lynch 2004, 4). The book was written with the strong political accent of pro-western orientation, which tended to see de facto states mostly through the lens of useful entities for the narrative of Russian expansionism. The interconnection between organized crime and domestic political leaders was also mentioned by King (2001) and Collier and Hoeffler (2004). Their arguments rest on the theory of greed and grievance in civil wars, which assumes that many conflicts (not only in de facto states) are often kept alive by top political leaders, who are often connected to informal structures and benefit from the shadow economy.

With a certain degree of generalization, it could be said that researchers at the turn of the millennium mostly focussed on the external relations of de facto states. The internal dynamics of the development in unrecognized states was somewhat neglected by researchers, and these issues only began to gain more attention in around 2005–2008 (Caspersen 2008a, 114–115). At that time, some authors also started to concentrate their attention on state-building and nation-building processes inside de facto states and found out that the lack of internal sovereignty does not necessarily mean the impossibility of democratic, institutional, and political development inside these entities. Caspersen (2008a, 117) agrees that Abkhazia and Nagorno-Karabakh are far from being liberal democracies, but she claims that the level of democracy in these regions is almost the same or even better than in their parent states Georgia and Azerbaijan. Broers (2005) and Popescu (2006) were among those who originally started to stress the economic, political, and social changes that de facto states have undergone in the last decade. They also observed that recognition bids that are based solely on the right to self-determination remain powerless. Broers (2005) claimed that some de facto states employ the so-called "democratization-for-recognition strategy", which is based on the assumption that the international recognition of de facto states could be earned by a successful democratization processes. Justification claims for the international recognition of independence also appeared in the works of Chirikba (2006) and Isachenko (2008). The most influential paper from this period was probably the article entitled *The Sustainability and Future of Unrecognized Quasi-States* written by Pål Kolstø. He claims that the main reasons why these states have not collapsed (though they have generally weak economies, weak state structures, and an absence of international recognition) are the facts that

> they have managed to build up internal support from the local population through propaganda and identity-building; channel a disproportionately large part of their meager resources into military defense; enjoy the support of a strong patron; and, in most cases, have seceded from a state that is itself very weak.

> (Kolstø 2006, 723)

18   *Tomáš Hoch*

These factors of a de facto states sustainability were followed up with the possible ends of de facto states.[2] Even though the social reality has changed considerably over the past thirteen years since the publication of this article, his factors of sustainability and possible ends of de facto states are largely still valid. Without mentioning them, there is almost no text devoted to the topic of de facto statehood in the post-Soviet area.

Since roughly 2006, a growing number of studies have focussed on the internal development taking place within de facto states. To a large extent this shift in focus is due to the fact that de facto states are no longer considered as merely a passing phenomenon which emerged for a short time as a consequence of the dissolution of the Soviet Union and that these entities are capable of existing for a relatively long time, despite their complete (or almost complete) lack of international recognition. The second reason for the growth of academic interest in the internal dynamics of development within de facto states is the fact that access to these territories has become easier. During the 1990s they were essentially closed to foreign researchers, but in the past decade the practicalities of visiting these entities have become much simpler (Blakkisrud and Kolstø 2012, 282).

Another milestone, which meant greater interest in the events in de facto states, was the August 2008 war in South Ossetia. This war utterly transformed the geopolitical map, not only of the South Caucasus but also of the entire post-Soviet space. Just the fact, that after some fifteen years of effort, Abkhazia and South Ossetia received formal recognition of their independence by the Russian Federation and subsequently by several other countries, has considerably changed the conflict dynamics. These changes have meant that the topics of sovereignty, international recognition, separatism, and security came into the spotlight for many academics and policymakers. Caspersen and Stansfield (2011) mentioned in the introduction of their edited volume, that de facto states can survive for a relatively long time despite the lack of international recognition. Furthermore, they pointed out that ethno-nationalist mobilizations provided an important driving force for the emergence of de facto states, but they are also very much the product of the international system, which constrains, shapes, and perhaps even enables these aspiring states. One year later Nina Caspersen wrote the book *Unrecognized States: The Struggle for Sovereignty in the Modern International System* (2012). Her book represents a valuable attempt to understand the links between sovereignty, statehood, and conflict, trying to find answers to the fundamental questions: how do these entities survive, how are they dealing with the fact of non-recognition, and what are the possibilities to reach a peaceful solution of prevailing conflicts connected with de facto statehood. Her book is concluded by the claim, that "current policy based on a rigid conception of sovereignty and territorial integrity is not producing results, so it might be time for a rethink, not only of sovereignty, but also ways of dealing with unrecognized states" (Caspersen 2012, 155).

Overview of the research 19

This brings us to the research direction focussed on the strategy of engagement without recognition. One of the first studies in this sense was the article *Engagement without recognition: A new strategy toward Abkhazia and Eurasia's unrecognized states* written by Cooley and Mitchell in 2010. They advocated a more tangible engagement of the West in post-Soviet de facto states, in the economic, social, and cultural spheres. They argued, that if the United States and the EU do not act quickly, post-Soviet de facto states would be more increasingly tied to Russia, which will be a strong barrier to any kind of future cooperation with Georgia, Azerbaijan, and Moldova. Other authors have spoken in a similar manner. Fischer (2010) expressed that from a long-term perspective it is fully in a parent states interest to support a strong EU position in de facto states because only then could a small window of opportunity be opened, leading to possible conflict transformation; though in reality, stronger involvement in de facto states is often hindered by parent states, concerned by the possibility that such actions could imply recognition. Ker-Lindsay (2015) rejected the often articulated objection to possible meetings with de facto state authorities or cooperation with them on cultural or economic issues as being unjustified. "There cannot be accidental recognition. As long as a state insists that it does not recognize a territory as independent, and does not take steps that obviously amount to recognition ... then it does not do so" (Ker-Lindsay 2015, 284). Other authors who have recently focussed on the possibilities of engagement with de facto states include Berg and Pegg (2018), Axyonova and Gawrich (2018), Coppieters (2018), or Berg and Vits (2018).

Since the war in South Ossetia in 2008, a lot of international attention has also been focussed on the role of patron states, upon whom de facto states depend on for their survival. Because the patron of most de facto states is Russia, this area of research mostly covered the issue of the intensification of relations between de facto states and Moscow. Many authors (e.g. Ó Beacháin 2012; Broers 2013; O'Loughlin, Kolossov, and Toal 2014; Hoch, Souleimanov, and Baranec 2014; Ambrosio and Lange 2016 or Ó Beacháin, Comai, and Tsurtsumia-Zurabashvili 2016) were trying not to perceive the research on this topic via the lens of geopolitical rivalry between Russia and the West, instead, they have tried to explain that Russia's policy towards de facto states has always been multi-dimensional. In addition to political aspects, it also included economic, military, security, and humanitarian dimensions and underwent significant changes over the course of time. Thus it is far more complex than to be perceived on the black and white dichotomic scale. However, as Pegg (2017) and Broers (2013) rightly pointed out

> Once geopolitical rivalry became the dominant way to frame understanding of de facto states, the rich academic scholarship on these entities was ignored. Instead, de facto states were "often understood in terms of what they symbolize, rather than what they are.
>
> (Broers 2013, 69; Pegg 2017, 19)

20 Tomáš Hoch

For western journalists and policymakers, this situation resulted in the oversimplification of the question: to what extent can we speak about post-Soviet de facto states as puppets in the hands of Moscow? Not surprisingly, authors differed in their answer to the question. However, the result of this approach has been the loss of the ability to distinguish between individual de facto states, and the general perception of their homogeneity in prevailing western discourse.

An extremely valuable contribution to the study of the internal processes in de facto states is represented by the research made by O'Loughlin, Kolossov, and Toal, in the first few years following the 2008 war in South Ossetia. They conducted rare, independent public opinion surveys of the local populations in South Ossetia, Abkhazia, Nagorno-Karabakh, and Transnistria. They examined attitudes towards parent states, the possibility to settle the conflict down, economic well-being, inter-group relations, geopolitical knowledge, and identity formation. The results of their extensive survey in Abkhazia, South Ossetia, Transnistria, and Nagorno-Karabakh have been published continually since 2011 (e.g. O'Loughlin, Kolossov, and Toal 2011, 2014; Toal and O'Loughlin 2013a, 2013b).

During the past ten years of de facto statehood research, a significant amount of studies has been based on the empirical material collected on fieldtrips in the region, with the subsequent qualitative interpretation of key findings. A special exception in this regard, and a completely different approach to the study of de facto statehood, is represented by the research conducted by Florea (2014). In his article *De Facto States in International Politics (1945–2011)*, he has tried to develop a large-N quantitative dataset dedicated to understanding the behaviour of de facto states. His intended goal was that this dataset could be used as "a stepping stone toward more comprehensive efforts at understanding the entire constellation of alternative forms of political organization in the international system" (Florea 2014, 808). However, his inclusion of 34 entities into the dataset, twice as many as other authors identified (e.g. Caspersen 2012, Kolstø and Paukovic 2014), stretched the whole concept of de facto statehood and contributed to confusion and dead end discussions about precise definitions. Another author who conducted quantitative analysis for the study of de facto statehood is Raul Toomla. In his paper *Charting informal engagement between de facto states: a quantitative analysis*, he examined the position of de facto states in the international system and the factors that determine this position by using fuzzy-set qualitative comparative analysis (Toomla 2016).

However, as has been mentioned in the first sentence of the previous paragraph, most of the papers from the past decade stood on qualitative methods and tried to explore, in depth, small numbers of variables in one or two regions. This paragraph is intended as a brief overview of the studies into the phenomenon of de facto statehood in the post-Soviet area that have deepened our knowledge and understanding of the development in these enduring yet unrecognized, and to a certain extent, still isolated regions.

Overview of the research 21

Bakke, O'Loughlin, and Ward (2011) explored the conditions that facilitate internal legitimacy in de facto states on the case study of Abkhazia. Berg and Mölder (2012) used group interviews in Abkhazia and Nagorno-Karabakh in order to analyse the formation of demos, which can help to consolidate de facto states by the provision of legitimacy and regime support. Blakkisrud and Kolstø (2012) analysed the processes of state-building and nation-building and the identification of a local population with their country in the South Caucasian de facto states. Caspersen (2008b) and Fabry (2012) wrote comparative studies on the legitimization of statehood in de facto states and on strategies that focus on gaining wider international recognition in Abkhazia, South Ossetia, and Kosovo. Whilst the prevailing view in the literature on de facto states is that these entities strive for internationally recognized independence, Kosienkowski (2017) argues that the Gagauz Republic's leaders did not pursue the goal of independence and rather they strived for autonomism. Internal narratives supporting, on the one hand, the idea of independence and, on the other hand, attempts to justify a possible unification with the Russian Federation have recently been examined in Abkhazia and South Ossetia by Hoch (2018) and Smith (2018). Harvey and Stansfield (2011) emphasized the contrast between domestic sovereignty and missing international recognition. Ó Beacháin (2012) explained how and why pluralistic and competitive elections occurred in Abkhazia. Trier and Szakonyi (2010) and Matsuzato (2011) focussed on the rights of minorities and inter-ethnic relations also in a case study of Abkhazia. The issue of refugees and IDPs from post-Soviet de facto states appeared recently in an analysis made by Lundgren (2016) and Prelz Oltramonti (2016). Case studies of the role of civil society in conflict transformation connected with de facto states appeared in Mikhelidze and Pirozzi (2008) or Kopeček, Hoch, and Baar (2016). The issue of counter-recognition strategies used by parent states (in their text called base states), in an attempt to prevent the recognition of seceded entities, was elaborated by Ó Beacháin, Comai, and Tsurtsumia-Zurabashvili (2016). Since 2008 a relatively frequent topic of research is the political status of Kosovo and its impact on the future development of post-Soviet de facto states (e.g. Fawn 2008; Krueger 2009; Tsurtsumia 2010). Blakkisrud and Kolstø (2012) and Berg (2012) have focussed their research interests on the relationship between secession, sovereignty, and political legitimacy in de facto states. Finally, in a brief overview, monographs covering the area of prolonged conflicts in the post-Soviet space should not be omitted. Among the most valuable recent books are certainly *Understanding Ethnopolitical Conflict: The Wars in Karabakh, Abkhazia, and South Ossetia Reconsidered* written by Emil Souleimanov; *Secessionist Rule: Protracted Conflict and Configurations of Non-state Authority* from Franziska Smolnik, *Unrecognized States and Secession in the 21st Century* edited by Martin Riegl and Bohumil Doboš; and *From conflict to autonomy in the Caucasus: The Soviet Union and the making of Abkhazia, South Ossetia and Nagorno-Karabakh*, written by Arsène Saparov.

22   *Tomáš Hoch*

In 2001 Charles King labelled post-Soviet de facto states as "information black holes". As is apparent from the preceding paragraphs, the last twenty years of social science research in post-Soviet de facto states have documented many aspects of internal political, social, and economic dynamics and also their external relations with the outside world. But despite growing interest in the topics connected with de facto statehood, there are still some aspects of this issue that remain relatively under-researched and suggest interesting prospects for future research. One of them has been offered by Giorgio Comai. He argues that in many ways post-Soviet de facto states are behaving similarly to small-sized-dependent jurisdictions in other parts of the world. He claims that reconceptualization of post-Soviet de facto states as small dependent jurisdictions would contribute to a "more nuanced understanding of their state-building project, their relationship with the patron state, their political economy, as well as their long-term path of development" (Comai 2018a, 181). In his chapter issued later that year, the same author has developed this idea, claiming that scholars focussing on the issue of de facto statehood are locked in a way of thinking oriented to the contested status of these entities and compare them mostly with other unrecognized states or conflict regions (Comai 2018b). A similar need for more comparative work, including not only de facto states but also other adjacent phenomena, has been voiced by Scott Pegg. He concludes his article entitled *Twenty Years of De facto State Studies: Progress, Problems, and Prospects* with a statement:

> More diverse comparative work, a renewed openness to the conflict resolution potential of de facto states and an enlarged focus on their respective civil societies all suggest interesting prospects for future research that should generate significant returns in the coming years.
>
> (Pegg 2017, 24)

Another direction may also be a historical approach that would focus to similarities and differences with entities that existed in the past. It remains to be said that the very nature of a topic focussed on a variable social reality, which changes dynamically with a dependence on many internal and external phenomena, constantly brings the need for new knowledge.

Notes

1 However, it should be noted that the author focussed primarily on de facto states located outside the post-Soviet space; his case studies involved Tamil Eelam, Eritrea, Northern Cyprus, and Somaliland.
2 In his 2006 text, Kolstø does not denote these entities as de facto states but as quasi-states; however, it is clear from the context that he is referring to de facto states. Kolstø himself uses the term de facto states in his texts from 2010 onwards (see Blakkisrud and Kolstø 2012 or Pegg and Kolstø 2015).

Literature

Ambrosio, Thomas, and William A. Lange. 2016. "The Architecture of Annexation? Russia's Bilateral Agreements with South Ossetia and Abkhazia." *Nationalities Papers* 44 (5): 673–693.

Axyonova, Vera, and Andrea Gawrich. 2018. "Regional Organizations and Secessionist Entities: Analysing Practices of the EU and the OSCE in Post-Soviet Protracted Conflict Areas." *Ethnopolitics* 17 (4): 408–425.

Bakke, Kristin M., John O'Loughlin, and Michael Ward. 2011. "The Viability of De Facto States: Post-War Developments and Internal Legitimacy in Abkhazia." APSA 2011 Annual Meeting Paper. Washington: American Political Science Association.

Berg, Eiki. 2012. "Parent States versus Secessionist Entities: Measuring Political Legitimacy in Cyprus, Moldova and Bosnia & Hercegovina." *Europe-Asia Studies* 64 (7): 1271–1296.

Berg, Eiki, and Martin Mölder. 2012. "Who Is Entitled to 'Earn Sovereignty'? Legitimacy and Regime Support in Abkhazia and Nagorno-Karabakh." *Nations and Nationalism* 18 (3): 527–545.

Berg, Eiki, and Scott Pegg. 2018. "Scrutinizing a Policy of 'Engagement without Recognition': US Requests for Diplomatic Actions with De Facto States." *Foreign Policy Analysis* 14 (3): 388–407.

Berg, Eiki, and Kristel Vits. 2018. "Quest for Survival and Recognition: Insights into the Foreign Policy Endeavours of the Post-Soviet de facto States." *Ethnopolitics* 17 (4): 390–407.

Blakkisrud, Helge, and Pål Kolstø. 2012. "Dynamics of De Facto Statehood: The South Caucasian De Facto States between Secession and Sovereignty." *Southeast European and Black Sea Studies* 12 (2): 281–298.

Broers, Laurence. 2005. "The Politics of Non-recognition and Democratisation." *Accord* 17: 68–71.

Broers, Laurence. 2013. "Recognizing Politics in Unrecognized States: 20 Years of Enquiry into the *De Facto* States of the South Caucasus." *Caucasus Survey* 1 (1): 59–74.

Caspersen, Nina. 2008a. "Separatism and the Democracy in the Caucasus." *Survival* 50 (4): 113–136.

Caspersen, Nina. 2008b. "From Kosovo to Karabakh: International Responses to De Facto States." *Südosteuropa* 56 (1): 58–83.

Caspersen, Nina. 2012. *Unrecognized States: The Struggle for Sovereignty in the Modern International System*. London: Polity.

Caspersen, Nina, and Gareth Stansfield (eds.) 2011. *Unrecognized States in the International System*. London: Routledge.

Chirikba, Viatcheslav. 2006. "The International Legal Status of the Republic of Abkhazia in the Light of International Law." *Abkhaz World*, September 2. www.abkhazworld.com/articles/analysis/285-int-legal-status-abkhazia-vchirikba.html.

Collier, Paul, and Anke Hoeffler. 2004. "Greed and Grievance in Civil War." *Oxford Economic Papers* 56 (4): 563–595.

Comai, Giorgio. 2018a. "Conceptualising Post-Soviet De Facto States as Small Dependent Jurisdictions." *Ethnopolitics* 17 (2): 181–200.

Comai, Giorgio. 2018b. "Developing a New Research Agenda on Post-Soviet De Facto States." In *Armenia, Caucaso e Asia Centrale*, edited by Aldo Ferrari and Carlo Frappi, 145–159. Venice: Università Ca' Foscari.

24   Tomáš Hoch

Cooley, Alexander, and Lincoln A. Mitchell. 2010. "Engagement without Recognition: A New Strategy toward Abkhazia and Eurasia's Unrecognized States." *The Washington Quarterly* 33 (4): 59–73.

Coppieters, Bruno. 2018. "Statehood, De Facto Authorities and Occupation: Contested Concepts and the EU's Engagement in Its European Neighbourhood." *Ethnopolitics* 17 (4): 343–361.

Fabry, Mikulas. 2012. "The Contemporary Practice of State Recognition: Kosovo, South Ossetia, Abkhazia, and Their Aftermath." *Nationalities Papers* 40 (5): 661–676.

Fawn, Rick. 2008. "The Kosovo and Montenegro effect." *International Affairs* 84 (2): 269–294.

Fischer, Sabine. 2010. "How to Engage with Abkhazia?" *ISS Analysis November 2010.* www.iss.europa.eu/uploads/media/How_to_engage_with_Abkhazia.pdf.

Florea, Adrian. 2014. "De Facto States in International Politics (1945–2011): A New Data Set." *International Interactions* 40 (5): 788–811.

Harvey, James, and Gareth Stansfield. 2011. "Theorizing Unrecognized States: Sovereignty, Secessionism, and Political Economy." In *Unrecognized States in the International System*, edited by Nina Caspersen and Gareth Stansfield, 11–26. London: Routledge.

Hoch, Tomáš. 2018. "Legitimization of Statehood and Its Impact on Foreign Policy in De Facto States: A Case Study of Abkhazia." *Iran and the Caucasus* 22 (4): 382–407.

Hoch, Tomáš, Emil Souleimanov, and Tomáš Baranec. 2014. "Russia's Role in the Official Peace Process in South Ossetia." *Bulletin of Geography. Socio-economic Series* 23: 53–71.

Isachenko, Daria. 2008. "The Production of Recognized Space: Statebuilding Practices of Northern Cyprus and Transdniestria." *Journal of Intervention and Statebuilding* 2 (3): 353–368.

Ker-Lindsay, James. 2015. "Engagement without Recognition: The Limits of Diplomatic Interaction with Contested States." *International Affairs* 91 (2): 267–285.

King, Charles. 2001. "The Benefits of Ethnic War: Understanding Eurasia's Unrecognized States." *World Politics* 53 (4): 524–552.

Kolossov, Vladimir, and John O'Loughlin. 1998. "Pseudo-States as Harbingers of a New Geopolitics: The Example of the Trans-Dniester Moldovan Republic (TMR)." *Geopolitics* 3 (1): 151–176.

Kolstø, Pål. 2006. "The Sustainability and Future of Unrecognized Quasi-States." *Journal of Peace Research* 43 (6): 723–740.

Kolstø, Pål, and Davor Paukovic. 2014. "The Short and Brutish Life of Republika Srpska Krajina: Failure of a De Facto State." *Ethnopolitics* 13 (4): 309–327.

Kopeček, Vincenc, Tomáš Hoch, and Vladimír Baar. 2016. "Conflict Transformation and Civil Society: The Case of Nagorno-Karabakh." *Europe-Asia Studies* 68 (3): 441–459.

Kosienkowski, Marcin. 2017. "The Gagauz Republic: An Autonomism-Driven De Facto State." *The Soviet and Post-Soviet Review* 44 (3): 292–313.

Krueger, Heiko. 2009. "Implications of Kosovo, Abkhazia and South Ossetia for International Law: The Conduct of the Community of States in Current Secession Conflicts." *Caucasus Review of International Affairs* 3 (1): 121–142.

Lundgren, Minna. 2016. "Place Matters: Return Intentions among Forcibly Displaced Young Georgians from Abkhazia Living in Tbilisi and Zugdidi." *Caucasus Survey* 4 (2): 129–148.

Lynch, Dov. 2004. *Engaging Eurasia's Separatist States*. Washington: United States Institute of Peace.

Matsuzato, Kimitaka. 2011. "Transnational Minorities Challenging the Inter-state System: Mingrelians, Armenians, and Muslims in and around Abkhazia." *Nationalities Papers* 39 (5): 811–831.

Mikhelidze, Nona, and Nicoletta Pirozzi. 2008. "Civil Society and Conflict Transformation in Abkhazia, Israel–Palestine, Nagorno-Karabakh, Transnistria and Western Sahara." Microcon Policy Working Paper 3. Brighton: University of Sussex.

Ó Beacháin, Donnacha. 2012. "The Dynamics of Electoral Politics in Abkhazia." *Communist and Post-Communist Studies* 45 (1): 165–174.

Ó Beacháin, Donnacha, Giorgio Comai, and Ann Tsurtsumia-Zurabashvili. 2016. "The Secret Lives of Unrecognised States: Internal Dynamics, External Relations, and Counter-recognition Strategies." *Small Wars & Insurgencies* 27 (3): 440–466.

O'Loughlin, John, Vladimir Kolossov, and Gerard Toal. 2011. "Inside Abkhazia: Survey of Attitudes in a *De Facto* State." *Post-Soviet Affairs* 27 (1): 1–36.

O'Loughlin, John, Vladimir Kolossov, and Gerard Toal. 2014. "Inside the Post-Soviet De Facto States: A Comparison of Attitudes in Abkhazia, Nagorny Karabakh, South Ossetia, and Transnistria." *Eurasian Geography and Economics* 55 (5): 423–456.

Pegg, Scott.1998. *International Society and the De Facto State*. Aldershot: Ashgate.

Pegg, Scott. 2017. "Twenty Years of De Facto State Studies: Progress, Problems, and Prospects." In *The Oxford Encyclopedia of Empirical International Relations Theory*, edited by W. R. Thompson et al., 1-30. Oxford: Oxford University Press.

Pegg, Scott, and Pål Kolstø. 2015. "Somaliland: Dynamics of Internal Legitimacy and (Lack of) External Sovereignty." *Geoforum* 66: 193–202.

Popescu, Nicu. 2006. *Democracy in Secessionism: Transnistria and Abkhazia's Domestic Policies*. International Policy Fellowship – Policy Studies. Budapest: Open Society Institute and Central European University.

Prelz Oltramonti, Giulia. 2016. "Securing Disenfranchisement through Violence and Isolation: The Case of Georgians/Mingrelians in the District of Gali." *Conflict, Security & Development* 16 (3): 245–262.

Riegl, Martin, and Bohumil Doboš (eds.) 2017. *Unrecognized States and Secession in the 21st Century*. Cham: Springer.

Saparov, Arsène. 2014. *From Conflict to Autonomy in the Caucasus: The Soviet Union and the Making of Abkhazia, South Ossetia and Nagorno Karabakh*. London: Routledge.

Smith, Mary E. 2018. "De Facto State Foreign Policy 'Social Moves' in Abkhazia and South Ossetia." *Iran and the Caucasus* 22 (2): 181–205.

Smolnik, Franziska. 2016. *Secessionist Rule: Protracted Conflict and Configurations of Non-State Authority*. Frankfurt: Campus Verlag.

Souleimanov, Emil. 2013. *Understanding Ethnopolitical Conflict: Karabakh, South Ossetia, and Abkhazia wars Reconsidered*. New York: Palgrave Macmillan.

Toal, Gerard, and John O'Loughlin. 2013a. "Inside South Ossetia: A Survey of Attitudes in a De Facto State." *Post-Soviet Affairs* 29 (2): 136–172.

Toal, Gerard, and John O'Loughlin. 2013b. "Land for Peace in Nagorny Karabakh? Political Geographies and Public Attitudes inside a De Facto State." *Territory, Politics, Governance* 1 (2): 158–182.

Toomla, Raul. 2016. "Charting Informal Engagement between De Facto States: A Quantitative Analysis." *Space and Polity* 20 (3): 330–345.

Trier, Tom, and David Szakonyi. 2010. *Under Siege: Inter-Ethnic Relations in Abkhazia*. New York: Columbia University Press.

Tsurtsumia, Ann. 2010. *Conflicts in Kosovo and Abkhazia, Georgia. Should Kosovo Serve as a Precedent for Abkhazia?* Berlin: VDM.

1.3 De facto states and other unrecognized entities in Eurasia

Vincenc Kopeček

The concept of a de facto state is mostly applied to unrecognized entities which were formed after the Second World War (Yemelianova 2015). However, a number of entities which resembled present-day de facto states existed even in the more distant past (Fabry 2010). In Eurasia, there were two periods during which a number of de facto states or other non-recognized entities emerged. The first one followed the collapse of tsarist Russia, whereas the second followed the dissolution of the Soviet Union. Although we argue that the concept of a de facto state should only be applied to cases prior to the Second World War with caution, the analysis of these cases enables us to make important comparisons with present-day de facto states. This chapter will briefly discuss the concept of a de facto state from the historical perspective, and then will introduce the two periods of political-territorial restructuring of the analysed territory and identify those entities which fulfil, at least partially, the defined criteria of a de facto state as used in this book.

Recognizing states – past and present

The definition criteria for a de facto state were coined at the turn of the 20th and 21st centuries, and although the nature of the phenomenon, that is, the non-recognition of secessionist entities, remains virtually the same, the practice of state recognition and its context, that is, the international system and international law, changed significantly. Thus, it is debatable if the recent concept of a de facto state can also be applied to historical cases of break-away entities. The nature of the problem is similar to the question of whether totalitarianism is an inherently modern phenomenon, or if this concept can be applied to some historical cases of autocratic regimes, exercising strict control over their populations (Stanley 1987; Shorten 2012). Where it would be pointless to treat ancient Sparta as a modern totalitarian regime, one cannot discount Popper's (1947) argument that Plato's ideal state, apparently inspired by Sparta, is based on a form of "totalitarian" principles. We argue that in the case of de facto states this argument is quite similar. Whereas secession and state recognition have been common

28 Vincenc Kopeček

phenomena for millennia, the application of the concept of a de facto state to any unrecognized break-away entity, regardless of its historical context, would be nothing else than conceptual stretching (cf. Sartori 1970; Collier and Mahon 1993).

In fact, the practice of state recognition changed twice during the last 200 years. Although, from about 1815 to the beginning of the 20th century, "self-determination was expressed through, and externally gauged by, self-attainment of effective control over a claimed entity to the exclusion of other claimants, most often previous sovereign governments" (Fabry 2012, 663), in the first half of the 20th century the practice of state recognition underwent a significant change. This was due to two important events which happened in the 1930s: the signing of the Montevideo Convention on Rights and Duties of States in 1933 and the refusal of the recognition of Manchukuo by the United States in 1931. Whereas the Montevideo Convention formulated empirical criteria which an emerging political entity has to fulfil in order to become a state, the precedent set by the refusal to recognize Manchukuo not only by the United States but also by other Western powers was based on Japan's violation of *jus cogens* – that is, that the Japan-sponsored separation of Manchukuo (Manchuria) from China was a serious breach of international law. This later became the so-called Stimson doctrine which was taken over not only by the League of Nations but also by the United Nations (Ryngaert and Sobrie 2011, 472–473).

Thus, we can agree with Fabry (2012, 663) that in the second half of the 20th century the practice of state recognition shifted from the acknowledgement of effective, de facto achievement of independence to "acknowledgment of an entitlement to independence in international law". However, it would be somewhat naïve to expect that there were no deviations from the two practices as were noticed by Fabry. Besides the recognition of the factual existence of the entity or its legal right for secession, the practice of recognition has also always been a question of policy (cf. Lauterpacht 2013, 1).

In the second half of the 20th century, the practice of state recognition was quite consistent. This was caused not only because of the Montevideo Convention and Stimson doctrine, but above all due to the process of decolonization, which brought relatively clear principles on which the former colonies were recognized as independent states (Rich 1993, 55). The situation changed, however, in early 1990s, when the practice of state recognition became a question of policy more than in the previous decades. When the two communist federations, Yugoslavia and the Soviet Union, collapsed, the European Community issued guidelines, a political document, which formulated principles on which the emerging states in post-Communist Eastern Europe should have been recognized (Rich 1993; Ryngaert and Sobrie 2011). Also the limited recognitions of Kosovo, Abkhazia, and South Ossetia in the first decade of the 21st century confirmed that at present, state recognition is granted selectively (Worster 2009: 119–120). The entities which separated in the 1990s and at the beginning of the 21st century with the consent of the parent state and/or under the de-colonization paradigm, such as Eritrea, East Timor, South Sudan, or Montenegro, were promptly recognized by the majority of states; however, the recognition of entities whose separation was largely contested, such as Kosovo, Abkhazia, or South Ossetia, is limited. Their recognition is a question of policy – or – better to say – it is a question of the political interpretation of international legal principles (cf. Fabry 2012, 671). Thus, we should get used to the fact that de facto states do not constitute a temporary anomaly in the Westphalian system of states, but they are rather "a permanent part of the international system" (Relitz 2016, 96).

It was, however, not only the practice of state recognition, which has been changing throughout the centuries but also the meaning of the recognition for the newly formed political entities. In a globalizing world, international recognition has become of crucial importance for any break-away entity. It is a crucial precondition for break-away entities to fully enjoy security guarantees provided by international law and also to participate freely and without intermediaries in the globalized economy (cf. Lynch 2004, 4; Jakša 2017, 35).

Despite the shift in the practice of state recognition, and also in its importance for break-away entities, we argue that there are useful parallels between the unrecognized entities of the past and modern de facto states which help us to better understand the formation and also the sustainability of present-day de facto states. Thus, we call these historical entities as de facto state-like entities and three of them – the Bukharan People's Republic, Mongolia, and Tannu-Tuva – will be analysed in Section 2.

Collapse of tsarist Russia and formation of the Soviet Union

The first period of political-territorial restructuring in Eurasia started with the Bolshevik coup d'état in October 1917, after which dozens of more or less independent or at least self-governing political entities appeared in various places of the collapsing Russian empire. These entities differed in size, lifespan, and purpose of formation, but most of them would fit into one of the two following categories. First, entities which regarded themselves as provisional or revolutionary bodies. Their ultimate goal was not gaining independence, but joining either the emerging Soviet state or becoming part of a potentially renewed anti-Bolshevik Russian state. These were, for example, the Baku Commune, the Donetsk-Krivoi Rog Soviet Republic, the Odessa Soviet Republic, the Don Soviet Republic, or their anti-Bolshevik counterparts such as the Centrocaspian Dictatorship, the Don Republic (also known as the Almighty Don Host), the Idel-Ural State, etc. Second, ethnically defined political entities, which clearly formulated aspirations for becoming independent states. Whereas Finland and the Baltic states were successful in their separation from Russia, most similar attempts ended up

30 Vincenc Kopeček

in the reintegration of respective territories into the emerging Soviet state. This was, for example, the case of the Ukrainian People's Republic, the Belarussian People's Republic, the Mountainous Republic of the Northern Caucasus, the Democratic Republic of Georgia, the Azerbaijani Democratic Republic, and the Democratic Republic of Armenia.[1]

Some political entities which emerged after the collapse of tsarist Russia, however, did not fit into any of the two categories. This was, for example, the case of the Kuban People's Republic, whose political and military elite were split into pro-Russian and pro-independence/pro-Ukrainian factions (Smele 2015b, 636–637), the Far Eastern Republic, created by the Bolsheviks as a buffer state against Japan (Valliant 1997; Smele 2015a, Loc. 1332), the Republic of North Ingria, created by Ingrian Finns in order to join an independent Finland (Kurs 1994), the Aras Republic, a puppet state created by the Azerbaijani Democratic Republic in the contested territory of Nakhchivan (Smele 2015b, 130), the Duchy of Courland and Semigallia, later absorbed by the United Baltic Duchy, a pro-German state declared on the territory occupied by the German forces (Kasekamp 2010, 95–100), or the Bukharan People's Soviet Republic (see Chapter 2.2 for details), which was indeed a Bolshevik state, however, remained nominally independent until 1924 (Pipes 1997, 254–255). Moreover, there were also political entities, which emerged in the territories adjusting the former Russian empire, such as Mongolia, Tannu-Tuva, the West Ukrainian People's Republic, or the Lemko-Rusyn Republic. Although they emerged on the (former) territory of China and Austria-Hungary, respectively, they also became involved in the political struggle after the collapse of tsarist Russia. Whereas the territory of the western Ukraine (including the pro-Russian Lemko-Rusyn Republic) was conquered by the Polish army and become a part of the interwar Polish Republic (see e.g. Magocsi 1993), Mongolia and Tannu-Tuva gained, with Soviet support, independence from their former masters as will be discussed in detail in Chapter 2.3.

If we put aside those political entities which existed for less than two years and thus proved to be just ephemeral episodes of the complex political-territorial restructuring of the territory of the former Russian empire, a number of the remaining ones, above all the ethnically defined entities, show certain similarities with the present-day concept of de facto state. They controlled most of the territories they claimed, they had their own governments, demonstrated a strong determination to become independent states, but had only limited international recognition (cf. Balaev 1998, 146–147; Hille 2010, 143). However, in the given historical period the *de jure* recognition of newly formed state entities was perceived as far less important than in the present; thus, the term de facto state, if referring to these entities – although there are a number of similarities between these states and the present-day cases of de facto states – should be used with caution.

However, three of these entities will be put under scrutiny in Section 2: Mongolia, Tannu-Tuva, and the Bukharan People's Soviet Republic.

Unrecognized entities in Eurasia 31

The aim of the inclusion of these entities is to demonstrate that Russian state, be it tsarist Russia, the Soviet Union, or the Russian Federation, have been using de facto states and similar entities in order to reach its goals in the "Near Abroad" for decades. However, history has shown that this strategy has not always been successful, and that at least one of the entities which were formed thanks to Russian/Soviet support eventually became an internationally recognized state.

Dissolution of the Soviet Union

The second period of emergence of de facto states in Eurasia started in the last years of the Soviet Union. According to the 1977 Soviet Constitution, the individual SSRs – that is, subjects of the Soviet Union – had a right to secede. Whereas such a move would have been unthinkable in the reality of Brezhnev's Soviet Union, in the late 1980s the liberalization and democratization of political life under Gorbachev made secession of individual SSRs possible.[2] When the USSR dissolved finally at the end of 1991, the international community recognized fifteen former SSRs as independent states. There were, however, more entities with various political statuses, which strove for more political rights, if not complete independence. Their endeavours gained momentum after the adoption of the Law on Secession (see Chapter 3.1 for details) and Boris Yeltsin's support for the "sovereignty from the bottom up" (Walker 2003, 95). From December 1989 to September 1991, twenty-nine entities in total, mostly autonomous republics and regions (*oblasts*), but also two territories without an autonomous status (Gagauzia and Transnistria),[3] passed sovereignty declarations giving the territory's laws priority over the Union or SSR laws (Walker 2003, 96). Seven of these territories even went one step further and officially declared independence (Walker 2003, 165). They were, Abkhazia and South Ossetia (ethnic autonomies within the Georgian SSR), Nagorno-Karabakh (an Armenian-populated autonomous region within the Azerbaijan SSR), Chechnya (an autonomous republic within the Russian SFSR), Crimea (a peninsula in the Ukrainian SSR inhabited by an ethnic Russian majority), and, finally, Transnistria (a strip of land on the left bank of the Dniester River with a significant Russian and Ukrainian population) and Gagauzia (a set of enclaves inhabited by ethnic Gagauz, Christians speaking a Turkic language), both of whom were challenging the Moldavian/Romanian national project and demanding separation from Chisinau. With the exception of Chechnya, which was seeking independence from Russia, the remaining entities which were inhabited by ethnic groups that had strong relations to Russia or, in the case of Nagorno-Karabakh, to Armenia, did not initially strive for complete independence, but their main goal was to change their administrative status within the Soviet Union (Cornell 2001, 195; Walker 2003, 157–165; Saparov 2015, 149–165) – which the Law on Secession had just made possible, at least in theory.

32 *Vincenc Kopeček*

However, during the second half of 1991, when the Union republics were, one by one, declaring independence and the Soviet Union was finally dissolved by the ratification of the Belavezha Accords in December 1991, all the entities mentioned above, had to decide whether to come to terms with their parent SSR or to struggle for complete independence. Whereas in the case of Crimea a peaceful solution was negotiated soon after the formal declaration of independence and the territory retained its recently achieved autonomous status within Ukraine (Walker 2003, 168), the remaining six entities took the road to de facto statehood.

Transnistria, Abkhazia, and South Ossetia, supported by Russia, and Nagorno-Karabakh, supported by Armenia, managed to preserve their *de facto* separation from their parent states, former SSRs, by the use of force, and have been existing as de facto states until the present (see Chapters 3.2, 3.3, 4.3, and 4.5). However, the fate of Gagauzia and Chechnya was different. Whereas Gagauzia (see Chapter 5.4), after three years of de facto statehood, was peacefully reintegrated into Moldova as an "autonomous territorial unit" (see e.g. Kolstø and Malgin 1998; Roper 2001), Chechnya refused to sign a Federation Treaty and insisted on its independence from Russia (Walker 2003, 164). Although the Chechens were able to drive out Russian forces in 1996 and negotiate a treaty on peace and the principles of Russian-Chechen relations, which effectively meant a *de facto* sovereignty of the Chechen Republic of Ichkeria (Cornell 2001, 217–218), the Second Chechen War, which officially lasted from 1999 to 2009 (Schwirtz 2009), brought Chechnya back under Russia's jurisdiction (see Chapter 5.3). Several Chechen leaders, however, formed a Chechen government in exile. In 2007, Dokka Umarov, the then president of Ichkeria, dissolved this political entity and declared himself the emir of the Caucasus Emirate, which was to encompass the whole North Caucasus. Despite its name, the Caucasus Emirate has never had a character of de facto state. Instead, it has acted as a jihadist organization, which later declined in influence and swore loyalty to the Islamic State, becoming its "Caucasus Province" (Souleimanov 2011, 2015).

None of the entities discussed above were successful in gaining wider international recognition. The international community prefers to respect the inviolability of borders between the former Soviet republics – with the exception of Russia, Venezuela, Nicaragua, Nauru, and Syria – states, which after the August 2008 Russian-Georgian war officially recognized the independence of Abkhazia and South Ossetia (Ker-Lindsay 2012, 29, 53).[4]

Besides the previously mentioned Crimea, there were more entities, which in the early 1990s enjoyed a certain degree of self-rule, but they are definitely not cases of de facto states as the concept is understood in this book. It was, for example, the case of Tatarstan, which, similarly to Chechnya, refused to sign the Federation Treaty. Unlike Chechnya, Tatarstan finally came to terms with the Russian Federation and negotiated a special status in 1994 (Malik 1994). However, in 2007 the powers of the Tatarstan authorities were

Unrecognized entities in Eurasia 33

reduced and in 2017 the republic completely lost its special status (Smirnova 2017).[5] In the South Caucasus, only two of the five autonomous entities[6] did not secede from their parent states – Ajaria and Nakhchivan. However, until 2004, when the newly elected Georgian president Mikheil Saakashvili forced the long-time leader of the Ajarian autonomy, Aslan Abashidze, to leave for Moscow, Ajaria was effectively out of control of the Georgian government (Marten 2012, 68–86). A similar situation remains in Nakhchivan, the Azerbaijani exclave possessing the status of an autonomous republic. In January 1990, in the midst of the chaos after the crackdown on the anti-Communist Azerbaijani Popular Front in Baku earlier that month, Nakhchivan ASSR declared its intention to secede from the Soviet Union. The intention went in vain, as the KGB units promptly took over Nakhchivan (O'Ballance 1997, 46); however, in the following years the exclave appeared to be under the control of Vasif Talibov, a relation of Azerbaijani president Heydar Aliyev, who himself was born in Nakhchivan. Talibov has been enjoying substantial autonomy from Baku (Kopeček 2016, 72–73), and in fact turned Nakchivan into a state-within-a-state (Caspersen 2012, Loc. 300). Even this case, indeed, cannot be treated as de facto state, as the 1990 Nakhchivan declaration of independence had a rather symbolic meaning and the Talibov government remains loyal to his relation in the Azerbaijani capital.

Even the remaining territories which in the South Caucasus somehow wrestled out of governmental control in the 1990s or early 2000s cannot be interpreted as de facto states. They were too ephemeral, their attempted governments did not really control declared territory, or they did not declare independence at all. In June 1993, the Talysh-Mughan Autonomous Republic was declared in the south of Azerbaijan by Alakram Hummatov, an ethnic Talysh and Azerbaijani military officer. Hummatov was apparently a pro-Russian figure attempting to destabilize Azerbaijan by provoking another separatist movement, but when the newly elected president Heydar Aliyev stabilized the situation in the country, the "republic", which did not even possess local support, was dissolved three months after its formation (Shafee 2008, 204–205).

The Pankisi Valley, the Upper Kodori Valley, and Javakheti in Georgia were in certain periods of Georgia's independence out of control of the Tbilisi government. Although Javakheti had certain potential for irredentism, as discussed in Chapter 3.3, representatives of the local Armenian community have never declared independence (Lohm 2007, 14), and after the turbulent early 1990s the central government gradually re-established its presence there (Kopeček 2019, 64). The cases of Pankisi and Upper Kodori were rather examples of what Stanislawski et al. (2008, 366) call black spots – territories controlled by regional warlords who did not seek independence, but preferred to be "forgotten islands of international disorder". In Kist[7] inhabited Pankisi, where thousands of Chechen refugees as well as a number of Chechen fighters (*boeviki*) fled from war-torn Chechnya, several years of warlord domination ended in 2002 (Wheatley 2005, 177–178). In Upper

34 Vincenc Kopeček

Kodori, part of Abkhazia which used to be out of control of the Abkhazian *de facto* government, the domination of local warlord Enzar Kvitsiani ended in 2006. He was forced to flee during an operation by Georgian forces in 2006, which then administered the territory until the August 2008 war (Marten 2012, 86–99). Similar black spots also existed in Russia's Dagestan in 1998–1999 – the "Wahhabi Republic" in Kadar Jamaat region – or in Tajikistan's Gorno-Badakhshan autonomous region in 1993–1999 (Stanislawski et al. 2008, 376–377).[8]

The crisis in Ukraine: Crimea and beyond

At the beginning of the 21st century, the list of post-Soviet de facto states seemed to be definitive. However, in 2014, a political crisis in Ukraine followed by the Russian military intervention led to the formation of other break-away entities in Eurasia. Three or four (if Sevastopol is included) distinct entities emerged in 2014. At first, the Autonomous Republic of Crimea and the city with special status of Sevastopol declared independence and were promptly and unilaterally annexed by the Russian Federation in March 2014. The annexation of Crimea was followed by the de facto secession of parts of the Donetsk and Luhansk regions in the East of Ukraine. This took the form of the Donetsk People's Republic and the Luhansk People's Republic, which declared independence from Ukraine in April 2014. Both entities managed, with apparent Russian support, to gain control over significant portions of the Donetsk and Luhansk regions and even tried to set up a larger confederative state which also had to encompass other Ukrainian territories; however, the power of separatist leaders remains restricted to the southeastern part of the two Ukrainian regions, including the Donetsk and Luhansk agglomerations (Toal 2017, 237–268). The intentions of the leaders of the two break-away republics are unclear. Their political declarations vary between calls for a formation of the so-called Little Russia (Malorossiya), a kind of alternative government to the one in Kiev, and calls for integration with Russia (BBC 2017; RFE/RL 2018). However, Russia has so far rejected both calls and both entities thus remain in a kind of limbo. Thus, it is debatable whether to include the Donetsk and Luhansk People's Republics into the list of de facto states as interpreted in this book; but definitely they are either emerging de facto states or borderline cases and they will be put under scrutiny in Chapter 3.4.

Crimea and Sevastopol are a rather different case. The annexation was formally preceded by a brief period of nominal independence; however, the two days in February 2014 between the formal declaration of Crimean independence and the official annexation by Russia (Englund 2014) cannot be, in any way, seen as a period of de facto statehood. Although the Crimea has been a specific territory for decades, enjoying differing political statuses, nor Crimea, or Sevastopol have ever been de facto states. The contested character of Crimea dates back to the Russian Civil War, when a number of short-lived political entities existed in the peninsula and the surrounding mainland (the Crimean People's Republic, the Taurida Soviet Socialist Republic, the Crimean Regional Government, and the Crimean Socialist Soviet Republic). In 1921, the Crimean Autonomous Soviet Socialist Republic was declared as a part of the Russian Soviet Federative Socialist Republic. After the expulsion of the Crimean Tatars in 1944, the Crimean ASSR was converted into the Crimean Region in 1945 and in 1954 it was transferred to the Ukrainian SSR. The autonomous status was restored in February 1991 in the form of the ASSR. During the dissolution of the Soviet Union, the Crimea was seen as a potential separatist entity; however, the imminent conflict between the prevalently Russian-speaking Crimea and the Ukrainian government was avoided. After a period of searching for an appropriate political status, in 1995, the peninsula was granted the status of the Autonomous Republic of Crimea, whereas Sevastopol, the seat of the Russian Black Sea Fleet, was made a city with special status. Despite the seemingly calm situation of the 1990s and 2000s in Crimea, a number of studies pointed out that the status of the peninsula was far from being accepted by Russia as well as the Crimean Russians (Kuzio 2010; Roslycky 2011; Malyarenko and Galbreath 2013). The events from early 2014 have proven that these studies were right (Table 1).

Table 1 Post-Soviet de facto states (including borderline cases)

facto state	Controlled area (sq. km)	Population	Capital	Years of existence	Recognized by UN member states
khazia	8,640	244,000 (2015)	Sukhumi (Sukhum)	1992–	Russia, Venezuela, Nicaragua, Nauru, Syria (Vanuatu and Tuvalu withdrew)
echen Republic of chkeria	17,000	1,200,000 (1996)	Grozny (Jokhar-Gala)	1991–2000	
netsk People's Republic	8,700	2,300,000 (2017)	Donetsk	2014–	
gauzia	1,832	135,000 (2014)	Comrat (Komrat)	1991–1994	
hansk People's Republic	8,100	1,470,000 (2017)	Luhansk (Lugansk)	2014–	
gorno-Karabakh Artsakh)	11,430	146,000 (2016)	Stepanakert (Khankendy)	1991–	
ith Ossetia	3,900	53,000 (2015)	Tskhinvali (Tskhinval)	1991–	Russia, Venezuela, Nicaragua, Nauru, Syria (Tuvalu withdrew)
insnistria Pridnestrovie)	4,163	475,000 (2015)	Tiraspol	1992–	

irces: UGS RYUO (2016); Pridnestrovie (2017); STAT NKR (2016); UGS RA (2016); Goskomstat LNR 8); Glavstat DNR (2018); Statistica Moldovei (2014); UNPO (2006, 60).

36 Vincenc Kopeček

Notes

1 For details on political entities which emerged after the collapse of tsarist Russia see, for example, Smele (2015a, 2015b).
2 For details on the dissolution of the Soviet Union see, for example, Walker (2003) or Lapidus, Zaslavsky, and Goldman (1992).
3 Crimea, which also passed the sovereignty declaration, was given the autonomous status only in February 1991 (Walker 2003, 165).
4 Abkhazia was also recognized by Tuvalu and Vanuatu and South Ossetia by Tuvalu. Both countries, however, later withdrew their recognitions (Civil Georgia 2014).
5 There were, however, more subjects of the Russian Federation which used to possess special status inspired by the Tatarstan model – see Sakwa (2016).
6 Within the Georgian SSR, there were two ASSRs – Abkhazia and Ajaria – and one autonomous region – South Ossetia. Within the Azerbaijan SSR, there was one ASSR – Nakhchivan, and one autonomous region – Nagorno-Karabakh. Nakhchivan and Ajaria were special cases within the structure of Soviet autonomies because they were not based on an ethnic principle as it was understood in the Soviet Union. Nakhchivan is an Azeri-populated exclave separated from Azerbaijan proper by a strip of land belonging to Armenia, whereas Ajarians, who were counted as a separate ethnic group until 1920s, differ from the Georgian majority not by language, but by religion.
7 Kists are ethnic Chechens (Vainakhs), who migrated to Georgia's Pankisi about 200 years ago (Sedlářová 2011, 264).
8 In the midst of the Tajik civil war, the Gorno-Badakhshan autonomous region declared independence in 1992. However, it remained rather proclamatory, and the regional government called it back in 1997 (Asim, Roofi, and Mahesar 2017, 331). Instead of virtually non-existent Gorno-Badakhshan government, the region was until 2000 administered by Agha Khan Foundation, an organization led by local Ismaili spiritual leader, which substituted institutions of the failed Tajik state (Stanislawski et al. 2008, 376–377).

Literature

Asim, Muhammad, Yasmin Roofi, and Shuja A. Mahesar 2017. "Ethnic Dilemma in Badakhshan Region: Implications on Pamiri Ethnic Group in Pakistan." *Grassroots* 51 (1): 331–344.

Balaev, Aidyn. 1998. *Azerbaidzhanskoe Natsionalnoe Dvizhenie v 1917–1918 Gg* [Azerbaijani National Movement in 1917–1918]. Baku: ELM.

BBC. 2017. "Ukraine Conflict: Russia Rejects New Donetsk Rebel 'State'." *BBC News*, July 19. www.bbc.com/news/world-europe-40653913.

Caspersen, Nina. 2012. *Unrecognized States. The Struggle for Sovereignty in the Modern International System*. Cambridge: Polity Press.

Civil Georgia. 2014. "Tuvalu Retracts Abkhazia, S. Ossetia Recognition." *Civil Georgia*, March 31. http://civil.ge/eng/article.php?id=27093.

Collier, David, and James E. Mahon. 1993. "Conceptual 'Stretching' Revisited: Adapting Categories in Comparative Analysis." *The American Political Science Review* 87 (4): 845–855.

Cornell, Svante E. 2001. *Small Nations and Great Powers. A Study of Ethnopolitical Conflict in the Caucasus*. Richmond: Curzon Press.

Englund, Will. 2014. "Kremlin Says Crimea Is Now Officially Part of Russia after Treaty Signing, Putin Speech." *The Washington Post*, March 18. www.washingtonpost.

Unrecognized entities in Eurasia 37

com/world/russias-putin-prepares-to-annex-crimea/2014/03/18/933183b2-654e-45ce-920e-4d18c0ffec73_story.html?utm_term=.1819d11e54f9.

Fabry, Mikulas. 2010. *Recognizing States: International Society and the Establishment of New States since 1776.* New York: Oxford University Press.

Fabry, Mikulas. 2012. "The Contemporary Practice of State Recognition: Kosovo, South Ossetia, Abkhazia, and Their Aftermath." *Nationalities Papers* 40 (5): 661–676.

Glavstat DNR. 2018. "Chislennost naseleniya DNR na 1 marta 2018 goda." Glavnoe upravlenie statistiki DNR. http://glavstat.govdnr.ru/pdf/naselenie/chisl_naselenie_0318.pdf.

Goskomstat LNR. 2018. "Chislennost naseleniya Luganskoi Narodnoi Respubliki." Gosudarstvennyi komitet statistiki LNR. www.gkslnr.su/files/chisl_260318.pdf.

Hille, Charlotte M. L. 2010. *State Building and Conflict Resolution in the Caucasus.* Leiden and Boston: BRILL.

Jakša, Urban. 2017. "Ontological Security of the Post-Soviet De Facto States." In *Unrecognized States and Secession in the 21st Century,* edited by Martin Riegl and Bohumil Doboš, 35–51. Cham: Springer International Publishing.

Kasekamp, Andres. 2010. *A History of the Baltic States.* Houndmills: Palgrave Macmillan.

Ker-Lindsay, James. 2012. *The Foreign Policy of Counter Secession: Preventing the Recognition of Contested States.* Oxford: Oxford University Press.

Kolstø, Pål, and Andrei Malgin. 1998. "The Transnistrian Republic: A Case of Politicized Regionalism." *Nationalities Papers* 26 (1): 103–127.

Kopeček, Vincenc. 2016. "How to Capture a State? The Case of Azerbaijan." *Politické vedy* 19 (2): 64–89.

Kopeček, Vincenc. 2019. "Trapped in Informality? A Study of Informal Politics in Georgia's Javakheti." *Caucasus Survey* 7 (1): 60–78.

Kurs, Ott. 1994. "Ingria: The Broken Landbridge between Estonia and Finland." *GeoJournal* 33 (1): 107–113.

Kuzio, Taras. 2010. *The Crimea: Europe's Next Flashpoint?* Washington, DC: The Jamestown Foundation.

Lapidus, Gail W., Victor Zaslavsky, and Philip Goldman, eds. 1992. *From Union to Commonwealth: Nationalism and Separatism in the Soviet Republics.* Cambridge: Cambridge University Press.

Lauterpacht, Hersch. 2013. *Recognition in International Law.* Reprint. Cambridge: Cambridge University Press.

Lohm, Hedvig. 2007. *Javakheti after the Rose Revolution: Progress and Regress in the Pursuit of National Unity in Georgia.* ECMI Working Paper # 38. Flensburg: European Centre for Minority Issues. www.ecmi.de/uploads/tx_lfpubdb/working_paper_38.pdf.

Lynch, Dov. 2004. *Engaging Eurasia's Separatist States: Unresolved Conflicts and De Facto States.* Washington: United States Institute of Peace Press.

Magocsi, Paul Robert. 1993. "The Ukrainian Question between Poland and Czechoslovakia: The Lemko Rusyn Republic (1918–1920) and Political Thought in Western Rus'-Ukraine." *Nationalities Papers* 21 (2): 95–105.

Malik, Hafeez. 1994. "Tatarstan's Treaty with Russia: Autonomy or Independence." *Journal of South Asian and Middle Eastern Studies* 18 (2): 1–36.

Malyarenko, Tetyana, and David J. Galbreath. 2013. "Crimea: Competing Self-Determination Movements and the Politics at the Centre." *Europe-Asia Studies* 65 (5): 912–928.

38 *Vincenc Kopeček*

Marten, Kimberly. 2012. *Warlords: Strong-Arm Brokers in Weak States*. Ithaca and London: Cornell University Press.

O'Ballance, Edgar. 1997. *Wars in the Caucasus 1990–1995*. New York: New York University Press.

Pipes, Richard. 1997. *The Formation of the Soviet Union: Communism and Nationalism, 1917–1923*. Cambridge and London: Harvard University Press.

Popper, Karl. R. 1947. *The Open Society and Its Enemies. Volume I. The Spell of Plato*. London: George Routledge & Sons.

Pridnestrovie. 2017. "Pridnestrovie v tsifrakh [Transnistria in Numbers]." *Gazeta Pridnestrovie*, March 1. http://pridnestrovie-daily.net/archives/16304.

Relitz, Sebastian. 2016. "De Facto States in The European Neighbourhood: Between Russian Domination and European (Dis)Engagement. The Case of Abkhazia." *EURINT* 3: 96–113.

RFE/RL. 2018. "Separatist Leader in Eastern Ukraine Vows Closer Russia Integration after 'Sham' Polls." *Radio Free Europe/Radio Liberty*, November 15. www. rferl.org/a/separatist-leader-pushilin-eastern-ukraine-vows-closer-integration-russia/29601673.html.

Rich, Roland. 1993. "Recognition of States: The Collapse of Yugoslavia and the Soviet Union." *European Journal of International Law* 4 (1): 36–65.

Roper, Steven D. 2001. "Regionalism in Moldova: The Case of Transnistria and Gagauzia." *Regional & Federal Studies* 11 (3): 101–122.

Roslycky, Lada L. 2011. "Russia's Smart Power in Crimea: Sowing the Seeds of Trust." *Southeast European and Black Sea Studies* 11 (3): 299–316.

Ryngaert, Cedric, and Sven Sobrie. 2011. "Recognition of States: International Law or Realpolitik? The Practice of Recognition in the Wake of Kosovo, South Ossetia, and Abkhazia." *Leiden Journal of International Law* 24 (2): 467–490.

Sakwa, Richard. 2016. "Devolution and Asymmetry in Russia." In *Federalism Beyond Federations: Asymmetry and Processes of Resymmetrisation in Europe*, edited by Ferran Requejo and Klaus-Jürgen Nagel, 155–176. London and New York: Routledge.

Saparov, Arsène. 2015. *From Conflict to Autonomy in the Caucasus: The Soviet Union and the Making of Abkhazia, South Ossetia and Nagorno Karabakh*. Kindle Edition. Abingdon and New York: Routledge.

Sartori, Giovanni. 1970. "Concept Misformation in Comparative Politics." *The American Political Science Review* 64 (4): 1033–1053.

Schwirtz, Michael. 2009. "Russia Ends Operations in Chechnya." *The New York Times*, April 16. www.nytimes.com/2009/04/17/world/europe/17chechnya.html.

Sedláŕová, Lenka. 2011. "Kists Facing Language Policy in Georgia." In *The Scale of Globalization. Think Globally, Act Locally, Change Individually in the 21st Century*, edited by Přemysl Mácha and Tomáš Drobík, 292–302. Ostrava: University of Ostrava.

Shafee, Fareed. 2008. "Inspired from Abroad: The External Sources of Separatism in Azerbaijan." *Caucasian Review of International Affairs* 2 (4): 200–211.

Shorten, Richard. 2012. *Modernism and Totalitarianism: Rethinking the Intellectual Sources of Nazism and Stalinism, 1945 to the Present*. Basingstoke and New York: Palgrave Macmillan.

Smele, Jonathan D. 2015a. *The "Russian" Civil Wars, 1916–1926: Ten Years That Shook the World*. Kindle Edition. New York: Oxford University Press.

Smele, Jonathan D. 2015b. *Historical Dictionary of the Russian Civil Wars, 1916–1926*. Lanham: Rowman & Littlefield.

Smirnova, Lena. 2017. "Tatarstan, the Last Region to Lose Its Special Status under Putin." *The Moscow Times*, July 25. http://themoscowtimes.com/articles/tatarstan-special-status-expires-58483.

Souleimanov, Emil. 2011. "The Caucasus Emirate: Genealogy of an Islamist Insurgency." *Middle East Policy* 18 (4): 155–168.

Souleimanov, Emil. 2015. "Caucasus Emirate Faces Further Decline after the Death of Its Leader." *Central Asia – Caucasus Analyst*, April 29. www.cacianalyst.org/publications/analytical-articles/item/13188-caucasus-emirate-faces-further-decline-after-the-death-of-its-leader.html.

Stanislawski, Bartosz H., Katarzyna Pełczyńska-Nałęcz, Krzysztof Strachota, Maciej Falkowski, David M. Crane, and Melvyn Levitsky. 2008. "Para-States, Quasi-States, and Black Spots: Perhaps Not States, but Not 'Ungoverned Territories,' Either." *International Studies Review* 10 (2): 366–396.

Stanley, John L. 1987. "Is Totalitarianism a New Phenomenon? Reflections on Hannah Arendt's Origins of Totalitarianism." *The Review of Politics* 49 (2): 177–207.

STAT NKR. 2016. *Nagorno Karabakh in Figures*. Stepanakert: National Statistical Service of the NKR.

Statistica Moldovei. 2014. "Population and Housing Census in 2014." *Population and Housing Census in the Republic of Moldova, May 12–25, 2014*. www.statistica.md/pageview.php?l=en&idc=479&.

Toal, Gerard. 2017. *Near Abroad: Putin, the West and the Contest over Ukraine and the Caucasus*. 1st edition. New York: Oxford University Press.

UGS RA. 2016. *Abkhazia v tsifrakh 2015 goda [Abkhazia in Numbers in 2015]*. Sukhum: Upravlenie gosudarstvennoi statistiki Respubliki Abkhaziya. http://ugsra.org/abkhaziya-v-tsifrakh/2015-0.pdf.

UGS RYUO. 2016. *Itogi Vseobshchei perepisi RYUO 2015 [Results of the General Census of the RSO]*. Tskhinval: Upravlenie gosudarstvennoi statistiki Respubliki Yuzhnaya Osetiya. http://ugosstat.ru/itogi-vseobshhey-perepisi-naseleniya-respubliki-yuzhnaya-osetiya-2015-goda/.

UNPO. 2006. "Background and Present Situation of the Talysh." *Unrepresented Nations and Peoples Organization*. www.unpo.org/article/3910.

Valliant, Robert. 1997. "Moscow and the Russian Far East. The Political Dimension." In *Politics and Economics in the Russian Far East: Changing Ties with Asia-Pacific*, edited by Tsuneo Akaha, 3–22. London and New York: Routledge.

Walker, Edward W. 2003. *Dissolution: Sovereignty and the Breakup of the Soviet Union*. Lanham: Rowman & Littlefield.

Wheatley, Jonathan. 2005. *Georgia from National Awakening to Rose Revolution: Delayed Transition in the Former Soviet Union*. Aldershot and Burlington: Ashgate Publishing.

Worster, William T. 2009. "Law, Politics, and the Conception of the State in State Recognition Theory." *Boston University International Law Journal* 27 (1): 116–171.

Yemelianova, Galina. 2015. "Western Academic Discourse on the Post-Soviet De Facto State Phenomenon." *Caucasus Survey* 3 (3): 219–238.

Section 2

Russian territorial expansion and de facto states in the first half of 20th century

2.1 Introduction to Russian and Soviet territorial expansion

Vladimír Baar and Slavomír Horák

Bukhara, Mongolia, and Tuva are three examples of de facto state-like entities, which emerged during Russian/Soviet expansion to Central Asia and the Far East. During the 16th and 17th centuries Russia annexed vast territories of Siberia, invoking the concept of *terra nullius,* and finally reached the Pacific coast in 1647. However, its further expansion to the south and east had to wait until the beginning of the 19th century, when Russia's expansion to the west was halted by the European powers. Russia thus turned its attention to the Caucasus, Central Asia, and the Far East.

Unlike the earlier Eastern Expansion, which had been more a struggle against the harsh natural environment than against the small and dispersed population, this time Russia faced relatively strong consolidated states. This included the Ottoman Empire, Iran, and China as well as other colonial powers – most significantly Britain and Japan. The expansion had thus become a complex chess game in which Russia had to carefully consider what forms of pressure it should exert in order to continue expanding its influence.

History shows that during its colonial expansion, Russia usually annexed newly conquered territories immediately – simply expanding its administrative structures into newly created governorates (*guberniya*) or regions (*krai, oblast*). In the occupied territories with more densely concentrated populations and firmer state structures, however, Russia contented itself with the formation of protectorates, territories of influence, and buffer zones. Protectorate status was also used if the claimed territory formed part of another state which was unwilling to relinquish it. This was, for example, the case of the South Caucasus and Central Asia, where a number of conquered khanates, emirates, and principalities which used to be independent or were under the suzerainty of the Ottoman Empire or Iran, formally existed even decades after they were subjugated by the Russian Empire (Allworth 1994, 165–166; Kopeček and Jelen 2015, 145–146). For example, the principality of Abkhazia was conquered by the Russian army in 1810, but it was abolished only in 1864, and the neighbouring principality of Odishi, which became Russia's protectorate in 1803 was abolished only in 1867 (Mikaberidze 2007, 460–461; Souleimanov and Hoch 2012, 41). Although most of these entities existed in a form of pre-stage before their full annexation by Russia, some

44 Vladimír Baar and Slavomír Horák

of these entities survived for a longer period, such as the emirate of Bukhara and the khanate of Khiva, which as protectorates even survived the fall of the Russian empire, and were later transformed into people's republics (see Chapter 2.2). The formation of specific political entities in Mongolia and Tuva at the turn of the 20th century followed a similar pattern. However, as tsarist Russia collapsed before it was able to completely wrestle these territories from China, they took the opportunity presented by the weakening of the Chinese and Russian states and declared independence which was preserved for at least several decades (see Chapter 2.3).

During the Russian Civil War of 1917–1922 a number of territories declared independence on Russia (see Chapter 1.3). Most of them were ephemeral short-lived entities, however, some of them gained virtual independence. Whereas Poland, the Baltic States, and Finland preserved their independence and became recognized by the international community (Rich 1993, 37), Ukraine, Belarus, Armenia, Azerbaijan, and Georgia, despite possessing limited international recognition (Talmon 1998, 288–289; Michaluk and Rudling 2014; Yusifova 2014; Gachechiladze 2016, 23) were conquered by the Red Army, and Sovietized. This meant that the national governments were replaced by Bolshevik-led governments which declared the individual republics as Soviet Socialist Republics. Although they nominally remained independent, they were de facto controlled by the Bolsheviks and finally became the founding republics of the Soviet Union in 1922. A similar pattern was also applied to some Central Asian territories, for example, Khiva and above all Bukhara, which will be analysed in Chapter 2.2.

The aim of this section is to demonstrate on the cases of Bukhara, Mongolia, and Tuva that although existing in a different historical context and the *de jure* recognition of newly formed state entities was perceived as less important than in the present, these entities shared a number of similarities with present-day de facto states and thus can serve as useful historical analogies. Above all, in this section we demonstrate which circumstances led to the incorporation of bygone "de facto states" into their powerful patron – The Soviet Union – and which helped some of them to eventually become fully recognized states.

Literature

Allworth, Edward A. 1994. *Central Asia, 130 Years of Russian Dominance: A Historical Overview*. Durham and London: Duke University Press.

Gachechiladze, Revaz. 2016. "Geopolitics and Foreign Powers in the Modern History of Georgia: Comparing 1918–1921 and 1991–2010." In *The Making of Modern Georgia, 1918–2012. The First Georgian Republic and Its Successors*, edited by Stephen F. Jones, 17–34. London and New York: Routledge.

Kopeček, Vincenc, and Libor Jelen. 2015. "Jižní Kavkaz – od tradice k modernitě pod vlivem ruského kolonialismu [The South Caucasus – From Tradition to Modernity under the Influence of Russian Colonialism]." In *Prekolonialismus, kolonialismus a postkolonialismus: impéria a ti ostatní ve východní a jihovýchodní*

Evropě [Pre-colonialism, Colonialism, and Post-Colonialism: Empires and the Others in the Eastern and Southeastern Europe], edited by Stanislav Tumis and Hanuš Nykl, 143–162. Prague: Charles University, Faculty of Philosophy.

Michaluk, Dorota, and Per A. Rudling. 2014. "From the Grand Duchy of Lithuania to the Belarusian Democratic Republic: The Idea of Belarusian Statehood, 1915–1919." *The Journal of Belorusian Studies* 7 (2): 3–36.

Mikaberidze, Alexander. 2007. *Historical Dictionary of Georgia*. Lanham, Toronto, and Plymouth: The Scarecrow Press.

Rich, Roland. 1993. "Recognition of States: The Collapse of Yugoslavia and the Soviet Union." *European Journal of International Law* 4 (1): 36–65.

Souleimanov, Emil, and Tomáš Hoch. 2012. *Role Ruska v konfliktech a oficiálních mírových procesech v Abcházii a Jižní Osetii v letech 1991–2008* [Russia's Role in Conflicts and Official Peace Processes in Abkhazia and South Ossetia in 1991–2008]. Prague: Auditorium.

Talmon, Stefan. 1998. *Recognition of Governments in International Law*. Oxford: Oxford University Press.

Yusifova, Shabnam. 2014. "The Recognition of the Independence of Azerbaijan Democratic Republic in Paris Peace Conference and the Attitude of Iran." *Mediterranean Journal of Social Sciences* 5 (19): 355–364.

2.2 Bukharan People's Soviet Republic
From protectorate to SSR

Slavomír Horák

The history of the Bukharan People's Soviet Republic has been explored in several different discourses. In the Soviet era, this entity was viewed in the context of the official concept of history; it was deemed to have been a bourgeois republic that represented a transitional phase between the overthrow of the Bukharan Emir – associated with the struggle against imperialism and British colonialism – and the building of a genuine Soviet state (Ishanov 1955, 32–33). From this perspective, Soviet historiography considered the so-called Bukharan Communist Party to have been the only progressive force in Bukhara; they treated the Jadidist concept of the Bukharan state as merely an element in the development of the Bukharan Communist Party, which, in turn, was viewed through the wider prism of the development of all communist parties in the USSR. Western historiography from previous decades (d'Encausse 1966; Becker 2004) likewise views the Bukharan People's Soviet Republic primarily as a transitional state between the overthrow of the Emir and the incorporation of Bukhara into the USSR. More recently, the Bukharan People's Soviet Republic has been studied by the American historian Adeeb Khalid (2010, 2015), who views it from the perspective of Jadidist concepts – that is, as a viable project which represented the culmination of the Jadids' long-term struggle to establish a modern nation state in Central Asia (Khalid 2015, 257–258).

Examination of Soviet and Bukharan sources reveals substantially differing interpretations of the birth, existence, and eventual extinction of the Bukharan People's Soviet Republic. Taking this comparative approach, it is also necessary to consider to what extent we can speak of de facto states in the case of historical entities. Fabry (2010, 69–70) convincingly demonstrates that the emergence of de facto statehood was undoubtedly a typical phenomenon of the initial decolonization stage of Latin America. And though it is quite difficult, in the narrow sense, to talk about the de facto states before the Second World War, according to the logic of their internal and external sovereignty, we can find a number of similarities between these historical entities and present-day de facto states (Map 2).

This chapter does not set out to provide an exhaustive analysis of the Bukharan People's Soviet Republic from 1920 to 1924. Instead it gives an account of the internal development and external relations of this entity with

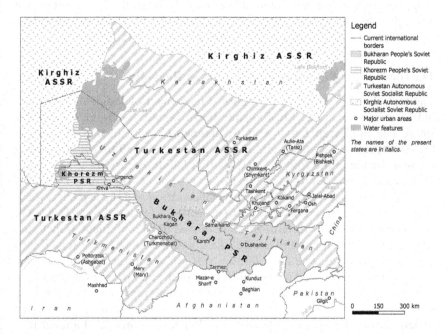

Map 2 Bukharan People's Soviet Republic (1920–1924).
Source: Authors.

regard to the concept of de facto states. It focusses on the different perceptions of statehood by the Bukharan elites on the one hand, and the Soviet regime on the other hand. Although the main representatives of both Bukhara and Russia (in Tashkent and Moscow) viewed the Bukharan People's Soviet Republic as part of the October Revolution, the two sides had differing opinions on the internal structure and external context of the republic. At the level of the local elites, the Bukharan People's Soviet Republic was viewed as a temporary entity, a precursor to the formation of a permanent, internationally recognized state entity based on the Jadidist concept of a modern Muslim state in Central Asia. However, this concept was at odds with the Soviet concept of Bukhara as a nominally independent state, but under the control of a patron state[1] – the USSR. This chapter demonstrates that given Bukhara's almost complete military and economic dependence on Russia, it was inevitable that the second concept would ultimately gain the upper hand – that is, the Soviet concept of patronage, viewing the Bukharan state as a transitional phase between the dictatorship of the Emirate and the building of a genuine Soviet state. Bukhara's internal weakness, combined with the existence of a strong patron state, was the main factor that led to the demise of the Bukharan statehood in the mid-1920s. The following text discusses the clash between these two opposing concepts, demonstrating that developments in Bukhara not only represented the successful fulfilment

48 *Slavomír Horák*

of Soviet goals in the region but also ultimately led to the fulfilment of one of the Jadids' main goals – the creation of a modern (at least by contemporary standards) state with a settled population in Central Asia.

The roots of the Bukharan People's Soviet Republic

The republic was rooted in the political movement of Jadidism, which set out to create a modern Muslim state in Turkestan and Bukhara (Khalid 1999). The Bukharan Jadids initially planned to build such a state within the structures of the existing Emirate; at the end of the 19th century and in the first decade of the 20th century, leading Jadids discussed the possibility of reforming the Emirate to enable this to take place. However, in 1917 this approach was abandoned following the declaration and subsequent revocation of the Emir's reformist manifesto in April 1917 (Shestakov 1927, 82–83). Conservative forces within the Emirate proved to be so influential that they were able to have the manifesto revoked, and the Jadids were forced into exile or imprisoned. The Emir himself was not a genuine proponent of reform; he had only agreed to the publication of the manifesto under pressure from the (still influential) Russian administration, represented by the Russian political agent Miller. For the Jadidist movement (and primarily for its left-leaning wing headed by Faizullo Khojayev), this development represented a turning-point for the Jadids' ambition to build a modern state. It convinced the leading forces within Bukhara's Jadidist movement that the Emirate was fundamentally unreformable, and led them to pursue their goals without the participation of the Emirate (Khalid 1999, 295).

The Jadids who had fled from persecution in 1917 found refuge in nearby Russian cities such as Chardzhou or Samarkand. In the autumn of 1917 their organization – better known as the Young Bukharan Party (*Yosh bukhoroliklar*) – was essentially reconstituted, along with a new manifesto created by one of the most prominent representatives of the Bukharan Jadids, Abdurauf Fitrat (Dimanshteyn 1930, 361–372; Kasymov and Ergashev 1989). Faizullo Khojayev headed the Young Bukharans' radical wing. Young, energetic, and radical, Khojayev understood that the new state would need a strong patron to provide both political and military support. Ideologically, Khojayev favoured the idea of a Muslim nation state – such as the Kokand Autonomy in 1918. However, unlike the Kokand Autonomy – whose leader Mustafa Chokai was critical of the Bolsheviks – Khojayev declared his loyalty to Bolshevik Russia from the very outset; this later helped him to rise to a prominent position in Soviet Uzbekistan and make Uzbekistan one of the leading Central Asian SSRs (Norling 2014, 65–66). Khojayev had been brought up in a Russian environment, and he was one of the most pro-Russian figures among the Jadids (Chika 2001, 99). Soviet-era documentaries characterized him as

> a person who wanted to combine both nationalism and communism in one person, very young (aged 26) and inexperienced. At the same time

he was the son of a rich local merchant, one of the monopolists under the Emir's government. He made no secret of his nationalism and his pride in Bukhara.

(RGASPI, f. 62, op. 2, d. 5, l. 18)

The conquest of Kokand by Bolshevik troops in 1918 showed that the idea of a multinational democratic state existing without the support of external forces (or the Bolsheviks) was an illusion. Although the Bolsheviks' victory at this point was still not yet secure (there would later be several uprisings against Bolshevik rule in Tashkent itself), the Soviet administration proved to be the most powerful force in the region. After fleeing Bukhara, Khojayev lived in Tashkent, where he definitively committed himself to the Bolshevik cause with the aim of creating a modern Bukharan state in the Jadidist sense. However, the Bukharan Jadids proved unable to recruit the support of more than a few hundred people, so they were heavily outnumbered by supporters of the Emir. The Bolshevik leadership in Tashkent was convinced that after the fall of the Kokand Autonomy, Bukhara would be an easy target – especially as the Bolsheviks had been promised support from Bukharan troops (though these troops did not actually exist). However, the failure of the Bolsheviks' attempt to take Bukhara (with the participation of Bukharan Jadids) showed that the Young Bukharans' plans were unrealistic (Genis 1993, 41, 2001).

Even after this failed attempt, Bukhara and its prospective pro-Soviet regime played an important role in Soviet policy – not only in Central Asia itself but also in the Bolsheviks' plans to "export the Revolution to the Orient". Bukhara was to serve as a springboard for extending Soviet political control into European colonies within Asia (Persic 1999, 20). In 1918–1920 the Bolshevik regime continued to view the Bukhara Emirate as a British puppet state; it was considered "a caravanserai of counter-revolution" (Ishanov 1969, 164). For this reason, the Bolsheviks considered Bukhara a key element in their ambition to extend their control. Unlike the Bukharan Jadids, they did not view the formally independent, pro-Soviet Bukharan republic as a final goal, but rather as a tool in Soviet policy, an entity which would be controlled by Soviet Russia, acting as the patron state. The conquest of Bukhara and the establishment of the Bukharan People's Soviet Republic in September 1920 was the result of a momentary symbiosis between Jadidist and Soviet positions on the new Bukharan state, combined with the Soviets' ability to use military force to establish and maintain the entity.

The decisive factor in the birth of the Bukharan People's Soviet Republic was the Soviet Army – primarily its Turkestan division. The plans for the overthrow of the Emir were drawn up in the spring and summer of 1920. Although the Turkestan government continued to reassure the Emir of its tolerant stance towards Bukhara until the last moment, the Turkestan Front – led by Mikhail Frunze – was already readying troops in garrisons close to the Emirate's borders, in the cities of Qarshi, Termez, Chardzhou, and the border town of Kagan (Genis 1993, 46–47, 2001). The mission led by

50 *Slavomír Horák*

the special envoy Hopner in July 1920 persuaded the Emir that the Russians were willing to make significant compromises, which the Emir viewed as a sign of weakness. However, the Bolsheviks' goal was to lull the Emir into a false sense of security by ostensibly making concessions which in reality the Soviet government had no intention of implementing (Persic 1999, 70–81).

The operation was launched by local Jadids (though their numbers were only small); this was intended to confer legitimacy on the new state. Representatives of the Young Bukharans gathered in Kagan and other cities, from where they orchestrated a propaganda campaign against the Emir. In line with Soviet ideology, the ostensible role of the Red Army was merely to "provide assistance" to the local revolutionary forces. This Soviet intervention played a crucial role in determining the course of development of the Bukharan state in the following years. In reality, it was not local representatives, but rather the military and political forces of the patron state which determined the development, maintenance, or transformation of the Bukharan state.

The formation of the Bukharan People's Soviet Republic

If we view the birth and persistence of the Bukharan People's Soviet Republic from the present-day conceptual perspective of de facto states, we can draw on the definition offered by Kolstø (2006, 729), combined with the notion of the sustainability of de facto states (Kolstø and Blakkisrud 2008, 484). According to these concepts, a de facto state and its sustainability are defined by the following key factors: the effectiveness of state- and nation-building, functioning state administration, military force, the existence of a patron state, the weakness of the parent state, and the role played by the de facto entity in the international community. The internal sustainability of de facto states is determined primarily by their ability to create functioning political, economic, and security entities. Of course, these aspects do not remain static; they can change over time, affecting the degree of independence enjoyed by the de facto state (or even its very existence).

In the case of Bukhara, the birth of the Bukharan People's Soviet Republic was not the case of separatism from a parent state, but was more akin to an internal coup d'état supported by opposition forces (the Jadids). The Emirate of Bukhara was a Russian protectorate, though its degree of dependency changed substantially between 1868 and 1920. The establishment of the Bukharan People's Soviet Republic was an attempt to reduce dependency on the Tsarist Russia and to orientate its ties on the Soviets. The necessity of at least some kind of future relationship with Russia has remained, only in the meantime the governing elite in the patron state has changed. The power of actors allied with the former regime has significantly decreased and the Emir was forced to leave Bukhara in 1920. In the following year he had to leave also the territory known as East Bukhara (later Tajikistan), though Basmachi units (opponents of the new regime) remained active in the region until the incorporation of the Bukharan People's Soviet

Republic into the USSR (Fraser 1988; Fitrat 1991, 53–54), in isolated cases even into the 1930s (Wanner 1997).

The republic declared itself an independent entity. Partial international recognition was granted by a 1921 treaty between Russia and Afghanistan (Arunova and Shumilov 1998, 66) and de facto recognition by Germany and Turkey which accepted Bukharan emissars and students (Khalid 2010, 352). Bukharan Ministry of Foreign Affairs also sent consuls to Petrograd, Tbilisi, Baku, and Tashkent (Khalid 2015, 135). Bukhara was capable of implementing state-building processes (creating its own institutions, ideology, etc.), albeit fully in accordance with the policies of the patron state. The internal politics of the newly created republic were determined by a number of factors. Most importantly, the new Bukharan government was not able to gain control over the majority of its claimed territory. The government was only able to control (with the assistance of the Red Army) the region around the city of Bukhara, Qarshi, Shahrisabz, and other large cities. Until 1922 the territory known as East Bukhara remained almost entirely under the control of the Basmachi units.

The formation of power structures – both at state level and party level – in the newly established republic essentially followed the Soviet model. In the first days of the new state's existence, a Council of Ministers (in Bukhara known as the Council of People's Nazirs – *khalq nozirlar shorosi/kengashi*) was appointed, in line with Soviet practice; the Bukharan Communist Party was also appointed (albeit formally) as the leading government institution. Likewise following Soviet practices (and under the guidance of representatives of Soviet Russia stationed in Bukhara), the Constitution of the Bukharan People's Soviet Republic was approved in 1921 – though it did include a number of provisions which deviated from standard Soviet ideology, such as the right of private ownership or the right to conduct private enterprise (Syezdy Sovetov Soyuza... 1960, 566–579).

The security organs of the new republic were also established according to Soviet models. In the first phase of the republic's existence, the main security organs were the Special Investigation Commission (*Chrezvychainaya sledstvennaya komissiya*), which initially arrested and executed the most influential figures from the Emir's entourage who had not managed to flee the country. Among the most prominent figures executed at this time were qazi kalan Molla Badriddin and qazi kalan Molla Burhanuddin (Khoshimov, Iminov, and Turakhodzhaev 2016, 101). The Special Investigation Commission later usurped substantial powers by collecting fees (and bribes) from traders; it was possible to import goods to Bukhara, but non-Bukharan traders were subjected to considerable harassment when attempting to export goods (RGASPI, f. 62, op. 2, d. 5, l. 37–38). In 1922, a Special Dictatorial Commission was set up in East Bukhara to combat the Basmachi movement; the Commission attempted to take de facto control over the territory (Gafurov 2008, 59–62). There were also repressive organs such as the Revolutionary Tribunal (established 1922) and the GPU intelligence service (1922), which likewise copied Soviet models.

52 Slavomír Horák

However, the informal division of power within Bukhara was dynamic and fluid, and underwent a number of changes. Although most Bukharan politicians were Jadids, there were substantial differences and internal conflicts within the Bukharan government – and here again the Soviets played an important role. Before their intervention in Bukhara, the Bolsheviks instigated an alliance between the Young Bukharan Party and the Bukharan Communist Party; the latter had been a relatively small group, lacking important contacts or influence within Bukhara and enjoying only low levels of support (Khalid 2015, 117). However, this alliance proved ineffective because the Communist Party members did not consider Khojayev and the other Young Bukharans to be genuine communists, citing their bourgeois origins. This dispute was already on open display at the joint congress of both parties held in Chardzhou in August 1920 (Khodzhaev 1970, 181–184). The distrust between the Young Bukharans and the original members of the Bukharan Communist Party led Khojayev – as the Chairman of the Council of Ministers – to refuse to appoint even one of the communists as a member of his government; the communists' position on the Bukharan political scene thus remained marginal. Khojayev and his Council of Ministers largely ignored Party meetings (Sokolov CK VKS "O polozhenii del v Bukhare", March 15, 1922, RGASPI, f. 62, op. 2, d. 5, l. 143). Nevertheless, the Soviets considered the Bukharan Communist Party to be the main political power in Bukhara, and the main partner in negotiations with Soviet Russia (and later the Soviet Union). This difference in the perception of the Bukharan Communist Party by the Jadids and the Soviets was also manifested in the incorporation of the Bukharan Communist Party into the All-Russian Communist Party. The Bukharan government did not view the incorporation as an attack on Bukhara's independence, but for the Bolsheviks it tied Bukhara even more closely to Soviet Russia. The difference in perception of the Bukharan republic meant that the Soviets largely refrained from interfering in internal conflicts within the Bukharan government. For the Bukharan elites, these conflicts became the cornerstones of their political careers. The conflicts mainly involved disputes among a number of influential Bukharan families; indeed, Khojayev's family was one of the wealthiest in the country. Other important figures included Abdulqodir Muhiddinov, who became the Agriculture Minister after the Young Bukharans' victory. The rivalry between Khojayev and Muhiddinov continued until the foundation of the Uzbek SSR, when Muhiddinov was dispatched to serve on the Tajikistan Revolutionary Committee in Dushanbe (Fedtke 2007). Another figure who wielded considerable influence in the Bukharan government until 1921 was Usmonkhoja Pulotkhojayev – initially the Finance Minister, then the Chairman of the Bukharan Central Executive Committee, and later one of the leading representatives of the Turkestan emigres. Besides Pulotkhojayev's supporters also included the Defence Minister Abdulhamid Arifov. This situation changed dramatically in the spring of 1922 when Pulotkhojayev and Arifov defected to the Basmachis; they later fled to Afghanistan. Khojayev thus remained in Bukhara surrounded by opponents or other persons who he

Bukharan People's Soviet Republic   53

could not be sure were not collaborating with the Basmachis (RGASPI, f. 62, op. 2, d. 5, l. 205). Despite this situation, the Soviets backed Khojayev, as they considered him to be a more reliable and loyal partner. In any case, given the internal rivalries within the Bukharan political scene, Khojayev was hardly in a position to choose his allies, and he had to rely increasingly on support from the Red Army and the Turkestan Soviet. In 1922–1923 Bukhara thus became increasingly dependent on the Soviet Union; not only was Khojayev reliant on the Soviets, but Soviet representatives in Bukhara were ratcheting up their influence over the cadre policies of the new state. The cadre changes of June 1923 took place entirely under the control of Soviet agents in Bukhara. One of the aims of these changes was to bring Khojayev and Muhiddinov closer together; the latter was appointed Deputy Chairman of the Council of Ministers (Voprosy Sredazbyuro Ts.K. January 15, 1925, RGASPI, f. 17, op. 3, d. 485, l. 6–8).

The internal instability of the Bukharan political apparatus, the defection of several key figures to the opposition, the conflicts among various political representatives (ideological, familial, and personal), as well as the Soviets' interference in Bukharan affairs – all these factors substantially reduced the Bukharan government's options for forming an independent state. As a result, the power wielded by the government gradually waned, creating a situation in which it was relatively easy for the Bolsheviks to instigate the transformation of the Bukharan republic into the Uzbek SSR.

External relations of the Bukharan People's Soviet Republic and the influence of the patron state

Although the Soviets played the key role of patron for the Bukharan People's Soviet Republic, this does not mean that the Bukharan government initially conducted foreign policy entirely according to instructions from Tashkent or Moscow. Besides its clear pro-Soviet stance, the Bukharan government also attempted to form alliances with other similar groups pursuing the Jadids' pan-Turkic ideals. For the Jadids, the concept of homeland (*watan*) was associated with the entire region of Turkestan, and Bukhara was just the foundation-stone of this structure. Moreover, the Bukharan state also attempted to establish contacts – including diplomatic relations – with other states.

These contacts occurred without the participation of the Soviet authorities – and often without consulting the Soviets. Regardless of Bukhara's role in pro-Soviet pan-Turkic initiatives such as the Congress of Eastern Nations in Baku (1920), Bukharan representatives also participated in (or organized) other pan-Turkic activities. In August 1921, Bukhara thus hosted the inaugural congress of the Turkestan National Union (*Türk Milli Birligi*), where delegates from Bashkortostan, Khorezm, Kazakhstan (Alash Autonomy), and Turkestan voted to create a Turkestani/Kokand Autonomy in Central Asia and to establish contacts with European culture without Russian mediation (Togan 2012, 286). Another example was the Bukharan

54 Slavomír Horák

economic and educational delegation in Berlin – though this was closed in 1922 under pressure from the Soviet Union, and the education centre was taken over by the Soviet embassy (Khalid 2015, 154).

Developments in Afghanistan – and interventions by Afghan representatives in Bukhara – played an important role in Bukhara's own development. The Afghan influence became particularly strong following the signature of the Soviet-Afghan treaty in 1921, in which both parties recognized Bukhara's independence and the republic's right to maintain its current structures. Afghanistan thus recognized the revolution that had taken place in Bukhara, and Soviet Russia granted *de jure* recognition of the new state's independence. The Afghan consul in Bukhara was especially active, often backing one or another of the feuding factions within the Bukharan government. The consul came from an aristocratic background, and according to contemporary accounts he was primarily concerned with plotting intrigues from which he could extract personal benefits (RGASPI, f. 62, op. 2, d. 5, l. 18). Nevertheless, the Afghan consul was considered one of the most important figures in the republic – alongside Khojayev, the Basmachis (fighters against the Soviet Army), and the Red Army (RGASPI, f. 62, op. 2, d. 5, l. 26). The Bukharan republic maintained a diplomatic mission in Kabul until 1922, when its consulate was downgraded to an agency (following Soviet pressure). Bukhara's last representative in Kabul was recalled in 1923 (Panin 1998, 65–68; Protokol No. 5 o zasedanii Prezidiuma Soveta narodnykh nazirov ot 7 iyulya 1923, RGASPI, f. 62, op. 2, d. 46, l. 84).

Intervention by the patron state (in this case Soviet Russia, acting through the Turkestan government in Tashkent) was inevitable from the very outset of the Bukharan republic. The planning of the coup d'état in Bukhara was considered by the Red Army to be part of the Sovietization of Bukhara, though this process was still in its transitional phase (Genis 1993, 44–45). The Turkestan Soviet government viewed itself not only as the protector of the new state but also as its actual initiator. The coup against the Emir could not have succeeded without military support from the Red Army. On the political level, the former Tsarist diplomatic mission in the Emirate became the Bolshevik mission.

The Jadids acted merely as a front during the occupation, bombing, and subsequent looting of Bukhara; the most visible participants in this operation were units of the Red Army, whose troops were often completely out of control. As a result, the Young Bukharan government took power in a city that had been conquered by force, with many buildings destroyed. The Bukharan People's Soviet Republic was thus born out of an armed intervention by the army of its patron state – even though the entire operation ostensibly took place under the banner of (and with the consent of) Bukharan representatives.

Moreover, for a long time the newly created state was unable to control its territory using its own resources. For example, only 400 people were available to defend the city of Bukhara itself: just 80–100 cavalry troops, plus militias (Pismo Sokolova CK VKP "O polozhenii v Bukhare", March 15, 1922, RGASPI, f. 62, op. 2, d. 5, l. 140). The task of taking control thus had to be

Bukharan People's Soviet Republic   55

entrusted to units of the Red Army, acting in the name of the Bukharan republic. Between 1920 and 1923 the number of Red Army troops involved in these operations grew tenfold (from 3,000 to around 30,000), and they were the only militarily capable force that could guarantee control over a large part of the state's territory and resist the Basmachi armed units.

Despite this situation, relations between the Bukharan government and the Red Army remained very tense throughout the existence of the republic. The Red Army behaved in a highly undisciplined manner in the state's territory; its troops were involved in looting, and they also destroyed mosques and religious texts. As a result, much of the local population – despite their negative stance towards the Emir and his forces – gave their support to the Basmachi movement (Wanner 1997, 155–156; Pylev 2006, 152–153). Throughout its entire existence, the Bukharan government tried in vain to rein in the Red Army's excesses in its struggle against the Basmachis, and the government also launched an information campaign among the local population (Kasymov and Ergashev 1989).

Despite the Red Army's indiscipline, the Bukharan republic could not exist without the military, economic, and financial assistance of its patron state. It was not in the interests of the Soviets to withdraw their troops from Bukhara, as such an act would probably have led to the collapse of the republic and the restoration of the old regime under the Emir or another form of theocratic monarchy. Neither of these outcomes would have been in the interests of either the patron state or the Bukharan government led by Khojayev.

The Bukharan republic's internal economic development essentially followed the same course as its domestic and foreign policy. During the first years of its existence, the republic succeeded in increasing its trade with Persia and Afghanistan. Indian products also appeared at Bukharan markets. The main source of foreign currency was the export of cotton and Karakul wool; exports of these goods were deemed strategic, and they were placed under the exclusive control of the Bukharan government's Revolutionary Committee (Ekonomicheskie otnosheniya 1996, 188). As a result of reduced demand for both these commodities on the Russian market, the focus of trade shifted westwards or southwards. Before the war, Bukhara had had manufacturing facilities that processed cotton for export, but the government proved unable to re-open these factories (O sostoyanii promyshlennosti v Bukharskoi respublike, RGASPI f. 62, op. 2, d. 46, l. 44) and most resources that had remained from the era of the Emirate (money, gold, and other assets) were stolen between 1920 and 1922 (O sostoyanii promyshlennosti v Bukharskoi respublike, RGASPI f. 62, op. 2, d. 46, l. 65–66).

Bukhara's foreign trade (with the exception of trade with Soviet Russia) was substantially restricted following the signature of an economic treaty between Russia and Bukhara in August 1922; this treaty created a single customs area and gave the Soviet authorities control over the customs posts on the Bukharan/Afghan border. Trade with Persia thus ceased completely, and trade with Afghanistan was severely reduced. The Soviet government

56 *Slavomír Horák*

took control of Bukhara's foreign trade, and most of the country's production was again exported to Russian Soviet markets.

Despite its attempts to revive foreign trade, the Bukharan government remained heavily dependent on financial subsidies from the Soviet Union. As soon as the Emir was overthrown, discussions were launched on the conditions for sending funds from Tashkent to Bukhara. In 1922 alone, Turkestani Central Committee sent over 3 million gold roubles to Bukhara – covering almost half of Bukhara's total expenditure (Tezisy doklada o byudzhete B.N.S.R. RGASPI, f. 62, op. 2, d. 46, l. 124–131). A major problem for the Bukharan economy was the high degree of corruption and embezzlement of state funds, as well as an unreliable tax collection system. Much of the Soviet financial aid thus ended up in the bank accounts of high-ranking state officials, including members of the government (Zapiska t. Lyubimovu, RGASPI, f. 62, op. 2, d. 46, l. 65–69).

Another problem facing the Bukharan economy was the chaotic currency situation. Soviet roubles from different issues (1919, 1922) were in circulation both in Turkestan and Bukhara itself. Bukhara also used the inflation-prone Bukharan currency, as well as temporary Turkestan coupons issued in 1919. Until 1923, old roubles issued in 1917 (*kerenka* roubles) remained the most stable currency; their value remained largely unchanged, and they could also be used to a certain extent in Afghanistan and Persia. From 1921, the Soviet authorities in Tashkent made regular payments to Bukhara in Soviet roubles (1919 issue), but these were exchanged for the more stable *kerenka* roubles on the local market. The simultaneous circulation of different currencies ended in 1923 when the Central Asian Bureau (*SredAzByuro*) of the Russian Communist Party's Central Committee ruled that only one currency could legally be used in Bukhara, and incorporated the Bukharan budget into the USSR budget (O politicheskom i ekonomicheskom polozhenii Bukhary, RGASPI, f. 62. op. 2, d. 40, l. 2–6). From May 1923 onwards, Soviet currency was thus the only legal tender in Bukhara (Masov et al. 2004, 308). Together with the incorporation of the Bukharan banking system into the Russian system in 1923, this step marked the end of Bukhara's fiscal independence, which was clearly unsustainable. It also meant that the inflation-prone Bukharan currency was no longer printed. The de facto integration of the Bukharan financial and currency systems into the Soviet system made a Bukharan currency redundant (O polozhenii del v Buchare, RGASPI, f. 62, op. 2, d. 46, l. 40, Tezisy doklada o byudzhete B.N.S.R. 1923, RGASPI, f. 62, op. 2, d. 46, l. 124–131).

The dire state of the Bukharan economy – which from the very establishment of the republic had remained completely dependent on outside assistance (in this case primarily from Tashkent) – was ultimately one of the main factors behind the extinction of Bukhara's modern statehood in 1924 and its incorporation into what would become the USSR. Bukhara's dependence on Soviet Russia meant that it had no option but to fulfil the patron state's demands – a situation which ultimately led to the complete extinction of Bukhara's economic (and later political) independence.

The transformation from the Bukharan People's Soviet Republic to the Uzbek SSR

Once the Soviets had stabilized their power base in Turkestan, they began to discuss the future of the entire region – a future which would ultimately bring widespread changes to existing borders. The main principle applied by the Soviets was that of nationality; however, this principle could not be applied with complete reliability because the distribution of national populations in the region had not yet been fully mapped, and there were not always clear ethnic dividing lines between the different nationalities (Farrant 2006). The main identifying criteria were religion and language, though even here substantial discrepancies existed. Some Kara-Kirghiz people (today the Kyrgyz) were considered to be Uzbeks (and their children were sent to Uzbek schools), despite the fact that their physiognomy was clearly Kyrgyz (Vypiska iz stenogrammy plenuma CK KPT ot 23 marta 1924 gg. RGASPI, f. 62, op. 2, d. 101, l. 96). Additionally, the Central Asian languages were not codified until after their speakers had been assigned to their respective nationalities (Roy 2007, 168–171). The division of Central Asia into national entities was primarily intended to transform the existing traditional states – Bukhara and Khorezm – into smaller structures; this was to prevent the emergence of a strong Turkic state (the goal of the Jadidist movement) and to discourage the further spread of pan-Islamism and pan-Turkism (Abdullaev 2009).

The decision to delimitate separate nationalities in Central Asia and create the Uzbek, Turkmen, and Kirghiz (today Kazakh) SSRs was initially received poorly in Bukhara, despite the fact that it was already clear that full independence for the Bukharan state was not sustainable. Khojayev favoured incorporation into the USSR in the form of a Bukharan Soviet Socialist Republic. According to Chika (2001, 108–110), the decisive factor in Khojayev's decision to abandon his backing for Bukhara and instead support the creation of an Uzbek SSR was fierce criticism from Stalin at a meeting between the Central Committee of the Russian Communist Party and representatives of national republics and regions in June 1923.

After this meeting, Khojayev increasingly began to favour the project to create an Uzbek SSR. Ideologically, he justified this change of opinion as a continuation (or culmination) of the national project pursued by the Jadidist Bukharan intelligentsia (Khalid 2015, 15). The Central Asian Bureau of the Russian Communist Party's Central Committee set up territorial committees and subcommittees based on national lines. Representatives of the Bukharan republic had the strongest influence within the so-called Uzbek Subcommittee for National Delimitation, including Khojayev himself (Zhurnal soveshchaniya uzbekskoi komissii Sr.Az.Biuro RKP, 10 maya 1924, RGASPI f. 62, op. 2, d. 101, l. 47–48). Unlike its counterparts, the Uzbek subcommittee managed to achieve most of its territorial objectives (RGASPI f. 62, op. 2, d. 104, l. 4247). The Uzbek SSR eventually incorporated the

58   *Slavomír Horák*

majority of the Bukharan and Khorezm republics and the former Khanate of Kokand. The new Uzbekistan included the main commercial, economic, and cultural centres in the region – Tashkent, the areas around the main rivers (the Syr Darya – Khujand, later part of the Tajik SSR; the Zeravshan – Samarkand; and the Amu Darya – Termez, Khorezm), the oasis around Bukhara itself, and the fertile Fergana Valley (apart from several areas under the control of the Kara-Kirghiz SSR). The only areas not given to Uzbekistan were the Turkmen regions, including the important Bukharan city of Chardzhou (Dokladnaya zapiska k proektu vyklyucheniya Turkmenskoi i Uzbekskoi respublik i prisoedineniya Kirgizskikh chastei Turkestana k Kirrespublike, RGASPI f. 62, op. 2, d. 101, l. 125–126). Some towns in the Tashkent region (Osh, Jalal-Abad) were given to the Kara-Kirghiz SSR (later the Kyrgyz SSR). East Bukhara – which during the existence of the Bukharan republic had mostly remained outside the control of the central government and which was home to a strong Basmachi presence as well as Red Army units from Turkestan – became the Tajik Autonomous SSR after pressure from the Tajik territorial subcommittee, which Khojayev had attempted to marginalize (Vypiska iz stenogrammy plenuma CK KPT ot 23 marta 1924. RGASPI, f. 62, op. 2, d. 101, l. 97–98).

In view of the broad definition of Uzbeks as a Turkic nation incorporating primarily settled populations in Central Asia – and in general terms all settled populations of local origin (Khalid 2015, 258) – we can therefore state that the extinction of the Bukharan state was not in fact the genuine end of this entity, but rather its transformation into a new state entity – the Uzbek SSR (Dokladnaya zapiska k proektu vyklyucheniya Turkmenskoi i Uzbekskoi respublik i prisoedineniya Kirgizskikh chastei Turkestana k Kirrespublike, RGASPI, f. 62, op. 2, d. 101, l. 126 et seq.).

Conclusion

Examination of Soviet and Bukharan sources reveals substantially differing interpretations of the birth, existence, and eventual extinction of the Bukharan People's Soviet Republic. From the Bolsheviks' perspective, the Bukharan republic represented a transitional phase on the path to a new state; this phase had to be temporarily accepted in order to overthrow the Emir and prepare the ground for the establishment of a genuine Soviet state. This state was to be a reflection of the right to national self-determination within the boundaries stipulated by the Communist Party. Unlike other regions which were more ethnically homogeneous (Ukraine), or in which it was possible to retain previous state entities (the South Caucasus), Central Asia was to be divided into entirely new state entities, which had never previously existed on maps. Although the ethnic principle was to be given the main priority in this process of territorial division, the blurred boundaries between ethnic groups (or even the definition of ethnic groups as such) led to conflicts among the representatives of the individual national groups. In reality, the

Soviets were able to exploit Bukhara's dependence on external assistance (both military and economic) in order to ensure that the Bukharan People's Soviet Republic would remain closely tied to the Soviet Union until it eventually ceased to exist. From this perspective, the Bukharan republic should be considered an example of a de facto state, whose existence was entirely dependent on its patron state. The patron state thus wielded the power and resources to terminate the state's independent existence. Throughout the areas where territorial delimitation was in progress, the Soviets always had several key figures who were loyal to the current Soviet policy (including Khojayev in Bukhara). However, it was not ultimately the Soviet leadership who determined the precise borders in the region. This task depended primarily on the negotiating skills of the individual delegates in the territorial subcommittees; Moscow's role (via its *SredAzByuro*) was merely to give final approval to the decision (Keller 2003; Abashin 2012).

By contrast, Bukharan sources indicate that the Bukharan government retained a certain degree of autonomy in its internal affairs (and partly also in international relations), and that leading representatives of the republic – including Khojayev – were concerned primarily with the long-term prospects for the state. In internal politics, Bukharan representatives on the one hand cooperated with the Soviet authorities, but on the other hand their actual activities within the republic may have been at odds with the situation as described in the documents held in Soviet and Russian archives (Khalid 2010, 338–339). From this perspective, the Bukharan republic possessed attributes of formal independence – a status that was recognized not only by the patron state but also by other states (mainly Afghanistan but also to some extent by Germany and Turkey).

However, Bukhara's economic and military dependence on its patron state led to a gradual reduction in sovereignty – both with regard to foreign policy (the closure of diplomatic representations in other countries, the cessation of independent foreign trade, the control of the borders by Soviet authorities) and also with regard to internal affairs. The state's internal weakness gave it little room for manoeuvre in foreign relations – and moreover it had to take account of the preferences of its patron state. The Bukharan elite – headed by Faizullo Khojayev – intended for the republic to be incorporated into the USSR as a formally independent Bukharan SSR (Chika 2001, 110). The rejection of this idea, and the decision to implement a process of national delimitation in Central Asia, led the Bukharan leaders to re-evaluate their plans for the country's future. They intended Bukhara to become the basis for the new Uzbekistan, which would extend beyond the boundaries of the Bukharan republic itself. The Uzbek SSR did indeed go on to become a major political, economic, ideological, and religious centre during the Soviet era. The most prominent Bukharan political figures during the existence of the republic, and also fierce rivals during the 1920s – Faizullo Khojayev and Abdulqodir Muhiddinov – later left a major mark on the post-Soviet historiography of Uzbekistan and Tajikistan, respectively; Muhiddinov – who

60   *Slavomír Horák*

was dispatched to Dushanbe – became one of the founding fathers of today's Tajikistan (Shakuri Bukhara'i 2013, 75–76), as did Khojayev in the case of Uzbekistan (Rajabov 2011).

The Uzbek SSR and the Turkmen SSR became the only Union Republics in Central Asia – that is, they were formally of equal status with Russia (the Russian Soviet Federal Socialist Republic), making them more than mere Russian protectorates. The Bukharan representatives – above all Faizullo Khojayev – could thus have considered the national delimitation of Central Asia to be the most effective solution with regard to achieving Jadidist goals – that is, the creation of a strong Turkic state in the new Russia (transformed into the Soviet Union). The extinction of the Bukharan republic should therefore not be viewed as the genuine end of this entity, but rather its transformation. At the time there was no international agreement on the preservation of borders, and in 1923–1924 Central Asia was deemed by the dominant global powers to form part of the Soviet sphere of influence, so this process of incorporating the Bukharan People's Soviet Republic into its patron state was much simpler than would be the case today. Several similar de facto state-like entities came into existence during the Civil War period. However, none of them possessed a comparable degree of internal legitimacy, or internal/external independence (at least in the early phase of its existence), as Bukhara.

Note

1 We use the term patron state for the role Bolshevik Russia/USSR played in the Bukharan case, although the term patron state, in the present theory, usually denotes the external power which helps de facto state to secede from its parent state. In this case, there was no parent state, just the former Russian government, of which Bukhara was a protectorate.

Literature

Abashin, Sergei. 2012. "Natsionalnoe razmezhevanie v Ferganskoi doline: kak vse nachinalos [National delimitation in Ferghana Valley: how did it begin]." *Islam v Sodruzhestve Nezavisimykh Gosudarst* 7 (2). www.idmedina.ru/books/islamic/?4695.

Abdullaev, Kamoluddin. 2009. *Ot Sintszyana do Khorasana. Iz istorii sredneaziatskoi emigratsii XX veka* [From Xinjiang to Khorasan. From the history of Central Asian emigration in the 20th century]. Dushanbe: Irfon.

Arunova, Mariana R., and Oleg M. Shumilov. 1998. *Granitsa Rossii s Afganistanom: Istoricheskii ocherk* [Borders of Russia with Afghanistan. Historical Overview]. Moskva: Institut vostokovedeniya RAN.

Becker, Seymour. 2004. *Russia's Protectorates in Central Asia: Bukhara and Khiva, 1865–1924*. London: Routledge.

Chika, Obiya. 2001. "When Did Faizulla Khojaev Decided to Be an Uzbek." In *Islam in Politics in Russian and Central Asia (Early Eighteen to Late Twentieth Centuries)*, edited by Stephane A. Dudoignon and Komatso Hisao, 99–118. London, New York and Bahrain: Kegan Paul.

Bukharan People's Soviet Republic 61

Dimanshteyn, Semyon M., ed. 1930. *Revolyutsiya i natsionalnyi vopros: dokumenty i materialy po istorii natsionalnogo voprosa v Rossii i SSSR v XX veke* [Revolution and National Question: Documents and Materials on History of National Question in Russia and USSR in the 20th Century]. Moskva Izdatelstvo Kommunisticheskoi akademii.

Ekonomicheskie otnosheniya. 1996. *Ekonomicheskie otnosheniya Sovetskoi Rossii s budushchimi sovetskimi respublikami 1917–1922. Dokumenty i materialy* [Economic Relations of Soviet Russia with future Soviet Republics 1917–1922]. Moskva: Vostochnaya literatura.

d'Encausse, Heléne C. 1966. *Réforme et Révolution chez les Musulmans de l'Empire russe* [Reform and Revolution among Muslims of the Russian Empire]. Paris: Presse de la Fondation Nationale des Sciences Politique.

Fabry, Mikulas. 2010. *Recognizing States: International Society and the Establishment of New States since 1776.* New York: Oxford University Press.

Farrant, Amanda. 2006. "Mission Impossible: The Politico-Geographical Engineering of Soviet Central Asia's Republican Boundaries." *Central Asian Survey* 25 (1–2): 61–74.

Fedtke, Gero. 2007. "How Bukharans Turned into Uzbeks and Tajiks: Soviet Nationalities Policy in the Light of Personal Rivalry." In *Patterns of Transformation in and around Uzbekistan,* edited by Paul Sartori and Tommaso Trevisani, 19–50. Reggio Emilia: Diabasis.

Fitrat, Abdulrauf. 1991. *Davrai hukmronii amir Olimkhon* [The Period of Amir Olimkhon Rule]. Dushanbe: Palatai davlatii kitobho.

Fraser, Glenda. 1988. Alim Khan and the Fall of the Bokharan Emirate in 1920. *Central Asian Survey* 7 (4): 47–61.

Gafurov, Abdullo. 2008. *Revkomy Tadzhikistana (1917–1924 gg)* [Revolution Committee of Tajikistan (1917–1924)]. Dushanbe: Institut istorii, arkheologii i etnografii AN Tadzhikistana.

Genis, Vladimir. 1993. "Razgrom Bukharskogo emirata v 1920 godu [Defeat of Bukharan emirate in 1920]." *Voprosy istorii* 7: 39–53.

Genis, Vladimir. 2001. *S Bukharoi nado konchat... K istorii butaforskikh revolyutsii* [It is Necessary to Terminate Bukhara... o the History of Fake Revolutions]. Moscow: MNPI.

Ishanov, Atabai I. 1955. *Sozdanie Bukharskoi narodnoi sovetskoi respubliki (1920–1924 gg.)* [The Formation of Bukhara National Soviet Republic]. Tashkent: Izdatel'stvo Akademii nauk Uzbekskoi SSR.

Ishanov, Atabai I. 1969. *Bukharskaya Narodnaya Sovetskaya Respublika* [Bukhara National Soviet Republic], Tashkent: Uzbekistan.

Kasymov, Farhad, and Bahodyr Ergashev. 1989. "Bukharskaya revolyutsiya [Bukharan revolution]." *Rodina* 11.

Keller, Shoshana. 2003. "The Central Asian Bureau, an Essential Tool in Governing Soviet Turkestan." *Central Asian Survey* 22 (2–3): 281–297.

Khalid, Adeeb. 1999. *The Politics of Muslim Cultural Reform. Jadidism in Central Asia.* Berkeley, Los Angeles, and Oxford: University of California Press.

Khalid, Adeeb. 2010. "The Bukharan People's Soviet Republic in the Light of Muslim Sources." *Die Welt des Islams* 50 (3–4): 335–361.

Khalid, Adeeb. 2015. *Making Uzbekistan: Nation, Empire, and Revolution in the Early USSR.* Ithaca: Cornell University Press.

Khodzhaev, Faizullo. 1970. *Izbrannye trudy v trekh tomakh* [Selected Works in Three Volumes]. Tashkent: Fan.

62 Slavomír Horák

Khoshimov, Soibjon A., Zh. Iminov, and S. Turakhodzhaev. 2016. "Politicheskie Repressii v Uzbekistane v 20–30-kh godakh XX veka [Political Repressions in Uzbekistan in 1920s–1930s]." *Nauka i sovremennost* 43: 100–108.

Kolstø, Pål. 2006. "The Sustainability and Future of Unrecognized Quasi-States." *Journal of Peace Research* 43 (6): 723–740.

Kolstø, Pål, and Helge Blakkisrud. 2008. "Living with Non-Recognition: State and NationBuilding in South Caucasian Quasi-States." *Europe-Asia Studies* 60 (3): 483–509.

Masov, Rahim, et al., eds. 2004. *Istoriya tadzhikskogo naroda* [The history of Tajik nation]. Dushanbe: Institut istorii, arkheologii i etnografii AN Tadzhikistana.

Norling, Nicklas. 2014. *Myth and Reality: Politics in Soviet Uzbekistan.* Ph.D. Dissertation. Baltimore, MD: Johns Hopkins University. https://jscholarship.library. jhu.edu/bitstream/handle/1774.2/37030/NORLING-DISSERTATION-2014.pdf.

Panin, Sergei. 1998. *Sovetskaya Rossiya i Afganistan 1919–1929 gg* [Soviet Russia and Afghanistan 1919–1929]. Irkutsk: Izdatelstvo Irkutskogo universiteta.

Persic, Moysei A. 1999. *Zastenchivaya interventsiya. O sovetskom vtorzhenii v Iran i Bucharu v 1920–1921 gg* [Timid intervention. About Soviet intervention to Iran and Bukhara in 1920–1921]. Moskva: Muravej Gaid.

Pylev, Aleksandr. 2006. *Basmachestvo v Srednei Azii. Etnopoliticheskii srez (Vzglyad iz XXI veka)* [Basmachi movement in Central Asia. Ethnopolitical cut (The View from the 21st Century)]. Bishkek: Kyrgyzsko-slavyanskii universitet.

Rajabov, Kahramon. 2011. *Faizullo Xo'jayev (Tarixiy Esse)* [Faizullo Khojayev (Historical Essay)]. Toshkent: Abu Matbuot-Konsalt

Roy, Olivier. 2007. *The New Central Asia: Geopolitics and the Birth of Nations.* New York: New York University Press.

Shakuri Bukhara'i, Muhammadjon. 2013. *The Imperialist Revolution in Bukhara.* Dushanbe: Shujaiyan.

Shestakov, A. 1927. "Bukhara v 1917 godu [Bukhara in 1917]." *Krasnyi arkhiv* 1: 80–122.

Syezdy Sovetov Soyuza… 1960. *Syezdy Sovetov Soyuza SSR, soyuznykh i avtonomnykh sovetskikh i sotsialisticheskikh respublik. Sbornik dokumentov v trekh tomakh 1917–1936 gg., t. 2 (1917–1922 gg.)* [The Congresses of Soviet of SSSR, Union and Autonomous Soviet and Socialist Republics. The Collection of documents in three volumes 1917–1936, Vol. 2 (1917–1922)]. Moskva: Izdatelstvo yuridicheskoi literatury.

Togan, Zeki V. 2012. *Memoirs. National Existence and Cultural Struggles of Turkistan and Other Muslim Eastern Turks.* North Charleston, NC: Createspace Independent Publishing Platform.

Wanner, Jan. 1997. Politicko-vojenská nestabilita sovětské moci v muslimských oblastech II. Boj s konzervativní muslimskou opozicí a basmačkým hnutím ve Střední Asii (1918–1933) [Political and military instability of Soviet power in Muslim region II. The fight with conservative Muslim opposition and Basmachi movement in Central Asia (1918–1933)]. In *Armáda jako nástroj státní integrace SSSR (1923–1941)*, edited by Bohuslav Litera, 121–184. Praha: Historický ústav.

2.3 Tuva and Mongolia
Between annexation and independence

Vladimír Baar, Barbara Baarová and Jaroslav Kurfürst

Whereas Russia stabilized its western border at the Vienna Congress of 1815, and subsequently also its borders in Transcaucasia and Central Asia (including the formation of the protectorate over Bukhara), at the same time it also expanded its influence in southern Siberia and the Amur region. This sparsely populated area came under Russian control during the 18th century, bringing Russia into direct contact with the Mongolian vassals of Manchu China and Manchuria itself (the home region of the ruling Qing dynasty). Russia took advantage of China's weakness after the Opium Wars to conclude the Treaty of Aigun (1858) and the Treaty of Peking (1860), gaining effective control over the entire region known as Outer Manchuria (the lower Amur region). Here, the direct contact with Manchu China – that is, with territories settled by Mongols and Manchus – represented a substantial obstacle to Russia's further expansion. In this case, the Russians were unable to invoke the concept of *terra nullius*, and instead they had to rely on military force and diplomacy.

The result of these Russian policies was, in course of several decades, the formation of two specific political entities – Tuva and Mongolia – which bear a number of similarities with present-day de facto states, above all Abkhazia and South Ossetia, for which Russia is a patron state. Whereas Mongolia, after decades of de facto statehood finally joined the UN in 1961, Tuva was annexed by Russia, its patron, in 1944. These century-old examples may, however, serve as unique model cases, which have demonstrated the possible trajectories of Abkhazia's and South Ossetia's development (Map 3).

The roots of Tuvan and Mongolian People's Republics

The long-lasting crisis of the Qing monarchist government, culminating in its collapse in late 1911 and early 1912, sparked an extensive disintegrative processes throughout China. The newly created republican government did not wield the necessary power to suppress these centrifugal tendencies. Especially Tibet considered the fall of the Manchu monarchy to be a good reason to terminate its present vassal status and renew its independence. This was a logical reaction because the Tibetans viewed their political

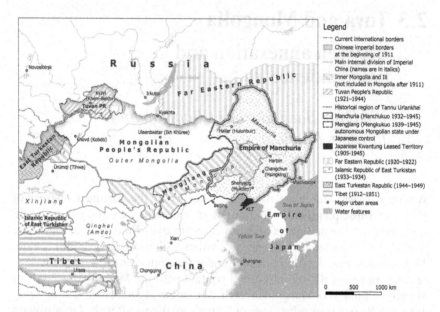

Map 3 Tuva and Mongolia between the First World War and the Second World War.
Source: Authors.

subordination to China as a contract with the Manchu (Qing) dynasty, and they rejected the continuation of Chinese suzerainty over Tibet under the new republican government (Zhagabpa 2000). Remote Tibet indeed managed to retain its de facto independence until the military invasion by the later Chinese communist government. The situation in Mongolia was considerably more complex; since its subjugation by the Manchu Qing in the 17th century Mongolia had not existed as a single political entity with its own monarch and government (as had been the case in Tibet).

The last Mongolian Khan Ligden died in 1634, after which the western parts of the territory were seized by the Dzungars and the eastern by Manchus, who themselves conquered (ten years later) China. Mongolia thus lost its statehood, and although in 1724 the Manchus allowed Mongolia to have its own spiritual leader (the Bogd Gegen), his position was never equal to that of the Dalai Lama, who was not only the Tibetan spiritual leader but also its secular ruler and the symbol of Tibetan statehood. The Manchus divided Mongolia into two parts – the so-called Inner Mongolia (which was open to Han immigration) and Outer Mongolia, which consisted of three (later four) autonomous *aimags* with dynasties of khans. The western and northern border areas of Outer Mongolia were made up of smaller administrative units – *khoshuns* and *sums*. Manchu governors known as *ambans* supervised the administration of the territory.

Russia too took a very cautious approach, waiting to see how the situation in China would develop. In the summer of 1911 some Mongolian aristocrats contacted the Tsar with a request for assistance in seceding from China, but the response was diplomatic – Russia promised merely to act as a mediator between the Mongols and the Qing, which did not satisfy the more radical aristocrats. In November 1911 they therefore formed (after consultation with the Bogd Gegen) a Provisional Government, which on 1st December issued a declaration of Mongolian independence. It should be noted that the Mongolian representatives understood Mongolia in the sense of its entire historic territory, that is, including the Sinicized Inner Mongolia and the Uriankhai (future Tuva).

However, Russia did not view Mongolia in these terms – either in 1911 or later. For them, Mongolia was restricted to just Outer Mongolia (Srba and Schwarz 2015, 191), that is, the territory with ethnic Mongolian majority, but at this time of crisis they decided to open up the issue of the Mongolian status of Uriankhai too. The local aristocrats mostly refused to submit to the Mongolian government, despite the fact that on 29 December the Bogd Gegen was ceremonially declared the Mongolian Khan – that is, the secular ruler. He was also recognized as the spiritual head of the Mongol Buddhist sect Gelupta by the Tuvans, but many of them rejected his authority in the secular sphere. One factor influencing this stance was undoubtedly the fact that the Tuvan language did not belong to the Mongolic group of languages, but to the Turkic group (which also includes Uyghur, Kazakh, Kyrgyz, and other Central Asian languages). On the other hand, the Tuvans had been part of the Mongolian Empire since the time of Genghis Khan, though they only gained joint control over their territory under the Manchus in 1762 (Dongak 2010, 194).[1] The Mongols felt their independence very intensely; for example, they abolished the use of the designation "Manchu period" and introduced the Mongolian "period of the Great Elect" (Kuzmin 2016, 147). They also removed the Chinese *ambans* from office and instructed them to leave Mongolia. The Russians continued to take a very cautious approach, diplomatically describing the Mongolians' declared independence as a form of autonomy which should be confirmed by a treaty between Russia and the new Chinese government. In Moscow's view, such a treaty would prevent interference from third parties, especially Japan. On the other hand, it should be noted that Russia and Japan had already delineated their spheres of interest in two secret treaties of 1907 and 1910; Manchuria and Inner Mongolia fell within the Japanese sphere, and Outer Mongolia within the Russian sphere (Plotnikov 2007). The attempts by many Inner Mongolian aristocrats to join the "independent" Mongolia led Russia to take a particularly cautious approach.

The Republic of China certainly had no intention of relinquishing control over any part of its territory that had been controlled by the Qing. The constitution of 16 March 1912 declared Mongolia (including Uriankhai) and Tibet to be integral parts of China, and this status is still formally declared by the constitution of the Republic of China on Taiwan.[2] Nevertheless, a

66   *Vladimír Baar et al.*

century later, on 21 May 2012, Taiwan's Mainland Affairs Council issued a report stating that (Outer) Mongolia is not a part of the Republic of China (MAC 2012).

The Mongolians naturally had no idea that Russia and Japan had concluded secret agreements delineating their respective spheres of influence, and they continued to strive for an independent state that would include Inner Mongolia. In the event that the Empire were to collapse, the *noyons* of the largest *khoshuns*, in conjunction with the Manchu aristocrats, planned to create an independent Mongolian-Manchurian state as a joint Japanese-Russian protectorate (Kuzmin 2016, 186–187). They offered the increasingly weak imperial court the option of relocating beyond the Great Wall of China and consolidating the historic territory of Manchuria after seceding from China (Boyd 2008, 114–115). Although the Inner Mongolian aristocracy was partially Sinicized by this time, after the declaration of Mongolian independence as many as 35 Inner Mongolian *khoshuns* (out of a total 49) declared their support for independence (Zhugder 1974, 277–278), on condition that they would be able to retain their autonomy. In April 1912 a demand was made for the creation of an autonomous Eastern Mongolia; a year later, on 20 August 1913, this entity was indeed declared to be an independent state during an uprising which involved the occupation of several towns. The Chinese army quashed the rebellion within a month, and its leaders fled to Outer Mongolia (Srba and Schwarz 2015, 197). The Chinese Republicans were willing to grant the Mongolians and the Tibetans autonomous rights, and on 1 August 1912 they established the Committee for Mongolian and Tibetan Affairs, which on 17 August drew up a list of "Rules for Engaging with the Mongolians"; this document accepted most of the Mongolians' demands for cultural autonomy, including a certain degree of territorial autonomy. The rules also acknowledged Mongolian claims over Uriankhai. This concession was not welcomed by Russia (Rossiya i Tibet 2005, 184–186). At the time, Uriankhai still had direct territorial contact (via Kobdo in western Mongolia) with the Chinese province of Xinjiang; however, on 20 August 1912 the Mongolians occupied Kobdo (modern Khovd), thus cutting Uriankhai off from China (Vasilenko 2013, 66). This situation subsequently enabled Russia to declare Uriankhai its protectorate.

Although Mongolia displayed attributes of statehood – including a defined area and population under its control as well as a government and a Khan (or the Bogd Gegen) and from February 1914 also an unelected dual-chamber parliament (*ulsyn khural*) – it did not receive international recognition as an independent state.[3] Nevertheless, it continued to hope for assistance from Russia; Mongolia and Russia were negotiating the content of a treaty which would define their mutual relations. The preparation of the treaty took several months; one of the problems was the distinction between Outer and Inner Mongolia. The Mongolians eventually succeeded in incorporating their preferred (more general) term "Mongolia" into the text of the treaty, which could be interpreted by each party at their discretion. The treaty was signed on 3 November 1912, and each party interpreted the wording on Mongolia's status in its own way. The Mongolians interpreted it as a recognition of independence, the Russians merely as an acknowledgement of Mongolia's autonomous status within China. This interpretation was supported by a Russo-Chinese declaration signed on 5 November 1913. Russia gave the same explanation to the Japanese, who were concerned by the use of the unspecific term "Mongolia" (Kuzmin 2016, 159–161).

The differing interpretations of Mongolia's status were brought to an end by the Kyakhta Conference featuring representatives of China, Mongolia, and Russia. The treaty signed in Kyakhta on 25 May 1915 confirmed China's sovereignty over Mongolia while retaining the territory's wide-ranging autonomy; it also acknowledged Russia's economic interests in Mongolia. The Mongolians were not satisfied with this outcome, as they had hoped that – even in the absence of genuine independence – they would at least achieve the unification of Outer and Inner Mongolia. They also lost Uriankhai, over which Russia had declared a protectorate in the previous year (29 June 1914). The Chinese were likewise dissatisfied with this development, but they left the issue open. They were, however, satisfied with the restoration of sovereignty over Mongolia, and in the west they had also managed to acquire part of the Altai Uriankhai and incorporate it into Xinjiang. The Russians too were satisfied, as they were currently occupied with the war in Europe. Besides enjoying economic advantages thanks to the treaty, in November 1915 they also reached an agreement with the Chinese granting the north-easternmost Inner Mongolian *khoshun* Hulunbuir the status of a special autonomous region.[4] Russia was keen that this region – inhabited by the Barga, who spoke a language similar to Buryat[5] – should not fall under Mongolian control; the main reason was that the Trans-Manchurian Railway (a continuation of the Trans-Siberian Railway, whose route through Russian territory was not yet complete) passed through this region.

In the following years Russia was brought to the point of collapse by the First World War, and the Chinese took advantage of this situation to exert pressure on the Mongolians. Chinese troops entered Mongolia under the command of General Xu Shuzheng (Hsu Seu-Cheng), and the Mongolian representatives realized that without outside help they had no hope of even maintaining their autonomy; under this pressure, they requested the revocation of their own autonomous status. This officially came into effect on 22 November 1919, when the Bogd Gegen-Khan had to swear his allegiance to the Republic of China and relinquish his secular authority. The Mongolian government and parliament were also dissolved, and the country was subjugated to central rule from Peking. Although by this point Russia was embroiled in a civil war, the Bolsheviks viewed Mongolia's subjugation to China as an expansion of the Japanese sphere of influence because General Xu belonged to the pro-Japanese wing of the Chinese political spectrum (Beloff 1963, 241). At the next available opportunity, the Bolsheviks therefore played a very active role in the developing situation in Outer Mongolia. The most complex situation emerged in Uriankhai, where a temporary regional council was formed after the ousting of the monarchy in March

68   *Vladimír Baar et al.*

1917; however, only some of the *noyons* joined this body, while others began secret negotiations with the Mongolians; the future founder of "Tuvan statehood" Mongush Buyan-Badyrgy even negotiated secretly with the Chinese (Mollerov 2014, 54). Following the Bolshevik coup, the very sparsely inhabited territory was also infiltrated by Soviet agents, who in March 1918 formed the Uriankhai Regional Soviet. Some *noyons* responded to this situation by requesting help from the Mongolian Bogd Gegen-Khan. However, by this time he was already under pressure from China, whose troops had not only entered Mongolia but also (in the autumn of 1918) Uriankhai itself. In January 1919 the Chinese set up a new official position – the Special Commissar for Uriankhai Affairs – and during the course of the year they gained control over most of the territory (Lamin 2007, 91). It appeared that the Republic of China had managed to suppress the centrifugal tendencies in its northern territories; only Tibet still remained beyond its control.

Neither Mongolia nor Uriankhai were fully independent states during the analysed period. However, there were substantial differences between them. Uriankhai never sought genuine independence because the local *noyons* were aware that independence was a highly specific notion in the Central Asian context. Mongolia was a very different case; there were still vivid memories of the Mongols' glorious dominance across a much larger area than their present homeland. For a long time they viewed their subjugation to the Manchus in a positive light because the Qing dynasty allowed them a very large degree of cultural and economic autonomy. However, the Sinicization of the dynasty, combined with a departure from China's formerly accommodating policy towards Mongolia, radicalized the Mongolians, and it is no surprise that they attempted to exploit the weakening and subsequent collapse of the Qing dynasty to create their own state. In the first years after its declaration of independence (up to the Kyakhta treaty of 1915) Mongolia resembled present-day de facto states. The Mongolians' focus on Russia was a result of their awareness that the concepts of independence and sovereignty took on a very specific meaning in the sparsely populated, open steppe landscapes of Central Asia. In such an environment the decisive role was always played by current military strength and the ability to forge alliances with neighbours (and to exploit conflicts between them). The Mongolians and the Tuvans were well aware of China's relative size and power, and it was logical for them to ally themselves with a strong Russia. Alliance in this region is associated with protection when necessary, which also somewhat undermines the concept of independence. The Mongolians essentially sought the same outcome, but their efforts ran up against Russia's highly cautious stance, which reflected its defeat in the Russo-Japanese war. Russia had to respect Japan's interests as set out in the above-mentioned secret treaties (Tang 1959). Moscow was also waiting to see how the situation in the Republic of China would develop. Eventually, political changes in Russia itself radically changed the balance of power in the region, and China exploited this fact to regain control over Mongolia and Uriankhai.

The formation of Tuvan and Mongolian People's Republics

In most regions of Russia the civil war ended in 1920–1921, but in the Asian part of Russia it took longer for the Soviet regime to become stabilized. Anti-Soviet resistance in the Central Asian protectorates of Bukhara and Khiva (Khorezm) (see Chapter 2.2) led to the ousting of the local monarchs and the establishment of Soviet People's Republics whose aim was to pacify the Muslim rebels. The remotest Asian regions were still being attacked by Japanese forces; in response to this, on 6 April 1920 Russia created the Far Eastern Republic (FER), whose purpose was to expel enemy forces, stabilize the area, and prepare it for reunification with Russia. This political entity was entirely exceptional because Russia had voluntarily removed it from Russian territory and recognized it as an independent state. Nevertheless, the motivation for this unprecedented act was clear – Soviet Russia faced numerous problems along its western and southern borders, and it was not prepared for war with Japan.[6]

The situation in Mongolia and Uriankhai, which changed its name to Tandy-Tyva (in Russian Tannu-Tuva) after its main ethnic group, was considerably more complex. People in Mongolia and Tuva reacted in different ways to the events of these years. The population's poor experiences with Chinese officials and troops hardly helped to create positive attitudes towards China while attitudes to Russia ranged from support to rejection. For many people the new communist ideology – delivered by ordinary people and incorporating rhetorical statements about the right of nations to self-determination – was attractive (also due to its promises of economic and social improvements). Moreover, at this time the communists did not interfere with local traditions and religious customs. By contrast, the Cossack armies fighting against the Bolsheviks often treated the local population very harshly (including confiscations of food); this discredited them in the eyes of the public, even though under the leadership of Baron Ungern-Sternberg (from February 1921) they had managed to secure strategic locations in Mongolia. From there the Cossacks advanced into Tuva (in April), where the Ataman Kazantsev formed the Uriankhai Yenisei Cossack Army. In both cases the Cossacks managed to expel some of the Chinese troops and restore the autonomous Mongolian government, but several months later they were defeated by the Red units, in which Buryats and Mongolians fought side by side with Russian troops. The same situation occurred in Tuva, where several local Tuvans fought for the Siberian partisans (Lamin 2007, 99–101).

In early March 1921, while Ungern was still operating in Mongolia, the Russian city of Kyakhta hosted the inaugural congress of the Mongolian People's Party. The exile government of the restored Mongolian state was subsequently appointed; in June, once the White forces had been expelled, the government entered the Mongolian capital. Uriankhai was also considered a part of Mongolia, though the majority of Tuvans refused to accept

70   *Vladimír Baar et al.*

this. In mid-August around 300 representatives from all Tuvan *khoshuns* gathered in Sug-Bazhy for the inaugural All-Tuvan *Khural*. Delegates of the Russian Soviet Federative Socialist Republic (RSFSR) were also present, as were representatives of the Comintern's Far Eastern Secretariat in Mongolia (Baiyr-ool 2011, 39–40). On the first day, the *Khural* accepted a resolution on the formation of a Tuvan state, and on the following day (14 August 1921) the Republic of Tannu-Tuva declared independence and adopted its first constitution – which stated *inter alia* that the Republic was under the protection of Soviet Russia. The second constitution (adopted in 1924) no longer contained this provision, but the USSR continued to interfere in the Republic's internal affairs (Lamin 2007, 130–131).

The Mongolians were irritated by Tuvan independence, and on 14 September 1921 their government issued a new declaration of independence calling on Russia and China to engage in peaceful coexistence. However, the Soviets were angered by some of the articles in this declaration, particularly the unilateral revocation of previous treaties and the rejection of suzerainty to the Republic of China. This was not in accordance with Russia's policy towards China, so the Soviets responded coolly, refraining from commenting directly on the declaration. The People's Commissar for Foreign Affairs Chicherin merely expressed his appreciation for Mongolia's trust in Russia and expressed sympathy for "the self-determination of the Mongolian people" (Srba and Schwarz 2015, 230). The Mongolians therefore quickly dispatched a delegation to Moscow where they hoped to secure Russia's support against China, the annexation of Tuva and other demands. The Soviets rejected these conditions, and the agreement signed with the Mongolians merely promised financial support in the form of loans, plus support for mutual trade. Nevertheless, in the first article of the treaty (signed on 5 November 1921), Russia recognized the legitimacy of the Mongolian government, and Mongolia likewise reciprocally recognized the Russian government. The treaty also contained provisions on the appointment of new ambassadors and the creation of a committee to delineate the Mongolian-Russian border. The Mongolians (entirely logically) considered the treaty to be an international act and a recognition of full independence (Datsyshen 2016, 68).[7] However, China deemed the treaty to be illegal, as it still considered Mongolia an integral part of its own territory. The Soviets were aware of the problematic nature of the treaty, and kept its signature a secret. However, the Chinese found out about its existence via the international press, and the Russians decided to sign a treaty with China committing them to respect Chinese claims on Mongolia. They kept this treaty a secret from Mongolia, but the Mongolians likewise soon found out about it; however, their protests were in vain (Srba and Schwarz 2015, 231).

The problem in the case of Tuva was somewhat different. Here the Russians rejected both Mongolian and Chinese claims, but at the same time Chicherin promised the Tuvans that Russia would not make any claims to their country. The situation was complicated by the fact that the representatives of some border areas were keen to be incorporated into Mongolia – and indeed this eventually happened, though after years of negotiation. The first of these territories was transferred to Mongolia in 1929, and Tuva lost a larger part of its territory in 1935 (Lamazhaa 2011, 62).[8] Mongolian-Tuvan relations thus remained tense in the 1920s. When the Tannu-Tuva government gave written notification to Mongolia (on 7 March 1922) that the Tuvans had freely created an independent state named Tannu-Tuva under the patronage of the RSFSR, the Mongolian government replied (on 15 November) with a note of protest stating that a session of the government had confirmed that Tannu-Uriankhai was part of Mongolia, and that it would be sending a representative there "to evaluate what rights and freedom are being discussed, and to what extent they are necessary for the nation of Tannu-Uriankhai" (Khertek 2016, 67–68). In a note dated 30 March 1923, the Tuvan government rejected the Mongolian claims, stating that "the Tannu-Tuvan nation exists outside the borders of Khalkha-Mongolian territory, and is a separate nation with its own language" (Mollerov 2005, 76). This was true, yet the Tuvan language still lacked an official written form, and official documents – including the constitution – were written in Mongolian using the traditional script (Bicheldei 2010). In October 1925 it was decided that this practice would continue until a standard form of the Tuvan language was developed; the first Tuvan newspapers were therefore published in Mongolian, and schools taught in Mongolian (and later also in Russian). There were wide-ranging discussions about which script should be used for the Tuvan language. Mongolia still laid claim to the territory (though not overtly), and this led to the rejection of the traditional Mongolian script. At the same time, the Turkic nations of the USSR were introducing the Latin alphabet for their languages, so on 30 June 1930 Tuva officially adopted this script (Otroshenko 2015, 22). Teaching in Tuvan was then introduced in all schools, and basic literacy improved dramatically during the following decade; in the 1920s just 1.5% of the population could read and write (though only Mongolian or Russian), in 1940 the figure was an incredible 85% (Bicheldei 2010, 225). The Soviet influence was also growing during this period, hand in hand with Russian immigration. In January 1922 the Russian population of Tuva won wide-ranging cultural autonomy in the form of a self-governing Russian labour colony. This institution did not have territorial autonomy, but its members were subject to Soviet legislation. This practice continued even after the introduction of the new constitution in 1930. Subsequently, on 24 May 1932, the Soviet Union and the Tuvan People's Republic (TPR) signed a declaration on the reorganization of the labour colony to create committees of Soviet citizens (Datsyshen 2016, 31). It is evident that a copy of the Soviet system existed in the TPR by this time (Lamin 2007, 158–160).

Mongolian-Tuvan relations during the first years of "independence" were thus burdened by mutual disputes, which in April 1924 actually escalated into an armed rebellion in Khemchik, accompanied by calls for incorporation into Mongolia (Khertek 2016, 68). The Tuvan government called on

72 *Vladimír Baar et al.*

Moscow for assistance but also sent its own negotiators to Khem-Beldir (Tuvan capital, from 1926 Kyzyl) and to Mongolia. In July and August there were tripartite talks, at which Mongolian claims to Tuva were rejected. However, the Mongolians still refused to give up. After the death of the Bogd Gegen, the first session of the Great *Khural* (26 November 1924) declared the foundation of the Mongolian People's Republic and emphasized "the association of all Mongolian tribes, including the Tannu-Uriankhai" (Khertek 2016, 69). The Soviets decided to take a harder line, and forced the Mongolian communists to change their stance. Exactly one year later, the second session of the Great *Khural* approved a declaration addressed to the government and the people of the TPR recognizing its sovereignty (Khertek 2016, 70). Subsequently, in July and August 1926, talks were held in Ulaanbaatar to solve some disputed issues; these culminated on 16 August in a treaty of mutual recognition. The treaty was ratified by Mongolia on 25 September and Tuva[9] on 28 November. The Sovietization of both countries had brought its first results, with two otherwise unrecognized states reciprocally recognizing each other's independence.[10]

The differing ends of Mongolian and Tuvan People's Republics

Although nominally independent, Tuva and Mongolia remained subjugated to Soviet control. Soviet-style practices in terms of dispensing with political opponents had already appeared in Mongolia in 1922 (when Prime Minister Bodo was executed), and such practices continued in the following years with the killing of several dozen leading state representatives and political opponents. Mass repression began following Stalin's consolidation of his power, culminating in 1936–1939. In Mongolia, this form of repression is associated mainly with the names of the Prime Minister Khorloogin Choibalsan and the Chairman of the Mongolian People's Revolutionary Party Yumjaagiin Tsedenbal. The repression was exceptionally thorough, and the number of people affected is estimated at over 100,000 (i.e. 13%–15% of the entire population), of whom over a third were executed.[11] The repression in Tuva was much less widespread (with around 1.5% of the population killed), and was associated with Salchak Toka – the politician who brought Tuva into the Soviet Union and remained the highest-ranking representative of Soviet Tuva until his death in 1973.

The incorporation of Tuva into the Soviet Union is often viewed as an act of violence through which Stalin completed the Sovietization of this small country. It is difficult to assess the extent to which Stalin influenced the decision-making of Tuvan politicians – especially Salchak Toka, with whom he had been friends for many years. It is certain that Toka had been an ardent Russophile since his youth, and he preferred speaking Russian to Tuvan.[12] From 1932 he was also the Secretary-General[13] of the Tuvan People's Revolutionary Party, and it was in this capacity, in April 1941, that his Central Committee requested the incorporation of Tuva into the USSR. The Soviet

Tuva and Mongolia 73

government did not respond to the request immediately, and the invasion of the USSR by Germany caused the matter to be postponed indefinitely (Lamin 2007, 389). The last constitution of the Tuvan People's Republic (1941) also declared a strong affiliation with the USSR; under the constitution, citizens of the Soviet Union were granted active and passive suffrage (Kharunova 2009, 148). During the war, Tuva sent as much food and other goods to the USSR as it was able to, and many Tuvans volunteered to fight for the Red Army. In July 1944, when the Soviet forces launched an offensive, Toka visited the Foreign Minister Molotov and discussed the matter of Tuva's incorporation. According to Lamin, Molotov asked about Tuva's relations with Mongolia and China, the attitudes of the local population and other matters; Toka assured him that the incorporation enjoyed mass support (with the exception of feudal elements). Molotov naturally agreed to the incorporation (Lamin 2007, 392–393). After returning home, Toka first arranged the Party's approval of the change, which was followed by unanimous approval from the Small *Khural* (17 August 1944). It is clear that this was a standard Party directive from the fact that the request for incorporation was sent to the Secretary of the Central Committee of the Soviet Communist Party Malenkov, who convened a session of the Presidium of the Supreme Soviet for 14 September, where the Tuvan delegation could present its request and explain the grounds for it. However, the incorporation of Tuva was not formally approved until the next session of the Presidium on 14 October, and it was not granted the status of a Soviet Socialist Republic (SSR, member state of the Soviet Union) or an Autonomous Soviet Socialist Republic (ASSR, an autonomous unit within an SSR), but merely an autonomous region (*oblast*). This status reflected the relatively small population at the time (just 95,400). This brief account of the legal steps taken to enact the incorporation demonstrates that even during the war, the USSR placed great emphasis on formal procedure – though objections have been voiced that the process was not entirely in accordance with contemporary legislation either in Tuva or the USSR. These objections focus on the fact that the declaration on the revocation of Tuva's own statehood and its incorporation into the USSR was approved only by the Small *Khural* and not by the Great *Khural*, and that on the Soviet side it was approved only by the Presidium of the Supreme Soviet and not by the Supreme Soviet itself (Kharunova 2009, 148) – though given the level of discipline within the Party, the result would have been the same. The issue of the approval by the Small *Khural* (a body similar to the Presidium of the Supreme Soviet) rather than the Great *Khural* has still not been satisfactorily resolved because neither of these Tuvan bodies predicted the revocation of Tuva's statehood and its incorporation into a different state. The fact that the change was not approved by the Supreme Soviet is explained by the fact that this body did not convene even once during the war, but instead delegated its powers to the Presidium (Lamin 2007, 391).

Tuva's revocation of its own statehood can be explained not only with reference to Toka's Russophile stance (Toka was in complete control of the single

74 *Vladimír Baar et al.*

party and thus the entire state) but also with reference to the fact that the Tuvans themselves were aware of their strong economic ties with Russia[14] and feared that the USSR would possibly leave Tuva to become part of Sovietized Mongolia (after all, the Soviets supported Mongolia in border disputes). It is very likely that Stalin wanted to solve the issue of Tuva (to which China only laid a formal claim) before the end of the war; along with Toka, he exploited the fact that the allies were not interested in Tuva. Mongolia was a different case. Although the Mongolian leadership and opposition had been decimated by the repression, leaving Tsedenbal and Choibalsan in firm control of the country, Mongolia's efforts to maintain its newly won statehood, the persistent Chinese claims on its territory, and fears of the allies' reaction made it impossible to repeat the Tuva scenario. Nevertheless, the Soviet Union made a strategic move to retain its influence in Mongolia after Mongolia had declared war on Japan (12 August 1945, two days after the USSR). Mongolian units helped the Soviets to occupy Manchuria including the Kwantung region, which was an integral part of Japan.[15] The Mongolians' role in this episode eventually made Jiang Jeshi (Chiang Kai-shek) willing to recognize Mongolia's independence. This concession was made in return for the Soviets halting their southward march to liberate Peking. In August 1945 Soviet-Chinese Treaty, China acknowledged that Outer Mongolia was not subject to Chinese sovereignty, though Manchuria was. The USSR also committed to cease its interference in the Xinjiang region (Opolev n.d.). China made its recognition of Mongolian sovereignty conditional upon the result of a referendum, which was held on 20 October 1945. The Mongolian government left no other option for voters except to express their support for independence. 98.5% of eligible voters participated in the referendum, with 100% of them supporting independence (Nohlen, Grotz, and Hartmann 2001, 490). Subsequent experience of other totalitarian regimes has shown such an overwhelming result to be not unusual (though a 100% result has not been common). Jiang Jeshi indeed recognized Mongolian independence on the basis of this referendum (in January 1946), but he later rescinded this recognition when Stalin backed the communists in the civil war (Radchenko 2015). The government of the Republic of China then successfully blocked Mongolia's membership of the United Nations. It was not until 1960 – when the USSR threatened to block the membership of all newly decolonized countries – that the other Security Council members pressured China into withdrawing its opposition; in 1961 Mongolia became a UN member and gained full international recognition.

However, Tuva and Mongolia were not the only de facto state-like entities, which emerged during the collapse of Manchu China and the Second World War. It was also Tibet, which declared independence after the fall of the Qing dynasty in 1912, Manchuria,[16] a Japan dominated entity existing in the territory of north-eastern China in 1931–1945, and the East Turkestan Republic, an entity under the Soviet influence existing in the north-west of present-day Xinjiang in 1944–1949. Nevertheless, during several years, all the de facto state-like entities formed between 1912 and 1945 had ceased to exist. The Manchurian state ceased to exist when its patron state lost the war, and East Turkestan (Xinjiang) never managed to become fully stabilized without a strong patron. Tibet, which never managed to find a patron to protect its independence, and in fact never even sought to find a patron – was militarily pacified by communist China in 1951, having received no support from other states.

Conclusion

Although the concept of de facto states had not yet emerged at the time when the Tsarist Russia disappeared and the above-mentioned entities of Bukhara, Tuva, and Mongolia with the strong ties to the forming Soviet Union appeared, this chapter rests on the assumption that it is indeed possible to define them as a historical examples of a de facto states.

The initial ease of the Russian eastward expansion was gradually replaced by a complex strategic game in which Russia/the USSR ran up against the interests of regional powers (China and Japan) and Britain (in Afghanistan and Tibet). Russia had to choose its tactics and develop new ways of strengthening its influence. It had traditionally exploited local disputes and offered a form of protection; in this regard the tactics used by Tsarist Russia and the USSR did not differ significantly. What did differ were the narratives that underpinned the expansionist policy.

In the case of Bukhara, the republic was intended from the outset to be a long-term project, not merely a temporary entity. Moreover, it was not a transient phenomenon that ceased to exist just a few months after its establishment; it thus fulfils the criterion of long-term sustainability that is viewed as an essential element of a de facto state. The republic followed its own autonomous internal course of development as a newly built state, yet it also had to deal with the legacy of the former Emirate – as well as with strong opposition from the former Emir and his entourage, plus other figures opposed to the Bukharan revolution. However, it was an external intervention (by the Red Army) which enabled the new system to be created, and the Soviet Union's role as the patron state enabled it to survive; these factors substantially limited the options open to the new republic. Indeed, it was ultimately the patron state (the USSR) which stood behind the extinction of the de facto entity – though the precise parameters of this extinction were determined by the elites from the Bukharan state.

In the case of Mongolia and Tuva, Russia's tactical approach and careful diplomacy led to the creation of de facto states that were loyal to Russia/ the USSR. The different status of Tuva and Mongolia can be explained by the decisions made by their patron state, the USSR, which had to respect the fact that China had gained the status of a victorious power at the end of the war. The USSR therefore resolved the status of Tuva before the war ended. The communists' victory in China represented a huge success for the Soviet Union, which expected to apply the tried-and-tested Mongolian and

76 *Vladimír Baar et al.*

Tuvan model (with a formally independent state actually run from Moscow via Party structures) to other states. Although the USSR did successfully apply this approach in Eastern Europe (with the exception of Yugoslavia and later Albania), in China its success was only short-lived. However, Mongolia remained a Soviet vassal until the disintegration of the USSR.

The steps which led to the emergence of these historical de facto states provide a fascinating insight into the late phase of Russian expansion and offer an innovative perspective on the period of transition from Tsarist to Bolshevik rule. Russia applied a similar model during its transformation from a communist regime to the Russian Federation. Russia's support for separatism in Abkhazia and South Ossetia led it to legally recognize these states' independence from Georgia while also retaining control over these de facto states by ensuring that they remained dependent on Moscow in a practically identical way to Tuva and Mongolia. It will be interesting to observe whether a similar course of development awaits these two present-day breakaway entities.

Notes

1 The administration was headed by an official with the title *amban-noyon*.
2 The case of Tuva is specific because it is part of Russia, and the case of Mongolia is specific because it became a recognized subject under international law. Taiwanese-Mongolian relations are nevertheless amicable, and on the diplomatic level economic and trade representation offices have been created in Ulaanbaatar (2002) and then in Taipei (2003). Taiwanese-Russian relations have followed a similar course.
3 The only "international agreement" was a treaty with Tibet signed on 2 February 1913, in which both states reciprocally recognized each other's independence; this was of enormous importance to the Mongolians because the treaty ranked the Bogd Gegen on the same level as the Dalai Lama.
4 This status was revoked in 1920.
5 From the 18th century, the Buryats had mainly been subjects of the Russian Tsar, but their shared faith and the similarity of their languages made them culturally close to the Mongolians (at least to some Mongol tribes). The Russians therefore attempted to designate the Buryats (and the Barga) as a separate nation, in the hope of dampening the desire for the unification of all Mongolian ethnic groups (Pan-Mongolism).
6 The issue with the "independence" of the FER was not only that it only controlled part of its claimed territory at the time of its declaration but also that its internal and foreign policies were under the control of the Bolsheviks in Moscow. Shortly after the FER army had expelled the last Japanese troops from Vladivostok, on 14 November 1922 the FER government requested incorporation into the RSFSR. It is evident that this process was managed from Moscow because on the very next day the FER was dissolved and its territory became part of Soviet Russia.
7 However, at the time the Bolshevik government lacked international legitimacy.
8 In 1935, it had to change its state emblem, which since 1930 had included a map of Tuva. The last border change took place in 1958 when small areas of territory were exchanged by mutual agreement.
9 Shortly before, on 24 November 1926, the word Tannu had been removed from the state's name under the new constitution.

10 The fact is that the USSR only enjoyed limited international sovereignty at this time; in 1926 it was recognized by just twenty-four states, and the next recognition only came in 1933.
11 The precise numbers of people persecuted were not made public; various estimates are given, for example, by Srba and Schwarz (2015, 262–263).
12 His pro-Russian sentiments are evident in the fact that he gave all his children Russian names (Valentin, Anna, Viktor, and Vladimir).
13 After Tuva's incorporation into the USSR he became the First Secretary of the Regional Committee of the Soviet Communist Party, subsequently holding this position until his death.
14 Ties with Russia have remained dominant up to the present day. The only major road from Tuva runs to Abakan in Khakassia; the other road, to Mongolia, is of much poorer quality. There is only one border crossing, which is currently only open for Russian and Mongolian citizens (modernization began in 2016 to create an international border crossing, but on the Mongolian side of the border the road remains unsurfaced). The only air links are with Russia. The airport in Kyzyl can only handle small aircraft, and there are flights to Novosibirsk, Krasnoyarsk, and Irkutsk 2–3 times a week.
15 The USSR then officially leased this region from China for a thirty-year period, but in 1955 it terminated the lease and returned the region to the People's Republic of China.
16 In 1934 this Manchurian state (known as *Manchukuo* in Chinese and *Manshukoku* in Japanese) was recognized by just three Central American countries (El Salvador, the Dominican Republic, and Costa Rica), followed by Italy and Spain (1937), Germany (1938), and Hungary (1939). After the outbreak of the Second World War, a further ten puppet governments of Germany and Japan also recognized the state. It was recognized by the USSR in May 1941.

Literature

Baiyr-ool, Mongush S. 2011. "Tri stolpa tuvinskoi gosudarstvennosti [The Three Pillars of Tuvan Statehood]." *Novye issledovaniya Tuvy* 3 (2–3): 37–62.

Beloff, Max. 1963. *The Foreign Policy of Soviet Russia 1929–1941, Volume I*. London, New York, and Toronto: Oxford University Press.

Bicheldei, Kaadyr-ool A. 2010. "80 let tuvinskoi pismennosti: stanovlenie, razvitie, perspektivy [80 Years of Tuvan Literature: Emergence, Development, Perspectives]." *Novye issledovaniya Tuvy* 2 (4): 210–229.

Boyd, James F. 2008. *Race and Strategy: Japanese-Mongolian Relations 1873–1945*. Perth: Murdoch University.

Datsyshen, Vladimir G. 2016. "Russkaya samoupravlyayushchayasya trudovaya koloniya v Tuvinskoi narodnoi respublike kak unikalnyi opyt rossiiskogo regionalizma [Russian Self-Governing Labour Colony in Tuvan People's Republic as a Unique Experience of Russian Regionalism]." *Novye issledovaniya Tuvy* 8 (3): 19–33.

Dongak, Venera S. 2010. "Problemy istorii i sovremennoi situatsii tuvinsko-mongolskikh otnoshenii [Problems of History and Presence of Tuvan-Mongolian Relations]." *Novye issledovaniya Tuvy* 2 (1): 188–205.

Kharunova, Marianna M.-B. 2009. "Tuva i SSSR: protses politicheskoi integratsii [Tuva and the USSR: A Process of Political Integration]." *Novye issledovaniya Tuvy* 1 (3): 139–163.

Khertek, Lyubov K. 2016. "Tuvinsko-mongolskie svyazi i otnosheniya v period Tuvinskoi Narodnoi Respubliki [Tuvan-Mongolian Contacts and Relations in the Period of Tuvan People's Republic]." *Novye issledovaniya Tuvy* 8 (3): 65–81.

78 *Vladimír Baar et al.*

Kuzmin, Sergey L. 2016. *Buddizm i gosudarstvennost Mongolii v nachale XX v.: transformatsia otnoshenii religii i gosudarstva v protsesse stanovlenia nezavisimosti* [Buddhism and Statehood of Mongolia at the Beginning of the 20th Century: Transformation of Relations between the State and the Religion in the Process of Emerging Independence]. Moskva: Institut vostokovedenia RAN.

Lamazhaa, Chimiza K. 2011. *Tuva mezhdu proshlym i budushchim* [Tuva between the Past and the Future]. Sankt Peterburg: Aleteiia.

Lamin, Vladimir A., ed. 2007. *Istoriya Tuvy, Tom II* [History of Tuva, Volume I]. Novosibirsk: Nauka.

MAC. 2012. "Press Release on Republic of Mongolia" (in Chinese). Taipei: Mainland Affairs Council, www.mac.gov.tw/public/Attachment/252122204856.pdf.

Mollerov, Nikolai M. 2005. *Istoriya sovetsko-tuvinskikh otnoshenii (1917–1944)* [History of Soviet-Tuvan Relations]. Moskva: Izdatelstvo Moskovskogo gumanitarnogo universiteta.

Mollerov, Nikolai M. 2014. "Protektorat Rossii nad Tuvoi v 1914–1924 gg. (istoriko-pravovoi aspekt) [Russian Protectorate over Tuva in 1914–1924 (Historical and Law Aspect)]." *Novye issledovaniya Tuvy* 6 (3): 47–57.

Nohlen, Dieter, Florian Grotz, and Christof Hartmann. 2001. *Elections in Asia and the Pacific: A Data Handbook, Volume II*. London and New York: Oxford University Press.

Opolev, Vitalii. n.d. "Dogovor o druzhbe i soyuze mezhdu Sovetskim Soyuzom i Kitaem ot 14 avgusta 1945 goda. Obyavlenie SSSR 8 avgusta 1945 goda voiny Yaponii [A Treaty on Friendship and Union between the Soviet Union and China, 14th August 1945. Declaration of War by the Soviet Union on Japan, 8th August 1945]." In *Istoriya sovetsko-kitaiskikh otnoshenii*. http://tank.uw.ru/books/opolev/.

Otroshenko, Ivanna V. 2015. "Yazykovaya politika i kulturnoe stroitelstvo v Tuvinskoi narodnoi respublike [Language Policy and Cultural Establishments in Tuvan People's Republic]." *Novye issledovaniya Tuvy* 7 (2): 16–32.

Plotnikov, Aleksei Y. 2007. *Russkaya dalnevostochnaya granica* [Russian Far Eastern Border]. Moskva: KomKniga.

Radchenko, Sergey. 2015. "The Truth about Mongolia's Independence 70 Years Ago. A referendum in Mongolia Seventy Years Ago Sheds Light on the Country's Path since." *The Diplomat*, October 22. http://thediplomat.com/2015/10/the-truth-about-mongolias-independence-70-years-ago/.

Rossiya i Tibet [Russia and Tibet]. 2005. Sbornik russkikh arkhivnykh dokumentov 1900–1914 [Proceedings of Russian Archive Documents 1900–1914]. Moskva: Izdadelstvo Vostochnaya literatura RAN.

Srba, Ondřej, and Michal Schwarz. 2015. *Dějiny Mongolska* [History of Mongolia]. Praha: Nakladatelství Lidové noviny.

Tang, P. S. H. 1959. *Russian and Soviet Policy in Manchuria and Outer Mongolia 1911–1931*. Durham: Duke University Press.

Vasilenko, Viktoria A. 2013. "Tanu-Uryankhaiskii krai v 1911–1912 gg.: rozhdenie trekhstoronnego sopernichestva [Tannu-Uryankhai Region in 1911–1912: A Birth of a Three-Party Rivalry]." *Novye issledovaniya Tuvy* (5) 3: 47–68.

Zhagabpa, Cipön W. D. 2000. *Dějiny Tibetu* [History of Tibet]. Praha: Nakladatelství Lidové noviny.

Zhugder, Chuluuny. 1974. *Razvitie obshchestvenno-politicheskoi mysli v Mongolii (XIX i nachalo XX v.)* [Development of Social-Political Thinking in Mongolia (19th and the beginning of 20th Century)]. Moskva: IF AN SSSR.

Section 3

The emergence of de facto states

3.1 Factors of de facto states' formation in the post-Soviet area

Tomáš Hoch

Although there are several studies focussing on factors which contribute to the formation of de facto states, this particular field remains somewhat understudied. One of the first authors who attempted to present a systematic theoretical account of the existence of de facto states in the international environment was Scott Pegg. Two chapters of Pegg's monograph International Society and the De facto State are devoted to several macro-level factors, which he discusses in general terms with reference to how de facto states emerge and are sustained, and to several micro-level factors, which he applies to specific case studies (Pegg 1998, 120–172). The six macro-level factors mentioned by Pegg (1998, 120) are "the new normative environment on territory; changing conceptions of sovereignty; the shift from empirical to juridical statehood; state recognition policies; the 'weak state' security problematic; and the principle of self-determination". While the first four of these factors ensure that de facto states remain in a position which limits their options for achieving widespread international recognition, the last two factors prevent de facto states from being incorporated into their parent state and thus ceasing to exist. The existence of de facto statehood thus results from a combination of all six macro-level factors – which create conditions enabling a de facto state to emerge and sustain its existence. Pegg notes that a number of these factors are interrelated. It would be impossible, for example, to understand the dynamics involved in the weak state security problematic without considering the changing normative environment on territory (Pegg 1998, 120). Among the micro-level factors which contributed to the emergence of the de facto states studied by Pegg are "foreign invasions, external political involvement, external humanitarian involvement, indigenous secession attempts, state collapse, the role of UN peacekeepers in separating warring parties, and the demonstration effect of already existing de facto states" (Pegg 1998, 148). As in the case of the macro-level factors, these micro-level factors are interrelated, and not all of them necessarily exist in all de facto states. According to Pegg, the emergence of de facto states thus results from a combination of several macro-level factors, which frame the picture and provide permissive conditions for the birth of de facto states in general, while the micro-level factors are more directly related to the actual

82 Tomáš Hoch

events leading up to the birth of specific entities (Pegg 1998, 171). However, it should be pointed out that Pegg's monograph focusses primarily on de facto states located outside the post-Soviet area; his case studies involve Tamil Eelam, Eritrea, Northern Cyprus, and Somaliland.

Other authors exploring aspects of de facto statehood in the post-Soviet space approach the factors enabling the emergence of de facto states with a considerably lower degree of theoretical abstraction. Essentially all of them agree that the existence of de facto states in the post-Soviet area is due to a combination of several factors, but they do not agree on the precise delineation of these factors. Among the factors mentioned by Berg and Toomla (2009, 27) are (a) incomplete and contested state-formation in the intermediate zones of great power rivalry and (b) the external influence of a power which is pursuing its own interests in the conflict between a de facto state and its parent state. Harvey and Stansfield (2011, 17–18) argue that the wars of Soviet succession are all examples of conflicts in which state weakness and instability of parent states paved the way for conflict and provided the necessary openings for secessionist movements to secure territory and engage in processes of separation. According to Caspersen (2012, 26) in most cases ethno-nationalism provided an important driving force, state breakdown was often an important factor, and external assistance was crucial.

A similar explanation of the factors leading to the emergence of de facto states in the post-Soviet space is given by Zabarah (2012) – who also adds another factor, the degree of institutional organization within the separatist group. According to him well-organized groups with institutionalized structures at their disposal, such as labour unions, parties, churches, or paramilitary organizations, would have a competitive advantage over groups still being in their formative process (Zabarah 2012, 183). Cornell (2002) is another scholar who considers the degree of institutional organization to be an important factor contributing to the armed conflicts in the post-Soviet space which ultimately led to the emergence of de facto states. Cornell notes that all present-day post-Soviet de facto states are located in regions which, during the Soviet era, were either autonomous republics (Abkhazia 1931–1991; Transnistria as the Moldavian ASSR 1924–1940) or autonomous regions (South Ossetia 1922–1990, Nagorno-Karabakh 1923–1991).[1]

The factor of institutional organization means that the population of Abkhazia, South Ossetia, Transnistria, and Nagorno-Karabakh had already undergone a process of ethno-national mobilization long before the eventual disintegration of the Soviet Union. After all, the de facto states that emerged during the 1990s were not the first such entities to appear within the region now known as the post-Soviet space; similar entities also emerged during the collapse of the Tsarist Empire and the formation of the USSR (see Chapter 1.3).

The disintegration of the USSR had the most problematic consequences in the wider Caucasus-Black Sea region. The population of this region was characterized by a high degree of ethnic and religious heterogeneity, and

Factors of de facto states' formation   83

memories of numerous historical injustices were vivid and persistent (Jelen 2014, 117). Due to the Soviet policy, any public discussion of violent chapters of history was strictly taboo; however, not even seventy years of Soviet rule could erase memories of past enmity. Hostility among different ethno-national groups remained latently present throughout the Soviet era, and when the USSR collapsed it returned to the surface in overt form. Gorbachev's *perestroika* created a vacuum of both power and ideology, giving free rein to formerly suppressed nationalist sentiments (Souleimanov and Hoch 2012, 38).

According to the last Soviet constitution (1977), the right to self-determination was only guaranteed to the inhabitants of the Union Republics. In 1991 these republics thus became fifteen independent states, and they quickly gained widespread international recognition. Their right to independence was enshrined in Article 72 of the 1977 Soviet constitution, which stated: "Each Union Republic shall retain the right freely to secede from the USSR". However, besides the Union Republics, several other entities of the USSR also attempted to gain independence, even though the 1977 constitution did not grant them this privilege: these included Gagauzia, Chechnya, Tatarstan, Abkhazia, South Ossetia, Nagorno-Karabakh, and Transnistria. These entities frequently based their argumentation on Article 3 of the 1990 Law on Secession, which states that "[t]he people of autonomous republics and autonomous formations retain the right to decide independently the question of remaining within the USSR or within the seceding Union Republic, and also to raise the question of their own state-legal status". The law also stipulated that the status of "territories not belonging to the seceding republic at the moment of its entry into the USSR" and "territories densely populated by the ethnic groups constituting a majority of the population of the locality in question" had to be resolved during the transitional period between the referendum and the factual secession of the individual Union Republic. The chaos unleashed by the disintegration of the USSR was thus reflected in the existence of numerous conflicting interpretations of these entities' legal status, and the elites of many of the Soviet Union's smaller nations began to call into question the established ethnic-territorial order.

The independent states born out of the wreckage of the USSR were thus immediately faced with the challenge of retaining their own territorial integrity. This was a particularly difficult task because their political institutions were still in their infancy and the dramatic economic transformation had led to a sharp decline in living standards. Another important factor in the escalation of ethno-national conflicts was the fact that while Georgian, Moldovan, and Azerbaijani nationalism (and with twenty years delay also Ukrainian nationalism) were essentially anti-Russian in their struggle to form their own nation states, the political elites in the regions now known as de facto states saw the Russian Federation as a guarantor of their rights, and took a stance against their parent states. It is therefore

84 *Tomáš Hoch*

no surprise that in the public discourse of these newly independent states (especially Georgia and Moldova), the elites of Abkhazia, South Ossetia, and Transnistria were typically viewed as a fifth column of Moscow. This brings us to another key factor already mentioned above: the existence of an external actor, pursuing its own interests through the conflicts. In the post-Soviet space, by far the most significant external actor is Russia, which has played an important role in the escalation of conflicts, the fighting itself, and the subsequent peace processes. In addition to Russia's political role, its activities in the conflict regions have also had strong economic, cultural, military/security, and humanitarian dimensions. For Abkhazia, South Ossetia, and Transnistria (and later on, also for Donetsk and Luhansk Peoples' Republics), Russia has become a patron state, offering an inseparable combination of political, diplomatic, military, and economic assistance that has represented an important source of support for their separatist ambitions. However, it would be overly simplistic to describe all post-Soviet de facto states as mere Kremlin puppets, or as mere tools enabling Moscow to pursue its foreign policy objectives. As has been mentioned in introduction of this monograph, de facto states differed from each other in many respects at the time of their emergence – not only in their geographical location, demographic homogeneity, or economic characteristics but also in terms of their relations with their parent state and with Russia. This still remains the case today. All the post-Soviet de facto states share several common features – they are active in attempts to gain international recognition, build their own economies, and form a coherent national identity. However, they differ in their degree of willingness to submit to Russian interests.

This section provides three comparative studies which demonstrate the process of formation of de facto states in the post-Soviet area. Each study focusses on the key factors identified in this theoretical introduction, which enabled the emergence of de facto states within the post-Soviet area: the legal and social chaos created by the disintegration of the USSR; the political and economic weakness of the newly formed independent states; the ethno-national ambitions of nations in current or former autonomous entities, bolstered by memories of historical enmity; and the patron state's direct or indirect support for the separatists. The first chapter focusses on the two de facto states which separated from Georgia – Abkhazia and South Ossetia – and shows how Russia (mis-)used the already existing ethnopolitical conflicts in the two Georgian autonomies. The second chapter focusses on Nagorno-Karabakh and Javakheti, two Armenian-populated regions, and identifies factors which led to the emergence of the Nagorno-Karabakh de facto state and which prevented a similar development in the case of Javakheti. Finally, the last chapter in this section provides an empirical insight into the ongoing conflict in Ukrainian Donbass, which seems to have resulted in the formation of two more de facto states – the Donetsk and Luhansk People's Republics.

Note

1 The Donetsk and Luhansk People's Republics could be seen as exceptions; however, during the Russian Civil War the Donetsk-Krivoi Rog Soviet Republic existed in the territory of present-day eastern Ukraine. See Chapter 3.4 for details.

Literature

Berg, Eiki, and Raul Toomla. 2009. "Forms of Normalisation in the Quest for De Facto Statehood." *The International Spectator* 44 (4): 27–45.

Caspersen, Nina. 2012. *Unrecognized States. The Struggle for Sovereignty in the Modern International System*. Cambridge: Polity Press.

Cornell, Svante E. 2002. "Autonomy as a Source of Conflict: Caucasian Conflicts in Theoretical Perspective." *World Politics* 54 (2): 245–276.

Harvey, James, and Gareth Stansfield. 2011. "Theorizing Unrecognized States: Sovereignty, Secessionism, and Political Economy." In *Unrecognized States in the International System*, edited by Nina Caspersen and Gareth Stansfield, 11–26. London: Routledge.

Jelen, Libor. 2014. "Spatial Analysis of Ethnopolitical Mobilisation in the Caucasus in the 1980s and 1990s." *Bulletin of Geography. Socio-economic Series* 25: 115–128.

Pegg, Scott. 1998. *International Society and the De Facto State*. Aldershot: Ashgate.

Souleimanov, Emil, and Tomáš Hoch. 2012. *Role Ruska v konfliktech a oficiálních mírových procesech v Abcházii a Jižní Osetii v letech 1991–2008* [Russia's Role in Conflicts and Official Peace Processes in Abkhazia and South Ossetia in 1991–2008]. Praha: Auditorium.

Zabarah, Dareg A. 2012. "Opportunity Structures and Group Building Processes: An Institutional Analysis of the Secession Processes in Pridnestrovie and Gagauzia between 1989 and 1991." *Communist and Post-Communist Studies* 45 (1): 183–192.

3.2 Formation of de facto states in Abkhazia and South Ossetia

Tomáš Hoch and Emil Aslan Souleimanov

The first years of Georgian independence following the disintegration of the USSR were far from idyllic. The turbulent course of events in this small Black Sea country was framed by two civil wars, unrest in regions with sizeable minority populations, an economic slump (impacting upon living standards), and armed conflicts with separatists in Abkhazia and South Ossetia. With regard to these two separatist regions, it is important to note that although both situations escalated into armed conflicts in the first half of the 1990s (ultimately giving rise to two de facto states), the roots of the conflicts went deeper, reaching back further into the past. This chapter sets out to describe the milestones in the complex development of Ossetian-Georgian and Abkhazian-Georgian relations which in the early 1990s led to the escalation of conflict in both separatist regions, and to identify the factors which ultimately led to the birth of the two de facto states.

The Ossetians and South Ossetia: ethnogenesis, demographics, and historiography of conflict

South Ossetia is a separatist republic in northern Georgia, bordering on the Republic of North Ossetia-Alania in the Russian Federation. It is *de iure* a part of Georgia, though since the early 1990s Ossetian separatists have been attempting to achieve independence. South Ossetia was the scene of a war in 1991–1992, since when the situation in this de facto state has been similar to that in Abkhazia. It covers an area of 3,900 km^2, and its capital is Tskhinvali. The last Soviet census (held in 1989) recorded 164,000 Ossetians living in Georgia, that is, 3% of Georgia's total population. However, the demographic problem facing Ossetia was that the South Ossetian Autonomous Region was home to just 65,000 Ossetians – that is, less than 40% of Georgia's total Ossetian population. In 1989 South Ossetia had just 100,000 inhabitants, with Ossetians making up around two-thirds of the population (66%) and less than a third (29%) made up by Georgians. Around half of families were mixed (Georgian-Ossetian). The remaining 5% of the population was made up of Russians, Armenians, and Jews (Zverev 1996). After the 2008 war, the population of South Ossetia shrank to an estimated 54,000 inhabitants (O'Loughlin, Kolossov, and Toal 2011, 3). The same number was also found by the 2015 census in South Ossetia (Kozaeva 2016) (Map 4).

Georgian historiographers consider the Ossetians to be an allochthonous nation which began to settle in the lowland areas of today's Georgia in significant numbers during the 17th and 18th centuries; the Georgian Prince Machabeli allowed them to settle on his estates. A common Georgian name for South Ossetia – *Samachablo* – is derived from Machabeli's name (Totadze 2008, 7–9). However, the Ossetians seek to demonstrate the autochthonous nature of their own population in today's South Ossetia with reference to the Scythian (proto-Alanic, later Alanic) presence in both the North and South Caucasus, claiming that an Ossetian population has lived in today's South Ossetia since time immemorial. However, though even Georgian historiographers acknowledge the existence of ancient Alania in the northern part of the Caucasus Mountains as an undisputed fact, the Ossetians' claim that the Alans also controlled mountain regions in the southern part of the range during some historical periods, and that they settled in these regions permanently, is considered problematic. The Georgians generally acknowledge the possible existence of an Ossetian population in the southern part of the Greater Caucasus, but they emphasize that the Alans' presence in today's south Ossetia was marginal, and that from 1008 onwards the southern parts of the mountains were under the political control of the Georgian state. In view of the absence of written documents concerning the ethnic composition of this region in ancient and medieval times, it is difficult to provide evidence for this claim based on available sources (cf. Schnirelman 2003, 461–503).

The modern-day conflict between the Tbilisi government and the South Ossetians has its roots in the Democratic Republic of Georgia (1918–1921).

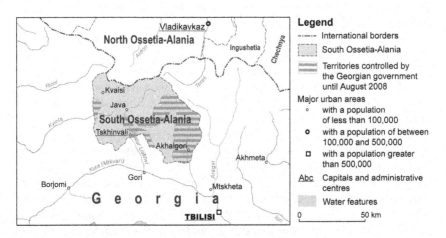

Map 4 South Ossetia.
Source: Authors.

88   *Tomáš Hoch and Emil Aslan Souleimanov*

During this period there were three large-scale uprisings by the inhabitants of South Ossetia (1918, 1919, 1920). These were initially motivated by dissatisfaction with the economic policies pursued by the central government, which in the South Ossetians' opinion unfairly prioritized the interests of large Georgian landowners over the Ossetian peasants. The conflict quickly escalated into an armed phase.[1] The combatants were two ethnically homogeneous groups – the South Ossetians (landless peasants who, under Russian influence, sought greater freedom and land rights) and the local Georgian aristocracy (to whom the land had traditionally belonged) – so the conflict quickly gained an ethnic dimension.

The first armed operation by the Georgian military was repelled by the South Ossetian rebels, who soon took control of the administrative centre of the region, the city of Tskhinvali. The city's Georgian population was subjected to attacks. The fighting continued, with both sides achieving temporary successes; gains by the Georgian army brought reprisals from the Ossetians, and hundreds of civilians died. Ethnically motivated killings and purges of the civilian population intensified nationalist sentiments on both sides, and mutual hatred between the two groups escalated. From 1918 onwards, a growing proportion of the South Ossetian population felt that their only source of support against the Georgians was Soviet Russia, which was keen to take control of South Ossetia – a strategically located region linking the North Caucasus with Transcaucasia. The socio-economic interests of the South Ossetian peasants thus predetermined their ethnic and political sympathies and antipathies to a substantial degree. Their dissatisfaction with the policies pursued by the Menshevik government in Tbilisi in areas with a majority Ossetian population strengthened their sympathies for the Bolsheviks; given the traditionally warm relations between Ossetians and Russians[2] and the Soviets' strategic interest in regaining control over Georgia, the Ossetians were able to count on both military and political support from Moscow (Souleimanov 2013, 113).

During the 1919 uprising, and especially in the major uprising of 1920, the South Ossetian rebels received clandestine yet substantial material support from the Red Army, and the Ossetian political elite overtly declared their desire to become part of Soviet Russia. However, in mid-1920, Moscow – reluctant to become involved in open military conflict on Georgian territory – distanced itself from its protégés in South Ossetia, and Georgian forces launched a major counter-offensive against the South Ossetian positions.[3] This operation was accompanied by widespread ethnic cleansing[4]; estimates range from 3,000 to 7,000 deaths, mainly of civilians, and 20,000 South Ossetians had to flee to Soviet Russia as the Georgian army advanced (Lang 1962, 228). South Ossetian volunteers joined the advancing Red Army, which in February of the following year occupied Georgia, crushing the country's new-found independence. The Red Army's advance was likewise accompanied by widespread ethnic killings. In 1922 the South Ossetian Autonomous Region was formed within Sovietized Georgia. As a concession to South Ossetian politicians who had hoped to be united with North Ossetia (and thus with Russia itself), the administrative boundaries of South Ossetia were expanded to include numerous towns and villages with predominantly Georgian populations (Souleimanov and Hoch 2012, 33).

The era of Soviet rule passed largely without conflict. One reason for this was the high percentage of inter-ethnic marriages, the similarity of Georgian and Ossetian traditions and culture, and the Orthodox faith shared by both nations. The peace was also bolstered by the official Soviet stance which viewed the tragic events of 1918–1921 as a taboo subject – though memories of ethnically motivated violence remained alive among the older generation for a time.

The Abkhazians and Abkhazia: ethnogenesis, demographics, and historiography of conflict

Abkhazia is a separatist republic in the north-western part of Georgia, covering an area of 8,700 km² (around 12% of Georgia's total territory). The most recent census took place in Abkhazia in 2011; it recorded 240,705 inhabitants, consisting of 50.8% Abkhazians, 19.3% Georgians, 17.4% Armenians, and 9.17% Russians (Abkhaz World 2011) (Map 5).

The Abkhazian (Abkhaz) language belongs to the Abkhazo-Adyghean language family[5]; the languages of this family are spoken in the western part of the North Caucasus. The Georgian language belongs to the Kartvelian family, spoken in the western part of the South Caucasus[6]; this means that the two languages are mutually unintelligible. However, the Abkhazians share more anthropological features with the Georgians than with the nations of the North Caucasus – even though logically one would expect the

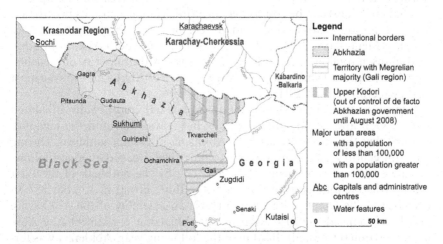

Map 5 Abkhazia.
Source: Authors.

90 *Tomáš Hoch and Emil Aslan Souleimanov*

opposite to be the case. There are essentially two possible (and conflicting) explanations for this situation. Either the tribes considered to be the ancestors of today's Abkhazians[7] originated in a Georgian environment, and over the centuries adopted the language of migrants from the North Caucasus, or the distant ancestors of the Abkhazians acquired some anthropological features of the Georgians as a result of living side by side with them. This dispute among historians, anthropologists, linguists, and ethnographers does not exist solely on the academic level; it also has a significant political dimension.[8] In Georgia we can thus frequently hear the opinion that today's Abkhazians have nothing in common with the historical tribes mentioned by Plinius Secundus, but are instead migrants from the North Caucasus, who stole the territory from the historical Abkhazians (who were of Georgian origin) and did not assimilate with them until the end of the 17th century.[9] Linguists – and not only those of Abkhazian origin – oppose this theory, noting that a nation which in ancient times lived in the ranges of the North Caucasus would hardly have had in their vocabulary words for concepts such as sea, ship, fishing net, tide, and so on, that is, concepts which would only be known by coastal communities (Amichba n.d.; Hewitt 1989; Anchabadze 2010).

On the other hand, the popular Abkhazian ethnogenetic account – that today's Abkhazia was inhabited solely by Abkhazians from ancient times, and that the sizeable Georgian population did not arrive until the late 19th and early 20th centuries as part of a policy of planned assimilation of the Abkhazians (Bhaghzba and Lakoba 2007) – is likewise untenable. Even in ancient times, there was a state entity on the Black Sea coast called Lazica. It can be deduced from the name alone that the Lazi[10] played a significant role in the state. Not even the Kingdom of Abkhazia (formed in the 8th century by merging the four above-mentioned proto-Abkhazian tribes) can be considered an ethnic state because its population included not only Abkhazians and Greeks but also ethnically Kartvelian peoples (Megrelians, Svans, and Lazi). Not only are both Abkhazians and Georgians autochthonous Caucasian nations; for the majority of their history, both nations lived together in the territory of Abkhazia – for the most part peacefully (Hoch 2011).

Georgians (or rather Megrelians in Abkhazia) traditionally inhabited today's Gali and Ochamchira districts, but it was not until the late 19th century that they began to settle in Abkhazia in greater numbers. During the 20th century they continued to colonize the areas abandoned following the exodus of the Muslim Abkhazians[11]; by the outbreak of the First World War Georgians were the majority ethnic group in Abkhazia.[12] In response to the October Revolution (1917) an assembly of the Abkhazian people announced the formation of an Abkhazian parliament (the Abkhazian National Council). In May of the following year, Abkhazia was formally declared a part of the newly emerging Mountainous Republic of the Northern Caucasus, but it remained embroiled in clashes between various political factions – pro-Russian Bolsheviks, pro-Turkish aristocrats, and pro-Georgian socialists (Mensheviks). In the spring of 1918, the administrative centre of Abkhazia, Sukhumi (formerly Sokhumi) was occupied by pro-Bolshevik Abkhazian militias; however, Georgian units immediately regained control over the city and the surrounding area. Unlike South Ossetia, Abkhazia was guaranteed autonomous status by the constitution of the independent Democratic Republic of Georgia.[13] Abkhazian-Georgian relations took a turn for the worse after an unsuccessful attack mounted by a Turkish-Abkhazian regiment in Sukhumi (the operation was organized by Abkhazian aristocrats and nationalists) and a failed coup by several Georgian officers of Abkhazian origin.[14] Tbilisi responded with repression: Abkhazia's autonomous status was temporarily suspended, and many Abkhazians supporting the separatist movement were imprisoned. This was followed by a wave of local uprisings, the largest of which was a peasant revolt of 1920 (which also affected the neighbouring Samegrelo region of Georgia). This revolt was bloodily suppressed by government forces. As Russian-Georgian relations became increasingly tense, the Abkhazians received support first from Denikin's Volunteer Army (February 1919) and two years later by the Red Army.[15]

A month after the Bolsheviks occupied Georgia, the Abkhazian Soviet Socialist Republic was declared, and the original National Council was reinstated. Membership of the Council was restricted solely to Abkhazians. The Bolsheviks were viewed by the Abkhazian population as liberators, and their arrival was met with boisterous celebrations. In November 1921, under pressure from Stalin and Ordzhonikidze, the Supreme Caucasian Bureau decided that Abkhazia and Georgia would become a federation. Events took a rapid turn, and in less than a month (on 16 December 1921) a federation agreement between Abkhazia and Georgia was signed. Abkhazia thus joined the Soviet Union as an independent sovereign republic, linked to Georgia merely by a treaty of association. This status was re-asserted by the Abkhazian constitution of 1 April 1925, and it lasted until 7 January 1931, when the new constitution of the Transcaucasian Socialist Federative Soviet Republic degraded Abkhazia's status to that of an autonomous republic within Georgia.

After the repressive policies of 1918–1921, Abkhazia underwent a second wave of intense Georgianization from 1931 to 1953, this time under Stalin's supervision. As other parts of the USSR, Stalin introduced a policy of forced collectivization, and in 1932 he launched a purge of undesirable citizens, mainly *kulaks* and members of the intelligentsia. The repression in Abkhazia reached its peak in 1936–1937, when 2,186 people were imprisoned, of whom 794 were shot (Ozgan 1998, 186–187). This was followed by the closure of Abkhazian schools and the introduction of the Georgian alphabet[16] in schools to replace the Roman script – though the majority of the population had problems reading and writing in the Georgian alphabet. Stalin is even less popular in Abkhazia than in other parts of the former USSR – not only

92   Tomáš Hoch and Emil Aslan Souleimanov

due to the terror he unleashed but also due to the degradation of Abkhazia's status from a separate SSR to an autonomous republic within Georgia. Abkhazians often claim that if the Kremlin had not been dominated by two ethnic Georgians (Stalin and Beria), Abkhazia today would be an independent state.[17] However, what Abkhazians see as a clear manifestation of Georgian imperialism is viewed entirely differently from the Georgian perspective. For Georgians, Stalin is an exceptionally controversial figure. He was an ethnic Georgian, yet it was him – and Sergo Orjonikidze (also a Georgian) – who in 1921 not only permitted Abkhazia to secede from Georgia, but soon afterwards also ensured that Georgia was occupied by the Red Army and incorporated into the newly emerging USSR.

The deaths of Stalin and Beria in 1953 brought this repressive chapter in Abkhazian history to an end. Abkhazian schools were re-opened, the Georgian alphabet was replaced by Cyrillic, and Abkhazians were given greater access to certain high-ranking official positions. During the 1950s the Abkhazians thus regained most of the rights that they had lost during the Stalinist era. This was also made possible thanks to Khrushchev and his new administration, for whom Georgia was associated with Stalin and Beria.[18] However, not even these concessions were enough to satisfy the Abkhazians, whose main objection was to the fact that Abkhazia formed part of the Georgian SSR. For many years Abkhazian intellectuals and Party functionaries attempted to raise Abkhazia's status to that of an SSR – or to have Abkhazia incorporated directly into the Russian SSR – and they repeatedly addressed these demands to the central government authorities in Moscow (1956, 1967, 1978). Moscow responded by gradually raising the status enjoyed by the Abkhazian language, Abkhazian culture, and the Abkhazian minority in Georgia. However, the Georgians objected to the fact that the Abkhazians – who made up less than 20% of Abkhazia's total population – held more than 70% of the positions in the state administration. The Abkhazians also had their own television and radio broadcasts and their own education system, which was largely independent of Tbilisi. From the 1960s onwards, the First Secretary of the Central Committee of the local Communist Party was always an Abkhazian; previously the post (the most powerful position in the autonomous republic) had traditionally been held by a member of the Georgian community. Similarly, eight of the twelve ministries were headed by Abkhazians; only the Interior Minister, the Chief Prosecutor, and the Prime Minister were ethnic Georgians.

This dispute – which at first sight may appear relatively unimportant – ultimately became one of the main driving forces behind the escalation of tensions between both nations under *perestroika*. Since the inception of the USSR, Soviet policy on nationality-related issues had been based on the principle of a dual hierarchy of state administration. While politically the USSR was a centralized state rooted in communist ideology, certain nations were given considerable privileges in the administration of their territory. Not only the SSRs but also the autonomous republics and autonomous

Abkhazia and South Ossetia 93

regions were created and managed along ethno-territorial lines. In practice, this meant the creation of a titular nationality which was designated as the original ethnic group in the region. Under the Soviet constitution, the titular nationality did not have a superordinate position vis-à-vis the other national communities living in the region, but in practice members of the titular nation enjoyed much easier access to important posts in the administration. In a system as bureaucratic as the USSR undoubtedly was, being a member of a titular nationality gave one a far greater chance of achieving a better economic position. The ethnogenesis of nations in the USSR was thus not merely an academic question; it also had a material effect on everyday life (Hoch 2011).

Ethno-national mobilization, legal, and political chaos during the disintegration of the USSR

A strict information embargo prevented the story of the ethnic conflicts of the early 1920s from becoming common knowledge in Georgia. Like members of the other nations of the USSR, Georgians were brought up in the spirit of socialist internationalism. As had been the case under Tsarist rule, there was a particular emphasis on the key role played by Russia in Georgian history, while some dramatic events (such as the suppression of revolts in the 19th century) remained unmentioned. The occupation of Georgia in 1921 was interpreted in line with Marxist-Leninist dogma as the culmination of the desires of the Georgian proletariat and peasantry, and many negative aspects of Russian-Georgian history were attributed to Tsarism (and later to Stalinism). During the second half of the 20th century, the communist regime managed to dampen tensions between the Abkhazians and Ossetians on one side and the Georgians on the other. This remained the case until the time of Mikhail Gorbachev's government, when his policies of *glasnost* and *perestroika* lifted the lid from long-suppressed nationalist sentiments. In 1988 a series of protests took place in Georgia, with demonstrators calling for independence. Zviad Gamsakhurdia and Merab Kostava became the main representatives of the Georgian independence movement.[19] The pro-Russian orientation of Georgian society was shaken in the aftermath of the tragic events of 9 April 1989, when tanks from the Transcaucasian Military District under the command of General Alexander Lebed opened fire on a peaceful demonstration in central Tbilisi where protesters were chanting slogans in favour of Georgian independence and the "full integration" of Abkhazia. Nineteen people lost their lives.[20] The incident led to a significant radicalization of the public mood, and the reputation of the local communists suffered a severe blow – one from which it never recovered.

Alongside this public radicalization, Georgia's ethnic minorities (especially the South Ossetians and the Abkhazians) stepped up their efforts at emancipation, demanding increased autonomy from Tbilisi. The Abkhazians also appealed to Moscow to be granted the status of a separate SSR,

Tomáš Hoch and Emil Aslan Souleimanov

ıd there were also requests for integration into Russia in the form of an aunomous republic. Because the Russians did not immediately dismiss these ʲmands, the feeling grew among large sections of the Georgian population ʲat the irredentism of Georgia's ethnic minorities was being provoked or ʲen directly controlled by Moscow, in an attempt to disrupt Georgia's terʲtorial integrity. The Georgian national movement was thus strongly antiʲussian from its very inception – more so than in neighbouring countries.

Against this background, the anti-communist nationalist opposition ʲentred around Zviad Gamsakhurdia gained strength. In October and ʲovember 1990 Georgia held its first free parliamentary multi-party ʲlections. The clear winner in both rounds of voting was the opposition ʲloc Round Table – Free Georgia (*mrgvali magida – tavisupali sakartvelo*), ʲvhich won 54% of the votes in the first round and 64% in the second. The ʲommunists won just over 29% of the votes (Slider 1997, 176). The words 'Soviet" and "Socialist" were removed from the country's official name. A transitional period was set up during which a new constitution was to be ıdopted and independence declared. Zviad Gamsakhurdia was elected the Chairman of the Georgian Supreme Soviet by 232 votes to 5 (O'Ballance 1997, 98). This result reflected his enormous popularity at the time – both in political circles and among the Georgian population as a whole. When his party came to power, Georgia began to move in a nationalist direction, so it is no surprise that (already strained) relations between the government and Georgia's ethnic minorities deteriorated further. The Abkhazians – just like the Ossetians, Armenians, Azeris, and Russians – protested against a regime whose clear aim, in their eyes, was to Christianize and Georgianize the country's entire population.

At the level of internal politics, Gamsakhurdia was a proponent of a strong state, a form of symbiosis integrating modern democracy with autocratic features (Piknerová 2013, 53). He saw himself in the role of the charismatic leader and national hero who had been called by fate to unify Georgia and act as its saviour (Nodia 1996). It was his strong belief in his role as a unifying force that caused him to approach ethnic minority issues with a high degree of ruthlessness. Ethnic populism was also a means of winning respect and support from the radicalized Georgian population, which viewed the emancipatory efforts of minority populations in the country's peripheral regions as a process that was being controlled by Moscow's omnipresent hand. In the early 1990s, the radical camp was also joined by the remaining members of the communist *nomenklatura* who had managed to cling to power; for them, nationalism trumped communist ideals. The events of April 1989 had also damaged the communists' reputation, and adopting nationalist patterns of thought and rhetoric appeared to them to be the only way of prolonging their political careers at a time when all former certainties were collapsing around them. It was ultimately the extreme right – not the relatively unpopular liberals – who moved into the space vacated by the communists.[21]

Gamsakhurdia's intransigent approach to ethnic minorities – which he viewed as a "fifth column" of the Kremlin, and against which he frequently directed vehement verbal attacks – was thus shared by many Georgians. The proponents of the slogan "Georgia for the Georgians" described all ethnic minorities as "guests" on Georgian soil, and repeatedly threatened them (especially the Ossetians) with expulsion (Khutsishvili 1994). This type of rhetoric – which came not only from leading political figures but also from intellectuals – exacerbated the already tense inter-ethnic relations in Georgia, where around a third of the population were members of ethnic minorities, mainly concentrated in relatively distinct areas. The first months of Gamsakhurdia's rule were a catalyst for ethnic and political tensions in South Ossetia and Abkhazia. The populations of these areas were also experiencing their own national revival, but one which was anti-Georgian rather than anti-Russian or anti-communist. It is therefore no surprise that in the all-Union referendum on the preservation of the USSR as a renewed federation, held in March 1991, all minorities in Georgia voted by overwhelming majorities for the preservation of the Union. However, the Georgians boycotted the referendum entirely; they refused to acknowledge the result, and on 31 March 1991 they arranged their own referendum on independence. 91.5% of eligible voters participated in the referendum, of which 98% supported Georgian independence (O'Ballance 1997, 98). As a result, on 9 April 1991 the Georgian Supreme Soviet declared independence, making Georgia the first independent state out of all the former SSRs.

Georgian nationalist discourse naturally provoked an antagonistic response from the elites of South Ossetia and Abkhazia. In South Ossetia the catalyst for anti-Georgian sentiment was the language law passed in August 1989 by the Georgian Supreme Soviet, which made Georgian the sole official language of the country. In South Ossetia, where only 14% of Ossetians could speak Georgian, this led to a substantial weakening of the position of the Ossetian and Russian languages (Cornell 2001, 165). Several weeks later, Tskhinvali announced a proposal to grant Ossetian, Georgian, and Russian equal status as official languages in the region. However, this moderate proposal was soon abandoned in the wake of increasingly intense clashes between South Ossetian and Georgian forces in the region, and Ossetian was declared the sole official language. The South Ossetians also asked Moscow for unification with North Ossetia. In the same month, Zviad Gamsakhurdia and the member of the Georgian parliament Givi Gumbaridze organized a "March to Tskhinvali", whose aim was to declare Georgian unity. Around 15,000 ethnic Georgians were bussed into Ossetia for this event. In reality, the march did not result in any declaration of unity; instead it sparked clashes between Ossetians and Georgians, with several people injured on both sides. These events strengthened the position of the South Ossetian nationalists and radicals grouped together in the National Assembly (*Ademon Nykhas*) movement, and armed vigilante units began to be set up.

Another major milestone in the deterioration of Ossetian-Georgian relations came in August 1990, when the Georgian Supreme Soviet banned all regional parties (i.e. parties without a nationwide presence) from participating in the autumn parliamentary elections. This ban *de jure* excluded the ethnic Ossetian parties from political life at a time when these parties were becoming stronger due to the escalating conflict with Tbilisi. South Ossetian political representatives responded by declaring the South Ossetian Soviet Socialist Republic and requesting that Moscow incorporate it into the USSR as a separate republic, entirely independent of Georgia. However, the Georgian parliament revoked this request on the following day. The Georgian public, incensed by the events of the previous April and the escalating crisis in Abkhazia, interpreted this act as a further attempt to disrupt Georgia's territorial integrity. At the end of the year, Tbilisi not only imposed a blockade on South Ossetia but also annulled its autonomous status and declared a state of emergency in the region, which was then formally annulled by Moscow (Cornell 2001, 166). The Georgian parliamentary elections – won by Zviad Gamsakhurdia's Round Table – were boycotted by the Ossetians. In South Ossetia, elections were held for the regional Soviet, but Gamsakhurdia immediately annulled the results. On 7 January 1991 the President of the USSR Mikhail Gorbachev revoked the declaration of South Ossetian independence on the grounds that any decision altering the status of South Ossetia could only come into legal force once it had been approved by the highest authorities in the Soviet Union. Gorbachev also noted that the Georgian Supreme Soviet had failed to comply with Soviet legislation concerning the process for changes in autonomous status. He likewise declared that the state of emergency in South Ossetia was illegal (Pliev et al. 2008), and he revoked the resolutions accepted by the Georgian Supreme Soviet.[22]

The South Ossetian public, still with fresh memories of the clashes with Georgian nationalists, played an active role in the all-Union referendum on the preservation of the USSR as a renewed federation; Moscow hoped to rescue the USSR from disintegration by delegating greater powers to the Union republics. In South Ossetia the draft agreement was approved by 99% of voters. However, the South Ossetians (like the Abkhazians) ignored the referendum on Georgian independence which took place two weeks later, on 31 March 1991. The conflict flared up again in the spring of 1991, as Georgians expelled Ossetians from their homes and vice versa. These clashes left dozens of people dead or injured. From mid-1991 Tskhinvali was subjected to artillery bombardment from nearby hills, and in the autumn the city was encircled by Georgian units. This was despite the presence of around 500 troops of the Soviet Interior Ministry, who had been posted in South Ossetia since April 1991 (König 2004, 253–266). The conflict between the Georgians and the Ossetians lasted a year and a half. The war left a thousand people dead and a hundred missing; 100,000 Ossetian refugees fled to Russia, and 23,000 Georgian refugees to other regions of the country (ICG

Abkhazia and South Ossetia 97

2004, 4). The war was also one of the factors which led to the ousting of Zviad Gamsakhurdia and his replacement by Eduard Shevardnadze. The conflict was finally brought to an end on 23 June 1992 by the Sochi agreement. The agreement stated that fighting was to cease by 28 June 1992 and a Control Commission was to be set up with members from Russia, Georgia, South Ossetia, North Ossetia, and representatives of the Organization for Security and Cooperation in Europe, which was to ensure peace in the region.

A similar situation – characterized by political and legal chaos accompanied by escalating violence – prevailed in the early 1990s in Abkhazia too. Verbal skirmishes among political representatives moved from public speeches and press releases to the legislative and executive branches in early 1992, when the Abkhazian parliament took advantage of the war in South Ossetia to pass a law revoking all Georgian legislation within the territory of Abkhazia. The subsequent sessions of the Abkhazian parliament were completely boycotted by Georgian deputies. The key date in the deterioration of Georgian-Abkhazian relations at this time was 23 July 1992, when the Abkhazian parliament (minus its Georgian contingent) approved Abkhazian independence and a return to the Abkhazian constitution of 1925. Georgia refused to recognize both the legitimacy of this renewed constitution and the legality of the revocation of Georgian legislation in Abkhazia: only 36 out of 65 parliamentary deputies had voted for Abkhazian independence, which was less than the constitutionally required two-thirds majority. However, in reality the events of 23 July led to a loss of Georgian control over Abkhazia – exacerbated by the fact that the military and police were under the control of the Abkhazian authorities. The breach of previous agreements on the administration of Abkhazia (1991) should be seen in the context of wider developments in Georgia. From March 1990 Georgia systematically revoked all legislation introduced by the Bolsheviks, and in February 1992 it reinstated the country's February 1921 constitution. After the approval of an amendment stipulating that the documents that came into force after 25 February 1921 lacked legal legitimacy, there was essentially no legal framework requiring Abkhazia to remain a part of Georgia in the form of an autonomous republic (a status that had been defined in 1931).

However, despite all the complications described above, there was still hope for a peaceful solution of the crisis in Abkhazia. On 12 August 1992 the Abkhazian leadership issued an assurance that Abkhazia intended to continue in a union with Georgia, provided that both sides could agree on the details of a treaty ensuring a peaceful joint future and equal opportunities in the political and cultural spheres (Ozgan 1998, 189). The discussions on this federative treaty were to be held on 14 August, but events intervened to prevent them; in the early morning of 14 August Georgian forces entered Abkhazia, sparking a military conflict, and political negotiations on a possible federation were sidelined. The war more than halved Abkhazia's original population of 525,000, and radically altered its ethnic structure. After the war, the Abkhazians gained control over virtually the entire territory of historical Abkhazia

98 *Tomáš Hoch and Emil Aslan Souleimanov*

(with the exception of the Upper Kodori valley, which they did not gain until 2008), and they declared their sovereignty and independence from Georgia – a status which is currently recognized by just five United Nations member states (Russia, Venezuela, Nicaragua, Nauru, and Syria).[23]

Russia's support for separatism

Up to 1991, Kremlin policy had an entirely dominant influence on affairs in Transcaucasia. Even after the disintegration of the USSR, Moscow retained its dominant influence on the Transcaucasian political and economic scene, though with one significant difference. Russia was no longer the only power influencing developments in Transcaucasia; it now had to contend with other states that had emerged after the disintegration of the USSR as well as other important actors such as the United States, the EU, Turkey, the UN, and the OSCE. After a brief period of Euro-Atlantic idealism in the early days of Boris Yeltsin's rule, at the end of 1992 Russian foreign policy began to emphasize the maintenance of the Russian hegemony in the post-Soviet space. One of the most pressing tasks Russian policymakers were facing was the regulation of armed conflicts throughout the post-Soviet space – preventing such conflicts from spilling over onto Russian territory and supporting the rights of Russian-speaking populations living outside the Russian Federation (Roeder 1997, 227). Viewed from this perspective, the conflicts in Abkhazia and South Ossetia represented a security threat to Russia, which could have led to a spillover effect in the North Caucasus.

The basic principles of Russian foreign policy outlined by Yeltsin in March 1993 fully reflected Russia's stance towards its near abroad. The rhetoric used by the President – and the Ministers of Defence and Foreign Affairs – emphasized that the entire post-Soviet space was viewed as Russia's sphere of influence, and called for the newly emerged independent post-Soviet republics to be integrated into a structure which would enable Russia to continue playing its historical role (Lough 1993, 53–60). This was an evident attempt by Moscow to prevent the emergence of a political and power vacuum in the South Caucasus – a situation which could potentially be exploited by neighbouring countries, the United States, and the EU. A clear demonstration of Russia's gradual turn away from Western-oriented policies was Moscow's categorical demand to be given full control over the peacekeeping operations that were taking place in the territory of the former USSR.[24]

A characteristic feature of Russian foreign policy in relation to Abkhazia and South Ossetia during the first half of the 1990s was the considerable discrepancy between the political declarations of leading Russian political representatives (who used every available opportunity to speak about maintaining strict neutrality and the principle of Georgia's territorial integrity) and the *realpolitik* on the ground, which provided support to the separatists (Hoch, Souleimanov, and Baranec 2014, 60). Russia's assistance of the rebels

Abkhazia and South Ossetia 99

in South Ossetia and Abkhazia was never overtly confirmed by any Kremlin representative, but indirect evidence reveals a strong degree of material and political support (Hoch, Kopeček, and Baar 2017, 335–336).[25] During the first war in South Ossetia – and subsequently also during the war in Abkhazia – Georgian politicians repeatedly accused Russia of providing direct assistance to the separatists. Russian leaders systematically denied these claims, accusing Georgia of needlessly attacking Russian targets.[26] This gave rise to an opinion which still remains widespread in Georgia to this day – that the wars were not in fact waged against the Abkhazians and South Ossetians, but against Russia itself, as Abkhazia and South Ossetia were merely being exploited by Russia as a means of achieving its foreign policy goals.[27] Many Georgian politicians repeatedly declared that the Abkhazians and Ossetians did not win the wars, but were in fact on the losing side, along with the Georgians, and that the only victor was Russia itself (Civil Georgia 2003).

It should be added that these opinions on the role of Russia in Abkhazia and South Ossetia do not concern solely the period of military confrontation in the early 1990s; they are still strongly represented in the prevailing discourse of Georgia today. An illustrative example of this is Mikheil Saakashvili's 2004 speech to graduates of the National Military Academy in Senaki (i.e. four years before the five-day war in South Ossetia), where he noted the existence of "certain forces in the Russian political establishment" with an interest in the disintegration of Georgia and warned his audience of "wide-ranging foreign aggression" (Venediktov 2004).

This statement by the former Georgian President is fully in accordance with the findings of research into the causes of the armed conflicts in Abkhazia and South Ossetia, conducted by the author of this chapter in 2015 in Georgia. The research revealed that Georgian public opinion views the main factors in the escalation of violence as follows: (1) the historical interests of the USSR in the region, (2) Russia's geopolitical interests in the region following the disintegration of the USSR, and (3) Abkhazian and Ossetian separatism. With regard to the first factor, this prevailing Georgian narrative places the blame for the conflicts in Abkhazia and South Ossetia on the Bolshevik leadership of the Communist Party of the Soviet Union, which from 1921 onwards attempted in various ways to undermine Georgia's statehood.[28] The second factor viewed by Georgian public opinion as a catalyst for the escalation of the conflicts in Abkhazia and South Ossetia is the power interests of the Russian Federation shortly after the disintegration of the USSR. The third important factor viewed by Georgian public opinion as a catalyst for the escalation of the conflicts in Abkhazia and South Ossetia is the separatist ambitions of both breakaway nations (Hoch and Khundadze 2017).

If we view the development of both conflicts in the broader context of Russian-Georgian relations, it is evident that Georgia's loss of control over the secessionist regions was useful for Moscow. The nationalist discourse

100 *Tomáš Hoch and Emil Aslan Souleimanov*

of the first Georgian President Zviad Gamsakhurdia and his successor Eduard Shevardnadze detached Georgia from Russia's sphere of influence to a substantial degree. It was only the persistence of both conflicts – and the outbreak of the second Georgian civil war in September/October 1993 – that forced Shevardnadze to seek cooperation with Moscow. Responding to Shevardnadze's request for Russian assistance, Yeltsin replied that unless Georgia joined the CIS and permitted Russian troops to be stationed on its territory, Russia would not help it to resolve its internal problems (Cornell 2001, 173). The situation had become so acute that the only chance of preventing the complete disintegration of Georgia was to accept Moscow's ultimatum. After the signature of an agreement on the status of Russian troops in Georgia (9 October 1993) and an agreement on Georgia's accession to the CIS (20 October 1993), Moscow acted very quickly; in late October and early November 1993 Russian forces helped Shevardnadze to suppress a revolt in western Georgia, taking just two weeks to bring the situation under control.[29]

Despite these events, however, it would not be accurate to claim that Russia provided consistent unofficial support for the separatists throughout the 1990s. Around the middle of the decade, the Kremlin's previous unofficial support for separatism gave way to a new policy seeking greater rapprochement with Georgia. This shift can be attributed to two factors. First, the First Chechen War took place in 1994–1996, leading to de facto Chechen independence; this disrupted Russia's territorial integrity and threatened to spill over into other regions of the North Caucasus. Second, in 1994 Georgia joined the CIS and accepted the stationing of Russian troops on its territory under the Collective Security Treaty. In return for this thaw in Georgian-Russian relations, Georgia expected that the Kremlin would support Tbilisi's attempts to regain control over Abkhazia and South Ossetia. Under these circumstances, Russia's ability to continue its support for separatist movements in the South Caucasus was temporarily restricted. Nevertheless, it can be claimed that without Russian material and moral support, the de facto states in Abkhazia and South Ossetia would hardly have been able to come into existence (Kopeček, Hoch, and Baar 2016, 97).

The last major factor influencing the birth of de facto states in Abkhazia and South Ossetia was the political instability brought by the critical economic situation in Georgia. As part of the USSR, Georgia had been one of the Union's relatively advanced economies, but the period following independence was marked by severe economic decline. This was due to numerous factors. The civil war and the armed conflicts in Abkhazia and South Ossetia necessitated increased military spending. Moreover, some paramilitary units, for example, *mkhedrioni* (Horsemen), *tkis dzmebi* (Forest Brothers), and *tetri legioni* (White Legion), operated outside government control, and committed unprofessional and gratuitous acts in the areas they occupied. The war also devastated the country's infrastructure and led to a loss of income from formerly important sources such as tourism and the export

Abkhazia and South Ossetia 101

of tea, tobacco, wine, and citrus fruits. This was compounded by the disintegration of the system of export markets within the USSR and its raw material subsidies. Georgia was hit by hyperinflation; this peaked in 1993 at 56,000%. In the first years after the disintegration of the USSR, Georgia's industrial production fell by 75% and its agricultural production by 55% (Papava 1995, 53). In 1994 the country's GDP was just 23% of the 1989 level – the worst economic performance of all the post-Soviet republics (Herzig 1999, 123). This economic crisis was combined with political instability – which deterred even the bravest foreign investors – plus the disintegration of state institutions and high levels of corruption. Given these circumstances, it is no wonder that Georgia during its first years of independence was sometimes described as a failed state.

Conclusion

The de facto states in Abkhazia and South Ossetia emerged at the beginning of the 1990s following the end of the armed phase in both conflicts. The conflicts were motivated by prevailing public opinion in both separatist nations regarding their future political status. From the historical circumstances discussed in this analysis it is clear from the outset that conflict was unavoidable in both cases. However, conflicts may take various forms, and they need not necessarily escalate into an armed phase and bloodshed. If we take into account that the declared motivation for the Abkhazians' attempts at self-determination was their fear of the possible extinction of their own culture (similar fears were also voiced by the Ossetians, though to a lesser extent), it is clear that the issue of Abkhazia's political status – though complicated – could have been brought to a satisfactory solution if a compromise-based approach had been applied. However, viewed through the prism of the political radicalism which engulfed Georgia and its separatist regions in the early 1990s, any compromise whatsoever was seen as a display of weakness and cowardice. Looking back on the turbulent events of the early 1990s today, with a quarter-century of hindsight, it is evident that the nationalism and political radicalism that were associated with the newly independent Georgia's overall political and economic weakness can be considered the main reasons why the conflicts between the Georgians, Abkhazians, and South Ossetians became ethnicized and eventually escalated into an armed phase.

The complicated relations between the Ossetians, Abkhazians, and Georgians – exacerbated by numerous perceived historical injustices – had already become politicized during the era of the USSR. From the 1950s to the 1970s, the presence of sizeable ethnic minorities in peripheral regions of Georgia – combined with the USSR's traditional ethnic-territorial definition of statehood – meant that the South Ossetians and Abkhazians were viewed as "guests" on Georgian soil. This perception of ethnic minorities has since become an integral part of the Georgian national narrative.

102 Tomáš Hoch and Emil Aslan Souleimanov

The myth of Georgia as a hospitable mother was cultivated, assigning the South Ossetians and Abkhazians the status of mere guests who, during the millennium-long history of Georgian statehood, had only settled in Georgia relatively recently, and were thus required to respect the territorial integrity of their host state. Viewed from a Georgian perspective of "historical justice", the legitimacy of their separatist ambitions was practically nonexistent. This gave rise to slogans which were commonly voiced (especially around the turn of the 1990s) by Georgians with nationalist sentiments. Ossetians were told "If you don't like it in Georgia, get back to Iran" (an allusion to their Iranian origins), while Abkhazians were told to get back to the north-western Caucasus and rejoin their Adyghean kin.

However, the South Ossetians and Abkhazians rejected this Georgian version of history even more vehemently than their Georgian opponents were attempting to construct it. In accordance with a pattern that is typical of all ethnic-political conflicts, historians from both camps blamed those on the opposite side for politicizing the situation and taking a biased approach. The South Ossetians attempted to demonstrate the autochthonous nature of their own population in today's South Ossetia with reference to the Scythian (proto-Alanic, later Alanic) presence in both the North and South Caucasus, claiming that an Ossetian population has lived in today's South Ossetia since time immemorial. In Abkhazia mass anti-Russian rebellions of 1866 and 1877–1878 are considered as a milestone in its history; the reprisals included the deportation of thousands of Muslim Abkhazians who had participated in the rebellion to the Ottoman Empire. This gave Abkhazia's Orthodox community numerical dominance over the formerly dominant Muslim community. However, a much more important turning-point in Abkhazia's history came when the Russian colonial authorities began to resettle members of other ethnic groups in the depopulated areas vacated by deportees; these groups included Armenians, Pontic Greeks, Jews, and above all Georgians. This trend continued during the Soviet era, reducing the Abkhazians to just under a fifth of the total population of their own country. The Abkhazians were the only ethnic group to make up a minority of the population in their own autonomous republic, and this stoked their fears of assimilation and the demographic dominance of the Georgians. The large-scale repression that was unleashed in Abkhazia (as in the rest of the Soviet Union) during the 1930s – and that ultimately led to the revocation of Abkhazia's status as an SSR and its incorporation into Georgia – had a clear ethnic undercurrent here because both Stalin and the head of the NKVD Lavrenti Beria were ethnic Georgians. Historical injustices were thus felt strongly by Abkhazians and South Ossetians. In the initial (latent) phase of the conflicts, hostility focussed on Tbilisi and subsequently on Georgians as an ethnic community. This was enabled by an awareness of ethnic-linguistic and cultural-historical differences – a typical feature of small nations – which was articulated with increasing force by the Abkhazians and South Ossetians from the late 1980s onwards. The Georgian integrative

Abkhazia and South Ossetia 103

project – legitimizing the notion of a shared Georgian state by citing ethnic and cultural similarities – was in direct conflict with the exclusivist projects of the South Ossetians and Abkhazians.

During seven decades of Soviet rule, both the Abkhazians and South Ossetians became strongly oriented towards the political centre of the Soviet Union. Moscow was viewed as the only force that was able to stand up to Georgia's political-administrative and demographic dominance, guaranteeing the smaller nations' separate status and helping them gain the maximum possible degree of autonomy – which, in the case of Abkhazia, meant the much-coveted reinstatement of the territory as a separate Union Republic. These attempts by the Abkhazians – and to a lesser degree also by the South Ossetians – combined with their support for the Russian language (the ethnic minorities were vocally in favour of the widest possible use of Russian in public life, especially in education) – represented a source of constant tension between them and the Georgians (Nodia 1996). As Georgian society became mobilized, the emancipatory ambitions of ethnic groups inhabiting the country's peripheral regions were viewed by the majority of Georgians as the attempts of a Moscow-supported "fifth column" to undermine Georgia's territorial integrity at a historic moment when it finally had the chance to build an independent nation state. Minorities which were not loyal to Georgia were automatically considered to be allies of Moscow.

If we are to identify and generalize the key factors enabling the emergence of de facto states in Abkhazia and South Ossetia, they would be the following: (a) the ethno-nationalist ambitions of the nations in current or former autonomous units, fuelled by the perception of numerous historic injustices; (b) the legal and social chaos brought by the disintegration of the USSR; (c) the political and economic weakness of the newly emerging states; and (d) the direct or indirect support offered to the separatists by their patron state.

Notes

1 For example, the South Ossetian peasants refused to pay taxes to Tbilisi. It should be pointed out that following the February Revolution (1917) in Russia, an Ossetian National Council was formed in the parts of today's South Ossetia where Ossetians were the majority population. The Bolsheviks soon gained the upper hand within the Council, though their influence was initially not particularly significant; they demanded the incorporation of South Ossetia into Soviet Russia.

2 Like the Russians, the majority of Ossetians (including South Ossetians) are Orthodox Christians. This is particularly significant in the context of the North Caucasus, where the Ossetians – surrounded by Muslim neighbours – are traditionally considered agents of Russian colonization in the region. In 1918 the so-called Mountainous Republic of the North Caucasus was formed, its borders formally stretching from the Caspian Sea to the Black Sea. There were clashes between the North Ossetians and the Ingush; in the 19th century the North Ossetians – encouraged by the Russian colonial administration – had occupied fertile land owned by the Ingush, their eastern neighbours. In these local conflicts, the Orthodox North Ossetians frequently supported the military

104 *Tomáš Hoch and Emil Aslan Souleimanov*

operations launched by their Russian neighbours (the Cossacks) against the Vainakh people (a collective term for the Ingush and the Chechens); they later supported operations by Anton Denikin's Volunteer Army troops and (after the White Army's defeat in the second half of 1919) by the advancing Red Army.

3 At the time, Russia was still embroiled in a bloody civil war, and Moscow was keen to maintain stable relations especially with the United Kingdom, which verbally supported Georgian independence.

4 Ossetians generally refer to these events as the First Ossetian Genocide. The second and third genocides refer to the events of 1989–1992 and August 2008, respectively. The description of these events as three genocides has become part of the South Ossetians' national narrative, and in recent years members of the pro-Russian government in Tskhinvali have exploited the events as evidence of the perceived malice and brutality of their "ethnic enemies" and the impossibility of co-existing within a single state. See, for example, the website on the "genocide of the Ossetian nation" at www.osgenocide.ru.

5 In addition to the Abkhaz and Adyghe languages, this family also includes Abaza and Kabardian. The Ubykh language (which became extinct in the early 1990s) was also part of this family.

6 In addition to Georgian, the Kartvelian family also includes Megrelian, Svan, and Laz.

7 Proto-Abkhazian tribes are now considered to be the Apsilians, Abazgs, Sanigai, and Misimians. The names originated in the tribes' own names (Apsua, Abasgoi, Asai, and Misimai), which were then transformed by the Greeks into Apsilian, Abazgoi, Sanigai, and Misimian. These names were then adopted by the Romans, and from Latin they found their way into other European languages.

8 For details of conflicting theories of Abzhazian ethnogenesis see, for example, Schnirelman (2003, 368–385).

9 These opinions are based on the well-known theories of the Georgian historian Pavle Ingorokva. When they were published in 1954, they had to be retracted on the instructions of the central authorities in Moscow, on the grounds that they provoked conflicts among the fraternal nations of the Soviet Union; however, they remained well-known and highly popular in Georgian society. Their popularity was reflected in a speech given on 20 April 1991 by the first President of the Georgian Democratic Republic Zviad Gamsakhurdia, who rehabilitated Ingorokva's views.

10 The Lazi are ethnic Georgians now living in the Turkish-Ajarian border region.

11 In the 1860s and 1870s, two-thirds of the total Abkhazian population (which was around 50,000) were forced to leave their homes by the Russian administration. The large majority of these emigrants were Muslims, who fled to the nearby Ottoman Empire. Although around half of the ethnically Abkhazian émigrés returned to Abkhazia in the early 1880s, the demographic and religious situation had changed because the colonists had begun to move into their former homes. Whereas in the mid-19th century Muslims formed a majority of the Abkhazian population, by 1886 they accounted for just 14% (Gachechiladze 2014, 81–86).

12 The prevailing opinion in Abkhazia is that this was a planned policy by the Georgians to assimilate the Abkhazian nation. The Georgians reject such claims of deliberate attempts at assimilation, attributing the growing numbers of Georgians in Abkhazia to a spontaneous migration connected with the eradication of malaria in Abkhazia during the 1920s. At the end of the 1920s, Russians also began to move to Abkhazia. The Russian population grew from 12,000 (in 1926) to almost 75,000 (in 1989) – an increase of 600% in just six decades. During the same period, immigration brought a 350% increase in the Georgian population, over 300% in the Armenian population, and just under 70% in the Abkhazian population. The 1989 census showed that Abkhazians formed a majority only in

Abkhazia and South Ossetia 105

the Gudauta district, and made up more than one-third of the population only there and in Ochamchira. In the remaining districts, Abkhazians made up less than 10% of the population, and in Gali less than 1%. Except for Gudauta, all districts had Georgian majority populations (Gachechiladze 1995, 83–87).

13 Tbilisi also guaranteed autonomous status to the Batumi district (Ajaria) and the Zakatali district in south-eastern Georgia, which was claimed by neighbouring Azerbaijan (and which ultimately became part of Azerbaijan during the first years of Soviet rule).

14 It should be noted that the majority of the troops were Ottoman citizens of Abkhazian origin, that is, the descendants of the Muhadjirs (refugees from Abkhazia who mostly left in the 1860s).

15 In February 1919 Denikin's forces managed to expel Georgian units from the Sochi area, subsequently occupying part of north-western Abkhazia.

16 A new Abkhazian alphabet was devised based on the Georgian script; it shared thirty-three letters with the Georgian alphabet and had six different letters.

17 Interview with a representative of the Abkhazian Ministry of Foreign Affairs, Sukhumi, June 2014 and Interview with a Member of the Abkhazian Parliament, Sukhumi, July 2014.

18 Interview with a Georgian academic, Tbilisi, July 2015.

19 Gamsakhurdia and Kostava were writers and dissidents during the communist era. Kostava represented the more moderate wing of the Georgian independence movement (he died in a car crash in October 1989), while Gamsakhurdia headed the more radical wing.

20 The dead were mostly women. Up to a thousand demonstrators were also subjected to a nerve gas attack (Leaning, Barron, and Rumack 1990).

21 The Communist Party was eventually banned in Georgia following an attempted coup in Moscow in August 1991, which the leaders of the Georgian Communist Party had unwisely supported.

22 For a more detailed legal analysis of the issue of separatism in South Ossetia and Abkhazia see, for example, Walter, von Ungern-Sternberg, and Abushov (2014).

23 More on the issue of how internal legitimization strategies for Abkhazian statehood are constructed and how they impact upon the foreign policy of this de facto state see, for example, Hoch (2018).

24 When the UN attempted to post an armed contingent of peacekeeping forces in Abkhazia, the original mandate of the forces (who were fully equipped with military hardware and given extensive powers under UN Security Council Resolution 858/1993) had to be altered (under Russian pressure) by means of Resolution 881/1993; the forces were restricted to merely monitoring events in Abkhazia and the activities of the CIS peacekeeping forces. This reflected Russia's unwillingness to tolerate a foreign military contingent in one of its "near abroad", which would have weakened its influence in the region.

25 During the war the Abkhazian army received modern Russian T-72 tanks, cruise missile launchers, and other military hardware that it had lacked before the outbreak of the war. There are still no publicly accessible records of the acquisition of this technology, and responsible persons in Abkhazia and in Russia refuse to discuss the subject. During the war, Russian planes bombarded Georgian positions on several occasions, and after the renewal of hostilities in September 1993 the Abkhazians regained their weaponry – which according to the Sochi agreement was to be stored in Russian facilities far away from the front line. Likewise, the Abkhazians' two greatest military successes – the heroic captures of Gagra and Sukhumi – only occurred after the Georgians had withdrawn their military hardware from the cities following Russian guarantees. The Abkhazians were never held to account by the Russians for breaching the cease fire (cf. Cornell 2001, 171).

106 *Tomáš Hoch and Emil Aslan Souleimanov*

26 O'Ballance (1997, 128–129) states that in the winter of 1992–1993, forty-six Russians died in Georgian attacks on Russian research stations and military bases in Abkhazia.
27 Interview with a Georgian journalist, Tbilisi, June 2015.
28 Interview with a Georgian academic, Tbilisi, July 2015.
29 The leader of the revolt, Georgia's first democratically elected President Zviad Gamsakhurdia (who had been ousted in the January 1992 coup), died at the end of 1993 in a remote village in western Georgia under unclear circumstances.

Literature

Abkhaz World. 2011. "The Population of Abkhazia Stands at 240,705." *Abkhaz World*, December 29. http://abkhazworld.com/aw/current-affairs/534-the-population-of-abkhazia-stands-at-240705.

Amichba, Khibla. n.d. "The Abkhazian Language and Its Place in the Caucasian Family of Languages." *Abkhaz World*. http://abkhazworld.com/aw/abkhazians/language/662-the-abkhazian-language.

Anchabadze, Gia. 2010. "In XII–XIII Centuries Term Abkhaz Had Three Meanings." *Humanrights.ge*, December 20. www.humanrights.ge/index.php?a=main&pid=12696&lang=eng.

Bhaghzba, Oleg, and Stanislav Lakoba. 2007. *Istoriya Abkhazii s drevneishikh vremen do nashikh dnei* [The History of Abkhazia from Ancient Times to Our Era]. Sukhum: Alasharbaga.

Civil Georgia. 2003. "Nino Burjanadze: Normalization with Russia Number One Priority." *Civil Georgia*, March 30. www.civil.ge/eng/article.php?id=3094.

Cornell, Svante E. 2001. *Small Nations and Great Powers. A Study of Ethnopolitical Conflict in the Caucasus*. Richmond: Curzon Press.

Gachechiladze, Revaz. 1995. *The New Georgia: Space, Society, Politics*. 1st edition. London: UCL Press.

Gachechiladze, Revaz. (2014): *The New Georgia: Space, Society, Politics*. 2nd edition. London: Routledge.

Herzig, Edmund. 1999. *The New Caucasus. Armenia, Azerbaijan and Georgia*. London: Royal Institute of International Affairs.

Hewitt, George. 1989. "Abkhaz." In *The Indigenous Languages of the Caucasus Vol. 2*, edited by John Greppin and George Hewitt, 39–88. New York: Caravan Books.

Hoch, Tomáš. 2011. *Možnosti rozvoje de facto států prostřednictvím humanitární pomoci, rozvojové spolupráce a aktivit organizací občanské společnosti: případová studie Abcházie* [Options for the Development of De Facto States through Humanitarian Aid, Development Cooperation and the Activities of Civil Society Organizations: A Case Study of Abkhazia]. Prague: European Science and Art Publishing.

Hoch, Tomáš. 2018. "Legitimization of Statehood and Its Impact on Foreign Policy in De Facto States: A Case Study of Abkhazia." *Iran and the Caucasus* 22 (4): 382–407.

Hoch, Tomáš, and Tato Khundadze, 2017. Pravoslavné církve a transformace gruzínsko-abcházského konfliktu [Orthodox Churches and the Transformation of the Georgian-Abkhaz Conflict]. *Mezinárodní vztahy* 52 (3): 7–22.

Hoch, Tomáš, Vincenc Kopeček, and Vladimír Baar. 2017. "Civil Society and Conflict Transformation in De Facto States." *Problems of Post-Communism* 64 (6): 329–341.

Hoch, Tomáš, Emil Souleimanov, and Tomáš Baranec 2014. "Russia's Role in the Official Peace Process in South Ossetia." *Bulletin of Geography. Socio-economic Series* 23: 53–71.

ICG. 2004. *Georgia: Avoiding War in South Ossetia.* Europe Report N 159. Tbilisii/ Brussels: International Crisis Group. https://d2071andvip0wj.cloudfront.net/159-georgia-avoiding-war-in-south-ossetia.pdf.

Khutsishvili, George. 1994. "Intervention in Transcaucasus." *Perspective* 4 (3). www.bu.edu/iscip/vol4/Khutsishvili.html.

König, Marietta. 2004. "Der georgisch-südossetische konflikt [The Georgian-South Ossetian Conflict]." In *OSZE Jahrbuch 2004*, edited by Ursel Schlichting, Susanne Bund, and Graeme Currie, 253–266. Baden-Baden: Nomos Verlag.

Kopeček, Vincenc, Tomáš Hoch, and Vladimír Baar. 2016. "De Facto States and Democracy: The Case of Abkhazia." *Bulletin of Geography. Socio-economic Series* 32: 85–104.

Kozaeva, Diana. 2016. "Okonchatelnye dannye perepisi: v Yuzhnoy Osetii zhivut 53 532 cheloveka [Final census data: 53,532 people live in South Ossetia]." *Sputnik.ru* August 11. http://sputnik-ossetia.ru/South_Ossetia/20160811/2874839.html.

Lang, David M. 1962. *A Modern History of Georgia.* New York: Grove Press.

Leaning, Jennifer, Ruth Barron, and Barry H. Rumack. 1990. *Bloody Sunday: Trauma in Tbilisi: The Events of April 9, 1989 and Their Aftermath: Report of a Medical Mission to Soviet Georgia.* Somerville: Physicians for Human Rights.

Lough, John. 1993. Defining Russia's Relations with Neighbouring States. *RFE/RL Research Report* 2 (20): 53–60.

Nodia, Ghia. 1996. "Political Turmoil in Georgia and the Ethnic Policies of Zviad Gamsakhurdia." In *Contested Borders in the Caucasus,* edited by Bruno Coppieters, 73–89. Brussels: Vrije Universiteit Press.

O'Ballance, Edgar. 1997. *Wars in the Caucasus 1990–1995.* New York: NYU Press.

O'Loughlin, John, Vladimir Kolossov, and Gerard Toal. 2011. "Inside Abkhazia: Survey of Attitudes in a *De Facto* State." *Post- Soviet Affairs* 27 (1): 1–36.

Ozgan, Konstantin. 1998. "Abkhazia – Problems and the Paths to Their Resolution." In *Contrasts and solutions in the Caucasus,* edited by Ole Høiris, and Sefa Martin Yürükel, 184–189. Aarhus: Aarhus University Press.

Papava, Vladimer. 1995. "The Georgian Economy: Problems of Reform." *Eurasian studies* 2 (2): 52–62.

Piknerová, Linda. 2013. "Ekonomicko-geografický a sociální přehled zemí jižního Kavkazu [Economic-Geographic and Social Overview of the South Caucasus Countries]." In: *Jižní Kavkaz v bezpečnostní perspective* [The South Caucasus in Security Perspective], edited by Michael Romancov, 45–71. Praha: Metropolitan University Prague Press.

Pliev, Soslan M. et al. 2008. *O poiske prichin, dinamiki, putei uregulirovaniya i vozmozhnykh napravleniyakh razvitiya gruzino-osetinskogo konflikta* [On the causes, dynamics, resolution, and possible future development of the Georgian-Ossetian conflict]. Unpublished document. www.uasdan.com/engine/download.php?id=4.

Roeder, Philip. 1997. "From Hierarchy to Hegemony: The Post-Soviet Security Complex." In *Regional Orders: Building Security in a New World,* edited by David A. Lake and Patrick Morgan, 219–244. University Park: Pennsylvania State University Press.

Schnirelman, Viktor A. 2003. *Voiny pamyati. Mify, identichnos i politika v Zakavkazie* [The War of Memory. Myths, Identity and Politics in Transcaucasia]. Moscow: IKC Akademkniga.

108 *Tomáš Hoch and Emil Aslan Souleimanov*

Slider, Darrell. 1997. "Democratization in Georgia." In *Conflict, Cleavage, and Change in Central Asia and the Caucasus*, edited by Karen Dawisha and Bruce Parrott, 156–198. Cambridge: Cambridge University Press.

Souleimanov, Emil. 2013. *Understanding Ethnopolitical Conflict: Karabakh, South Ossetia, and Abkhazia wars Reconsidered*. New York: Palgrave Macmillan.

Souleimanov, Emil, and Tomáš Hoch. 2012. *Role Ruska v konfliktech a oficiálních mirových procesech v Abcházii a Jižní Osetii v letech 1991–2008* [Russia's Role in Conflicts and Official Peace Processes in Abkhazia and South Ossetia in 1991–2008]. Praha: Auditorium.

Totadze, Anzor. 2008. *The Ossets in Georgia: Myth and Reality*. Tbilisi: Universal.

Venediktov, Alexei. 2004. "Saakashvili vstupil na tropu voiny [Saakashvili set out on the road of war]. *Izvestiya*, July 12.

Walter, Christian, Antje von Ungern-Sternberg, and Kavus Abushov (eds.). 2014. *Self-determination and Secession in International Law*. Oxford: Oxford University Press.

Zverev, Alexei. 1996. Ethnic Conflicts in the Caucasus 1988–1994. In *Contested Borders in the Caucasus*, edited by Bruno Coppieters, 13–71. Brussels: Vrije Universiteit Press.

3.3 Nagorno-Karabakh and Javakheti

Two different trajectories of Armenian separatist movements

Vincenc Kopeček

Both Javakheti and Nagorno-Karabakh are regions outside the borders of the former Armenian SSR, which are inhabited mainly by ethnic Armenians. Following the Sovietization of Transcaucasia (the South Caucasus), Nagorno-Karabakh was granted the status of an autonomous region (*avtonomnaya oblast*) within the borders of the Azerbaijan SSR, whereas Javakheti remained an integral part of the Georgian SSR and lacked any formal autonomous status. During the disintegration of the Soviet Union, Armenian separatist (or more precisely irredentist) movements were active in both these territories. However, while in Nagorno-Karabakh the escalating tension between the ethnic communities ultimately gave rise to armed conflict and de facto separation, in Javakheti the situation remained relatively calm (despite several dramatic episodes), and today this region does not represent an immediate threat to Georgia's territorial integrity. This chapter therefore examines and compares Javakheti and Nagorno-Karabakh – two territories which at the beginning of the 1990s had similar potential for separatism – and seeks to explain which factors led to the birth of Nagorno-Karabakh as a de facto state and which factors led to the eventual decline of the separatist movement in Javakheti (Map 6).

Javakheti and Nagorno-Karabakh: a brief historical overview

Although both Javakheti and Nagorno-Karabakh lie outside the internationally recognized borders of today's Republic of Armenia, their ethnic Armenian inhabitants have not traditionally been considered members of the Armenian diaspora (Margaryan 2008, 56). In Armenia, both territories are traditionally considered to be historically Armenian, even though the continuity of historical Armenian populations with today's Javakheti and Karabakhi Armenians is a highly problematic notion; both Javakheti and Karabakh are border areas which have belonged to various states during the course of their history, and the ethnic and religious composition of their populations has changed frequently over the centuries. The different Armenian, Azerbaijani, and Georgian interpretations of these territories' history also play an important role in the Armenia-Azerbaijan conflict and (to a lesser extent) the disputes between Armenia and Georgia.

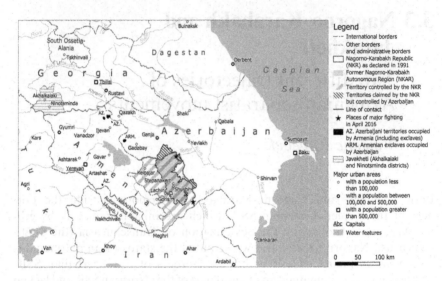

Map 6 Nagorno-Karabakh and Javakheti.
Source: Authors.

Javakheti is a volcanic plateau situated at an elevation of between 1,700 and 2,000 metres above sea level, encircled by the mountain ranges of the Lesser Caucasus whose highest peaks reach 3,000 metres. If we ignore the speculative claims regarding whether it was the ancestors of today's Georgians or today's Armenians who settled in the Javakheti Plateau first, it is clear that the direct ancestors of today's Javakheti Armenians arrived in the territory from the Erzurum Province of the Ottoman Empire in 1828–1829, after the territory had been abandoned by its previous inhabitants (Muslims of Georgian origin) as a result of the Russo-Turkish War (Gachechiladze 2012, 89). Another influx of ethnic Armenians into Javakheti (now controlled by Russia) occurred in 1897–1902 after the Hamidian massacres of Armenians in the Ottoman Empire, and some survivors of the Armenian Genocide also found refuge in Javakheti (Cornell 2001, 178; Gachechiladze 2012, 89). In addition to Armenians, the region's inhabitants also included Caucasian Greeks and the Dukhobors – a mystical, pacifist religious group of Russian origin who were considered heretics by the Orthodox Church (Lohm 2006, 5–6).

Nagorno-Karabakh is just a part of a more extensive historical region known as Karabakh, which stretches between the Zangezur Mountains and the Kura and Araxes Rivers.[1] Historically it was a border area between Armenia and Caucasian Albania (Alwan). The Caucasian Albanians evidently spoke a similar language to today's North Caucasian nations, though (to simplify matters somewhat) they were either Christianized and Armenianized or Islamized and Turkified between the 4th century and the 15th century A.D. (Kopeček 2008, 204; Walker 1991, 76–77). The western, mountainous part of Karabakh (known in the Armenian tradition as Artsakh) became Armenian, and thus also Christian. For a long time Artsakh remained under the dominance of several Armenian dynasties that became known as *meliks*; the territorial units under their control were known as melikates. The melikates were not independent states; they were autonomous entities that were subordinated to the rulers of neighbouring Muslim powers – then from the 15th century the reborn Persian Empire, and from the 18th century the semi-independent Karabakh Khanate, which had its capital in the city of Shusha/Shushi (Bournoutian 1997). The influx of ethnic Armenians to Karabakh in the modern era came after Russia took control of the territory at the beginning of the 19th century. In the 1830s, according to Swietochowski (1995, 10–12), the population of Karabakh included a total of 19,000 Armenians (mainly concentrated in the mountains) and 35,000 Muslims (mainly in the lowland areas).

After the collapse of Tsarist Russia and the birth of three independent South Caucasian states in 1918, both Javakheti and Nagorno-Karabakh became disputed territories; Javakheti was claimed by Armenia and Georgia, and Nagorno-Karabakh by Armenia and Azerbaijan. In both cases the disputes escalated into armed conflicts. The Georgian-Armenian War was soon brought to an end by a British-brokered ceasefire, and Javakheti (which had become part of Georgia) saw almost no fighting (the main theatre of conflict was the region of Lori, to the south) (Hovannisian 1971, 93–125). By contrast, Nagorno-Karabakh remained the scene of fierce fighting (with several temporary suspensions of hostilities) until 1920, when the region was seized by the Bolsheviks and (like the whole of the South Caucasus) Sovietized. Three Soviet republics (Armenia, Azerbaijan, and Georgia) were created, grouped together in the Transcaucasian Soviet Federative Socialist Republic. Javakheti became an integral part of the Georgian SSR, while in Nagorno-Karabakh – along with the neighbouring regions of Zangezur (Syunik) and Nakhchivan – the question of who should control the territory continued to be disputed. These disputes were eventually resolved by the direct intervention of Moscow: Zangezur was allocated to the Armenian SSR, while Nagorno-Karabakh and Nakhchivan were incorporated into the Azerbaijan SSR as (respectively) an autonomous region and an autonomous republic (Cornell 2001, 74–76; Saparov 2012; Altstadt 2015, 229).[2] All three of these regions on the border between the Armenian SSR and the Azerbaijan SSR originally had ethnically mixed populations; however, the Armenia-Azerbaijan War (and the subsequent incorporation of the territories into the Armenian SSR or the Azerbaijan SSR) reduced the size of the minority populations. Azeris thus gained a clear dominance in Nakhchivan, and Armenians in Zangezur (Troinitskii 1905; TSU 1929; RGAE, f. 1562, op. 336, d.d. 256–427, d.d. 966–1001). It was only in Nagorno-Karabakh – a type of enclave within the Azerbaijan SSR, without a land connection to the Armenian SSR – that a large percentage of Azeris continued to live

112 *Vincenc Kopeček*

alongside the majority Armenian population. Indeed, the size of the Azeri community in Nagorno-Karabakh actually grew slightly during the following decades; by the time the USSR collapsed, Azeris made up slightly under a quarter of the population (Jelen 2009, 138).

The conflicts in Nagorno-Karabakh and Javakheti were reignited during the final years of the Soviet Union. In the case of Karabakh, demands for the integration of both Armenian Soviet political entities had been voiced on several occasions even under Soviet rule (Tchilingirian 1999, 442); however, it was only when Mikhail Gorbachev's reforms ushered in a more open political climate that these demands began to intensify – both in Nagorno-Karabakh and in the Armenian SSR. Demonstrations calling for the Nagorno-Karabakh Autonomous Region (NKAR) to come under Armenian jurisdiction led to the so-called "war of laws", in which both sides "exchanged petitions, resolutions, and legal acts irrespective of whether they corresponded to the Constitution" (Gahramanova 2010, 135). The passion that this "war of laws" inflamed on both sides eventually escalated into the first armed clashes, which gained in intensity until they eventually (in early 1992, after the collapse of the Soviet Union at the end of 1991) developed into a full-scale war between Karabakhi self-defence units and Azerbaijani forces, which ultimately turned into an undeclared war between Armenia and Azerbaijan (de Waal 2003, 235–236). The Armenian units – who were more motivated and better organized – gained the upper hand; after the ceasefire in April 1994 they controlled not only most of the territory of the former NKAR but also the land between the NKAR and Armenia itself, plus extensive areas to the east and south of the NKAR (stretching as far as the Iranian border) from which the original Azeri and Kurdish populations were expelled, as also happened in Nagorno-Karabakh itself (see Chapter 4.5). However, the Nagorno-Karabakh Republic (NKR), formally declared in January 1992, failed to maintain control over the Shahumyan district, to the north of the NKAR. This Armenian-populated district too had declared itself a part of the NKR, but the Karabakhi forces lost control of its territory in the first months of the Karabakh war, and its population was expelled (de Waal 2003, 194). Ethnic violence in Nagorno-Karabakh also spilled over into Azerbaijan and Armenia; from 1988 onwards there were pogroms targeting members of the sizeable Armenian and Azeri minorities, respectively, leading to a de facto exchange of population between the two SSRs and the elimination of these minority communities (de Waal 2003, 62).

At the end of the 1980s, as in the NKAR, in Javakheti too there were demands for changes in the political-administrative status of the territory, where ethnic Armenians made up 95% of the population (Geostat 2010). However, these demands differed: the Karabakhi Armenians demanded incorporation into the Armenian SSR, while the Javakheti Armenians called primarily for Javakheti to be granted the status of an autonomous region within the Georgian SSR (Cornell 2001, 179). The latent conflict threatened to escalate particularly at the beginning of the 1990s, when the nationalist Zviad Gamsakhurdia was elected President of Georgia; this caused considerable anxiety among Georgia's ethnic minorities, as Gamsakhurdia's slogan was "Georgia for the (Christian) Georgians" and he was a fierce defender of the rights of the (allegedly) oppressed ethnic Georgians living in regions with mainly non-Georgian populations, such as Javakheti (Slider 1997, 170). Fearing the possible consequences of Gamsakhurdia's policies, the Javakheti Armenians took control of the territory's administration; during the Georgian civil war (sparked when Gamsakhurdia was ousted from power in early 1992) Javakheti remained practically outside the Tbilisi government's control. However, unlike their counterparts in Nagorno-Karabakh, the Javakheti Armenians did not declare independence, and – although they had managed to procure weapons – the conflict did not escalate into armed clashes (Lohm 2007, 14). The Tbilisi government did not manage to establish full control over the situation in Javakheti until 1994/1995, when – under the rule of President Eduard Shevardnadze – Javakheti was merged with the neighbouring Samtskhe region (which had a majority Georgian population) to create a single province (Guretski 1998; Lohm 2007, 17). Since then, the political and security situation in Javakheti has deteriorated on several occasions,[3] and demands for autonomy have continued to be voiced, but secession from Georgia has never been a realistic prospect.

Autonomy, liberalization, and the Law on Secession

Svante Cornell (2002) has pointed out that the existence of territories with autonomous status was one of the key sources of separatism in the South Caucasus. The creation of autonomous territorial entities for a particular titular nationality – whether in the form of an autonomous region (*avtonomnaya oblast*) or an autonomous republic (*avtonomnaya respublika*) – led to the emergence of political institutions on the legislative, executive, and also the party level. In the case of the NKAR, the basic political body was the Regional Soviet (*oblastnyi soviet*), which elected an Executive Committee (*ispolnitelnyi komitet*), whose Chairman (*predsedatel*) was the leader of the autonomous region. The Executive Committee had the right to set up departments and other executive-administrative bodies to direct individual branches of state administration, as stipulated in the law on the autonomous region. In the case of Nagorno-Karabakh, these institutions were capable of generating political leaders who officially formulated demands for a change in the territory's status; logically these demands were irredentist, and eventually separatist in nature. After all, it was the Nagorno-Karabakh Regional Soviet which in 1988 approved a resolution demanding the transfer of the NKAR out of the jurisdiction of the Azerbaijan SSR and into the jurisdiction of the Armenian SSR. Later, the Nagorno-Karabakh Regional Soviet, together with the Supreme Soviet of the Armenian SSR, declared the merger of the two entities to create a single entity within the USSR. And in January

114   *Vincenc Kopeček*

1992 the former Regional Soviet, now known as the National Council, declared the independence of the NKR (Croissant 1998, 35; Avakian 2010, 18; Saparov 2015, Loc 4164). High-ranking Karabakhi party officials also played an important role in Karabakhi separatism; they were not formally the leaders of the NKAR, but under the Soviet post-totalitarian regime the official NKAR leaders were their subordinates within the party structure. Boris Kevorkov, the long-serving First Secretary (*pervii sekretar*) of the Communist Party's Regional Committee (*obkom*) in Nagorno-Karabakh, remained loyal to Baku and Moscow; in February 1988 he attempted to prevent the Regional Soviet from approving the above-mentioned resolution. However, his successor Genrikh Poghosyan became one of the main driving forces behind the Karabakh Movement (de Waal 2003, 12–13).

Unlike Nagorno-Karabakh, Javakheti never had autonomous status. During the Soviet era, the territory of this historic region was more or less covered by the Akhalkalaki district (*raion*); in the 1960s, part of this district's territory was removed to create the Bogdanovka district. Both districts had District Soviets and other administrative bodies, but they were directly subordinate to the republic-level bodies in Tbilisi. Even after Georgia gained its independence in 1991, it essentially retained the same administrative model. In 2006 the districts (*raioni*) were renamed municipalities (*munitsipaliteti*), becoming the only local government units in Georgia; however, in the case of Akhalkalaki and Ninotsminda (the latter being the former Bogdanovka, renamed after Georgia's independence), their boundaries remained unchanged. In 1995 Akhalkalaki and Ninotsminda became part of the newly formed province (*mkhare*) of Samtskhe-Javakheti, in which ethnic Armenians make up only half of the population. However, the Georgian provinces are not part of the system of local government (which exists only at the level of municipalities); they are merely administrative subdivisions of national-level government, each headed by a Presidential Appointee (*sakhelmtsipo rtsmunebuli*), the so-called Prefect (Losaberidze, Kandelaki, and Orvelashvili 2002; Skorupska and Zasztowt 2014). For this reason, Javakheti lacks central political bodies which would be capable of generating a Javakheti political elite headed by a clear political leader with significant powers. In the Soviet era there were two District Soviets, and currently there are two local assemblies (*sakrebulo*) and two mayors (*gamgebeli* or *meri*) – none of them wielding a degree of power comparable to the power the officials of the former Karabakhi autonomy used to wield. The Javakheti political leaders were thus recruited not from the official structures of the Soviet political system but from elsewhere – and their demands were primarily for autonomy.[4]

However, the initial impulse for the Karabakhi irredentist movement did not emerge from the NKAR's formal political institutions, but rather from the burgeoning civil society that had taken root in the more liberal political environment ushered in by Gorbachev's reforms. These activists travelled to Karabakhi *sovkhozes* and factories collecting signatures on petitions (de Waal 2003, 20), and it was their demands that the formal Karabakhi

Nagorno-Karabakh and Javakheti   115

elite adopted as their own during 1988. Since the launch of Gorbachev's reforms in 1985, Karabakhi activists had become increasingly vocal in their demands for the incorporation of the NKAR into the Armenian SSR, and in 1987 this activism spilled over into Armenia itself. Important public figures in Armenia began to champion the Karabakhi cause: members of the Armenian Academy of Sciences, writers, historians, and even Gorbachev's economic advisor Abel Aghanbeghyan (Chorbajian, Donabedian, and Mutafian 1994, 146–148). It was only in response to grass-roots activism that the Nagorno-Karabakh Regional Soviet approved the resolution demanding incorporation into the Armenian SSR, and the subsequent development of Armenian-Azerbaijani relations was characterized by a kind of ping-pong between official bodies and institutionalizing civil society. The Karabakh Soviet's resolution was followed by the creation of the Karabakh Committee (*Gharabagh Komite*) in the Armenian SSR and the Krunk Committee (*Krunk Komite*)[5] in the NKAR. Their members – especially those of the Karabakh Committee – addressed their demands directly to the government in Moscow, and they became the de facto political leaders of Armenia; eventually, in 1990, they took power having been elected to the Armenian Supreme Soviet (Dudwick 1997, 80–81).

Emerging grass-roots political institutions also played a central role in the organization of the Javakheti Armenians; however, the lack of formal institutions endowed with significant powers meant that the political agenda formulated by civil society was not adopted by official political representatives. This led to the formation of separate political institutions which – at least for a time – acted as de facto substitutes for the non-existent autonomous political institutions. As early as 1988 the *Javakhk* organization[6] was established, originally as a coordinating committee of the emerging local non-government organizations. Its members initially included not only Armenians but also ethnic Georgians, Russians, and Caucasian Greeks; however, it soon became a purely Armenian organization that can be viewed as part of the broader ethno-political mobilization of Armenians in the Soviet Union and as an echo of events in the Armenian SSR and the NKAR (Wheatley 2004, 13). During the Karabakh war, *Javakhk* organized the formation of a unit of Javakheti Armenians who went to fight in Nagorno-Karabakh, but the organization's primary demand was the creation of an autonomous territorial entity of Javakheti. *Javakhk* was mainly active in the Akhalkalaki district. This was due to a number of factors – chief among them the fact that Akhalkalaki is the real centre of the Javakheti Armenian community, while Ninotsminda has a more peripheral status, having been originally settled mainly by the Dukhobors; at the end of the 1980s there were still over 3,000 Dukhobors in the Ninotsminda district (Lohm 2006, 10), and their pacifist ethos apparently influenced the local Armenians too.[7] In Akhalkalaki *Javakhk* opposed President Gamsakhurdia's attempts to appoint an ethnically Georgian prefect; in February 1991 this led to the formation of the Provisional Council of Representatives, which administered Akhalkalaki until

116   *Vincenc Kopeček*

November of the same year, when the *Javakhk* leader Samvel Petrosyan was appointed prefect (Cornell 2002, 164; Wheatley 2004, 14).

Javakhk's demands remained limited to autonomous status; even during the Georgian civil war they did not declare Javakheti a breakaway state (Guretski 1998). However, in other parts of the Soviet Union, two similarly vaguely defined territorial units did decide to declare independence. These were Gagauzia and Transnistria, which managed to break away from Moldova despite having no autonomous status – though in the case of Gagauzia (see Chapter 5.4) the territory's de facto independence only lasted from 1991 to 1994 (Caspersen 2012; Loc 352). Javakheti's lack of autonomous status therefore does not explain why the situation there remained relatively calm and did not escalate into an open ethno-political conflict.

In the final months of the USSR's existence, the primary impetus that led several autonomous territories (and even some territories without formal autonomous status) to declare independence was Gorbachev's Law on Secession, passed in April 1990. According to the Soviet constitution, only union republics (SSRs) could declare independence – not autonomous republics (ASSRs) or other autonomous entities. However, the Law on Secession did give "autonomous regions or any type of similar distinct territories" within the borders of union republics the right to conduct a referendum on their legal status if the union republic declared independence. The purpose of the law was actually to prevent the secession of the union republics by giving the autonomous units similar rights, though the entire process formulated by the law was in fact a violation of the Soviet constitution, which did not give autonomies the right of secession. The law was also too complex, and required "steps that the autonomies ... did not, and indeed could not, take" (Walker 2003, 166).

The Law on Secession is the document that formed the basis for the NKR's declaration of independence; although the former NKAR had a much higher political status than Javakheti, according to the Soviet constitution it could not unilaterally break away from the Azerbaijan SSR. Moreover, the ethnic Armenian population of Nagorno-Karabakh also spilled over into Azerbaijan itself, beyond the borders of the NKAR. Leaving aside the Armenian minority communities in large Azerbaijani cities such as Baku, Sumgait and Kirovabad (today Ganja), the main Armenian population centre outside the NKAR was in the Shahumyan district, directly adjacent to the NKAR. This district was considered by Armenians to be part of historic Artsakh, as its territory included Gulistan, one of the former Karabakh melikates (Bournoutian 1997, 91). It thus became involved in Armenian irredentism within the USSR, and from April to May 1991 it was the scene of Operation "Ring" (*Koltso*), during which the Armenian population was expelled by combined Soviet and Azerbaijani units (Croissant 1998, 41–42). The Armenian population of the Shahumyan district did manage to return to their homes in the following months, and the Shahumyan District Soviet approved the district's incorporation into the emerging NKR (Avakian 2010, 18); however, in the summer of 1992 the NKR lost control of the district – though it still

Nagorno-Karabakh and Javakheti   117

maintains a formal claim over the territory.[8] Here it should be mentioned that the Shahumyan District Soviet (which declared the district to be part of the NKR) was on the same level in the political hierarchy and had the same powers as the Akhalkalaki and Bogdanovka District Soviets, which never took such a step. In any case, at the height of the tensions (i.e. during 1991) these two District Soviets had effectively ceased to function, and the Akhalkalaki District Soviet had been replaced by the grass-roots-organized Provisional Council of Representatives.

Armenian stronghold vs. Armenian backwater

A simple comparison of the political status of Nagorno-Karabakh and Javakheti during the disintegration of the Soviet Union does not provide a satisfactory answer to the question of why Nagorno-Karabakh broke away but Javakheti did not. The NKAR itself was just a focal point for Armenian irredentism (or separatism), and the boundaries of today's de facto NKR are entirely different from those of the former NKAR. The autonomous political bodies enabled a Karabakhi political elite to emerge, but important representatives of the Karabakhi separatists who came to power in Nagorno-Karabakh (and who led the NKR during the war) were recruited from emerging grass-roots organizations, especially from the *Krunk* Committee – among them the NKR's first President, Robert Kocharyan (de Waal 2003, 56). In any case, even a cursory comparison with Gagauzia and Transnistria shows that autonomous status was not an essential precondition for a successful breakaway.

When seeking an explanation of why Nagorno-Karabakh and Javakheti developed along different trajectories, it is therefore necessary to take into account another aspect – the differing significance of both territories for the Armenian nation as such. Both territories are similar in terms of physical size and population (though Nagorno-Karabakh is slightly larger in both respects), and both are relatively isolated in terms of their physical geography. The difference between them is that while Javakheti's role in Armenian history has largely been that of a backwater, Nagorno-Karabakh (or Artsakh) is viewed as a territory of crucial national importance – a stronghold. This is despite the fact that at first sight, Nagorno-Karabakh may appear to be a backwater in the same manner as Javakheti: it is situated far from the heartlands of historical Armenia (the Ararat valley, the area around Lake Van, and the Shirak plain), but when these core lands lost all trace of the former Armenian political structures and the Armenian population lived under the control of the Ottoman or Persian Empires, the *meliks* of Karabakh were practically the last surviving members of the Armenian nobility, presiding over a territory which enjoyed a certain degree of autonomy from the Muslim rulers all around them. This meant that the Karabakhi Armenians became "the last line of defence against the Islamic east". They developed a strong military tradition, and in both Tsarist Russia

118   Vincenc Kopeček

and the Soviet Union some of the highest-ranking military positions were held by Karabakhi officers (de Waal 2003, 186). In the 19th century Shusha/Shushi (the capital of the Karabakh Khanate) became one of the main cultural centres of the Russian Caucasus Viceroyalty, and it was the city with the largest Armenian population after Tbilisi. Nagorno-Karabakh thus did become a major Armenian population centre, playing an important role both economically and culturally, albeit only for a few decades. During the Armenia-Azerbaijan War of 1918–1920 Nagorno-Karabakh was one of the focal points of the battles, and the Armenian quarter in Shusha/Shushi was entirely destroyed after the Karabakhi Armenians' uprising against temporary Azerbaijani rule. After the Sovietization of the South Caucasus, Nagorno-Karabakh became an autonomous component of the Azerbaijan SSR – a development which was never accepted by the Armenians, who consider the loss of Nagorno-Karabakh (along with the Armenian Genocide) to be one of the greatest tragedies in Armenian history. Even under Soviet rule, Armenian sources criticized alleged discrimination against the Karabakhi Armenians and drew attention to the growing number of ethnic Azeris living in Nagorno-Karabakh, the purpose of which was allegedly to tip the balance of the population so that Azeris would become the majority (Chorbajian, Donabedian, and Mutafian 1994, 142–144).

Nagorno-Karabakh (Artsakh) became a kind of symbol (cf. the Karabakhization of Armenian history, Chapter 4.2) around which the Armenian independence movement crystallized in the late 1980s. In the case of Javakheti there was no such interpretation of history, as Javakheti lacks a historical narrative that would be in any way comparable to that of Karabakh; it essentially functioned as a settlement location for Armenian refugees who had been expelled from their former homes in the 19th century and early 20th century. Javakheti also avoided the fighting during the brief Armenian-Georgian War of December 1918; this meant that Armenian-Georgian relations never became as hostile as Armenian-Azerbaijani relations (a hostility exacerbated by the failure to distinguish between Azeris and Turks).

Under Soviet rule, Javakheti formed part of a border zone that was subject to a special regime; this zone also included neighbouring areas of the Armenian SSR, but not the central part of the Georgian SSR, to which Javakheti belonged administratively (Lohm 2007, 6; Wheatley 2004, 7). Due to the military checkpoints on the roads to Tbilisi and other large Georgian cities, in practice it was easier for Javakheti Armenians to travel to the Armenian SSR (Leninakan – today Gyumri – or Yerevan) for education, work, or culture. During the Soviet era, Javakheti thus became de facto separated from the rest of the Georgian SSR: the main languages were Armenian and Russian, Tbilisi's influence over everyday life was restricted, and so the Armenian population did not have any particularly strong reasons to be dissatisfied with their status.[9] This situation changed with the upsurge of Georgian nationalism during the final year of the USSR's existence; the Javakheti Armenians felt threatened by this development, but there were

Nagorno-Karabakh and Javakheti   119

two key factors which mitigated against any serious attempts to undermine Georgia's territorial integrity: the conciliatory approach of the Republic of Armenia itself, and the pragmatic approach taken by Georgia.

Javakheti: a lifeline or the second front line?

The Karabakhi Armenians' demands received strong support from the Armenian cultural elite already in the late 1980s. The Karabakh Committee – made up of leading Armenian intellectuals – became the basis for the Pan-Armenian National Movement *(Hayots Hamazgayin Sharzhum)* (Croissant 1998, 33) which in 1990 took power in the Armenian SSR and guided the country to independence (Kopeček 2012, 45). The Karabakh Movement thus stood at the heart of the Armenian independence movement, and even though the newly independent Republic of Armenia, for pragmatic reasons, decided to withdraw its claims over Nagorno-Karabakh in 1991 (see Chapter 4.2), the first Armenian President Levon Ter-Petrosyan proved unable to broker a peaceful resolution of the Karabakh conflict (Libaridian 2004, 234). After the NKR's declaration of independence, Armenian society supported its struggle against the Azerbaijani units, and volunteers from Armenia (and to a lesser extent from the Armenian diaspora) went to Nagorno-Karabakh to join in the fighting (de Waal 2003, 206–207). The heroes of the Karabakh war were even appointed to positions in the Armenian government – mainly to ministries with connections to the armed forces, such as the Ministry of Defence or the Ministry of Internal Security; these posts were held by figures such as Vazgen Sargsyan, the most prominent commander of the Armenian volunteer units, and Serzh Sargsyan, the Commander-in-Chief of the Karabakh Defence Army (see Chapter 4.2). Levon Ter-Petrosyan eventually lost control over the Armenian army itself, which in 1993 – with the knowledge of the then-Defence Minister Vazgen Manukyan and the Armenian generals – became fully involved in the fighting in Kelbajar, clashing directly with the reorganized Azerbaijani army in the final months of the war. This intervention meant that both sides in the conflict were now evenly matched – a situation that ultimately led to the signing of a ceasefire agreement (de Waal 2003, 210–212, 235–240) which (despite frequent breaches) remains in place to this day.[10]

It is almost inconceivable that the Karabakhi Armenians could have overcome the more powerful Azerbaijani forces without support from the Republic of Armenia – both material support (via the Lachin corridor, secured by the Karabakhi forces in May 1992) and military support (in the form of volunteers and regular units). Indeed, even today the NKR could not continue to exist without economic, military, and political support from Armenia – as described in Chapter 4.4. By contrast, the Javakheti Armenians did not receive similar support for their demands, either from the Armenian SSR or from the independent Republic of Armenia – despite the fact that the activization of the Javakheti Armenians occurred at the same time as that

120   *Vincenc Kopeček*

of their counterparts in Karabakh, and despite the fact that the situation in Georgia during the first few years after independence was even more chaotic than in Azerbaijan, so any armed resistance against Georgian rule in Javakheti would have stood a reasonable chance of success. Moreover, until 2007 Akhalkalaki was the site of a Russian military base – which was viewed by the Javakheti Armenians as their primary security guarantee against any potential attack by Georgian nationalists (Lohm 2007, 14). Although many analysts warned against a potential escalation of the situation in Javakheti (Manning 2000, 24), concurrent developments in Nagorno-Karabakh paradoxically led the Republic of Armenia to become involved in Javakheti with the clear aim of calming the situation. The Armenian public's attention was logically focussed on Nagorno-Karabakh – for the reasons analyzed above. When the Karabakh conflict was in full flow, the Republic of Armenia simply could not afford to become involved in another separatist (or irredentist) movement – mainly due to economic reasons.

In 1992 and 1993 the Republic of Armenia found itself on the brink of economic collapse. Like other post-Soviet countries, it had experienced a dramatic economic slump caused by the disintegration of the USSR market; it was still coping with the effects of the 1988 earthquake; and it also had to contend with Azerbaijani (and later Turkish) blockade. In the spring of 1988 Azerbaijan closed the road between Armenia and the NKAR in response to the Karabakhi Armenians' demands. Armenia retaliated by staging a rail blockade of the Nakhchivan exclave, effectively cutting it off from the rest of Azerbaijan. In September 1989, Azerbaijan – which was under the de facto control of the Azerbaijani Popular Front (*Azarbayjan Khalk Jabhasi*) – declared a railway blockade of Armenia's entire territory. This caused Armenia serious economic problems, as the main supply route into the Armenian SSR had been by rail from Azerbaijan (Croissant 1998, 34). In January 1990 the Popular Front was removed from power after the intervention of Soviet units, and the blockade was partially relaxed. However, in November 1991 it was once more reinstated after an Azerbaijani helicopter crashed and Armenia was accused of shooting it down (Kaufman 2001, 69–73). Moreover, in April 1993 Turkey closed its border with Armenia in a display of solidarity with Azerbaijan; Armenia thus found itself to a large extent isolated from the outside world. In the early 1990s Georgia, Armenia's northern neighbour, was embroiled in a civil war which made transit routes through Georgian territory unreliable and cut off the railway line to Russia via Abkhazia. Armenia's short section of border with Iran thus became the only viable supply route for goods and raw materials (Croissant 1998, 87; de Waal 2003, 205–206; Libaridian 2004, 243).

When the situation in Georgia became calmer, Georgia – and its ports – became Armenia's main route to the outside world; over 70% of Armenia's foreign trade (including trade with Russia and Turkey) passes through Georgia (Killough 2008). Although Iran supplies natural gas to Armenia (Abrahamyan 2016), due to its international reputation it is not a particularly

Nagorno-Karabakh and Javakheti 121

attractive trade partner, and the land connection between Armenia and Iran is complicated. There is no railway, and although the road has been improved considerably in recent years, it leads through challenging terrain via three mountain passes, two of which are more than 2,300 metres above sea level. This makes the route particularly complicated in the winter months (Almasian 2014; Badalyan 2017).

In this context, it is clear that in the early 1990s the Armenian side could not afford to let the situation in Javakheti escalate. Any Armenian support for separatist demands (or even simply demands for greater autonomy) by the ethnically mobilized Javakheti Armenians would have poisoned Armenian-Georgian relations and cut off key land routes between Armenia and the outside world. Armenia's approach to Javakheti has therefore consistently sought to calm the situation. The first President of the Republic of Armenia Levon Ter-Petrosyan explicitly opposed Javakheti demands for autonomy (Wheatley 2004, 14), and his successor Robert Kocharyan emphasized the need for the Javakheti Armenians to integrate into Georgian society (Tonoyan 2010, 297). Under Kocharyan's presidency, Armenia even arrested one of the most prominent Javakheti activists, Vahagn Chakhalyan from the *Miatsyal Javakhk* (United Javakhk) movement, and extradited him to Georgia, where he was subsequently prosecuted (Lohm 2007, 14). Armenian rhetoric shifted somewhat under the presidency of Serzh Sargsyan, who in 2009 stated that Armenian should be granted the status of a regional language in Javakheti (Tonoyan 2010, 297–298). However, by that time the situation in Javakheti was entirely different to that in the early 1990s, when there had been a serious threat of ethnic conflict. By 2009 the policies of Georgia's President Saakashvili had begun to bear fruit: he had managed to at least partially integrate this formerly very isolated region into the rest of the country, he had co-opted key representatives of the Javakheti political elite, and he had used the state security forces to eliminate radical Javakheti activism (Wheatley 2009, 21).

The attitudes of the parent states: combating or co-opting the separatists

In the Soviet era, both Javakheti and Nagorno-Karabakh were territories with a special position. In the case of Nagorno-Karabakh this was due to its autonomous status, while the special nature of Javakheti was a result of its de facto isolation from the rest of the Georgian SSR – a result of its location within a border zone where access was restricted. Both territories were thus separate entities from the SSRs of which they were a part – and following Gorbachev's reforms in the late 1980s these SSRs had to respond to demands voiced by the ethnic communities that lived there. Azerbaijan and Georgia each took an entirely different approach – though it should be borne in mind that their choice of approach was determined by a range of circumstances (which are discussed in this section).

122   Vincenc Kopeček

Azerbaijan took a relatively hard-line approach to the demands of the Karabakhi Armenians. After all, the Nagorno-Karabakh Regional Soviet's declaration demanding incorporation into the Armenian SSR was an entirely unprecedented step – and indeed one which violated the Soviet constitution, which required the affected SSR (in this case Azerbaijan) to grant its consent in such cases. The subsequent responses by the Karabakhi side (and Armenia itself) likewise took a hard-line stance, causing the situation to escalate rapidly. The long-serving NKAR Party boss Boris Kevorkov, a Baku loyalist who was highly unpopular among the local Armenian population, was sidelined; power was seized by more popular politicians who continued to voice radical demands for a change in the NKAR's status (de Waal 2003, 13). The dialogue between representatives of the Karabakhi Armenians and the Azerbaijan SSR (which during 1989 came under the de facto control of the nationalist Popular Front) practically came to a halt, and the Azerbaijani authorities' approach to the Karabakhi Armenians was based on brute force – either economic blockades or the deployment of Azerbaijani armed units. This hard-line approach continued – and indeed became even harsher – when the Popular Front was removed from power by Soviet forces in January 1990 and the highest-ranking political posts in the Azerbaijan SSR were once again occupied by communists. Azerbaijan therefore did not even attempt to reach an agreement with the Karabakhi Armenians – though it should be mentioned that by this time the Armenia-Azerbaijan conflict had spread beyond the borders of Nagorno-Karabakh itself, and neither of the parties showed any willingness to engage in dialogue.

Georgia found itself in a somewhat more advantageous situation with regard to the Javakheti Armenians. Javakheti activists did not seek to break away from Georgia, but "merely" demanded autonomy – though there was no guarantee that such a status would be final. The Georgian side was unwilling to even discuss autonomy; indeed, the authorities attempted to appoint an ethnic Georgian as the prefect of the Akhalkalaki district. However, after realizing the strength of local opposition to this step, they relented and instead appointed the leader of the Javakheti Armenian nationalists to the post (Wheatley 2004, 14). This naturally had a calming effect on the situation, and it bought Georgia some time; in addition to the potential conflict in Javakheti, Tbilisi also had to contend with full-scale conflicts in South Ossetia and Abkhazia. After a change of government in Tbilisi caused the strongest wave of Georgian nationalism to subside, and in the knowledge that the Republic of Armenia had no interest in stoking the Javakheti conflict, the Georgian government was able to incorporate Javakheti into a larger province (diluting the influence of the Armenian community), and it also co-opted part of the Javakheti Armenian elites into its own power structures. This was a typical manifestation of the Shevardnadze regime in Georgia, which was based on a form of neo-feudal structure (Wheatley 2005, 109–110); the President allowed various sectoral or regional power groups to participate in power, in return for their loyalty.

Nagorno-Karabakh and Javakheti 123

Politics in Javakheti is often perceived as clan-based. However, these "clans" (or more precisely informal networks) "do not reflect any deep-seated sociological divisions within the population" (Sabanadze 2001, 17), but are rather a result of the competing business interests of Javakheti's co-opted elite (Wheatley 2009, 21–24). Divides among Javakheti's informal leaders, who know each other well from the Soviet past, seem to be the outcome of the Shevardnadze administration's deliberate strategy which played one group or network against another and supported weaker groups at the expense of the more powerful ones (Closson 2007, 189).

A shining example of this is the relative decline of Melik Raisyan's Akhalkalaki-based network, which in the late 1990s competed with Enzel Mkoyan's Ninotsminda-based network. Both networks were allied to the Union of Citizens of Georgia (UCG), Shevardnadze's party of power, and both their leaders were elected MPs (Sabanadze 2001, 17). However, Shevardnadze's support had a leaning towards Mkoyan's relatively weaker network, a fact which resulted into an inclination of Raisyan's network towards Zurab Zhvania, a long-time Speaker of the Parliament and Shevardnadze's crown prince. To Raisyan's misfortune, Zhvania left the President's camp in 2001 and established his own faction in the Parliament, which Raisyan also joined. Mkoyan's network was successful in utilizing Raisyan's relative decline of influence, and it became the dominant network in the whole of Javakheti (Wheatley 2009, 22).

The result of this policy was that in exchange for de facto control over Javakheti, regional informal leaders showed loyalty to the ruling regime, eventually turning a once restless region into Shevardnadze's political stronghold, where the local political elite always managed to secure electoral victory for him (Devdariani 2004, 99). This model even survived a change in the presidency. After the Rose Revolution, the new President Mikheil Saakashvili set out to break up the clientelistic networks on which Shevardnadze's regime had been based – yet Javakheti remained essentially unaffected by these changes. Assisted by the Interior Minister Vano Merabishvili (a native of Akhaltsikhe, the administrative centre of Samtskhe-Javakheti), the Javakheti elite – which in the 2003 election had supported Shevardnadze – essentially switched their loyalties to Saakashvili instead (Lohm 2007, 13; Wheatley 2009, 22). Similarly, after the defeat of Saakashvili's United National Movement in the 2012 parliamentary election, the large majority of the Javakheti elite shifted its support to the new government coalition Georgian Dream (*kartuli otsneba*) – again after having supported the incumbent government in the election. The Javakheti elite's loyalty to whichever government is currently in power – and also its willingness to be co-opted by the new government – is a manifestation of its pragmatic stance; the Javakheti elite views any current government as a guarantor of the *status quo* for Javakheti – a situation which it considers to be basically satisfactory, both in terms of the power held by the elite and in terms of the existence of a degree of informal Armenian autonomy. Although Javakheti

124 *Vincenc Kopeček*

is part of a larger province, the executive positions in the municipalities of Akhalkalaki and Ninotsminda are occupied primarily by ethnic Armenians, and the Armenian language plays the dominant role in state administration, the education system, and the public sphere as a whole. This is de facto at odds with Georgian legislation, which grants a similar status only to the Georgian and Abkhazian languages; however, the Georgian authorities tolerate the situation because the Javakheti Armenians generally have a poor command of the Georgian language (Wheatley 2009, 48).[11]

Under Saakashvili's presidency, several attempts were made to integrate Javakheti into the rest of Georgia. These included some relatively successful infrastructure projects which alleviated the region's physical isolation, as well as some less successful attempts to improve knowledge of the Georgian language among the Javakheti Armenians and to integrate them into the Georgian education system.[12] Even at the end of Saakashvili's presidency, Javakheti thus remained under the de facto administration of local informal leaders – though it became more integrated into the rest of Georgia. This has also reduced Javakheti's secessionist potential. In any case, formerly strong nationalist movements such as *Javakhk*, *Virk*, and *Miatsyal Javakhk* had become increasingly weakened through a combination of factors: the successful co-opting of several leaders of Javakheti nationalist movements; the essentially fabricated prosecutions of some of the nationalist leaders; the ban on registering political parties on an ethnic or regional basis (Lohm 2007, 17; Wheatley 2009, 26); and the ongoing integration of Javakheti into the rest of the country that had begun under Saakashvili's presidency.[13]

Russia's hidden hand

Although the Soviets' divide-and-rule policy was responsible for the complicated borders in the South Caucasus (and also elsewhere in the post-Soviet space) which ultimately helped to inflame tensions, the influence of Russia itself on the Karabakh conflict and the Javakheti situation is often overstated. Even so, it cannot be ignored. It is, however, important – especially in the case of Karabakh – to distinguish between the interventions by the Soviet government (whose aim was to hold the USSR together), the role of Russian military units (either during the latent or "hot" phases of conflict), and the policies of the Russian Federation (which is able or willing to use both conflict situations in order to promote its own interests in the region).

The Gorbachev government's interventions in the Karabakh conflict were motivated primarily by its efforts to prevent the disintegration of the USSR, and it should be pointed out that these interventions were not well-conceived. Moscow essentially always supported whichever side was more inclined towards it at any given time. Initially this generated false hopes on the Karabakhi side, and later it created the impression – on both sides of the conflict – that Moscow was backing the enemy. In the early stages of the conflict, Moscow appears to have inclined towards the Armenian side; for most of 1989 the NKAR was removed from the control of the Azerbaijan SSR and was governed directly from Moscow. However, in November 1989 this direct rule came to an end, and the NKAR came under the control of the authorities in Baku – sparking vehement opposition from the Armenian side which ultimately led to the declaration of the United Armenian Republic (also including Nagorno-Karabakh). When Soviet forces removed the Popular Front from power in Azerbaijan in January 1990 and replaced it with pro-Soviet communists, the Soviet units began to support the Azerbaijan SSR, because the nationalist Pan-Armenian National Movement had taken power in the Armenian SSR. Soviet units even became involved in Operation *Koltso*, whose aim was to expel ethnic Armenians from the territory adjacent to the NKAR (Croissant 1998, 31–42).

The involvement of the so-called "Russian" units in the fighting during the Karabakh war is a particularly complex issue. Both sides referred to the former Soviet army units that took part in the conflict (mainly as mercenaries) as "Russians", despite the diverse ethnic composition of these units (albeit dominated by ethnic Russian soldiers). Scholarly perspectives on this issue differ. De Waal (2003, 166–167) views the involvement of the "Russian" units not primarily as a deliberate interference by the Russian Federation, but rather as a consequence of the chaotic situation that ensued after the disintegration of the USSR, when tens of thousands of former Soviet army troops were left stranded in the former Soviet republics, attempting to earn a living by fighting as mercenaries or by selling or lending their weapons. By contrast, Cornell (2001, 355–356) views these "Russian" operations (supporting both sides) as a deliberate attempt by Moscow to add fuel to fire.

However, the Russian Federation's intervention in the Karabakh conflict should be viewed particularly in the context of Moscow's interference in the internal politics of Azerbaijan. In 1992–1993, under the rule of the Popular Front, Azerbaijan refused to join the CIS – an entity which the Russian government viewed as the basic tool for it to exert its influence within the post-Soviet republics. This is the background against which Russia's interference in Azerbaijan should be read – whether the activation of Talysh and Lezgin separatism or Surat Huseynov's 1993 coup against President Abulfaz Elchibey, after soldiers from the brigade that Huseynov had commanded in the Karabakh war obtained weapons from a unit leaving the Russian military base in Ganja and led an assault on undefended Baku (Cornell 2001, 356–357). Although the coup succeeded in ousting Elchibey, a combination of circumstances meant that Surat Huseynov never actually became President; instead the post went to the former Azerbaijan Communist Party First Secretary Heydar Aliyev. However, even Aliyev had to contend with situations that are generally considered to have been orchestrated by Moscow – such as the revolt by Interior Ministry units in 1995 (Kopeček 2012, 49–50). This Russian interference – especially the coup against Elchibey and the feeble attempts to stoke Talysh separatism – weakened Azerbaijan's position

126 Vincenc Kopeček

in the Karabakh conflict, so Russia can certainly be said to have exerted a certain influence over its course. However, Russia's double-dealing policy (supplying arms to both sides, Armenia's membership of the Russian-led Collective Security Treaty Organization, Moscow's maintenance of a Russian military base in the Armenian city of Gyumri, and its simultaneous insistence on Azerbaijan's territorial integrity) did not concern the birth of the NKR as a de facto state, but rather the subsequent phases of the Karabakh conflict (cf. Shirinyan 2013).

When speaking of the Russian influence on the situation in Javakheti, the most frequently mentioned topic is the Russian military base in Akhalkalaki. The base used to serve as a security guarantee for the Javakheti Armenians, who feared not only Georgian nationalist vigilantes but also (somewhat irrationally) Turkish invasion.[14] The base was also one of the pillars of the local economy; local Armenians were employed there as civilian or even military staff. According to Wheatley (2004, 28), 10.4% of Javakheti's population (over 6,000 people) were directly dependent on the military base for their livelihood, while thousands of others were dependent on it indirectly. The base was the main consumer of local agricultural production, provided light and heat for residential areas in its vicinity, enabled local children to attend the garrison school (with teaching in Russian), and even opened the military field hospital to the local public (Margaryan 2008, 57). The Russian rouble was the main currency in Javakheti, whereas the Georgian *lari* was accepted reluctantly and the prices in *lari* were higher.[15] Javakheti's lagging economy also became heavily dependent on remittances from Russia, where breadwinners would go for seasonal work. Life in Javakheti villages even became structured around the fact that large numbers of working-age men would migrate each spring to Russia and return in late autumn. Weddings and other village ceremonies were thus held during the winter. Many villages also became heavily dependent on remittances from individuals and families who reside in Russia permanently.[16]

In view of the development of the conflicts in Abkhazia and South Ossetia (see Chapter 3.2), there were understandable fears in Georgia that Russia may decide to offer military support to the separatists in Javakheti too. However, these fears ultimately proved unfounded – not only due to the situation in Javakheti itself but also due to the wider context of Georgian internal politics. At the beginning of the 1990s Georgia, like Azerbaijan, refused to join the CIS, and it is highly probable that the Russians' support for Abkhazian separatism, as well as its backing of the 1993 Zviadist uprising in Samegrelo, was Moscow's way of exerting pressure on Georgia in order to keep the country within the Russian orbit (Cornell 2001, 334–342). Once Shevardnadze's Georgia had eventually joined the CIS, Russia stopped supporting the Zviadists (the supporters of the ousted President Zviad Gamsakhurdia) and blockaded Abkhazia for over a decade, as Moscow officially recognized Georgia's territorial integrity (what changed only in 2008 after the August War). The simple explanation of why Russia did not make use of its military base in Akhalkalaki to support Armenian secessionism is therefore this: it did not have to. The above-mentioned steps were sufficient to keep Shevardnadze's Georgia within Russia's sphere of influence, and by the time Russian-Georgian relations broke down completely in 2008, the Russian troops had already been withdrawn from the base. However, fears persisted that the Javakheti Armenians, with their links to Moscow, could potentially act as a Russian fifth column. The issue was that many Javakheti Armenians had taken Armenian or Russian citizenship in addition to their Georgian citizenship (see the paragraph on passportization in Chapter 4.2 and the paragraph on Responsibility to Protect in Chapter 4.2); this made it easier for them to travel to Russia for work. However, this had serious consequences, as the Georgian government, fearing possible Russian aggression under the pretext of protecting Russian citizens, declared dual citizenship illegal (Wheatley 2009, 39–40). About 3,000 people in the Akhalkalaki district were thus deprived of Georgian citizenship. They were not allowed to vote, to receive pensions, etc. Whereas in Akhalkalaki most of them managed to regain their Georgian passports, in the Ninotsminda district 2015 there were still hundreds of people who had been deprived of Georgian citizenship.[17]

The influence of Russia on the current situation in Javakheti is only indirect, and it is also quite limited. Moreover, destabilizing the situation in Javakheti is against the interests of Armenia – an ally of Russia – and so in the foreseeable future Russia's main leverage on Georgia will continue to be exerted via the conflicts in South Ossetia and Abkhazia. However, Russia would have played a far greater role in Javakheti if plans to merge Javakheti and Ajaria into a single autonomous entity had ever become a reality. Russia maintained a military base in the Ajarian city of Batumi until 2007, and the Ajarian leader Aslan Abashidze has always been considered "Moscow's man" (Wheatley 2005, 115); indeed, after being forced by Mikheil Saakashvili to resign in the spring of 2004, he spent his exile in Russia.

Conclusion

Both Nagorno-Karabakh and Javakheti – two territories with predominantly ethnic Armenian populations in Azerbaijan and Georgia, respectively – held strong secessionist potential when the Soviet Union disintegrated at the beginning of the 1990s. Events in Nagorno-Karabakh escalated into a bloody ethnic war, accompanied by ethnic cleansing which created hundreds of thousands of refugees (or internally displaced people) on both sides and resulted in the birth of a de facto state. By contrast, the latent ethnic conflict in Javakheti – despite several moments of high tension – never escalated into military conflict, and today Javakheti is a relatively stable area which poses no significant threat to Georgia's territorial integrity.

The results of the analysis presented in this chapter show that the fact that one of these territories broke away from its parent state while the other did

128 Vincenc Kopeček

not (despite sharing similar starting conditions) was not due to a combination of sufficient conditions (factors); rather it was the result of a complex process which at different moments was affected to varying degrees by the individual factors analyzed here. Moreover, these individual factors interacted; whether one or another factor played a greater or lesser role depended on the broader context of political developments in both territories, in their patron or kin states, in the South Caucasus, and in the post-Soviet space as a whole.

In the case of Nagorno-Karabakh, the beginnings of the secessionist movement were rooted in feelings of grievance at how the territory had been incorporated into Azerbaijan rather than Armenia, and by the fear that the growing Azerbaijani population would, in the long term, threaten the Armenians' clear majority status in the NKAR. The local political elite, whose emergence had been facilitated by the NKAR's autonomous status, was able to formulate clear demands for a change in the territory's status. These demands sparked an armed response from the parent state Azerbaijan and generated a positive response from the kin-state Armenia – thanks to the traditional image of Nagorno-Karabakh as a mythical bastion of the Armenian nation. Support for the Karabakh Movement thus became part of the struggle for Armenian emancipation as a whole, and as a result of the historical context, it led not to irredentism but to more or less formalized Armenian support for the Karabakhi separatists. In Azerbaijan too, the Karabakh conflict played an important role in the process of emancipation from the Soviet Union, and the legitimacy of the current Armenian and Azerbaijani political elites is closely bound up with the events in Karabakh.

In Javakheti, the initial impulse for the emergence of a secessionist or autonomist movement was the Armenian community's fear of attack by Georgian nationalist vigilantes. The actions of the Javakheti political elite (which emerged in the early 1990s mainly in Akhalkalaki, and less so in Ninotsminda) were thus motivated primarily by a concern for the protection of the local Armenian population. In view of the fact that no such attacks actually took place, and the Georgian side was willing to make compromises, the two sides eventually reached an informal agreement. The Javakheti Armenians were not formally granted their desired autonomy, but for over two decades the territory preserved a status quo in which it was under the de facto rule of local clientelist groups. There was therefore no reason for widespread radicalization, either by the elites or by the Javakheti population as a whole. The Georgian government and the Javakheti elites thus had the opportunity to find a viable mutual *modus vivendi* – a process that was facilitated by the fact that Javakheti does not hold the same historical significance as Nagorno-Karabakh in the Armenian consciousness, and also by the fact that the Republic of Armenia had become internationally isolated by the Karabakh war and so could not afford to support another secessionist movement.

There are several candidates for the decisive factors that caused Nagorno-Karabakh to break away and form a de facto state while Javakheti remained an integral part of Georgia. The first is autonomous status. As is demonstrated by the cases of Transnistria and Gagauzia, this was not a necessary precondition in all cases of post-Soviet separatism. Nevertheless, the autonomous status of the NKAR enabled a political elite to emerge which ultimately guided the territory to its breakaway, while the absence of autonomous status in Javakheti was quite possibly responsible for the fact that Armenian nationalism in the early 1990s developed particularly in Akhalkalaki but to a lesser extent in Ninotsminda.

Another factor with at least the same degree of importance (or possibly an even greater degree) was the different image of the two conflict zones in the eyes of the population of Armenia itself. As a key component of Armenian national mythology, Nagorno-Karabakh inspired much greater interest than Javakheti, which was far less historically significant. The Javakheti Armenians themselves supported the Karabakhi Armenians, and some went to Karabakh to fight as volunteers.

Another important factor is the Republic of Armenia's calming influence on the situation in Javakheti, where its conciliatory approach brought very different results than in Karabakh. More than the other factors discussed here, this factor was highly dependent on the context of events. If the situation in Karabakh had not escalated, or if the Armenian side had suffered a rapid defeat (e.g. due to the withdrawal of regular Armenian army units in the second phase of the war), Javakheti could easily have become the next battleground for the irregular Armenian units returning from Karabakh.

The fourth key factor is the influence of external actors, especially Russia – though this influence should be viewed in the broader context, and individual aspects of it should be distinguished. Russia did influence both conflicts, though this influence was exerted more strongly on the parent states – which were attempting (with varying degrees of success) to extricate themselves from the Russian sphere of influence. Russia could potentially have offered much greater direct military support in the case of Javakheti than it did in Karabakh, but this never happened because the Russian troops had already withdrawn from the base before the outbreak of the 2008 Russo-Georgian War – an event which would have offered an opportunity for such an intervention. Nagorno-Karabakh remains a special case in terms of Russian influence on the post-Soviet de facto states, as Moscow exerted its influence in an indirect way. By contrast, the situation in Javakheti followed a similar pattern to that in Abkhazia and Transnistria (passportization, Responsibility to Protect, Russian military bases), but the context in Javakheti meant that Russia did not make use of these instruments.

The final factor is the fact that Georgia took a much more conciliatory approach to its Armenian minority than Azerbaijan; it was relatively successful in co-opting a critical mass of the local elite, and it ultimately managed to integrate Javakheti into the rest of the country to a large degree.

130 *Vincenc Kopeček*

This policy should, however, also be viewed in the context of the Georgian civil war, which weakened the Georgian government's capacity to deal with the Javakheti situation by force and meant that the Georgian irregular units were mainly tied up with the fighting in Abkhazia. For Azerbaijan, the unrest in Nagorno-Karabakh (especially in the late 1980s and early 1990s) represented a fundamental problem. Even while the Soviet Union was still in existence, Baku – with the partial support of Moscow and against the background of escalating ethnic violence even outside the NKAR itself – decided to confront the problem with force. This meant that Azerbaijan no longer realistically had the option of applying a similar policy with the Karabakhi Armenians as the Tbilisi government had done with the Javakheti Armenians. This does not mean that the escalation of the Karabakh situation into war and separation was an inevitable process, but rather that the tool used by Georgia (which had proved to be effective) could not realistically be used in Karabakh once the military conflict had begun.

Notes

1 The name Karabakh is of Turko-Persian origin. It is more recent than the traditional Armenian name Artsakh, which evidently originated in the name of the historical Urartian province of Urtekhe (Walker 1991, 71). In the Turkic languages, kara means black, and bakh in Persian means a garden. The name "black garden" clearly refers to the fertile land of the region, especially its lowland areas. However, the history of the toponym Karabakh as the name of an administrative unit only dates back to the 16th century, during the reign of the Persian Safavid dynasty, which created the so-called beglarbegate of Karabakh. The semi-independent Karabakh Khanate existed in the 18th century (Chorbajian, Donabedian, and Mutafian 1994, 71–78).
2 The complicated – and seemingly pointless – territorial division of this part of the South Caucasus into several enclaves/exclaves and autonomous entities was a consequence of the complex geopolitical situation, the Soviet doctrine of ethnic federalism, and the Bolsheviks' divide-and-rule policy. Nakhchivan was allocated to the Azerbaijan SSR on the basis of the 1921 Treaties of Kars and Moscow between Atatürk's Turkey and Bolshevik Russia. The incorporation of Zangezur into the Armenian SSR effectively cut the Azerbaijan SSR off from ethnically similar Turkey while also partially compensating Armenia for its losses of territory to Turkey (especially Kars and Ardahan). The division of the Armenians into two different political entities – one of them subordinated to the Azerbaijan SSR – also weakened Armenian resistance to Bolshevization. (The division of the Azeris into two territorially separate – if politically linked – entities had a similar effect.) Moreover, the demarcation of borders in the region was accompanied by contradictory declarations on the future political affiliation of the individual disputed territories by the central government in Moscow and by local Bolshevik leaders; this helped to strengthen grievances on both sides (Croissant 1998, 18–20; Cornell 2001, 74–76; Saparov 2012; Altstadt 2015, 229).
3 For example, in 1998, when a Georgian army unit was heading to the Akhalkalaki base for joint military exercises with the Russian army, it was met by a group of heavily armed Armenians, who had not been informed about the exercises and thought this was the beginning of an ethnic cleansing (Cornell 2001, 179). Large-scale protests organized by the Miatsyal Javakhk (United Javakhk) movement were held in 2005 in response to the planned closure of the Russian

military base in Akhalkalaki. In 2008 a bomb exploded outside the house of the Javakheti Member of Parliament Samvel Petrosyan, and two police officers were killed during the subsequent security operation targeting Miatsyal Javakhk activists who were considered suspects (Wheatley 2009, 26–28).

4 In September 1998 the Speaker of the Parliament and de facto leader of the Autonomous Republic of Ajaria Aslan Abashidze offered the Javakheti Armenians the option of becoming part of Ajaria. The proposal – a potential threat to Georgia's territorial integrity – never became a reality (Cornell 2001, 181).

5 Krunk is the Armenian word for a crane; in Armenia this bird is a symbol of homesickness. KRUNK is also an acronym of the Russian phrase Komitet za revolutsionnoe upravlenie Nagornogo Karabakha (Committee for the Revolutionary Administration of Nagorno-Karabakh).

6 Javakhk is the Armenian name for Javakheti.

7 Interview with a specialist on minority issues, Tbilisi, Georgia, June 2015.

8 The Armenia-Azerbaijan War could conceivably have affected a much larger territory. The Armenian population originally extended north of the Shahumyan district into the Shamkhor district as far as Kirovabad, but most Armenians fled these areas as a result of Armenian-Azeri ethnic violence in 1988–1989 (Chorbajian, Donabedian, and Mutafian 1994, 154).

9 Interview with a specialist on minority issues, Akhaltsikhe, Georgia, July 2015.

10 Even after the May 1994 ceasefire between Armenia, the NKR, and Azerbaijan, the line of contact between the Karabakh Defence Army and the Azerbaijani army has remained a genuine front line, the scene of frequent exchanges of fire despite the officially valid ceasefire agreement. From time to time these exchanges escalate into more serious clashes using heavy weaponry; in April 2016 they gave rise to the so-called four-day war, which led to a slight change in the course of the front line (giving more territory to the Azerbaijanis) and caused heavy losses of life on both sides (Souleimanov 2016). The Armenia-Azerbaijan border itself – which is currently closed and partially mined (HRW 2001, 850–851) – also occasionally witnesses exchanges of fire or diversionary operations (especially by the Azerbaijani side). One documented diversionary operation took place in December 2016 near the village of Chinari, in Tavush province (Petrosyan 2016), and the village of Baghanis (in the same province) has repeatedly been fired on (Lragir 2016, 2017; Paremuzyan 2016); Baghanis is located near to Yukhari Askipara, an Azerbaijani exclave occupied by Armenia. Besides Yukhari Askipara, Armenia also occupies two other Azerbaijani exclaves – Barkhudarly-Sofulu (near Ijevan) and Karki (renamed Tigranashen) on the border of Nakhchivan. Armenian forces also occupy the village of Ashaghi Askipara, which was not an exclave but an integral part of the Azerbaijani province of Kazakh (Lenta.ru 2012). Azerbaijan occupies the Armenian exclave of Artsvashen (Bashkend), to the north of Lake Sevan.

11 The situation has improved somewhat from the time of Wheatley's research, however, based on author's own observation, the number of people who can speak Georgian fluently is still limited. For example, an Akhalkalaki-based Georgian-Armenian state officer explained (November 2017) that s/he was selected to the particular job because of his/her knowledge of Georgian. S/he was reportedly the only officer in the respective department who was able to write and speak Georgian.

12 Interview with a specialist on minority issues, Akhaltskihke, Georgia, July 2015. Interview with an ethnic Armenian journalist, Ninotsminda, July 2015.

13 Interview with an ethnic Armenian civil activist and former politician, Ninotsminda, July 2015.

14 Interview with a specialist on minority issues, Akhaltskihke, Georgia, July 2015.

132 *Vincenc Kopeček*

15 Interview with a specialist on minority issues, Akhaltskihke, Georgia, July 2015.
16 Interview with a parish priest, Akhalkalaki district, Georgia, July 2015.
17 Interview with an ethnic Armenian journalist, Ninotsminda, Georgia, July 2015.

Literature

Abrahamyan, Gayane. 2016. "Armenia: Looking to Receive an Economic Boost from Iran." *Eurasianet*, February 10. www.eurasianet.org/node/77266.
Almasian, Mher. 2014. "The Highway System – Transportation Infrastructure in Armenia: Part I." *The Armenite*, April 2. http://thearmenite.com/2014/04/transportation-infrastructure-armenia-part-highway-system/.
Altstadt, Audrey L. 2015. "Ethnic Conflict in Nagorno-Karabagh." In *Ethnic Conflict in the Post-Soviet World: Case Studies and Analysis*, edited by Leokadia Drobizheva, Rose Gottemoeller, Catherine McArdle Kelleher, and Lee Walker, 227–253. London and New York: Routledge.
Avakian, Shaken. 2010. *Nagorno-Karabakh: Legal Aspects*. Yerevan: Tigran Mets Publishing House.
Badalyan, Hakob. 2017. "Iran-Armenia Railway Is Gone." *Lragir*, March 15. www.lragir.am/index.php/eng/0/comments/view/36888.
Bournoutian, George. 1997. "Eastern Armenia from the Seventeenth Century to the Russian Annexation." In *The Armenian People from Ancient to Modern Times, Volume II. Foreign Dominion to Statehood: The Fifteenth Century to the Twentieth Century*, edited by Richard G. Hovannisian, 81–107. New York: St. Martin's Press.
Caspersen, Nina. 2012. *Unrecognized States. The Struggle for Sovereignty in the Modern International System*. Cambridge: Polity Press.
Chorbajian, Levon, Patrick Donabedian, and Claude Mutafian. 1994. *The Caucasian Knot. The History and Geo-Politics of Nagorno-Karabagh*. London and New Jersey: Zed Books.
Closson, Stacy R. 2007. *State Weakness in Perspective: Trans-Territorial Energy Networks in Georgia, 1993–2003*. Dissertation. London: London School of Economics and Political Science. http://etheses.lse.ac.uk/1941/1/U226529.pdf.
Cornell, Svante E. 2001. *Small Nations and Great Powers. A Study of Ethnopolitical Conflict in the Caucasus*. Richmond: Curzon Press.
Cornell, Svante E. 2002. *Autonomy and Conflict: Ethnoterritoriality and Separatism in the South Caucasus: Cases in Georgia*. Uppsala: Department of Peace and Conflict Research, Uppsala University.
Croissant, Michael P. 1998. *The Armenia-Azerbaijan Conflict. Causes and Implications*. Westport and London: Praeger.
de Waal, Thomas. 2003. *Black Garden. Armenia and Azerbaijan through Peace and War*. London and New York: New York University Press.
Devdariani, Jaba. 2004. "Georgia: Rise and Fall of the Facade Democracy." *Demokratizatsiya: The Journal of Post-Soviet Democratization* 12 (1): 79–115.
Dudwick, Nora. 1997. "Political Transformations in Postcommunist Armenia: Images and Realities." In *Conflict, Cleavage, and Change in Central Asia and the Caucasus*, edited by Karen Dawisha and Bruce Parrott, 69–109. Cambridge: Cambridge University Press.
Gachechiladze, Revaz. 2012. *The New Georgia: Space, Society, Politics*. 2nd edition. New York: Routledge.

Gahramanova, Aytan. 2010. "Paradigms of Political Mythologies and Perspectives of Reconciliation in the Case of the Nagorno-Karabakh Conflict." *International Negotiation* 15 (1): 133–152.

Geostat. 2010. "Ethnic Groups by Major Administrative-Territorial Units." *Geostat.* www.geostat.ge/cms/site_images/_files/english/census/2002/03%20Ethnic%20 Composition.pdf.

Guretski, Voitsekh. 1998. "The Question of Javakheti." *Caucasian Regional Studies* 3 (1). http://poli.vub.ac.be/publi/crs/eng/0301-05.htm.

Hovannisian, Richard G. 1971. *The Republic of Armenia: The First Year, 1918–1919.* Los Angeles: University of California Press.

HRW. 2001. *Landmine Monitor Report 2001: Toward a Mine-Free World.* Washington: Human Rights Watch.

Jelen, Libor. 2009. "Změny etnické struktury v kavkazském regionu od konce 80. let: primární statistický rozbor [Changes in ethnic structure in the Caucasus region since the end of the 1980's: Primary statistical analysis]." *Geografie* 114 (2): 130–144.

Kaufman, Stuart J. 2001. *Modern Hatreds: The Symbolic Politics of Ethnic War.* Ithaca and London: Cornell University Press.

Killough, Ashley Corinne. 2008. "Armenia in Need of an Alternative Export-Import Route." *Eurasia Daily Monitor* 5 (195). https://jamestown.org/program/armenia-in-need-of-an-alternative-export-import-route/.

Kopeček, Vincenc. 2008. "Hledání Ázerbajdžánského pupku [A Quest for Azerbaijani Navel]." *Geografická revue* 4 (2): 196–213.

Kopeček, Vincenc. 2012. *Jižní Kavkaz mezi demokracií a autoritarismem* [The South Caucasus between Democracy and Authoritarianism]. Praha: European Science and Art Publishing.

Lenta.ru. 2012. "Pyatero Azerbaidzhanskykh voennykh pogibli v boyu na granice s Armeniei [Five Azerbaijani soldiers died in fighting on the Armenian border]." *Lenta.ru*, June 5. https://lenta.ru/news/2012/06/05/dead/.

Libaridian, Gerard J. 2004. *Modern Armenia. People, Nation, State.* London and New York: Transaction Publishers.

Lohm, Hedvig. 2006. "Dukhobors in Georgia: A Study of the Issue of Land Ownership and Inter-Ethnic Relations in Ninotsminda Rayon (Samtskhe-Javakheti)." ECMI Working Paper #35. Flensburg: European Centre for Minority Issues. www.ecmi.de/uploads/tx_lfpubdb/working_paper_35_en.pdf.

Lohm, Hedvig. 2007. *Javakheti after the Rose Revolution: Progress and Regress in the Pursuit of National Unity in Georgia.* ECMI Working Paper # 38. Flensburg: European Centre for Minority Issues. www.ecmi.de/uploads/tx_lfpubdb/working_paper_38.pdf.

Losaberidze, David, Konstantine Kandelaki, and Niko Orvelashvili. 2002. "Local Government in Georgia." In *Developing New Rules in the Old Environment, Local governments in Eastern Europe, in the Caucasus and Central Asia*, edited by Igor Munteanu and Victor Popa, 265–322. Budapest: Local Government and Public Service Reform Initiative.

Lragir. 2016. "Azerbaijan Fired at Baghanis Village, Armenia." *Lragir.am*, June 9. www.lragir.am/index.php/eng/0/country/view/35874.

Lragir. 2017. "Baghanis Village Was Under Intensive Fire by Azerbaijan." *Lragir. am*, April 29. www.lragir.am/index.php/eng/0/country/view/37030.

Manning, Robert A. 2000. "The Myth of the Caspian Great Game and the 'New Persian Gulf.'" *The Brown Journal of World Affairs* 7 (2): 15–33.

134 *Vincenc Kopeček*

Margaryan, Sara. 2008. "Preservation of Identity through Integration: The Case of Javakheti Armenians." In *Caucasus Studies 4: Migration-Society-Language*, edited by Karina Vamling, 52–61. Malmö: Malmö University.

Paremuzyan, Larisa. 2016. "Baghanis, an Armenian Border Village in the Line of Fire." *Hetq*, April 9. http://hetq.am/eng/news/67185/baghanis-an-armenian-border-village-in-the-line-of-fire-two-azerbaijani-gun-positions-must-be-dealt-with.html/.

Petrosyan, Tigran. 2016. "Armenia States Diversion Attempt by Azerbaijan." *Caucasian Knot*, December 29. www.eng.kavkaz-uzel.eu/articles/37977/.

Sabanadze, Natalie. 2001. *Armenian Minority in Georgia: Defusing Interethnic Tension*. ECMI Brief # 6. Flensburg: European Centre for Minority Issues. http://mercury.ethz.ch/serviceengine/Files/EINIRAS/34193/ipublicationdocument_singledocument/824f5bca-e34a-4188-81bb-81bcbdcad3f3/en/brief_6.pdf.

Saparov, Arsène. 2012. "Why Autonomy? The Making of Nagorno-Karabakh Autonomous Region 1918–1925." *Europe-Asia Studies* 64 (2): 281–323.

Saparov, Arsène. 2015. *From Conflict to Autonomy in the Caucasus: The Soviet Union and the Making of Abkhazia, South Ossetia and Nagorno Karabakh*. Kindle Edition. Abingdon and New York: Routledge.

Shirinyan, Anahit. 2013. "Assessing Russia's Role in Efforts to Resolve the Nagorno-KarabakhConflict:FromPerceptiontoReality." *JournalofConflictTransformation*, no. February. http://caucasusedition.net/analysis/assessing-russias-role-in-efforts-to-resolve-the-nagorno-karabakh-conflict-from-perception-to-reality/.

Skorupska, Adriana, and Konrad Zasztowt. 2014. *Georgia's Local Government Reform: How to Escape from the Soviet Past (and How Poland Can Help)*. PISM Policy Papers. Warszaw: Polish Institute of International Affairs. www.pism.pl/files/?id_plik=16394.

Slider, Darrell. 1997. "Democratization in Georgia." In *Conflict, Cleavage, and Change in Central Asia and the Caucasus*, edited by Karen Dawisha and Bruce Parrott, 156–198. Cambridge: Cambridge University Press.

Souleimanov, Emil. 2016. "What the Fighting in Karabakh Means for Azerbaijan and Armenia." *Central Asia – Caucasus Analyst*, May 12. www.cacianalyst.org/publications/analytical-articles/item/13361-what-the-fighting-in-karabakh-means-for-azerbaijan-and-armenia.html.

Swietochowski, Tadeusz. 1995. *Russia and Azerbaijan: A Borderland in Transition*. New York: Columbia University Press.

Tchilingirian, Hratch. 1999. "Nagorno Karabagh: Transition and the Elite." *Central Asian Survey* 18 (4): 435–461.

Tonoyan, Artyom. 2010. "Rising Armenian-Georgian Tensions and the Possibility of a New Ethnic Conflict in the South Caucasus." *Demokratizatsiya* 18 (4): 287–308.

Troinitskii, Nikolai A. 1905. *Pervaya vseobshchaya perepis naseleniya Rossiiskoi Imperii 1897 g* [The First General Population Census of the Russian Empire 1897]. Tablitsa XIII: Raspredelenie naseleniya po rodnomu yazyku i uezdam Rossiiskoi Imperii krome gubernii evropeiskoi Rossii [Table XIII: Structure of Population According to the Mother Tongue and Districts of the Russian Empire, without the Provinces of the European Russia]. Sankt-Peterburg: Tsentralnyi Statisticheskii Komitet.

TSU. 1929. *Vsesoyuznaya perepis naselenia 1926 goda. Tom 10–16* [All-Union Population Census 1926. Volume 10–16]. Tablitsa VI: Natsionalnyi sostav naseleniya po regionam respublik SSSR, naselenie po polu, narodnosti [Table VI: National Structure of the Regions of the Union Republics, Population According to Sex and Nationality]. Moskva: Izdanie TSU Soyuza SSR.

Walker, Christopher J. 1991. *Armenia and Karabagh: The Struggle for Unity.* London: Minority Rights Group.

Walker, Edward W. 2003. *Dissolution: Sovereignty and the Breakup of the Soviet Union.* Lanham: Rowman & Littlefield.

Wheatley, Jonathan. 2004. *Obstacles Impeding the Regional Integration of the Javakheti Region of Georgia.* ECMI Working Paper # 22. Flensburg: European Centre for Minority Issues. www.ecmi.de/uploads/tx_lfpubdb/working_paper_22.pdf.

Wheatley, Jonathan. 2005. *Georgia from National Awakening to Rose Revolution: Delayed Transition in the Former Soviet Union.* Aldershot and Burlington: Ashgate Publishing.

Wheatley, Jonathan. 2009. *The Integration of National Minorities in the Samtskhe-Javakheti and Kvemo Kartli Provinces of Georgia.* ECMI Working Paper # 44. Flensburg: European Centre for Minority Issues. www.ecmicaucasus.org/upload/publications/working_paper_44_en.pdf

3.4 Unfinished story of the Donetsk and Luhansk People's Republics

Towards a de facto state?

Alexandra Šmídová and Tomáš Šmíd

After the disintegration of the Soviet Union, Ukraine – like other post-Soviet states – was the scene of conflict between nationalists and those who supported the preservation of the Soviet system. Immediately after Ukraine's independence, the question of federalization became a central issue; federalization would have given the Donbass region the status of an autonomous unit within the country. Differing opinions on this issue were also reflected in Ukraine's highly fragmented political landscape, which included pro-Russian, pro-Western, and Ukrainian nationalist political formations. Pro-Russian positions were dominant within the Donbass region, and they also frequently served as a platform for the expression of pro-Soviet nostalgia.

The stagnation of the economy, combined with the complicated political and security situation in the region, regularly led to protests and strikes by the local population – which were often accompanied by expressions of anti-Ukrainian sentiments. However, the most important impulse for the region's secession from Ukraine was ultimately a series of events which did not actually take place in Donbass itself. In November 2013 Kiev's Independence Square (*Maidan Nezalezhnosti*) was the scene of demonstrations in support of Ukraine's integration into European structures – specifically calling for the signature of an association agreement with the EU, which Mykola Azarov's government had blocked – and protests against the politics of the President Viktor Yanukovych. The demonstrations gave rise to a protest movement which became known as *Euromaidan* (Ukrayinska pravda 2013a). The wave of protests spread to all regions of Ukraine; part of the population supported *Euromaidan*'s ideas and demands, while another part – mainly in eastern and southern Ukraine – supported the government coalition and opposed the signature of the association agreement and any change of government (Ukrayinska pravda 2013b).

Following armed clashes between protesters and special forces from the Ministry of the Interior (*Berkut*), Yanukovych's government fell (Balmforth and Grove 2013). Dissatisfaction with the steps taken by the new government and the influence of Russia led to the so-called Crimean crisis, when the Crimean Peninsula was annexed by Russia (Gosudarstvennaya Duma 2014) on the basis of an illegitimate referendum (Tierney 2015, 534–535).

This sparked protests even in the eastern regions of Ukraine. Large industrial cities were the scene of pro-Russian demonstrations, and there were clashes between factions supporting the secession of the eastern regions and proponents of a united Ukraine. In the Donbass – the Donetsk and Luhansk regions (*oblasts*) – two new political entities were declared: the Donetsk People's Republic (*Donetskaya narodnaya respublika* – DPR) and the Luhansk People's Republic (*Luhanskaya narodnaya respublika* – LPR). These two newly formed entities formed a confederation known as New Russia (*Novorossiya*) (Laruelle 2016; O'Loughlin, Toal, and Kolossov 2017), though this confederation was later dissolved (Litvinova 2017). On 14 May 2014, the Ukrainian government launched the so-called anti-terrorist operation (ATO) in the east of the country; the operation consisted of a set of coordinated actions undertaken with the aim of destroying the armed non-state groups that were active in the unrecognized republics (Verkhovna rada Ukrayiny 2015). The intensity of the Donbass conflict has fluctuated during the past three years, yet a significant part of Ukraine's internationally recognized territory is controlled by breakaway groups represented by the unrecognized state entities of the DPR and LPR. These entities are the subject of the analysis presented in this chapter (Map 7).

The primary goal of the chapter is to evaluate whether these separatist entities can be considered genuine de facto states. We draw on the definition of de facto states presented in Chapter 1.1, so the following sections focus on

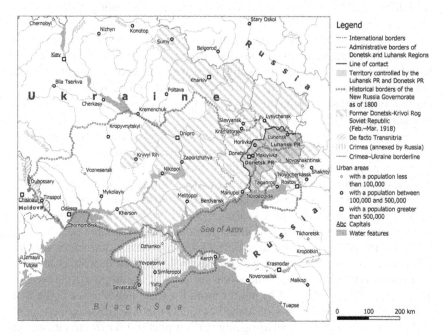

Map 7 Donetsk and Luhansk People's Republics.
Source: Authors.

138 *Alexandra Šmídová and Tomáš Šmíd*

individual criteria for the definition: control over a territory and its population, the functioning of state institutions, and attempts to gain international recognition (including the maintenance of relations with other states). The chapter then discusses the historical and ideological context from which both republics emerged, analyzing their historical continuity, ideological basis, and economy (cf. Møller 2003).

Population and territory

Despite the still-ongoing conflict (and the migration of a certain part of the Donbass population), the DPR has a population of around 2,300,000. Data from the DPR's Ministry of Justice and the Migration Department of its Interior Ministry state that as of March 2018, the territory controlled by the DPR had 2,299,385 inhabitants. Of this number, 2,189,988 lived in urban areas and 109,397 in rural areas. Donetsk itself had a population of 951,873 according to the same statistics. When the armed clashes became less intense, a large proportion of the refugees decided to return to their homes (Glavstat DNR 2018a, 2018b). In the LPR, according to the LPR State Statistical Committee (Gosudarstvennyi komitet statistiki LNR), there were 1,470,247 people living permanently in the territory under LPR control in March 2018, with 434,972 living in Luhansk itself (Goskomstat LNR 2018).

Ukrainian citizens who remained in the zone affected by the ATO and who do not hold the status of involuntary migrants are not entitled to welfare payments, pensions, or grants from the Ukrainian state. There also exist blacklists of citizens living in the territories of both breakaway republics who the Ukrainian authorities deem to be collaborators. These citizens have been accused of separatism, and they are being prosecuted in Ukrainian courts (Myrotvorec 2015). However, the DPR and LPR both have permanent populations living and working within their territories; the criterion of a stable population is thus met.

There are no significant internal divisions within these populations – either along religious, ethnic, or ideological lines (cf. Møller 2003, 17). This is mainly because most of the inhabitants who supported the Ukrainian side during the conflict were forced to leave the DPR and LPR and settled in areas under Ukrainian government control. On the other hand, not all of the people who moved to the Ukrainian side of the front line are supporters of the Kiev government. The dominant motivating factor for such relocations was the reality of war and material hardship, rather than ideology and political convictions.[1] In fact, we can currently observe a process of anti-Ukrainian radicalization among some sections of the population, even in areas controlled by Kiev.[2] The main reason for this phenomenon is the fact that after almost four years of armed conflict, the Ukrainian government still shows no interest in providing any real support to Ukrainian citizens in the Donbass region. Kiev has stopped the payment of pensions and welfare, and it has also blocked water and food shipments at checkpoints set up on the edge of the ATO zone. Moreover, some sections of the Ukrainian army have conspicuously lacked discipline in the zone, engaging in aggressive behaviour and harassment of ordinary local people; contrary to the information presented in the Western media, this type of behaviour has certainly not been restricted to the *Opolchenie*,[3] covert Russian troops, or the (formerly) pro-Kremlin Chechen units known as the Kadyrovites (*kadyrovtsy*). However, during the war there has not been any internal ethnic, religious, or other conflict within the territory controlled by the DPR and LPR – the concept of *russkii mir* (or *sovetskoe proshloe*) functions as an identitary-ideological bond regardless of nationality. From the demographic perspective, one future threat is a potential brain-drain of talented specialists who fled the Donbass region during the conflict, settling either in Ukraine, Russia, or outside the former USSR; this process is still continuing (Segodnya 2017).

The declared territory of the DPR is delineated by the borders of the Donetsk region of Ukraine; the region covers an area of 26,517 km^2 (Derzhstat Ukrayiny 2016). However, the breakaway structures control less than half of this territory (though it is difficult to give a precise figure). Even representatives of the DPR admit that they only control around one-third of the territory of the Donetsk region. According to the DPR ex-leader A. Zakharchenko,[4] "DPR territory under Ukrainian control" (i.e. the remainder of the Donetsk region) is occupied territory, and the armed struggle will continue until this territory is liberated and the republic's independence is recognized. Zakharchenko had been rejecting the idea of autonomous status for the Donetsk region or its membership of a federal structure as part of a united Ukraine (Zakharchenko 2015).

The Luhansk region has a total area of 26,683 km^2. As in the case of the DPR, it is difficult to give a precise figure for the area of this territory controlled by the *Opolchenie*. In 2014 the Ukrainian cabinet drew up a list of municipalities under the control of the unrecognized republics (Kabinet ministriv 2014). However, it is not possible to determine an exact area because the so-called grey zone – the line along which armed conflicts between the Ukrainian army and the *Opolchenie* are localized, and the area over which neither party has absolute control – is shifting almost on a daily basis (Kravchenko 2016). It can therefore be concluded that despite the still-ongoing armed conflict, the criterion of control over a defined territory is nevertheless met – though both breakaway entities control a smaller area than they originally declared as their territory.

Government and institutions

The state apparatus in both breakaway entities is still relatively weak. However, in the event of the cessation of armed conflict, their models for institutions and state bodies possess all necessary attributes potentially enabling them to function in a more stable manner – though it would be premature to engage in predictions. The DPR and the LPR have all the necessary elements of state power: a parliament (the People's Council), a government (the Council of Ministers), a head of state, and a supreme court. They also possess a state apparatus, local bodies, a military command structure, a prosecution service, and a security service. Comparing the two breakaway entities, the DPR has a more stable state apparatus and a stronger functional influence over its territory. The LPR – especially in terms of its external relations – is dependent on the DPR government, though it is debatable whether its attempts at external relations can genuinely be termed foreign policy. In essence, all (strategic) decision-making within the LPR's territory stems from an external actor, the Russian Federation; decisions made in Russia then filter downwards via the DPR central government. The LPR government has only limited influence over decision-making, which is essentially restricted to the local and municipal level (Kanygin 2017). Additionally, the situation is further complicated by fierce internal political struggles among the Luhansk elites, and also between the Luhansk elites and some representatives of the Kremlin (Snegirev 2017). A good example of these internal conflicts is the resignation of Igor Plotnitskii as the LPR leader, which was presented in the Ukrainian media as a conflict between the interior minister Kornet and Plotnitskii.[5] In the opinion of respondents with close links to high-ranking Kremlin officials, the resignation enabled Moscow to consolidate its influence in the LPR's state structures (TSN 2017; 112.ua 2017).

The last essential element of a state is its institutions. The main criteria here are the government's ability to perform its executive role, to possess a certain institutional structure, and to be elected by the population in free and democratic elections. The DPR and LPR governments – which from the Ukrainian perspective are elected illegally and illegitimately – are attempting to create a functional state apparatus, though due to the ongoing military conflict it is very difficult for them to perform their government duties. The internal structures of both entities are the scene of regular conflicts between officials, elites, criminal groups, and armed actors; this situation is further exacerbated by conflicts over spheres of influence and economic capital. The dire humanitarian situation and the weakness of the judiciary also play a role (Dialog.ua 2015; Kanygin 2017; Snegirev 2017). The populations of both republics are currently fighting for their own survival, so the rule of law has been replaced by a new slogan: "power and truth belongs to those who have guns".[6] Respect for even elementary laws is very weak. Currently the DPR and the LPR are not enforcing either Ukrainian legislation or the laws that they themselves have created (e.g. Glavred 2017; Kazanskii 2017).

A number of ministries have been established to enable the executive branch to function. There is also a security service, a military command structure, and a prosecutor's office. However, the weak economies of both entities do not enable these institutions (especially ministries) to perform all their functions. Now that Ukraine has stopped paying welfare, pensions, and salaries to the inhabitants of the DPR and the LPR, the new authorities in both republics are attempting to take over this role; however, their provision of these services

The Donetsk & Luhansk People's Republics   141

still remains limited and unstable. On the other hand, it should be noted that the new authorities are the only institutions which at least partly attempt to provide services for the local population. This fact has boosted public support for the breakaway republics, while support for the Ukrainian government has waned as a result of Kiev's refusal to provide basic social services and its determination to isolate the populations of the two territories.

In terms of the social contract between the leadership of both entities and the local population, the period of armed conflict brought serious breaches of public security, freedom, and private ownership rights. Despite the fact that the institutional structure and legal framework in both republics are designed to preserve these attributes, the protection provided to the population in the ATO-affected zone during the armed conflict has been weak; basic rights and freedoms are systematically violated. Reports from Human Rights Watch, Amnesty International, and the UN speak of illegal detention, kidnapping, physical and psychological torture, brutality towards the civilian population, the use of civilians as human shields, illegal treatment of prisoners-of-war, blockades of humanitarian aid, persecution of journalists, and other similar incidents. It should be pointed out that basic violations of human rights and freedoms of the population in the ATO zone have been committed not only by the *Opolchenie* but also by regular Ukrainian army units (OHCHR 2014; OON 2014; HRW 2015). With regard to personal property rights, there have been incidents in which local authorities, representatives of the breakaway republics, and armed rebels have confiscated property from the inhabitants of the territories in question; this was the official reason for Plotnitskii's dismissal of Kornet from his post as interior minister. Privately owned businesses, means of transport, and residential premises have been nationalized. Initially the governments of the new republics issued decrees nationalizing the property of oligarchs, but since then, property and businesses have also been confiscated from people who have left the breakaway republics to settle in Ukrainian-controlled territory (Kanal 24 2014; Tsenzor.net 2015). This fact has been confirmed by respondents living in the DPR who were interviewed by the authors.

The ability to enter into relations with other states

Neither the DPR nor the LPR are currently recognized by the international community. The only state that has recognized their independence is South Ossetia – itself a de facto state. The DPR's independence has also been recognized by the LPR; in 2014–2015 both breakaway republics formed a confederation known as the Union of People's Republics – New Russia (*Soyuz narodnykh respublik – Novorossiya*). Russia itself does not recognize the independence of either republic, though it does accept documents issued by their authorities – passports, birth certificates, university diplomas, and death certificates (BBC 2017). The DPR and LPR have recognized the independence of Abkhazia, the NKR, South Ossetia, Transnistria, Northern

Cyprus, and Palestine (SGOV Novorosii 2015). However, there is also interaction with other states due to the ongoing armed conflict. EU member states, the United States, Russia (as the patron state of both breakaway entities), and Ukraine (as the parent state) are all forced to negotiate with representatives of the DPR and LPR as part of their conflict-solving efforts. In view of the fact that the Donbass region is rich in natural resources, there are also economic contacts with Ukraine, despite Kiev's insistence that both entities are terrorist organizations occupying its own territory. The potential ability to interact with other states is also boosted by the fact that the international community does not view the region as a peripheral one.

However, it is debatable whether any of the global powers will be interested in such interaction. The West – supporting Ukraine – is highly unlikely to recognize the breakaway states' independence and thus legalize their secession. Likewise, it appears unlikely that their patron state Russia will recognize the DPR and LPR in the foreseeable future; if it were to do so, it would risk incurring even more severe sanctions from the West. Unlike the situation in Crimea, Russia is not attempting to secure the de facto independence of the DPR and LPR – and even less so their annexation to the Russian Federation – due to the threat of harsher sanctions. It should also be taken into account that Russia in general does not recognize de facto states, even though it may support them on the ground; Moscow only recognized the independence of Abkhazia and South Ossetia after these entities had been in de facto existence for fifteen years, as a response to Kosovo's declaration of independence and Saakashvili's anti-Russian policy stance. Russia still does not recognize the NKR or Transnistria. From the economic perspective too, it is more beneficial to Moscow to leave the status of the DPR and LPR unresolved, since – as in the case of Transnistria – such territories are suitable locations for politically problematic business dealings that are on (or beyond) the boundaries of legality; it is also cheaper for Russia to trade with such unrecognized territories (which are essentially dependent on Moscow's support) than it would be if they were internationally recognized. The comparison with Crimea is geopolitically invalid; Crimea has immensely more strategic value for Russia than the DPR or the LPR, and in simple terms it was Russia that instigated the Crimean crisis. For Russia, the value of the DPR and LPR is as a corridor to Crimea – facilitating transport links with the annexed peninsula, enabling Moscow to maintain a strong security presence there, and also helping to destabilize the situation in (anti-Russian) Ukraine. It is therefore unlikely in the foreseeable future that the international community will recognize the independence of the DPR and LPR even if the armed conflict ceases; in such a case both entities would probably remain de facto states for a long time.

The representatives of the DPR and the LPR officially declare their desire for international recognition, though in view of Russia's position (see above) and both entities' complete dependence on Russian support (mainly in economic terms), they are not in fact actively seeking to secure this recognition.

The Donetsk & Luhansk People's Republics 143

It is also unlikely that the current elites actually support international recognition; they are motived more by their own economic interests and desire for power than by a desire to accept the real responsibilities and duties that would come as a result of international recognition of their states' legality. The current breakaway groups are primarily motivated by the desire to profit from the situation; this places them close to the category of warlords. Secessionists (or irredentists) with genuine political motivations – who formed the elites in the DPR and LPR in the early phases of the conflict – have since been removed from their positions (such as Igor Girkin, known as Strelkov).[7]

Historical continuity

The DPR was formed during the Ukrainian crisis, when territory in the region came under the control of rebel groups. In early spring 2014, after Russia's annexation of Crimea, Donetsk was the scene of pro-Moscow demonstrations demanding the secession of the Donetsk region from Ukraine. Some of the demonstrators saw the region's future as echoing the irredentist scenario that had played out in Crimea, ending in the incorporation of the region into the Russian Federation. Other activists supported a secessionist path, leading to the independence of the Donetsk region (or the entire Donbass) (RBK 2014).

On 7 April 2014, pro-Russian activists occupied the region's administrative buildings in Donetsk. The DPR was established by popular ballot, and a date was announced for a referendum on independence. The so-called republican government asked the Russian President Vladimir Putin to dispatch a peace contingent of Russian troops (Malorossiya 2014). The referendum – which was in breach of the Ukrainian constitution and failed to meet international standards – was held on 11 May 2014; 89.07% of votes were cast for independence. According to the DPR's central electoral commission, participation in the referendum was 74.87% (Vesti 2014). On the following day the republic's government declared the DPR to be a sovereign independent state. The situation in Luhansk unfolded in a similar manner. At the end of March 2014 there were several protests against *Euromaidan;* on 6 April the Ukrainian security service (SBU – *Sluzhba bezpeki Ukrayiny*) building was occupied, and on 11 April the *Opolchenie* issued an ultimatum to the Luhansk Regional Soviet, instructing it to hold a referendum on independence within ten days. The referendum eventually took place on 11 May, though the LPR had already declared independence on 27 April. In the referendum, 96.2% of the votes were cast in favour of independence, and participation was 75% (Korrespondent.net 2014). On 24 May the DPR and the LPR formed the confederation known as New Russia.

The events of the spring of 2014 inevitably provoked a reaction from Ukraine; as soon as the regional administrative buildings in Donetsk and Luhansk were occupied, Kiev decided to declare both breakaway republics terrorist organizations, and the so-called ATO was launched in the Donbass

144 *Alexandra Šmídová and Tomáš Šmíd*

region (Generalna prokuratura Ukrayiny 2014). This marked the beginning of armed conflicts in eastern Ukraine. Fighting on one side were the Ukrainian army and (pro-)Ukrainian volunteers – mainly former *Maidan* activists and members of right-wing extremist movements. On the other side, fighting for the so-called separatists, rebels or (in the rhetoric of the Kiev government) terrorists, were regular Russian army units, plus (in lesser numbers) local militias. Later, fighters from abroad – mainly mercenaries but also some volunteers – joined both sides.[8]

From the perspective of historical continuity, one significant phenomenon is that the DPR and LPR completely reject all previous involvement with Ukraine and the preceding Ukrainian Soviet Socialist Republic. The DPR sees itself as a continuation of the Donetsk-Krivoy Rog Soviet Republic (*Donetsko-krivorozhskaya sovetskaya respublika* – DKSR), which was formed in February 1918 on the basis of economic principles, to combine the coal, iron, and steel industries in the region (Goncharenko 1991). However, Lenin did not support the new entity; in the following month he called a plenary meeting declaring the DKSR part of the Ukrainian People's Republic of Soviets (*Ukrainskaya narodnaya respublika sovietov* – UNRS).[9] Most of the territory of the UNRS formed the basis for the subsequent Ukrainian Soviet Republic (*Ukrainskaya sovetskaya respublika* – USR); the USR then became part of the Russian Soviet Republic (*Rossiiskaya sovetskaya respublika* – RSR), which was lost by the Bolsheviks in April 1918. The DKSR legally ceased to exist from the beginning of 1919. When the Bolsheviks retook the area in March 1919, they established the Ukrainian Soviet Socialist Republic, which on 30 December 1922 – after a chaotic period of armed conflict – became part of the USSR (Kornilov 2011).

A substantial part of the separatist elites and their supporters claim that the DPR and the LPR form the New Russia confederation, making them successors to the New Russian Governorate (*Novorossiiskaya guberniya* – *Novorossiya*), an entity which was incorporated into the Russian Empire in the second half of the 18th century. However, in terms of territorial delineation, the majority of the two breakaway republics do not fall within the boundaries of the former New Russian Governorate (Shubin 2014; Varov 2017). The leaders of the DPR and LPR therefore decided not to identify themselves as the successors to the former New Russia, but instead to the 1917–1918 Donetsk-Krivoy Rog Soviet Republic. All attempts to bring the two breakaway states together as a single entity have so far failed; the confederation known as the Union of People's Republics – New Russia (*Soyuz narodnykh respublik* – *Novorossiya*) ceased to exist in May 2015 (Derkachev and Karcev 2015). According to the former DPR foreign minister A. Kofman, the New Russia project has been shelved indefinitely (Gordon 2015). According to the original plans, New Russia was to be a confederative republic consisting of eight current Ukrainian oblasts: Donetsk, Luhansk, Zaporizhzhya, Odessa, Dnipropetrovsk, Kharkiv, Mykolaiv, and even Kiev.

The DKSR shares numerous features with the present-day DPR and LPR. The most important feature in the current context is the fact that the DKSR wanted to be an autonomous unit within Soviet Russia, not within Soviet Ukraine (though it ended up as part of Soviet Ukraine and completely lacked autonomous status). The existence of historical continuity is a key issue for the DPR – and this importance is evident from its propaganda and political statements. In all public communications, the current DPR government attempts to emphasize its separate status from the rest of Ukraine and to point out that it has always been a separate entity; the DKSR serves this line of argumentation much better than the New Russian Governorate. The existence of a similar historical precedent is viewed as reinforcing the territorial integrity and cohesion of the DPR (Kornilov 2011).

Despite the demise of the confederation, the term "New Russia" continued to be used both by the elites and by the mass population, even though the DPR and LPR exist separately from each other. From July 2017 they briefly formed part of a new confederative entity known as Little Russia (*Malorossiya*), which differed from the former New Russia only in its name. On 18 July 2017 Zakharchenko announced that both the DPR and the LPR would join this new entity. The project was never brought to full fruition because the local political elites of the LPR failed to reach an agreement on the proposed union with the DPR (which would have been the larger and more powerful partner). Nevertheless, the Kremlin (through Vladislav Surkov) expressed its support for Zakharchenko's idea (Karmazin 2017). Like the New Russia confederation, the Little Russia project has its roots in Russia's Tsarist history – especially the history of what is now Ukraine. Up to 1917, Little Russia comprised the governorates of Volhynia, Kiev, Podolia, Kharkov, Chernigov, and Poltava; however, in the present-day situation the precise territorial delineation of this historical entity is less important than the context in which the term "Little Russia" was used. The notion of a Little Russian identity emerged in the 17th century; the Little Russians were viewed as a regional branch of the single Russian nation (Dolbilov and Miller 2006, 465–502). Nevertheless, just one month after the new name of the potential new entity (which would have had Donetsk as its capital) was announced, Zakharchenko admitted that the new name had met with a very negative response from the population of both breakaway republics, so the confederation of the DPR and LPR was ultimately not renamed (Korrespondent.net 2017).

The ideological and religious basis

Ideology is considered a highly important attribute by the leadership of the DPR and LPR. According to the Article 9 of the DPR's constitution (Konstitutsiya DNR 2014, cf. Vremennyi osnovnoi zakon LNR 2014), no ideology (or religion) can hold an exclusive status or be an ideology/religion of the state. However, the concept of the "Russian world" (*russkii mir*), on which the republic is based, has become a core idea. The concept of *russkii mir* embodies a historic, geographical, and (ethno)cultural community declaring its association with Russia's inherited historical memory, using the Russian language, and preserving Russian culture and traditions – with the cooperation and support of the current Russian Federation (Laruelle 2015; Solik and Baar 2016; Kurfürst 2017). However, the mere existence of a large ally – in this case Russia – is not sufficient. From the ideological perspective, it should be added, the entire concept is founded on the conflict with Ukraine, that is, the creation of a shared enemy. Ukrainians are presented as Bandera-inspired nationalists and fascists, *karateli*[10] or a pro-Western junta against which the DPR is struggling. Propaganda plays an important role in creating this ideological basis, so the government controls local television and radio stations (whose main audience consists of pensioners); it also controls cyberspace (which is mainly used by young and middle-aged people). The main sources of the DPR's propaganda in cyberspace are the social networks VKontakte and Facebook, and the video server YouTube. These platforms include numerous profiles, pages, channels, and groups which direct the propaganda campaign to the public. There are several target groups; the largest comprises Russian- or Ukrainian-speaking young people, especially in eastern Ukraine.[11] Among the most resonant topics are front line propaganda reports (successful military campaigns by DPR armed forces and the demonization of Ukrainian troops) and the promotion of life and institutions in the new republics. The concept of New Russia also played a central role in cyberspace propaganda; it was intended to provide a single unified identity for the entire separatist/irredentist movement. However, despite massive propaganda efforts, New Russia never became a reality – mainly due to internal political developments within the two breakaway republics and a change of attitude in Moscow.

For a long time, religion did not play a major role in the case of the DPR and LPR; this was reflected in both republics' constitutions (Konstitutsiya DNR 2014; Vremennyi osnovnoi zakon LNR 2014). Representatives of both republics have attempted to win support from members of all religions and confessions – though the Orthodox Church (here represented by the Moscow Patriarchate) nevertheless holds the key position, and in the words of Zakharchenko it represents the spiritual foundation of the republic (Zakharchenko 2014). However, in January 2016 there was a mass demonstration outside a Greek Catholic church, which marked a change in stance towards other religions and confessions: a charity collection of both money and goods (humanitarian aid) for the Ukrainian army had been held in the church, which was subsequently closed and forbidden from holding religious services (DAN 2016). The Greek Catholic (Uniate) Church is viewed *en bloc* as a representative of the enemy Ukrainian regime. The Orthodox Church represented by the Kiev Patriarchate also holds the same position; indeed, it was viewed as a hostile element even earlier than the Greek Catholic Church.

The Donetsk & Luhansk People's Republics 147

From the perspective of the integration of the state and the nation, it is necessary to determine a criterion which is shared by the inhabitants of a defined territory, and which thus can unite them. Here it is important to mention that even prior to the conflict, around 40% of the region's population were ethnic Russians (Derzhstat Ukrayiny 2001). This means that ethnic origin or nationality cannot serve as the main criterion in this case. In order to gain the maximum possible support in the heterogeneous, multi-ethnic Donbass region, the governments of both entities not only had to create a shared enemy in the form of the "Ukrainian junta"; they also had to find an additional unifying feature. The local population had a strong connection with Ukrainian ethnicity – supported by family ties and the Soviet practice of identifying citizens by their nationality in official documents such as birth certificates and passports (the so-called *pyataya grafa*) – so for a period the breakaway governments stopped demonizing the enemy on the basis of their Ukrainian ethnicity, instead seeking shared points of contact with the Ukrainians – in the form of "Little Russian" identity.

Ultimately, it was the Russian language which became the main criterion for identitary links between the DPR/LPR and their populations. One reason behind the unrest and protests in the spring of 2014 was the revocation of Ukraine's law on regional languages – a change that had been pushed through by the government in Kiev. The effect of this revocation was to make the use of Ukrainian compulsory in schools, places of employment, and state institutions. This step provoked a very negative response in the Donbass region; it was perceived as a hostile act, an attempt at forced Ukrainianization and a ban on people's use of their native tongue (Russian). This helped the DPR and LPR governments to gain strong support from the local population, as they presented themselves as defenders of the Russian language – and, by extension, Russian culture as a whole (Kovalenko and Rezchikov 2017).

The economic base

When the current conflict comes to an end, it is debatable whether – and if so, how – the DPR and the LPR will be able to repair the damage caused by the war and renew local infrastructure. The republics' success in this matter will depend on whether Ukraine imposes sanctions on the breakaway states, whether they have access to international trade, how they deal with unemployment and create jobs, and whether they are able to support themselves without external assistance. Financial support from Russia currently represents one of the few resources available to the republics; other income streams include proceeds from limited trade in raw materials, as well as income tax revenues from companies operating within the republics' territory. However, Russian support has shrunk as a consequence of Russia's involvement in Syria. According to A. Tkachuk, the head of the Ukrainian security service (SBU), in March 2016 the republics were operating with just

148   Alexandra Šmídová and Tomáš Šmíd

53% of their expected budgetary resources. Almost 80% of the funds designated for local authorities remained under the control of the central governments, and were not in fact transferred to the local level (FaceNews 2016). The DPR leadership explains this financial shortfall as being due to the fact that the local population do not pay taxes (Donbass.ua 2016). According to an article in the German *Bild* magazine, Russia sends around 1 billion EUR per year in financial support to the DPR and LPR; of this sum, 79 million EUR goes to pay pensions and salaries for state-sector employees, plus gas, water, electricity, and other municipal expenditure (Thinktanks. by 2016). Due to the current problems faced by the Russian economy – as a result of both sanctions and the cost of its operations in Syria – it is difficult to predict what future levels of Russian support will be, though according to respondents working in the DPR's state administration, the majority of support from Moscow still involves providing troops, weapons, and ammunition for the DPR armed forces.

The economic base of the breakaway republics is weakened by the ongoing conflict, but even after the closure of the conflict it will be necessary to expend much time and effort repairing vital infrastructure and industrial facilities. The Donbass was always the industrial heartland of Ukraine – but following the disintegration of the USSR it faced problems due to outdated industrial technologies; there was almost no modernization, and the region's competitiveness continued to decline. For these reasons, the republics' declarations that they are economically independent entities, capable of creating viable long-term trading relations, must be viewed as a mere myth of separatist propaganda.

In 2017 the economic development ministries of both republics issued reports claiming that their economies were growing thanks to increased industrial production and volumes of coal mined and sold; however, according to unofficial statistics, just 30% of pre-war industry is still operating (Regnum 2017a). In March 2017 the DPR and LPR launched an extensive programme to nationalize privately owned industrial companies and infrastructure which had been paying tax to the Ukrainian state. The majority of these companies, especially those forming part of the Industrial Union of Donbass and System Capital Management corporations, are owned by the Ukrainian oligarch Rinat Akhmetov (Regnum 2017b). The grey economy also plays a major role in both republics, with its typical symptoms of corruption, fraud, and the influence of armed groups and criminal structures in economic life (Skorik 2018).

Conclusion

Among the general factors leading to the emergence of de facto states in the post-Soviet space are the political and economic instability of newly formed states, combined with ethnic-nationalist ambitions and supported by an awareness of the complexities of history, drawing on real or perceived

The Donetsk & Luhansk People's Republics 149

historical injustices. The DPR and the LPR differ from the other post-Soviet de facto states not only because they emerged almost two decades later but also because the conflict within society runs more along the line of linguistic identity than ethnic identity. Attempts to provoke hatred between Russians and Ukrainians on the basis of ethnic origin proved largely unsuccessful because a large part of the Donbass region's population is either of Ukrainian nationality or has close family ties with the Ukrainian community. A logical consequence of this fact is that a sizeable percentage of the population is of mixed Russian-Ukrainian origin. It is therefore unsurprising that the leadership of both de facto states sought to emphasize concepts with a historical-territorial dimension rather than an ethnic-national subtext – that is, the concepts of New Russia, and later Little Russia.

A key factor in the birth of the DPR and the LPR was the weakness of the Ukrainian state, combined with Russian support for separatism. In this context it should be mentioned that post-Soviet Ukraine was a fragile construct, which lacked a long-term tradition of statehood within its current borders. Moreover, the events of the 20th century – such as the Stalinist terror, the famine, and the Second World War – caused enormous losses and transfers of population, meaning that the state's inhabitants felt a relatively low level of emotional commitment to Ukraine; this, in turn, made the process of nation-building and state-building a more complicated one, particularly in the eastern and southern regions. Similar remnants of Soviet policy with regard to nationality and population, as well as the consequences of widespread Stalinist repression, can also be found to a substantial extent in all post-Soviet regions where de facto states have emerged. Another shared factor has been Russia's attempt to use de facto states as a tool for exerting pressure on the new successor states – especially in situations when the successor states' foreign policy is at odds with Moscow's preferences.

With regard to the criteria for de facto statehood, the DPR and LPR essentially meet most of these criteria. They do not control the majority of their claimed territory, but the territory they do control is home to the majority of the population of the Donbass region. The breakaway states also possess organized political systems which are able (at least to a certain extent, though not fully, due to the realities of the ongoing conflict) to provide the population of their territories with basic services. However, one issue that is currently highly debatable is whether the republics are genuinely attempting to establish relations with other states and to gain international recognition. In reality, relations with other states are being established only selectively – and this reflects that fact that the political elites of both republics are not in fact genuinely attempting to gain recognition. This is due to their substantial dependence on Russia, which does not wish to see the republics become independent, instead preferring them to remain part of the Ukraine, where they can act as a destabilizing force – thus serving Russia's interests. In this respect, the two republics cannot be considered genuine de facto states – despite having existed formally for more than two years.

Notes

1 For example, interview with a former police officer from Donetsk, now living in Mariupol, September 2015; interview with a pensioner from Donetsk, now living in Slavyansk, August 2016; interview with a former employee of the municipal authority in Donetsk, now living in Kramatorsk, April 2017.

2 For example, interview with a former nurse from Makiyivka, now living in Kramatorsk (age 50), 8 April 2017; interview with a former employee of the Ukraine health ministry from Makiyivka (age 49), now living in Kiev, 14 August 2016; interview with a former self-employed businesswoman from Donetsk (age 45), now living in Kiev, 15 August 2016; interview with a lawyer from Makiyivka (age 51), now living in Kiev, 15 August 2016; interview with a student from Makiyivka (age 22), now living in Kiev, 16 August 2016; interview with a student from Donetsk (age 20), now living in Brno, Czechia, 15 October 2017.

3 Historically, the *Opolchenie* were armed tribal formations, armed civilian units such as people's guards, or irregular (reserve) armed forces such as militias. Peter I introduced compulsory military duties for civilians as a way of increasing the size of his armed forces by recruiting ordinary people who were not trained soldiers; this system later developed into a form of military conscription. Under the Russian Empire, the *Opolchenie* were represented by so-called *Ratnik*s, who were called up for military service during the Crimean War, the Japanese-Russian War and the First World War. During the Second World War the concept of the *Opolchenie* shifted; currently the *Opolchenie* are no longer civilians recruited to carry out military duties during a war, but are instead "voluntarily mobilized" members of the population (Ivanov 2011). In the conflict in eastern Ukraine, the armed Donbass units present themselves as *Opolchenie*, and maintain that they are volunteers in the people's army.

4 Alexander Zakharchenko has died in August 2018 after an explosion at a cafe in Donetsk city.

5 The conflict between Igor Plotnitskii and Igor Kornet began in 2015 after the killing of the separatist military commander Alexander Bednov (known as Batman), apparently in retribution for his opposition to pro-Moscow policies. There was then an attempt on the life of Plotnitskii himself; Plotnitskii accused the interior ministry and Kornet himself of having deliberately allowed the assassination attempt to go ahead. Conflicts also began to emerge between the prosecutor's office and the interior ministry. In early November 2017 Kornet was dismissed from his post as interior minister, though Plotnitskii did not sign the official order until 20 November. On the following day, an armed group led by Kornet occupied a number of administrative buildings, including the interior ministry. Television and radio broadcasting was suspended. In the evening Plotnitskii resigned as the head of the LPR and fled, apparently to Russia. The current head of the LPR is Leonid Pasechnik, the former minister of state security.

6 Interview with a former technician from Donetsk who joined the *Opolchenie*, October 2014.

7 This fact was confirmed by an informal conversation with an assistant to a deputy of the DPR People's Council, February 2018, via Skype. Similar information was given by a former technician from Donetsk who joined the *Opolchenie*, January 2018, via Skype.

8 For details of Russian forces' involvement in the conflict see, for example, Sutyagin (2015) or Allison (2014).

9 This was a different entity than the Ukrainian People's Republic (*Ukrainskaya narodnaya respublika* – UNR), which was headed by Symon Petlyura; the UNR was a non-Bolshevik state entity which existed during the disintegration of Tsarist Russia.

The Donetsk & Luhansk People's Republics 151

10 A term used in the DPR and LPR to denote Ukrainian troops. It is based on the verb *karat* – to punish.
11 This information is based on an analysis of the content of VKontakte, Facebook and YouTube carried out by one of the authors and focussing on DPR and LPR propaganda in cyberspace.

Literature

112.ua. 2017. "Peredel vlasti v ORLO: SMI soobshili, chto Kreml vstal na storonu glavy MVD LNR Korneta [Redistribution of power in independent districts of the Luhansk region: Media informed that Kremlin turned to support the head of the Ministry of Interior Kornet]." *112.ua*, November 21. https://112.ua/obshchestvo/peredel-vlasti-v-orlo-smi-soobshhili-chto-kreml-vstal-na-storonu-glavy-mvd-lnr-korneta-421617.html.

Allison, Roy. 2014. "Russian 'Deniable' Intervention in Ukraine: How and Why Russia Broke the Rules." *International Affairs* 90 (6): 1255–1297.

Balmforth, Richard, and Thomas Grove. 2013. "Ukraine Police Smash Pro-Europe Protest, Opposition to Call Strike." *Reuters*, December 12. www.reuters.com/article/2013/11/30/us-ukraine-protest-idusbre9at01q20131130.

BBC. 2017. "Rossiya priznala dokumenty, vydavaemye v DNR i LNR." *BBC Russkaya sluzhba*, February 18, www.bbc.com/russian/news-39016068.

DAN. 2016. "Zhiteli na mitinge osudili propagandy voiny i pomosh donetskich greko-katolikov VSU [Residents at the Meeting Condemned War Propaganda and Help of Donetsk Greek Catholics to the Ukrainian Army]." *Donetskoe agenstvo novostei*, January 29. https://dan-news.info/obschestvo/zhiteli-dnr-na-mitinge-osudili-propagandu-vojny-i-pomoshh-doneckix-greko-katolikov-vsu.html.

Derkachev, Vladimir, and Dmitrii Karcev. 2015. "DNR nashla sebe istoriyu [DPR Found Its History]." *Novaya gazeta*, February 6. www.gazeta.ru/politics/2015/02/06_a_6402557.shtml.

Derzhstat Ukrayiny. 2001. "Vseukrayinskiy perepys naselennya [All-Ukrainian Population Census]." Derzhavnaya sluzhba statystyky Ukrayiny. www.ukrcensus.gov.ua/.

Derzhstat Ukrayiny. 2016. *Statystychnyi sbirnyk Regiony Ukrayiny 2016. Chastyna I* [Statistical Proceedings Regions of Ukraine. Part I]. Kiev: Derzhavna sluzhba statystyky. www.ukrstat.gov.ua/druk/publicat/kat_u/2016/zb/12/zb_ru12015pdf.zip.

Dialog.ua. 2015. "Peredel sfer vliyaniya v DNR. Zakharchenko sozdaet batalyon dlya zashchity ot Khodakovskogo [Redistribution of Spheres of Influence in DPR. Zakharchenko Founds Battalion as a Protection against Khodakovskii]." *Dialog.ua*, October 23. www.dialog.ua/news/69986_1445587089.

Dolbilov, Mikhail, and Aleksei Miller. 2006. *Zapadnye okrainy Rossiiskoi imperii* [Western Peripheries of Russian Empire]. Moscow: Novoye literaturnoe obozrenie.

Donbass.ua. 2016. "Rossiya urezala finansirovanie DNR [Russia Cut Financing of the DPR]." *Donbass.ua*, February 2. http://donbass.ua/news/region/2016/02/02/rossija-urezaet-finansirovanie-dnr.html.

FaceNews. 2016. "Rossiya sokratila finansirovanie LNR i DNR na 50% [Russia Reduced Financing of the LPR and DPR by 50%]." *FaceNews*, March 15. www.facenews.ua/news/2016/311755/.

152   *Alexandra Šmídová and Tomáš Šmíd*

Generalna prokuratura Ukrayiny. 2014. "Samoproholosheni respubliky u Donetskii ta Luhanskii oblastyakh kvalifikovano yak terorystychni organizatsiyi [Self-declarared Republics in Donetsk and Luhansk Regions Qualified as Terrorist Organizations]." www.gp.gov.ua/ua/news.html?_m=publications&_c=view&_t=rec&id=138582.

Glavred. 2017. "'Bezzakonie i korruptsiya'. 'Politseiskyi DNR' pytalsya sbezhat v Germaniyu iz-za 'bespredela' kolleg ['Unlawfulness and Corruption.' 'DPR's Policeman Tried to Escape to Germany because of 'Unbridled' Colleagues]." *Glavred*, December 26. http://glavred.info/ukraine/bezzakonie-i-korrupciya-policeyskiy-dnr-pytalsya-sbezhat-v-germaniyu-iz-za-bespredela-kolleg-478148.html.

Glavstat DNR. 2018a. "Osnovnye demograficheskie pokazateli DNR za yanvar–fevral 2018 goda [Basic Demographic Indicators of the DPR in January and February 2018]." Glavnoe upravlenie statistiki DNR. http://glavstat.govdnr.ru/pdf/naselenie/osn_dem_pokazateli_0218.pdf.

Glavstat DNR. 2018b. "Chislennost naseleniya DNR na 1 marta 2018 goda [Population of the DPR on 1 March 2018]." Glavnoe upravlenie statistiki DNR. http://glavstat.govdnr.ru/pdf/naselenie/chisl_naselenie_0318.pdf.

Goncharenko, Nikolai G. 1991. *K istorii obrazovaniya i deyatelnosti DKR* [About the History of Formation and Existence of the DKR]. Lugansk: Molodogvardeets.

Gordon. 2015. "'Ministr DNR': proekt 'Novorossiya' zakryt ['Minister of the DPR': The Project of 'New Russia' Terminated]." Gordon, May 18. http://gordonua.com/news/war/ministr-dnr-proekt-novorossiya-zakryt-81447.html.

Goskomstat LNR. 2018. "Chislennost naseleniya Luganskoi Narodnoi Respubliki [Population of the Luhansk People's Republic]." Gosudarstvennyj komitet statistiki LNR. www.gkslnr.su/files/chisl_260318.pdf.

Gosudarstvennaya Duma. 2014. "Federalnyi konstitutsionnyi zakon o prinyatii v Rossiiskuyu Federatsiyu Respubliki Krym i obrazovanii v sostave Rossiiskoi Federatsii novykh subyektov – Respubliki Krym i goroda federalnogo znacheniya [Federal Constitutional Law on Accession of the Republic of Crimea to the Russian Federation and about Formation of New Subjects of the Russian Federation – The Republic of Crimea and the City of Federal Significance]." Ofitsialnyi internet-portal pravovoi informatsii. http://pravo.gov.ru/proxy/ips/?docbody=&nd=102171897.

HRW. 2015. "Ukraine: More Civilians Killed in Cluster Munition Attacks. Both Sides Have Used Widely Banned Weapon." *Human Rights Watch News*, March 19. www.hrw.org/news/2015/03/19/ukraine-more-civilians-killed-cluster-munition-attacks.

Ivanov, Feodor N. 2011. "Periodizatsiya istorii rekrutskoi povinnosti v Rossii v XVIII–XIX vekakh [Periodization of the History of Conscription in Russia of the 18th and 19th Centuries]." *Vesnik Voennogo universiteta* 27 (4): 134–140.

Kabinet ministriv. 2014. "Rozporyadzhennya No 1085-r. Pro zatverdzhennya pereliku naselenykh punktiv na teritoriyi yakykh organy derzhavnoi vlady tymchasovo ne zdiisnyuyut svoyi povnovazhennya, ta pereliku naselenykh punktiv, shcho roztashovani na liniyi zitknennya [On approval of the List of Settlements in the Territory of Which the State Authorities Temporarily Fail to Exercise Their Powers, and on the List of Settlements Located on the Line of Contact]." Zakonodavstvo Ukrayiny. http://zakon3.rada.gov.ua/laws/show/1085-2014-%D1%80?test=4/UMfPEGznhhogc.ZiNqdmrbHI4oMs80msh8Ie6.

Kanal 24. 2014. "Samoprovozglashennye rukovoditeli DNR sobirayutsya natsionalizirovat imushchestvo nekotorykh oligarkhov [Self-declared Leaders of the

The Donetsk & Luhansk People's Republics   153

DPR Ready to Nationalize Property of Some Oligarchs]." *Kanal 24*, May 17. http://24tv.ua/news/showNews.do?samoprovozglashennie_rukovoditeli_dnr_sobirayutsya_natsionalizirovat_imushhestvo_nekotorih_oligarhov&objectId=443904&lang=ru.

Kanygin, Pavel. 2017. "DNR protiv LNR: v chem intriga? [DPR against LPR: Where is the Plot?]." *Novaya gazeta*, November 23. www.novayagazeta.ru/articles/2017/11/23/74655-dnr-protiv-lnr-nedruzhestvennoe-pogloschenie.

Karmazin, Igor. 2017. "Ot Novorossii do Malorossii [From New Russia to Little Russia]." *Lenta.ru*, July 18. https://lenta.ru/articles/2017/07/18/malorossia/.

Kazanskii, Denis. 2017. Official Facebook page. Post dated March 27. www.facebook.com/den.kazansky?fref=ts.

Konstitutsiya DNR [Constitution of the DPR]. 2014. Ofitsialnyi sait Narodnogo soveta Donetskoi narodnoi respubliki [Official Site of the People's Soviet of the Donetsk People's Republic]. https://dnrsovet.su/zakonodatelnaya-deyatelnost/konstitutsiya/.

Kornilov, Vladimir. 2011. *Donetsko-Krivorozsskaya respublika: rasstrelyannaya mechta* [Donetsk-Krivoi Rog Republic: A Dream Shot to Pieces]. Kharkiv: Folio.

Korrespondent.net. 2014. "Referendum 11. maya v Donetske i Luganske: vse sobytiya [Referendum in Donetsk and Luhansk on 11 May: All Events]." *Korrespondent.net*, May 11. https://korrespondent.net/ukraine/politics/3361134-referendum-11-maia-v-donetske-y-luhanske-vse-sobytyia.

Korrespondent.net. 2017. "Nazvaniya Malorossiya ne budet: Zakharchenko peredumal [The Name Little Russia Will Not Come Into Existence: Zakharchenko Changed His Mind]." *Korrespondent.net*, August 9. https://korrespondent.net/ukraine/3876197-nazvanyia-malorossyia-ne-budet-zakharchenko-peredumal.

Kovalenko, Nikita, and Andrei Rezchikov. 2017. "Donbass i Krym zabyvayut ukrainskii yazyk [Donbass and Crimea are Forgetting the Ukrainian Language]." *Vzgliad*, June 7. https://vz.ru/world/2017/6/7/286098.html.

Kravchenko, Valerii. 2016. "Seryezony voiny na Donbasse [Grey Zones of the War in Donbass]." *Labirinty voiny*, January 15. http://war.intsecurity.org/2016/01/%D1%81%D0%B5%D1%80%D1%8B%D0%B5-%D0%B7%D0%BE%D0%BD%D1%8B-%D0%B2%D0%BE%D0%B9%D0%BD%D1%8B-%D0%BD%D0%B0-%D0%B4%D0%BE%D0%BD%D0%B1%D0%B0%D1%81%D1%81%D0%B5/.

Kurfürst, Jaroslav. 2017. "Ruský svět a neoeurasianismus: dvě strany jedné mince [The Russian World and Neo-Eurasianism: Two Sides of the Same Coin]." *Mezinárodní vztahy* 52 (3): 23–46.

Laruelle, Marlene. 2015. *The 'Russian World': Russia's Soft Power and Geopolitical Imagination*. Washington, DC: Centre for Golbal Interests.

Laruelle, Marlene. 2016. "The Three Colors of Novorossiya, or the Russian Nationalist Mythmaking of the Ukrainian Crisis." *Post-Soviet Affairs* 32 (1): 55–74.

Litvinova, Daria. 2017. "Separatists in Ukraine Declare Creation of New 'State' Malorossiya." *The Telegraph*, July 18. www.telegraph.co.uk/news/2017/07/18/separatists-ukraine-declare-creation-new-state-malorossiya/amp/.

Malorossiya. 2014. "Deklaratsiya o suverenitete Donetskoi narodnoi respubliki [Declaration of Sovereignty of the Donetsk People's Republic]." *Malorossiya*, April 7. http://malaya-russia.blogspot.com/2014/04/blog-post_894.html.

Møller, Bjørn. 2003. *Conflict Theory*. Working Paper No. 122. Aalborg: Institute for History, International and Social Studies. http://vbn.aau.dk/files/33796614/122.pdf.

Myrotvorec. 2015. Centr doslidzhennya oznak zlochyniv proti natsionalnoyi bezpeki Ukrayiny, svitu, bezpeki lyudstva, ta mizhnarodnogo pravoporyadku

[Center for Research of Signs of Crimes against the National Security of Ukraine, Peace, Humanity, and the International Law]. https://psb4ukr.org/criminal/.

OHCHR. 2014. *Report on the Human Rights Situation in Ukraine.* Geneva: Office of the United Nations High Commissioner for Human Rights. www.ohchr.org/Documents/Countries/UA/OHCHR_sixth_report_on_Ukraine.pdf.

O'Loughlin, John, Gerard Toal, and Vladimir Kolossov. 2017. "The Rise and Fall of 'Novorossiya': Examining Support for a Separatist Geopolitical Imaginary in Southeast Ukraine." *Post-Soviet Affairs* 33 (2): 124–144.

OON (Organizatsiya Obyedinennykh Natsii). 2014. "V Ukraine segodnya gibnet v 3 raza bolshe ludei, chem mesyac nazad [In Ukraine, Three Times More People Dies today than Month Ago]." *Novosti OON*, August 24. www.unmultimedia.org/radio/russian/archives/173238/#.VVsXW0Z25nD.

RBK. 2014. "Prorosiiskie aktivisty provozglasili Donetskuyu narodnuyu respubliku [Pro-Russian Activists Declared Donetsk People's Republic]." *RBK (Rosbizneskonsalting)*, April 7. http://top.rbc.ru/politics/07/04/2014/916183.shtml.

Regnum. 2017a. "Ekonomika DNR: medlennyi rost posle padeniya [Economy of the DPR: Slow Growth after the Fall]." *Regnum*, September 1. https://regnum.ru/news/2316546.html.

Regnum. 2017b. "Khroniki natsionalizatsii ukrainskikh predpriyatii v Donbasse: itogi pervogo dnya [The Chronicle of Nationalization of Ukrainian Companies in Donbass: Results of the First Day]." *Regnum*, March 2. https://regnum.ru/news/2244517.html.

Segodnya. 2017. "Emigrirovat iz Ukrayiny: pochemu grazhdane khotyat pokinut stranu [To Emigrate from Ukraine: Why Citizens Want to Leave the Country]." *Segodnya*, January 25. www.segodnya.ua/ukraine/emigrirovat-iz-ukrainy-pochemu-ukraincy-hotyat-pokinut-stranu-791309.html.

SGOV Novorosii. 2015. Server gosudarstvennych organov Novorosii [Server of State Bodies of New Russia]. http://donr.su/.

Shubin, Alexandr V. 2014. *Istoriya Novorossii* [History of New Russia]. Moscow: Olma Media Group.

Skorik, Mikhail. 2018. "Kak dela delayutsya. Na chem derzhatsya ekonomika i finantsy DNR i LNR [How the Work is Going. What are the Economy and Finance of the DPR and the LPR?]." *Spektr*, April 19. http://spektr.press/kak-dela-delayutsya-na-chem-derzhatsya-ekonomika-i-finansy-dnr-i-lnr/.

Snegirev, Dmitrii. 2017. "Otstranenie Plotnitskogo ne tolko stavit pod udar reputatsiyu Surkova, no i lomaet vsyu geopolitiku RF na vneshney arene [Deposing of Plotnitskii Not Only Endangeres the Reputation of Surkov, but Breaks All Geopolitics of the Russian Federation in the International Arena]." *Gordon*, December 12. http://gordonua.com/blogs/snegirev/otstranenie-plotnickogo-stavit-pod-udar-ne-tolko-reputaciyu-surkova-no-i-lomaet-vsyu-geopolitiku-rf-na-vneshney-arene-220903.html.

Solik, Martin, and Vladimír Baar. 2016. "Koncept 'Ruského sveta' ako nástroj implementácie soft power v ruskej zahraničnej politike [The Concept of the 'Russian World' as an Instrument of the Implementation of Soft Power in the Foreign Policy of the Russian Federation]." *Politické vedy* 19 (1): 8–47.

Sutyagin, Igor. 2015. *Russian Forces in Ukraine.* Briefing Paper. London: Royal United Services Institute. https://rusi.org/sites/default/files/201503_bp_russian_forces_in_ukraine.pdf.

Thinktanks.by. 2016. "Na finansirovanie DNR i LNR Rossiya tratit okolo 1 mlrd evro v god [Russia losts 1 mld Euro Per Year on Financing DPR and LPR]."

Thinktanks.by, January 19. https://thinktanks.by/publication/2016/01/17/na-finansirovanie-dnr-i-lnr-rossiya-tratit-okolo-1-mlrd-evro-v-god.html.

Tierney, Stephen. 2015. "Sovereignty and Crimea: How Referendum Democracy Complicates Constituent Power in Multinational Societies." *German Law Journal* 16 (3): 523–541.

Tsenzor.net. 2015. "Terroristy DNR vvedut konfiskatsiyu imushchestva bezhencev i smertnuyu kazn [Terrorists DNR Will Introduce the Confiscation of Property of Refugees and the Death Penalty]." *Tsenzor.net*, January 23. http://censor.net.ua/video_news/321281/terroristy_dnr_vvedut_konfiskatsiyu_imuschestva_bejentsev_i_smertnuyu_kazn_video.

TSN. 2017. "Pauki v banke: kto i pochemu v LNR boretsya za vlast i zachem DNR vvela voiska [Spiders in a Bank: Who and Why in LPR Fights for Power and Why DPR Formed an Army]." *TSN*, November 21. https://ru.tsn.ua/ato/pauki-v-banke-kto-i-pochemu-v-lnr-boretsya-za-vlast-i-zachem-dnr-vvela-voyska-1044395.html.

Ukrayinska Pravda. 2013a. "Na Maidan pryishlo blyzko 1500 oburenykh zupynkoyu evrointegratsiyi [About 1,500 People Dissatisfied with an End of the Integration of Ukraine to the EU Came to Maidan]." *Ukrayinska pravda*, November 22. www.pravda.com.ua/news/2013/11/22/7002691/.

Ukrayinska Pravda. 2013b. "'Regionaly' zvezly byudzhetnykiv na svii anty-evromaidan [Party of Regions Have Brought Workers to their Anti-Euromaidan]." *Ukrayinska pravda*, November 24. www.pravda.com.ua/news/2013/11/24/7002847/.

Varov, Andrei. 2017. *Istoriya osvoeniya Novorossiiskogo kraya* [History of the Annexation of the New Russia]. Moscow: Izdatelskie resheniya and Ridero.

Verkhovna rada Ukrayiny. 2015. "Postanova pro vyznannya okremykh raioniv, mist, selyshch i sil Donetskoyi ta Luganskoyi oblastei tymchasovo okupovanymy terytoriyamy [Resolution on the Recognition of Individual Districts, Cities, and Villages of Donetsk and Luhansk Regions as Temporarily Occupied Territories]." *Vidomosti Verkhovnoyi rady* 17 (128). http://zakon1.rada.gov.ua/laws/show/25419?test=4/UMfPEGznhhaP1.ZixKBnfzHI4s.s80msh8Ie6.

Vesti. 2014. "Referendum na Donbasse. Khronika sobytii [Referendum in Donbass. Chronicle of Events]." *Vesti*, May 11. https://vesti-ukr.com/donbass/51063-referendum-na-donbasse-hronika-sobytij.

Vremennyi osnovnoi zakon LNR [Provisional Fundamental Law of the LPR]. 2014. Narodnyi Soviet LNR [Peoples's Soviet of the LPR]. https://nslnr.su/zakonodatelstvo/konstitutsiya/.

Zakharchenko, Aleksandr. 2014. "Aleksandr Zakharchenko o religii [Aleksandr Zakharchenko on Religion]." *Youtube channel of the DPR*, May 21. www.youtube.com/watch?v=uKA8so9wZTg.

Zakharchenko, Aleksandr. 2015. "A. Zakharchenko o zhitelyakh DNR nakhodyashikhsya pod ukrainskoi okkupatsiei [A. Zakharchenko about Citizens of the DPR Living under the Ukrainian Occupation]." *Youtube channel of the DPR*, May 11. www.youtube.com/watch?v=CncBJ5pfvcI.

Section 4

How de facto states are sustained and instrumentalized

4.1 Factors of de facto states' sustainability

Vincenc Kopeček

This section explores the factors that have enabled four de facto states in the post-Soviet space to sustain their existence for more than a quarter of a century. Unlike the popular discourse which often considers de facto states as mere puppets of their powerful patrons (e.g. Williams 2008; Hille 2015; Coffey 2016; Pender 2017; Riegl and Doboš 2017), we claim that the security guarantees provided by an external patron are just a part of the complex phenomenon of sustaining de facto states (cf. Caspersen 2009). We do not downplay or even deny the importance of a patron state, which often uses de facto states in order to promote its own goals and interests, but we claim that it is the capacity and ability of a de facto state to build its own political institutions, what also plays a role. Whereas the military, economic, or political support from a patron state is crucial for de facto state to prevent its reintegration into the parent state, the internal viability of de facto state is crucial for surviving as a distinct polity, and not being absorbed by its powerful patron.

The very fact that a de facto state is, by definition, excluded from the international community – which would be capable of offering the kind of security guarantees associated with international recognition (Caspersen 2012, Loc. 987) – means that reintegration into the parent state represents a genuine threat. For this reason, most de facto states have a patron state, which provides security guarantees on a unilateral basis. In cases when a de facto state has lacked a patron state (e.g. the Chechen Republic of Ichkeria), or when the patron state has proved to be weak, unable, or unwilling to invest the necessary funds and effort into protecting the de facto state (e.g. Serbian Kraina, Biafra, or Tamil Eelam), the de facto state has indeed been forcibly reintegrated into the parent state. The long-term existence of a de facto state without a patron state is only possible if the parent state collapses, and thus no longer represents a threat to the de facto state; this has been the case of Somaliland (Caspersen 2012, Loc. 1106), though Somaliland does maintain amicable relations with several neighbouring states – especially with Ethiopia, which to a large extent acts as a surrogate patron state (Kaplan 2008, 153; Záhořík 2008, 22; Rudincová 2016).

160   *Vincenc Kopeček*

If we exclude the case of Somaliland, the existence of a strong patron state, willing to undertake military intervention to protect the de facto state, is a key condition for the existence of any de facto state; in the post-Soviet space this dependence was clearly demonstrated during the five-day Russian-Georgian war, in which Russian troops intervened to support South Ossetia, defeated the Georgian army, and also assisted Abkhazian troops in seizing the Upper Kodori Gorge – the last territory to which Abkhazia laid claim but did not control (Felgenhauer 2009).

In practice, security guarantees by patron states in the post-Soviet space have taken two forms: either the deployment of international peacekeeping forces that are dominated by troops from the patron state or the direct deployment of troops from the patron state (fighting alongside troops from the de facto state). The choice between these two options appears to have been guided by a clear and simple logic. In cases when the patron state has assumed the role of the mediating party and denied its military involvement in the conflict, the ceasefire agreement has been followed by the deployment of mixed peacekeeping forces including a significant contingent of troops from the patron state. This occurred in Transnistria, Abkhazia, and South Ossetia during the 1990s (Cornell 2001, 170, 174; King 2001, 533). However, it should be noted that although Russian peacekeeping forces in South Ossetia were indeed deployed only after the ceasefire agreement had been signed (Cornell 2001, 336), in Transnistria the Russian component of the tripartite peacekeeping forces represented a de facto continuation of the presence of the 59th Division of the 14th Soviet (since 1992, Russian) Army, which fought alongside the Transnistrian separatists (King 2001, 533 and 539–540). Likewise, Russia already had a military base in Abkhazia, at Bombora near Gudauta; around 400 Russian troops remained at the base separately from the international peacekeeping forces even after 2006, when the base (along with the other Russian bases on Georgian territory) was to be closed (Socor 2006).

The other form of security guarantee by patron states has involved the direct, unilateral deployment of troops from the patron state within the territory of the de facto state, as in the five-day Russian-Georgian war and the war in Karabakh. In such cases, the forces deployed by the patron state have gradually become integrated with the forces of the de facto state itself – as has been the case in Abkhazia and South Ossetia from 2008 onwards. In Abkhazia, predominantly Russian "peacekeepers" were replaced by around 3,500 regular Russian troops and 1,500 armed members of the Russian Federal Security Service (FSB – *Federalnaya sluzhba bezopasnosti*); some of these work alongside Abkhazian border guards patrolling the administrative border line between Abkhazia and Georgia (ICG 2013, 3–6). A similar situation exists in South Ossetia, where around 3,500 members of the Russian armed forces are stationed (Rukhadze 2013). South Ossetia and Abkhazia (which were both officially recognized by Russia in 2008) signed an agreement with Russia to create joint armed units (RT 2015; Morrison 2016); this process has been facilitated by the fact that the Abkhazian armed forces have been led by retired Russian generals and the fact that the South Ossetian Defence Minister (like a large proportion of the South Ossetian government) is a Russian citizen (Gayoso 2013, 112; DFWatch 2015).

A similar case exists in the NKR. Although the Republic of Armenia officially claims that it is not (and has never been) a direct participant in the conflict, from 1990s until 2018 it did not act as a mediator but instead it promoted the interests of the Karabakhi Armenians on the international stage. In fact, from 1990s until the Armenian Velvet Revolution of 2018, which brought the change of government, leading representatives of the Republic of Armenia, such as presidents, prime ministers, or defence ministers, were of Karabakhi origin. Armenia's role in the Karabakh conflict, however, seems to change after the Armenian Velvet Revolution of 2018. Not only the leaders of Karabakhi origin were deposed, but the new Prime Minister of the Republic of Armenia, Nikol Pashinyan, stressed that Armenia's foreign policy should me more Armenia-centred and that in the talks with Azerbaijan, he would represent Armenia, not the NKR (Abrahamyan 2018). However, despite the partial shift in Armenia's policy towards the NKR, the Republic of Armenia still provides a direct security guarantee to the NKR as its troops serve in Karabakh alongside the forces of the Nagorno-Karabakh Defence Army (Kolstø and Blakkisrud 2008, 490).[1] There are also close links between the membership of both armies; high-ranking officers in the Armenian army are often Karabakhi Armenians, but this, again, seems to change as Pashinyan's government is probably preparing to dismiss generals of Karabakhi origin (Mejlumyan 2018).

As Chapters 4.2 and 4.3 demonstrate, the provision of security guarantees by patron states is not an end in itself; it is motivated either by the attempt to instrumentalize de facto states (i.e. to promote the patron state's own interests in the region by sustaining the existence of the de facto state) or by the need to intervene on behalf of ethnic kin-groups which created the de facto state. The first type of motivation is exemplified by Russia and its relationships with Transnistria, South Ossetia, Abkhazia, and to a certain extent also the NKR. The second type can be seen in the relation between the Republic of Armenia and the NKR. In cases of the second type we speak not only of a patron state but also of a kin-state. However, a patron kin-state does not merely use the de facto state as a means of promoting its own interests. The relationship between the two entities is a complex one, in which the de facto state, though weaker than the patron state, is nevertheless able to influence public opinion in the patron state (by appealing to notions of ethnic, cultural, or historical kinship) to such an extent that the patron state is willing to intervene on behalf of the de facto state – even if such intervention comes at a cost to the patron state. Even the overt instrumentalization of de facto states requires a certain degree of legitimization. In the case of Russia, this process is manifested in the issuing of passports to the inhabitants

162   *Vincenc Kopeček*

of de facto states, who are then considered to be Russian citizens; if they are threatened, Russia then cites the principle of Responsibility to Protect, and is willing to undertake military intervention to protect its citizens (see Chapter 4.3).

Besides direct or indirect military support, patron states are also crucial for de facto states from the economic point of view. All present-day post-Soviet de facto states (excluding the DPR and LPR) are relatively small entities with populations between tens of thousands and a few hundreds of thousands people, and despite the fact that some of them have certain economic potential, they are definitely not economically self-sufficient – the chief reason being the war devastation of industry and infrastructure, declining population, and a factual isolation from the rest of the world, which causes serious problems in foreign trade and investment (King 2001, 535–538; Kolstø and Blakkisrud 2008, 493–498).

All present-day post-Soviet de facto states count on patron states' direct budget support; however, there are significant differences among individual cases. Whereas the Russian direct subsidies to the South Ossetian budget make up incredible 98% (Chitadze 2013, 110; Rukhadze 2015), in the case of Transnistria it is "only" 70% (Puiu 2015), and in the case of Abkhazia between 35% and 60% (Rimple 2015). Finally, Armenia's subsidies to the NKR's budget make up about 50% (Krüger 2010, 111). The Abkhazian case is particularly interesting, as the amount of Russian subsidies seem to be directly related to Abkhazia's conformity to Russia's demands (Rukhadze 2015). However, Russia's financial generosity towards its client de facto states has been reportedly weakened after 2014. The reason seems to be twofold: declining Russian economy and the fact that there are two more entities Russia has to support financially – the Donetsk and Luhansk People's Republics.[2]

De facto states are also more or less integrated into their patron states' economies. In most cases, patron states are de facto states' main trade partners and provide the only trade link with the rest of the world, and de facto states also unilateraly adopted patron states' currencies (King 2001, 541–542; Gerrits and Bader 2016, 301). There is, however, one exception – Transnistria. Not only has Transnistria introduced its own (although nonconvertible) currency – the Transnistrian rouble (Popescu 2013, 123) – but its economy is more oriented towards Moldova and the EU than Russia and the EEU. There are several reasons for that: First, unlike South Ossetia, Abkhazia, and Nagorno-Karabakh, Transnistrian economy survived the brief war almost untouched. Second, unlike Georgia and Azerbaijan, Moldova did not close the "borders" with its breakaway region and enables Transnistrian companies to export not only to Moldova but also to the European and World markets. Third, thanks to the combination of cheap labour and relatively good quality of its products (mainly steel, textile, and cement), Transnistrian industry is quite competitive (King 2001, 537–538, 564; Kolstø and Blakkisrud 2008, 107; Eurasianet 2016).

Factors of de facto states' sustainability   163

Other factors enabling de facto states to be sustained and to develop as state entities must be sought within the de facto state itself – in its ability to build democratic political institutions through which it gains both external and (especially) internal legitimacy (Berg and Mölder 2012; von Steinsdorff and Fruhstorfer 2012; Kopeček, Hoch, and Baar 2016), thus preventing it from being absorbed not only by its parent state but also by its patron state. This applies particularly in the cases of Abkhazia and the NKR, which during the first decade of the 21st century adopted the so-called democratization-for-recognition strategy as a means of achieving international recognition (i.e. earned sovereignty). Although this strategy has not been successful *per se*, even the partial democratization of these two entities has enabled self-confident autonomous political communities to emerge (as Chapter 4.5 shows). While Transnistria and South Ossetia are seeking incorporation into their patron state (BBC 2014; Fuller 2016) – a solution which, especially in the case of South Ossetia, has not yet been implemented due to Russian instrumentalization of the conflict and also due to constrains of international politics and law – Abkhazia and the NKR are attempting to build their own separate state entities. South Ossetia signed an integration agreement with Russia in 2015, but in Abkhazia the plans to sign a similar document met with considerable public opposition; although ultimately Abkhazia was forced to sign an agreement, which in many respects makes it subordinate to Russia, the final version of the text omitted references to integration and spoke "merely" of strategic partnership. Indeed, the Abkhazian Parliament has still not yet approved draft legislation permitting the sale of real estate to foreign citizens (i.e. primarily Russians), even under the strongly pro-Russian presidency of Raul Khajimba (Rukhadze 2015; DFWatch 2016).

The NKR likewise takes a somewhat negative stance towards the possibility of integration into its patron state. When the Karabakh Movement was in its infancy, in the late 1980s, its aim was for Nagorno-Karabakh to become an integral part of what was then the Armenian SSR. However, sociological surveys indicate that for more than a decade, public opinion on this question within the NKR has been divided into two roughly equal camps (Regnum 2003; O'Loughlin, Kolossov, and Toal 2014, 449; IPSC 2016, 40); support for independence grew after the four-day war with Azerbaijan in April 2016. The goal of an independent NKR enjoys particularly strong support among younger people, up to the age of 31 (IPSC 2016, 41), and the idea of integration into the Republic of Armenia is highly unpopular among the NKR's political representatives. In 2015 only two small political parties (out of a total of five parliamentary parties) supported integration, neither of them government parties.[3] However, the support for the integration of the NKR into the Republic of Armenia may be a subject of change after the Armenian Velvet Revolution of 2018. The new Armenian Prime Minister, Nikol Pashinyan, has on one side, stressed that integration of the NKR into the Republic of Armenia is a desirable solution of the conflict, whereas on the other hand he verbally clashed with the Karabakhi leaders (Abrahamyan 2018; Mejlumyan 2018).

164   *Vincenc Kopeček*

The following chapters address some of the issues mentioned in the previous paragraphs. Chapters 4.2–4.4 focus on relations between patron states and de facto states. In Chapter 4.3, Eduard Abrahamyan provides a comprehensive empirical analysis of Russia's agenda in the South Caucasus and brings clear evidence that Russia's involvement in conflicts in Abkhazia, South Ossetia, and (in a way) in Nagorno-Karabakh is driven by the Kremlin's determination to use these conflicts and de facto states which have emerged from them as a leverage on the three South Caucasian states – Armenia, Azerbaijan, and Georgia. He identifies two instruments (military deployment and passportization), and two mechanisms (Responsibility to Protect and Alliance Politics), which Russia uses in order to pursue its interest in the region.

Chapters 4.3 and 4.4 challenge the prevailing discourse that it is a powerful patron state which is unidirectionally imposing its will on a much weaker de facto state. In Chapter 4.3, Marcin Kosienkowski analyzes the role Russia plays in sustaining the Transnistrian de facto state. However, he also pays attention to the mutually beneficial exchange of goods and services between Russia and Transnistria and he convincingly demonstrates that although Transnistria is the weaker partner in this relationship, it is definitely not mere Russia's puppet.

In Chapter 4.4, on the case of the NKR and the Republic of Armenia, Vincenc Kopeček shows that the patron state-de facto state relations are far more complex and much more colourful than is often expected. Whereas Russia's motives in its involvement in South Ossetia, Abkhazia, and Transnistria are driven by its great-power interests, Armenia's motivation for involvement in the Nagorno-Karabakh conflict is driven by ethnic solidarity and Karabakh's importance in Armenia's historical narrative. It does not mean, however, that the Republic of Armenia would not influence the Karabakhi internal politics. Nevertheless, besides the largely informal mechanisms used by the Republic of Armenia in order to tame their brethren in Nagorno-Karabakh, it is also the NKR which is conscious of its perceived importance and has developed its own informal mechanisms in order to secure Armenia's support.

Finally, in Chapter 4.5, Vincenc Kopeček focusses on internal factors which contributed to the sustaining of a de facto state. It demonstrates how Nagorno-Karabakh and Abkhazia have developed their political institutions which help them to survive as distinct political entities.

Notes

1 Although the Republic of Armenia continues to officially deny its deployment of troops in Karabakh, its direct involvement is essentially an open secret. Armenian forces are a clearly visible presence in the NKR, and Armenian troops are only distinguishable from their Karabakhi counterparts by wearing different insignia on their uniforms in the colours of the respective national flags: red-blue-orange in the case of Armenian troops, with a white pattern added to the NKR version (Interview with a Karabakhi official, October 2009).

2 Interview with a former Abkhazian politician, October 2015.
3 Interview with a representative of the *Dashnaktsutyun* party, October 2015, and interview with a representative of the *Sharzhum-88* political movement, October 2015.

Literature

Abrahamyan, Eduard. 2018. "Pashinyan Stiffens Armenia's Posture toward Karabakh." *Eurasian Daily Monitor* 15 (72). https://jamestown.org/program/pashinyan-stiffens-armenias-posture-toward-karabakh/.

BBC. 2014. "Moldova's Trans-Dniester Region Pleads to Join Russia." *BBC News*, March 18, sec. Europe. www.bbc.com/news/world-europe-26627236.

Berg, Eiki, and Martin Mölder. 2012. "Who is Entitled to 'Earn Sovereignty'? Legitimacy and Regime Support in Abkhazia and Nagorno-Karabakh." *Nations and Nationalism* 18 (3): 527–545.

Caspersen, Nina. 2009. "Playing the Recognition Game: External Actors and De Facto States." *The International Spectator* 44 (4): 47–60.

Caspersen, Nina. 2012. *Unrecognized States. The Struggle for Sovereignty in the Modern International System*. Cambridge: Polity Press.

Chitadze, Nika. 2013. "Georgia's National Security and Regional Policy after the August 2008 War." In *Reassessing Security in the South Caucasus: Regional Conflicts and Transformation*, edited by Dr Annie Jafalian, 105–116. Farnham, UK and Burlington, VT: Ashgate Publishing, Ltd.

Coffey, Luke. 2016. "South Ossetia Referendum is Not Legal." *Al Jazeera*, April 16. www.aljazeera.com/indepth/opinion/2016/04/south-ossetia-referendum-legal-160414060118260.html.

Cornell, Svante E. 2001. *Small Nations and Great Powers. A Study of Ethnopolitical Conflict in the Caucasus*. Richmond: Curzon Press.

DFWatch. 2015. "Russian General, Wounded in 2008, Appointed at Abkhazian Army Military Command." *Democracy & Freedom Watch*, May 19. http://dfwatch.net/russian-general-wounded-in-2008-appointed-at-abkhazian-army-military-command-35811.

DFWatch. 2016. "Abkhazia Shelves Proposal to Allow Sale of Real Estate to Foreigners." *Democracy & Freedom Watch*, April 22. http://dfwatch.net/abkhazia-shelves-proposal-to-allow-sale-of-real-estate-to-foreigners-41968.

Eurasianet. 2016. "Moldova: Separatist Transnistria Region Reorienting Trade from Russia to EU." *Eurasianet*, May 4. www.eurasianet.org/node/78636.

Felgenhauer, Pavel. 2009. "After August 7: The Escalation of the Russia-Georgian War." In *The Guns of August: Russia's War in Georgia*, by Svante E. Cornell and S. Frederick Starr, 162–180. Abidgdon and New York: Routledge.

Fuller, Liz. 2016. "South Ossetia Postpones Referendum on Accession to Russian Federation." *Radio Free Europe / Radio Liberty*, May 30, sec. Caucasus Report. www.rferl.org/content/georgia-russia-south-ossetia-accession-referendum-delay/27766068.html.

Gayoso, Carmen A. 2013. "The Promulgation of Anti-Democratic Norms in South Ossetia." In *International Dimensions of Authoritarian Persistence: Lessons from Post-Soviet States*, edited by Rachel Vanderhill and Michael E. Aleprete, 105–124. Plymouth: Lexington Books.

Gerrits, Andre, and Max Bader. 2016. "Russian Patronage over Abkhazia and South Ossetia: Implications for Conflict Resolution." *East European Politics* 32 (3): 297–313.

166 Vincenc Kopeček

Hille, Kathrin. 2015. "Georgia Wary of Moscow Deals with South Ossetia and Abkhazia." *Financial Times*, February 18. www.ft.com/content/cfa4e440-b78c-11e4-8807-00144feab7de.

ICG. 2013. *Abkhazia: The Long Road to Reconciliation.* Europe Report N 224. Brussels: International Crisis Group. https://d2071andvip0wj.cloudfront.net/224%20 Abkhazia%20-%20The%20Long%20Road%20to%20Reconciliation.pdf.

IPSC. 2016. *Opinion Polls in Nagorno-Karabakh: Comparative Results from 2015 and 2016.* Yerevan: Institute for Political and Sociological Consulting. www.eufoa. org/Comparative%20opinion%20polls_2015-2016__EN.pdf.

Kaplan, Seth. 2008. "The Remarkable Story of Somaliland." *Journal of Democracy* 19 (3): 143–157.

King, Charles. 2001. "The Benefits of Ethnic War: Understanding Eurasia's Unrecognized States." *World Politics* 53 (4): 524–552.

Kolstø, Pål, and Helge Blakkisrud. 2008. "Living with Non-Recognition: State- and Nation-Building in South Caucasian Quasi-States." *Europe-Asia Studies* 60 (3): 483–509.

Kopeček, Vincenc, Tomáš Hoch, and Vladimír Baar. 2016. "De Facto States and Democracy: The Case of Abkhazia." *Bulletin of Geography. Socio-Economic Series* 32: 85–104.

Krüger, Heiko. 2010. *The Nagorno-Karabakh Conflict: A Legal Analysis.* Heidelberg, New York, Dordrecht, London: Springer.

Mejlumyan, Ani. 2018. "Pashinyan Clashes with Nagorno-Karabakh Leaders." *Eurasianet* December 3. https://eurasianet.org/pashinyan-clashes-with-nagorno-karabakh-leaders.

Morrison, Thea. 2016. "Putin Signs Law on Ratification of Russian-Abkhazian Military Agreement." *Georgia Today*, November 26. http://georgiatoday.ge/news/5224/ Putin-Signs-Law-on-Ratification-of-Russian-Abkhazian-Military-Agreement.

O'Loughlin, John, Vladimir Kolossov, and Gerard Toal. 2014. "Inside the Post-Soviet De Facto States: A Comparison of Attitudes in Abkhazia, Nagorny Karabakh, South Ossetia, and Transnistria." *Eurasian Geography and Economics* 55 (5): 423–456.

Pender, Kieran. 2017. "Sukhumi in the Spotlight: Hope Amid the Ruins of a Pro-Russian Breakaway State." *The Guardian*, September 29. www.theguardian. com/cities/2017/sep/29/sukhumi-spotlight-hope-ruins-russia-abkhazia-georgia.

Popescu, Liliana. 2013. "The Futility of the Negotiations on Transnistria." *European Journal of Science and Technology* 9 (2): 115–126.

Puiu, Victoria. 2015. "Can Russia Afford Transnistria?" *Eurasianet*, February 18. www.eurasianet.org/node/72146.

Regnum. 2003. "44,9% Karabakhtsev – za suverennoe gosudarstvo, 48,3% – za prisoedinenie k Armenii [44,9% of Karabakhis – for Sovereign State, 48,3% – for Integration with Armenia]." *Regnum*, December 25. https://regnum.ru/news/ polit/197764.html.

Riegl, Martin, and Bohumil Doboš. 2017. "(Super)Power Rule: Comparative Analysis of Parent States." In: *Unrecognized States and Secession in the 21st Century*, edited by Martin Riegl and Bohumil Doboš, 85–108. Cham: Springer.

Rimple, Paul. 2015. "Economics Not Impacting Russian Support for Georgian Separatists." *Eurasianet*, February 13. www.eurasianet.org/node/7206.

RT. 2015. "Russia Signs Major Alliance Treaty with South Ossetia, Pledges Military Protection." *RT International*, March 18. https://www.rt.com/politics/241929-russia-ossetia-treaty-alliance/.

Rudincová, Kateřina. 2016. "Ethiopian Foreign Policy in the Horn of Africa: Informal Relations with Somaliland and their Possible Future Development." *Politeja* 42: 213–226.

Rukhadze, Vasili. 2013. "Russia Underscores Its Military Presence in Georgia's Breakaway Regions." *Eurasia Daily Monitor* 10 (101). https://jamestown.org/program/russia-underscores-its-military-presence-in-georgias-breakaway-regions/.

Rukhadze, Vasili. 2015. "In the Face of Recent Russian-Abkhaz Disagreements, Is Georgian-Abkhaz Dialogue Possible?" *Eurasia Daily Monitor* 12 (128). www.jamestown.org/single/?tx_ttnews%5Btt_news%5D=44139&no_cache=1.

Socor, Vladimir. 2006. "Russia's Retention of Gudauta Base – An Unfulfilled CFE TReatyCommitment." *Eurasia Daily Monitor* 3(99). https://jamestown.org/program/russias-retention-of-gudauta-base-an-unfulfilled-cfe-treaty-commitment/.

von Steinsdorff, Silvia, and Anna Fruhstorfer. 2012. "Post-Soviet de Facto States in Search of Internal and External Legitimacy. Introduction." *Communist and Post-Communist Studies* 45 (1–2): 117–121.

Williams, Paul. 2008. "No Comparison between Kosovo and South Ossetia." *Radio Free Europe / Radio Liberty*, August 17. www.rferl.org/a/No_Comparison_Between_Kosovo_And_South_Ossetia/1191723.html.

Záhořík, Jan. 2008. "Etiopie v současné severovýchodní Africe: vnitropolitický a mezinárodně-politický pohled [Ethiopia in Contemporary Northeastern Africa: A View from the Point of Internal and International Policy]." *Slovenská politologická revue* 8 (1): 2–33.

4.2 Unrecognized states as a means of Russia's coercive diplomacy? An empirical analysis

Eduard Abrahamyan

The collapse of the Soviet Union triggered the rise of a new political paradigm in the South Caucasus. In turn, ethnic conflicts and the emergence of de facto states determined the foreign policies and strategic objectives of regional actors and global powers as they dealt with the post-Soviet space. The post-Cold War order created a new security environment in which former geopolitical rivals found themselves engaged in cooperation and partnership, rather than competition. The situation did, however, offer scope for a re-emerging Russia to create certain instruments and mechanisms to exert political and economic influence upon its neighbourhood.

Russia occupies a rather specific position in this context, assigning to itself the role of the sole successor to the Soviet Union's geopolitical heritage. This assumption has in fact predetermined Moscow's political assertiveness and consistently defiant posture, as it has sought to radically reverse the post-Cold War order by imposing new rules designed to maintain Russia's dominance in neighbouring regions. This fundamental shift in Russia's foreign policy, which began gradually in the mid-2000s, became more evident in the 2008 Russian-Georgian war and was fully unveiled by the seizure of Crimea in 2014. In the scholarly literature it is termed "Russian revisionism" (Mead 2014).

Proactive involvement in the so-called peacekeeping and mediating initiatives targeted at territorial disputes and ethnic conflicts in the post-Soviet space has always been, and still remains, a priority of the Russian Federation (Chausovsky 2016). In fact, the dependency of de facto states on Russia has often been considered in Moscow as a core precondition for Russia's long-term involvement in states afflicted by ethnic and territorial conflicts (Van Herpen 2015).

Russia's realpolitik approach towards the de facto states in Transnistria, Abkhazia, South Ossetia, and Nagorno-Karabakh stands in stark contrast to the policies of the other key actors from the Western hemisphere. Realizing its critical role in the settlement of regional conflicts, Moscow, as part of its strategy, has embarked on a process of instrumentalizing the phenomenon of unrecognized states in an effort to bolster its influence over its nearest neighbours (Heritage Foundation 2016).

Unrecognized states and Russia 169

Russia's posture in this regard is fairly straightforward: Moscow maintains peacekeeping troops in Transnistria, standing behind the state institution-building of the breakaway region and being vocal against Moldova's Euro-Atlantic integration. Likewise, Russia recognized the de facto states in Abkhazia and South Ossetia in 2008 while continuing the incorporation and military-political absorption of their territories. It has deliberately sought to hinder Georgia's potential eligibility for and compatibility with NATO and the European Union (EU). Meanwhile, although it is one of the three mediators in the Minsk Group within the Organization for Security and Co-operation in Europe (OSCE), Moscow is bent on distributing lethal arms to both parties in the confrontation between Armenia and Azerbaijan. In this aspect, the situation surrounding the unrecognized state in Nagorno-Karabakh provides Russia's policymakers with a strategy for dealing with both Baku and Yerevan.

In order to retain the South Caucasus within its orbit, Moscow considered it both affordable and reasonable to utilize the de facto states in Abkhazia, South Ossetia, and Nagorno-Karabakh as instruments in order to regulate and limit the dynamics of integration by Georgia, Armenia, and Azerbaijan into Western institutions. To that end, Russia elaborated and imposed a range of instruments and mechanisms that facilitated the use of the unrecognized states as a means of coercive diplomacy vis-à-vis Tbilisi, Baku, and Yerevan (Breedlove 2016). This geopolitical ambition on Russia's part has to some extent determined the destiny of the de facto states.

Therefore, in order to convey a sense of the full spectrum of Russia's moves vis-à-vis the unrecognized states, it is essential to define and examine the key instruments and mechanisms that Moscow employs in connection with the phenomenon of de facto states. The term "instrument" in this particular case can be applied with reference to hardware or software means that Russia leverages to pursue its policy towards the political subjects and actors in the South Caucasus. The term "mechanisms" can be defined as the respective frameworks which enable Russia to enact the instruments it has devised. Analysis of these instruments and their confluence with the mechanisms will enable us to conceptualize and understand the specific framework of Russia's regional policy in the South Caucasus. In short, the main aim of this chapter is to unveil Russia's *modus operandi* in dealing with Georgia, Armenia, and Azerbaijan, whereby it uses the de facto states as instruments for purposes of intimidation and as coercive policy tools.

The instruments

Military deployments

The deployment of military boots on the ground is a vital component of the instruments used in the de facto states that are aimed at serving Russia's regional interests. This particular instrument exists in Transnistria, Abkhazia,

170   *Eduard Abrahamyan*

and South Ossetia, and it was imposed after the ceasefires there began. Likewise, Moscow has unambiguously confirmed its willingness and readiness to establish a military presence also in the NKR (Rustamov 2015). The ability of the warring parties there to wage new conflicts has kept open the question of whether to station an international peacekeeping contingent in Nagorno-Karabakh. This, in turn, has provided an opportunity for Russia to become involved and to design such an initiative (Sirkov and Baikova 2016).

A retrospective glance at the Kremlin's efforts to establish a military presence on the ground in Abkhazia and South Ossetia helps to shed light on Moscow's utilization of the breakaway unrecognized political entities to put pressure on Georgia. Having been involved to varying degrees in the South Ossetian and Abkhazian conflicts in 1991–1993, Moscow implicitly backed Shevardnadze in 1993 in his struggle for power against Zviad Gamsakhurdia. In return, it acquired the right to play a proactive role in the mediation between the fighting parties (Saakashvili 2013). In accord with Security Council Resolution 858, the UN established an Observer Mission in Georgia in August 1993. This mission, UNOMIG, aimed to ensure compliance with the ceasefire agreement between Georgia and Abkhazia that was reached on 27 July 1993 (UNSC Res. 858 1993).

However, the ceasefire was violated when the fighting escalated in September 1993. This escalation of the conflict led the UN to officially approve Russia's mediation and the deployment of peacekeeping military units from the Russian-backed Commonwealth of Independent States, at the official request and the consent of the warring sides (UNSC Res. 957 1994). In the short term, Moscow negotiated a ceasefire and a separation of forces agreement, thereby gaining broad scope for political manoeuvring and further influence. This, in turn, ultimately led to the gradual deterioration of Russia's relationship with Georgia. Interestingly, during the adoption of another Security Council resolution in 1994, Russia's involvement in the peace process was acknowledged to have been constructive. It was particularly stressed that the Russian Federation was facilitating the achievement of a "comprehensive political settlement of the conflict, including on the political status of Abkhazia, respecting fully the sovereignty and territorial integrity of the Republic of Georgia" (UNSC Res. 957 1994).

Almost the same process had taken place with regard to South Ossetia two years earlier, with one exception: the Joint Peacekeeping Force (JPKF) was made up of three battalions under Russian command, composed of Russians, Georgians, and North Ossetians. This peacekeeping body was agreed to during the negotiations held in Sochi in 1992 between Georgia and the South Ossetian forces, under the auspices of Moscow, in which the Russian side achieved a considerable – and in fact decisive – role in the further negotiation processes (Sammut and Cvetkovski 1996).

Needless to say, these steps provided a suitable rationale for Russia's regular interference in the internal affairs of the conflicting sides. The assurance of the status quo in both the Abkhazian and South Ossetian hotspots by the

Unrecognized states and Russia 171

stationing of military contingents made Russia indispensable to Georgia, and therefore made Georgia dependent on Moscow for several reasons.

In addition to the presence of Russian troops acting as peacekeepers, Moscow also dispatched its Railway Troops to Abkhazia in late 2007, with the aim of restoring the local infrastructure. Its political plan in the mid-term perspective was allegedly to de-blockade railway access to Georgia in order to restore direct communication with Armenia (Kobaladze 2008). This move sparked condemnation from Tbilisi because Moscow deliberately avoided seeking Georgia's approval to undertake this initiative. Incidentally, Russian railway troops in fact facilitated a later Russian military incursion, in August 2008 (Nichol 2008). This military contingent, posing as peacekeepers, primarily safeguarded Moscow's crucial role in the resolution of Georgia's territorial problems, cementing Russia's ability to interfere with Georgia's agenda for Abkhazia.

It is noteworthy that until the suspension of Russia's peacekeeping mandate in the aftermath of the conflicts in Abkhazia and South Ossetia in 2008, the Russian troops in the de facto states were officially responsible for the safety of their populations. This factor made the local populations increasingly dependent on Russia for their security (Ivannikov 2012). Furthermore, Russia's deployment of peacekeeping troops provided the momentum for rapid military action with the aim of irreversibly changing the strategic environment by creating a *fait accompli*; this has recently happened again, in Crimea (2014). Nevertheless, the instrument that was the Russian military presence on the ground acted first and foremost as a deterrent to any attempt by Georgia to recapture the breakaway territories. The biased attitudes of Russian peacekeepers surfaced in late May 2008 when Moscow's moves inexorably created scope for local military operations initiated by the South Ossetian authorities aimed at taking over the Georgian enclaves on Ossetian territory (Socor 2008). Located to the north and northeast of Tskhinvali, the capital of the de facto state of South Ossetia, the Georgian villages of Tamarasheni, Eredvi, Kehkvi, and Achabedi were (according to independently verified reports) attacked by the Ossetian militia literally a week prior to the large-scale Georgian offensive in August 2008 (HRW 2008; OSCE Report HDIM.DEL/320/08 2008; OSCE Report HDIM.DEL/321/08 2008).

While the South Ossetians sought to neutralize the Georgian enclaves, the Russian peacekeeping contingent did nothing to prevent or terminate the spreading hostilities (IIFFMCG 2009b). Later, it was accepted that the ambivalent stance taken by the Russian peacekeepers had the intention of provoking Georgia to take countermeasures (Nichol 2008).

As has been revealed by Moscow-based security and defence expert Pavel Felgenhauer, Russia had already planned in early June to trigger skirmishes in Abkhazia and South Ossetia in order to draw Georgia into a large-scale conflict, initially containing Georgian countermeasures by using its peacekeepers. Felgenhauer also asserted that the Russian military intervention into Georgia itself was pre-planned. Meanwhile, the headquarters of the

172 Eduard Abrahamyan

Russian peacekeeping contingent urged Georgia not to retaliate, vowing to act as a physical barrier between the belligerents if necessary. Simultaneously, the Russian command relocated its peacekeeping troops, stationing them along the line of contact between Tskhinvali and Georgia – thereby reinforcing the rear of the Ossetian militia, which, in turn, managed to gain control over the Georgian enclaves (Felgenhauer 2008a, 2008b).

Later, in the evening of 7 August, a heavy mortar bombardment of Georgian villages provoked Georgian President Mikheil Saakashvili to order a major assault on Tskhinvali. The de facto state's troops had thus been used as a "trap" to entangle Georgia in the conflict, clearly exposing the Russian peacekeeping mission to danger as an instrument for pushing Georgia off the NATO membership track. The de facto states in South Ossetia and Abkhazia were the operational environments where the "military deployment" instrument was utilized as a means of political coercion in regard to Tbilisi (Breedlove 2016).

To sum up, the Russian military deployment in Abkhazia and South Ossetia has become an important component in the instrumentalization of the de facto states in these breakaway regions of Georgia. This tool has been used in an attempt to keep Georgia vulnerable in its relations with Moscow and to dismantle Georgia's reformed army, in order to make NATO membership impossible and to undermine the stability of the Georgian state.

It is worth noting that since the outbreak of the conflict in 2008 and the subsequent unilateral recognition of Abkhazia and South Ossetia, the Russian presence on the ground in these territories has led to the emergence of a process known as borderization. The first attempt at borderization dates back to the spring of 2013, when Russian border guards erected border signs and barbed wire barricades in order to hinder movement between Georgia and South Ossetia. Borderization is a manifestation of Russia's pursuit of a strategy termed "escalation dominance" vis-à-vis Georgia. In the Russian strategic mindset, escalation dominance involves controlling the degree of conflict escalation in breakaway regions of Georgia in order to benefit Moscow's interests. Russia's concept of escalation dominance in the region is designed to manage the intensity of conflicts not only by preventing over-escalation but also in some cases by fomenting escalation. Borderization involves the regular seizure of territory, followed by the establishment of border controls along what is legally only an administrative boundary line – a process observed on multiple occasions and robustly condemned by the international community in 2010 and in 2015 (Horrell 2016). Russia stepped up borderization in 2015 and throughout the summer of 2016, encroaching on a Georgian village situated in the vicinity of the South Ossetian-Georgian demarcation line.

This chapter focusses predominantly on military deployment and passportization as key instruments in the utilization of de facto states by Russian foreign policy; it does not examine borderization in depth, as borderization is essentially an outcome of the efficient and systematic use of these two instruments.

Unrecognized states and Russia 173

Therefore, having previously reaped practical benefits from the activities of its troops in Abkhazia and South Ossetia, it is clear why Moscow is striving to deploy a similar contingent in the de facto state in Nagorno-Karabakh. Russia has attempted to set up a peacekeeping force in Nagorno-Karabakh, but so far it has been unable to do so. It is likely that the primary goal of Russia's mediation efforts between the conflicting parties in Armenia and Azerbaijan remains the deployment of troops to the contested de facto state of Nagorno-Karabakh.

Passportization

Passportization – the issuing of Russian passports to residents of the de facto states who want them – is the second important instrument that Moscow uses to ramp up its influence over the de facto states, laying a solid foundation for military intervention and direct involvement in the conflict. Passportization by a third country in a breakaway region represents a serious violation of the traditional state's territorial sovereignty. Georgia is a case in point.

In this regard, one of Vladimir Putin's remarks about the consequences of the Soviet Union's demise yields some useful context, indicating the core motivation for Russia's progressively more assertive posture in the unrecognized states. Speaking of the dissolution of the Soviet Empire as "the geopolitical catastrophe of the century", he stated, "as for the Russian people, it was a genuine tragedy. Tens of millions of our fellow citizens and countrymen found themselves beyond the fringes of Russian territory" (Putin 2015).

Putin set forth a concept according to which residents of the countries bordering on Russia, which share the Soviet heritage, would henceforth be treated as "fellow citizens and countrymen", spurred by the idea of re-establishing Russia's political, economic, and cultural superiority. This particular approach was the ideological basis for the passportization as practised in the de facto states of Abkhazia and South Ossetia, shortly after the separatist regimes in Abkhazia and South Ossetia were established (in 1992 and 1993, respectively).

The acknowledged constituent components of Putin's underlying strategy, which yields wide scope for the instrumentalization of the de facto states, are the so-called policy of passportization (which has been imposed since 2002–2003) and the Russian boots on the ground that facilitate the regions' military-political absorption, which has been discussed above (IIFFMCG 2009a). These two main components have turned the de facto states of Abkhazia and South Ossetia into client entities, re-designed as instruments in Russia's coercive policy towards Georgia.

While the political reasons for Russia's deployments of military troops posing as peacekeepers are more or less comprehensible, there is another instrument – passportization – which is less well-known but which has appreciably reinforced the process of instrumentalizing the de facto states.

174 *Eduard Abrahamyan*

Passportization means the mass granting of Russian citizenship, and consequently the issuing of passports to persons living in South Ossetia and Abkhazia. This means that the security of the vast majority of these Russian citizens, who do not live within the constitutional territory of the Russian Federation, is assured by the Russian military units that are fielded in that specific territory. These two components make up part of Russia's *modus operandi* vis-à-vis the de facto republics of Abkhazia and South Ossetia, both of which are breakaway states from Georgia. The phenomenon of passportization has resulted in the massive distribution of Russian Federation passports to the residents of Abkhazia and South Ossetia in the period 2002–2008, without Georgia's permission.[1]

From Georgia's perspective, the residents of the breakaway regions of Abkhazia and South Ossetia are Georgian citizens, even though they do not hold official documentation of that status. The authorities in Tbilisi have a reasonable belief that the policy of passportization is not only integral to Russia's attempt to coerce Georgia into abandoning its westward economic and political orientation, but that it also provides solid ground for a future Russian claim to sovereignty over these territories. Consequently, the passportization of Abkhazia and South Ossetia, their subsequent diplomatic recognition by Russia and a handful of other states, and the decision by Russia's policymakers to considerably reinforce their military assets on the ground have all been viewed as unlawful developments by Tbilisi.

Since 2003, Russia has utilized its policy of passportization as a tool to pressurize Georgia. It is worth mentioning that, at an earlier point in time, seeking to justify Vladimir Putin's preferred solution to the problem legally and in terms of international law, Russia's legislative body the Duma officially approved a new federal law on citizenship (Federalnyi zakon no. 18 cl. 2500). The law came into effect in 2002 and introduced a simplified procedure for conferring Russian citizenship on all those who had been (or whose ancestors had been) citizens of the Soviet Union. This notable amendment to Russia's citizenship law was soon exploited by tens of thousands of new applicants from South Ossetia and Abkhazia (IIFFMCG 2009a).

As has already been noted, the tensions between Georgia on the one hand and Abkhazia and South Ossetia on the other hand opened up an avenue for Russia's instrumental use of the de facto states in Georgia's breakaway regions, with the aim of disrupting Georgia's Euro-Atlantic path. Unrecognized Abkhazia and South Ossetia became convenient tools in Russia's strategy of coercive diplomacy by passportization and the consistent Russian military build-up, combined with economic and security dependence on Moscow.

In 2004 it became clear that the Russian-brokered peace talks between Abkhazia, South Ossetia and Georgia lacked any real prospects for success, and the talks eventually reached an impasse. Additionally, Russia increasingly indicated concern about and discontent with Georgia's westward path; this caused a deep crisis in bilateral relations and transformed Russia from

Unrecognized states and Russia   175

a broker/mediator in the process of conflict resolution to a direct party to the conflict. The main complaint from Moscow concerned Georgia's strong desire to join NATO, which in 2004–2006 became the critical point of contention in Russian-Georgian relations (German 2015).

In short, the existence of Russian citizens on the ground provided an opportunity for Russia to increase its direct control over the de facto states, making them in effect a part of Russia – a development which radically changed the logic of the conflict after the clashes in 2004. This has been an important instrument in Russia's coercive policy vis-à-vis the recognized states, as passportization has paved the way for Russia to "blackmail" Georgia if Tbilisi does not abandon its path of Euro-Atlantic integration. This has made the targeted states (Georgia, Moldova) politically insecure and much more susceptible to Moscow's regional ambitions. The passportization factor was put to effective use by Moscow on the eve of the South Ossetian war, providing Russia with a pretext of defending its own citizens and enabling it to intervene in Georgia via the mechanism of the Responsibility to Protect (R2P) concept that is advanced and accepted by the United Nations.

Mechanisms

Responsibility to Protect

Given the large number of Russian citizens who lived in both Abkhazia and South Ossetia by 2008, policymakers in Moscow started to push for Russia's sovereign right to engage directly in the conflict it was itself provoking, and which it believed was escalating. By doing so, Moscow counted on being able to exploit its instrument of passportization in order to enable it to apply the United Nations-approved concept of R2P. As a background condition to justify its military incursion into the de facto states and then into Georgia, Moscow alleged that the Russian peacekeepers' role had been disrupted by the Georgian offensive, which constituted an existential threat to Russian citizens on the ground. In particular, Moscow's commitment to "protect Russia's citizens", wherever they might live, was a core justification for the intervention in Georgia, which has been referred to as "Russia's 9/11" (Allison 2008).

The situation served as a convenient pretext for a military build-up, spurring the elaboration of a structural framework for the instrumental use of the de facto states by Russia. Russian officials' announcements and expressed standpoints frequently had an obvious pro-Ossetian and pro-Abkhazian character, provoking Georgia to consider a military solution to its territorial problems as inevitable.

Against this backdrop, the passportization process in Abkhazia and South Ossetia opened up an avenue for Moscow's policymakers to manipulate Georgia. It therefore came as no surprise that the more Georgia asserted its sovereign right to develop a closer relationship with NATO, the more often various officials in Moscow expressed "Russia's commitment to protect its citizens in Abkhazia and South Ossetia" (Van Herpen 2015).

Therefore, the international norm of R2P, in connection with Russia's regional interests, emerged as an active mechanism for instrumentalizing the passportization of the populations in the de facto states of Abkhazia and South Ossetia. A statement by Vitalii Churkin, Russia's UN representative, in which he explained the validity of Russia's military invasion of Georgia's internationally recognized territory, supports this argument. Specifically, Churkin stressed that "the Georgian military during the two days of operations committed war crimes and sought to initiate ethnic cleansing" (United Nations 2008). These two allegations paved the way for legitimizing the application of the R2P norm. Churkin unambiguously stressed that Russia was determined to defend its compatriots in South Ossetia in accordance with international law. Having created a strong basis for action via passportization, Russian armed forces invaded South Ossetia, expressly aiming to protect citizens of the Russian Federation from the Georgian offensive. As a consequence of the five-day conflict, the Russian President Medvedev emphasized that "historically, Russia remains a security guarantor for Caucasus nations", morally reinforcing the decision to intervene (Regnum 2008).

Moscow's use of the instrument of passportization to justify applying the R2P norm to intimidate and intervene in Georgia was entirely successful (Allison 2008). Although the key Western countries expressed immediate concern, and France raced to act as a mediator between Moscow and Tbilisi, neither NATO nor the EU were willing to offer a firm and robust deterrent to Russia's challenging actions. Using passportization to establish tangible, influential instruments, Russian policymakers adeptly instrumentalized the de facto states by exploiting a mechanism of international law.

Alliance Politics

As a consequence of the five-day conflict, Moscow officially declared its unilateral recognition of the independence of the breakaway regions of Abkhazia and South Ossetia as *de jure* states. It is highly likely that this particular move was made in order to ensure that Georgia remained perpetually vulnerable in terms of its territorial integrity, and therefore ineligible for NATO and EU membership. Although Moscow's military and political steps are acknowledged as the "obvious occupation" of the territories, in violation of Georgia's internationally recognized borders, from Russia's perspective, all the measures it applied were justified (OSCE Report HDIM. DEL/321/08 2008).

Following its recognition of the de facto states' independence, Moscow terminated the peacekeeping missions there and rushed to sign treaties of alliance, with the intention of harmonizing the establishment of military bases in Abkhazia and South Ossetia with Russia's constitution. This was possible because the de facto states in Abkhazia and South Ossetia are not sufficiently integrated into (or represented in) the international arena. Instead, these partially recognized states have fallen victim to the political ambitions of regional states – particularly Russia, which has emerged as a power challenging the post-Cold War order and questioning the political sovereignty of other post-Soviet states. Even though Moscow has formally recognized the independence of the de facto states in Abkhazia and South Ossetia, they are still not treated by Russia as independent entities under international law, but rather as clients or footholds for military retaliation against Georgia. In other words, Russia does not view them as truly independent states, as it loudly proclaims, even as it proceeds with its military build-up via the Alliance Politics mechanism discussed below.

Alliance Politics is the substantive mechanism that Putin's political elite has employed to create a range of military bases in Abkhazia and South Ossetia in order to strengthen its grip on the region. From Russia's perspective, Alliance Politics is directly linked to an entire spectrum of military deployments. A typical example of the utilization of Alliance Politics concerns one of the de facto states/frozen conflicts. It is the Armenian-Russian bilateral alliance signed in 1994, and subsequently cemented by Armenia's entry into the Moscow-orchestrated Collective Security Treaty Organization (CSTO) (Druzhinin 2016). In this case, Alliance Politics became the mechanism through which the instrument of military deployment was implemented. The existence of the de facto state/frozen conflict in Nagorno-Karabakh enabled Russia to establish its 102nd Military Base and 3624th Airbase in Armenia, which Russia has since used to exert pressure on Armenia with respect to other issues as well.

Alliance Politics is the most convenient mechanism for amplifying the political impact, economic dependence, and security incompetence of the de facto states – as well as of Russia's minor allies, such as Armenia. The perception that an existential threat emanates from Turkey, and the very real threat of the resumption of war in Nagorno-Karabakh, motivated Yerevan to grant Russia permission to maintain a military presence in Armenia. By exploiting such vulnerabilities and political disorientation, Moscow demonstrates that its military presence is an important guarantee of Armenia's security. In light of increasing tensions over the de facto state in Nagorno-Karabakh, and Moscow's cultivation of the concerns within Armenia, Russian troops have received the right of unlimited movement within the territory of Armenia. Taking into account Russia's unrestrained actions at its base in Crimea, the Russian base has morphed from a conceivable guarantor of Armenia's security into a grave threat to its sovereignty.

As has been stated by the former CSTO chief Nikolai Bordyuzha in February 2016, the central purpose of the Russian military base in Armenia is to serve Russia's regional interests, not to deter Turkey or Azerbaijan on Armenia's behalf (Badalyan 2016). Bordyuzha's confession buttresses the perception that if Yerevan were to be drawn into a conflict with Azerbaijan,

178 *Eduard Abrahamyan*

the Russian leadership – focussed as it is on manipulating both Yerevan and Baku via the de facto state in Nagorno-Karabakh – would see the military base in Armenia as a potential tool for applying pressure on either or both.

Until September 2013, Armenia explicitly sought to diversify its security and economic relationships through links to the EU and NATO. However, Alliance Politics and the military presence of Russia in Armenia have had psychological implications (see the following paragraph) amid continued and growing pressure from Moscow aimed at forcing Armenia to abstain from signing an Association Agreement with the EU. It is important to note that before September 2013, Russian officials frequently stressed their willingness to continue to supply arms to both Armenia and Azerbaijan, playing upon the most vulnerable aspect of both adversaries' foreign policies – the existence of the de facto state in Nagorno-Karabakh.

To substantiate and explain the psychological impact of Russia's Alliance Politics and military presence on Armenia's *populus*, it is important to acknowledge the appreciable effect of Russia's media in conjunction with the above-mentioned factors. For example, Russian or Russian-backed local media often emphasize the potential threat of Turkey (and recently also of the "Islamic State" terrorist organization) to Armenia's security. In this context, Armenia's alliance with Russia and the Russian military deployment are portrayed as a crucial prerequisite for Armenia's security and stability. The alleged threat from Turkey is portrayed as a repercussion of the situation with the de facto state in Nagorno-Karabakh. Such an approach is practical from Moscow's perspective, as Turkey's hypothetical threat to Armenia is the central narrative that is used in order to justify Russia's military projection and build-up on Armenian soil.

In 2010, as a result of the efficient use of such narratives to underpin Russia's Alliance Politics and military deployment, Moscow updated the conditions under which the 102nd military base operates in Armenia's territory. Russia's then-President Dmitrii Medvedev and his Armenian counterpart signed an extension to the lease up to 2044 (Grigoryan 2010). The basic document was also amended to redefine the conditions of Russia's military presence. This has provided Moscow with sufficient technical and legal capacity to "move into" any part of Armenia, potentially including the territory of the NKR. Therefore, the Russian military presence has significantly contributed to Moscow's influence over Yerevan and Baku.

As for Abkhazia and South Ossetia, shortly after Moscow's unilateral recognition of the independence of these breakaway territories, the Kremlin came up with a range of strategic agreements, officially making allies of the de facto states. In effect, Moscow has turned the territories of Abkhazia and South Ossetia into large-scale military training camps, stationing its bases no. 241 and no. 114 in their respective territories. In the shadow of this move, Moscow initiated an effort to boost its Anti-Access/Area Denial (A2/AD) capabilities along its Western strategic flank by stationing ballistic missile defence systems, accompanied by a large number of troops, in both Crimea and Abkhazia. In March 2015, the bilateral agreement of "Alliance and Strategic Partnership" between Russia and Abkhazia was put in place, which implies the strategic absorption of Abkhazia into Russia and the embedding of the de facto state into Russia's security and defence framework (Kavkazskii Uzel 2015). This situation has rendered Georgia's security even more vulnerable. In short, using Alliance Politics, Moscow has acquired the opportunity to use the de facto states' territory to deploy surface-to-surface ballistic missile systems – such as Tochka-U and Scud – that could easily reach Tbilisi (OSCE Statement PC.DEL/88/11 2011).

As for South Ossetia, Moscow appears to have exacerbated the current situation through its military build-up there. Vladimir Putin promised Abkhazia and South Ossetia "not declarative, but material support" and announced that Georgian aspirations for "speedy Atlantic integration" endangered their security (ICG 2008). In fact, Russia's alliance agreements with the de facto states merely give Russia wide scope for unlimited military deployments in Abkhazia and South Ossetia. Meanwhile, Russia has illustrated its reluctance to accept an initiative by the local authorities of South Ossetia to conduct a referendum on whether to join Russia, akin to the referendum in Crimea. Discussing the prospects for such a referendum, political analyst Sergei Markedonov has stressed that

> President Putin has always dodged the question of South Ossetia's status within Russia, hiding behind general statements about the will of the people and the responsibility of Georgian leaders for the loss of South Ossetia. The issue is neither rejected, nor receives serious consistent support.
>
> (Sorokina 2016)

Of course, if a referendum takes place, Russia could merely refuse to accept the de facto state, but the potential for a referendum functions as a means of amplifying the coercive nature of Moscow's policy towards Tbilisi. In other words, the referenda, in parallel with military deployments and passportization, represent an additional tool in the instrumentalization of the de facto states within the framework of Russia's regional policy.

Through its military build-up and its recognition of the de facto states, Moscow has complicated the future for Georgia even further by establishing the so-called "point of no return" in the security environment. In other words, the de facto states have actively become a new type of instrument in Russia's hands. This particular instrument entails pressuring Tbilisi in order to demonstrate that Russia is an "indispensable" participant in any effort to resolve the territorial conflicts, and to emphasize that the remedy for all of Georgia's ills is to be found in Moscow. Alternatively, as the military build-up proceeds, Moscow can use the de facto states as stepping stones for another potential military intervention in Georgia.

Conclusion

Based on a case study of Russia's policy towards the unrecognized states of Abkhazia, South Ossetia, and Nagorno-Karabakh, this chapter has sought to demonstrate how de facto states can be used by dominant actors as important tools for influencing regional politics in general, and the policies of nations affected by separatism in particular. A comprehensive empirical analysis of Russia's agenda in the South Caucasus since the early 2000s enabled the author to identify two distinct *instruments* and two *mechanisms* in Russia's regional agenda. The instruments of maintaining a military presence and granting Russian citizenship to the population of South Ossetia and Abkhazia enabled Moscow to strengthen its grip over the unrecognized republics prior to Russia's formal recognition of their independence in 2008. The mechanisms of military deployments and passportization have enabled Moscow to legitimize its presence in Georgia's breakaway republics, paving the way for the use of the principle of R2P, as proved useful in the South Ossetia War of August 2008.

Russia's military deployment in Armenia has enabled Moscow to draw Armenia – and to an extent also Nagorno-Karabakh – into its orbit, binding Yerevan to it by means of Alliance Politics. Consequently, while Russia's grip over South Ossetia and Abkhazia has been rather direct, its influence on the Nagorno-Karabakh conflict has been relatively indirect – because it is Yerevan, not Stepanakert, towards which Russia's influence has been directed. The existence of de facto states in the South Caucasus has allowed Moscow to maintain its influence in the region – and to take an increasingly assertive stance toward Armenia, Azerbaijan, and Georgia. This explains Moscow's interest in blocking a lasting solution to the region's "protracted conflicts" while keeping the de facto states alive both economically and politically. Although the findings of this chapter are predominantly empirical and context-bound, they can have general relevance in pointing to the use of the phenomenon of de facto states as a tool in the exercise of power politics.

Note

1 It is worth mentioning that the passportization has been primarily welcomed by the populations of the unrecognized states of Abkhazia and South Ossetia, since it ostensibly gives them a means to travel internationally as Russian citizens – something they would not otherwise be able to do. Nevertheless, in most cases, the passports are in effect issued by Russian authorities in Sukhumi and Tskhinvali – and this is clearly stated in these passports. While some countries probably accept these passports, it is difficult to obtain a Schengen visa with such a passport.

Literature

Allison, Roy. 2008. "Russia Resurgent? Moscow's Campaign to 'Coerce Georgia to Peace'." *International Affairs* 84 (6): 1145–1146.

Badalyan, Akob. 2016. "Rossiiskaya voennaya baza poteryala svoi smysl [Russian Military Base Lost Its Raison d'être]." *INOSMI.ru*, February 18. http://inosmi.ru/military/20160218/235442591.html.

Unrecognized states and Russia 181

Breedlove, Gen. Philip. 2016. "Document: 2016 U.S. European Command Posture Statement." *USNI News*, February 25. https://news.usni.org/2016/02/26/document-2016-u-s-european-command-posture-statement.

Chausovsky, Eugene. 2016. "Russia's Evolving Role in the South Caucasus." *Stratfor*, March 9. www.stratfor.com/sample/analysis/russias-evolving-role-caucasus.

Druzhinin, Aleksei. 2016. "Inter-state Relations between Russia and Armenia." *Ria Novosti*, April 7. http://ria.ru/spravka/20160407/1403365727.html.

"Federalnyi zakon no. 18 cl. 2500 O grazhdanstve Rossiiskoi federatsii [Federal Law No 18, cl. 2500 On citizenship of the Russian Federation]." Enacted May 31, 2002, as amended December 31, 2014. http://pravo.gov.ru/proxy/ips/?docbody=&nd=102076357.

Federalnyi, Pavel. 2008a. "Rossiya nachnet voinu protiv Gruzii predpolozhitelno v Avguste [Russia Will Start the War against Georgia Probably in August]." *Georgia-Online*, June 20. www.apsny.ge/news/1213985330.php.

Felgenhauer, Pavel. 2008b. "The Russian-Georgian War was Preplanned in Moscow." *Eurasia Daily Monitor* 5 (156). www.jamestown.org/single/?no_cache=1&tx_ttnews%5Btt_news%5D=33888.

German, Tracey. 2015. "Heading West? Georgia's Euro-Atlantic Path." *International Affairs* 91 (3): 601–614.

Grigoryan, Marianna. 2010. "Russia Signs Base Lease Extension with Armenia." *Eurasianet*, August 20. https://eurasianet.org/russia-signs-base-lease-extension-with-armenia.

Heritage Foundation. 2016. "Europe: As a Key Strategic Region, How Threatened are U.S. Interests in Europe?" *2016 Index of US Military Strength*. http://index.heritage.org/military/2016/assessments/threats/europe/.

Horrell, S. 2016. *A NATO Strategy for Security in the Black Sea region*. Washington, DC: The Atlantic Council.

HRW. 2008. "Georgian Villages in South Ossetia Burnt, Looted." *Human Rights Watch News*, August 12. www.hrw.org/news/2008/08/12/georgian-villages-south-ossetia-burnt-looted.

ICG. 2008. *Georgia and Russia: Clashing over Abkhazia*. Europe Report N 193. Tbilisi/Brussels: International Crisis Group. www.crisisgroup.org/file/1871/download?token=ddPc8xl0.

IIFFMCG. 2009a. *September 2009 Report 1*. Independent International Fact-Finding Mission on the Conflict in Georgia. http://news.bbc.co.uk/1/shared/bsp/hi/pdfs/30_09_09_iiffmgc_report.pdf.

IIFFMCG. 2009b. *September 2009 Report 3*. Independent International Fact-Finding Mission on the Conflict in Georgia. http://news.bbc.co.uk/1/shared/bsp/hi/pdfs/30_09_09_iiffmgc_report.pdf.

Ivannikov, Oleg. 2012. "Mirotvorcheskaya deyatelnost Rossii v Yuzhnoi Osetii v 1992–2008 gg: Predposilki, rezultaty, osnovnye uroki [Russia's Peacekeeping Operation in South Ossetia 1992–2008: Prerequisites, Results, Core Lessons]." *Ia Rex*, July 13. www.iarex.ru/articles/27439.html.

Kavkazskii Uzel. 2015. "Dogovor mezhdu Rossiiskoi Federatsiei i Respublikoi Abkhaziya o soyuznichestve i strategicheskom partnerstve [Treaty between the Russian Federation and the Republic of Abkhazia on Cooperation and Strategic Partnership]." *Kavkavskii Uzel*, March 5. www.kavkaz-uzel.ru/articles/252910/.

Kobaladze, Giorgi. 2008. "Zheleznodorozhnye voiska Rossii chinyat dorogi v Abkhazii [Railway Units of Russian Army are repairing railways in Abkazia]." *Radio Svoboda*, June 2. www.svoboda.org/content/article/450185.html.

182 *Eduard Abrahamyan*

Mead, Walter Russell. 2014. "The Return of Geopolitics: The Revenge of the Revisionist Powers." *Foreign Affairs*, April 17. www.foreignaffairs.com/articles/china/2014-04-17/return-geopolitics.

Nichol, J. 2008. *Russia-Georgia Conflict in South Ossetia: Context and Implications for U.S. Interests*. Washington, DC: Congressional Research Service. www.research.policyarchive.org/20063_Previous_Version_2008-08-29.pdf.

OSCE Report HDIM.DEL/320/08. 2008. Ethnic Cleansing of Georgians Resulted from Russian Invasion and Occupation since August 8, 2008. www.osce.org/odihr/34091?download=true.

OSCE Report HDIM.DEL/321/08. 2008. Violations of IHL and IHRL in Course of an International Armed Conflict: Torture, Inhuman and Degrading Treatment, Hostage Taking, etc. www.osce.org/odihr/34092?download=true.

OSCE Statement PC.DEL/88/11. (2011). On Installation by the Russian Federation of Tactical Operational Missile Launch System "Scarab B", also Known as "Tochka-U" on the Occupied Tskhinvali Region of Georgia. www.osce.org/pc/76807?download=true.

Putin, Vladimir. 2015. "Interview with Charlie Rose." *CBS News*, September 29. www.youtube.com/watch?v=83eJnDbnVQs.

Regnum. 2008. "Medvedev: Russia Has Been and Will Remain the Guarantor of the Security of the Peoples of the Caucasus." *Regnum*, August 8. https://regnum.ru/news/polit/1038419.html.

Rustamov, E. 2015. "Vafa Guluzade: Rossiia i v proshlom predlagala vvedenie mirotvorcheskikh sil v Karabakh [Vafa Guluzade: Even in the Past Year, Russia Offered Stationing of Peacekeeping Forces in Karabakh]." *1News.az*, 10 April. www.1news.az/authors/oped/20150410115902116.html.

Saakashvili, Mikheil. 2013. "Speech at the Sixty-eighth General Assembly of the UN." www.youtube.com/watch?v=B4vSocpB9no.

Sammut, Dennis, and Nikola Cvetkovski. 1996. *Confidence Building Matters: The Georgia-South Ossetia Conflict*. London: VERTIC.

Sirkov, Nikolai, and Tatiana Baikova. 2016. "Vladimir Putin postaraetsya oslabit karabakhskii uzel [Vladimir Putin Will Managed to Weaken the Caucasian Knot]." *Izvestiya*, April 18. http://izvestia.ru/news/610417.

Socor, Vladimir. 2008. "Moscow Encourages North-South Ossetian Irredentism Against Georgia." *Eurasia Daily Monitor* 5 (97). www.jamestown.org/single/?tx_ttnews%5Btt_news%5D=33639&no_cache=1#.V3wQlbgrLP4.

Sorokina, Irina. 2016. "Adjournment: South Ossetia Postpones Referendum." *Russian International Affairs Council*, June 6.

United Nations. 2008. "UN Security Council again Holds an Emergency Meeting on the Situation in South Ossetia." *UN News Centre*, August 8. www.un.org/russian/news/story.asp?newsID=10057#.V1XImZErLP4.

UNSC Res. 858. 1993. Resolution no. 858, Adopted by the United Nations Security Council at its 3268th Meeting. https://documents-dds-ny.un.org/doc/UNDOC/GEN/N93/466/03/IMG/N9346603.pdf?OpenElement.

UNSC Res. 957. 1994. Resolution no. 957, Adopted by the United Nations Security Council at its 3407th Meeting. https://documents-dds-ny.un.org/doc/UNDOC/GEN/N94/298/25/PDF/N9429825.pdf?OpenElement.

Van Herpen, M. H. 2015. *Putin's Wars: The Rise of Russia's New Imperialism*. New York: Rowman & Littlefield.

4.3 The patron-client relationship between Russia and Transnistria

Marcin Kosienkowski

The patron-client concept originated in anthropological studies to describe interpersonal relations in small communities and then it has been transferred to higher levels, including the international level. The patron-client relationship in the international sphere can be defined as a mutually beneficial exchange of goods and services between two international actors, mainly states that are unequal in terms of their military, economic, and political power. Benefits may be both tangible and intangible, for example, a patron (a stronger actor) may provide economic aid to a client (a weaker actor) in return for the latter's diplomatic support. Essentially, the resources exchanged are non-comparable; they are, however, valued by both parties. The international patron-client relationship has been studied more intensively, both theoretically and empirically, since the 1980s. The bulk of associated literature covers the Cold War era, focussing predominantly on patronage over client states from Africa, Asia, and Latin America by the two superpowers; the United States and Soviet Union (e.g. Shoemaker and Spanier 1984; Carney 1989; Efrat and Bercovitch 1991). The patron-client relations between various states in the contemporary post-Cold war era have also been afforded some consideration (e.g. Bar-Siman-Tov 1998, Ciorciari 2015, Veenendaal 2017).

While students of the patron-client relationship focus predominantly on relations between states, the international patron-client model has been extended to other types of international actors too. One example is collective patrons and clients consisting mainly of intergovernmental organizations and their member states (Ravenhill 1985). However, other actors are also included, such as "mini-states" that appeared at the beginning of the 1990s in Somalia when its central government collapsed; together they formed a collective client of the United Nations (Bariagaber 1996). Another example is Taiwan, acting as a patron of some microstates and, at the same time, as a client of the United States (Veenendaal 2017). Due to a higher level of international recognition, it can be classified as an entity sui generis, placed between universally recognized states and de facto states that lack international recognition or enjoy it only at a minimal level. Finally, more recently, attempts have been made to employ the international patron-client concept

184 *Marcin Kosienkowski*

to analyze relations between patron states and post-Soviet client de facto states, that is, relations between Russia and Abkhazia, South Ossetia, and Transnistria as well as between Armenia and Nagorno-Karabakh (Devyatkov 2017; Kolstø and Blakkisrud 2017; Berg and Vits 2018).

This chapter aims to analyse, in a more systematic way, the patron-client relationship between Russia and Transnistria since the beginning of the 21st century. While Russia (initially the Soviet Union) has arguably exercised patronage over Transnistria since its proclamation in September 1990 (see map 9), their special relationship has become more palpable since around 2003. More precisely, this work investigates Russia's and Transnistria's rationale behind the establishment of their patron-client relations, the benefits derived by both parties from their relationship, and the efforts to legitimize their association. It then discusses the dynamics of the patron-client relationship between Russia and Transnistria. The chapter draws on previous theoretical and empirical research on relations between patrons and clients, covering both the Cold War and post-Cold War periods, as well as on secondary sources on Transnistria and statements made by the Russian and Transnistrian authorities.

Russia's patronage: rationale, benefits, and legitimization

Rationale

The main reason why stronger states establish and maintain patronal relations with weaker countries is that they seek to advance their national interests in this way (cf. Bariagaber 1996, 171–172). During the Cold War the two superpowers formed the patron-client relationship with African, Asian, and Latin American states because they expected to gain certain advantages over each other in their competition for influence over the world (Shoemaker and Spanier 1984, 11–14; Bercovitch 1991, 14–19). As pointed out by Kunihiko Imai and Peggy Ann James (1996, 166) not long after the end of the Cold War, "the major actors and their relative power may change, but their structural competition for influence over weaker states will remain a constant factor".

One such post-Cold War era rivalry is the competition between Russia and the West over the post-Soviet area. Moscow considers this region a sphere of its exclusive influence or a zone of its privileged interest and seeks to counterbalance the involvement of external actors (Kanet and Sussex 2015). Transnistria has a role to play in this struggle: as a Russian client, it affords Russia certain advantages over its Western adversaries in the competition for influence in two former Soviet republics: mainly in Moldova, Transnistria's parent state but also in Ukraine, Transnistria's second neighbour (Dunn and Bobick 2014; Kennedy 2016; Rogstad 2016). Just as clients played a prominent role in the rivalry of their Cold War superpower patrons (Shoemaker and Spanier 1984, 13), so Transnistria plays a significant role in Russia's competition with the West, primarily over Moldova (Rodkiewicz 2012).

Russia's perception is that the competition over Moldova has intensified since late 2003 and since then Russia has enhanced its special, patron-client relationship with Transnistria, making it more tangible for observers. In 2003 the Moldovan Communist authorities dismissed the Kozak Memorandum shortly before the signing ceremony under pressure from the United States, the European Union (EU), the Organization for Security and Co-operation in Europe (OSCE), and a portion of Moldova's population. The Memorandum was a Russian-orchestrated plan for the settlement of the Transnistrian conflict, secretly negotiated with Moldova and Transnistria independently of other international actors. As pointed out by William H. Hill (2012, 7), the Head of the OSCE Mission to Moldova in 1991–2001 and 2003–2006,

> what Western leaders in 2003 saw as a minor matter of blocking an unworkable political settlement in a small, remote post-Soviet divided state, Kremlin leaders saw as a direct geopolitical challenge and defeat on turf that had been theirs, relatively unchallenged, for [a long time] ... Moldova may have been one of the first places in the former USSR where Russia–United States and Russia–European Union relations moved from an uneasy, peripatetic cooperation to a more clearly adversarial posture.

Moreover, the Western actors stepped up their engagement in Moldova in the 2000s. This especially concerned the EU. Ahead of the 2004 Eastern enlargement, the EU decided to develop a comprehensive policy towards its southern and new Eastern neighbours in order to promote a ring of stability in the neighbourhood, consisting of democratic and prosperous countries. This included Moldova – directly bordering the EU since 2007 when Romania had become a member, which was a potential source of security threats and a challenge for EU border integrity, being the poorest state in Europe with a hybrid political regime and a frozen conflict on its soil. Importantly, the idea of European integration has been in principle, promoted by the then and subsequent Moldovan governments, ultimately seeking EU membership (Całus and Kosienkowski 2018).

Since the launch of the European Neighbourhood Policy in 2004, relations between the EU and Moldova, being greatly about the EU assisting Moldova in converging and integrating with the EU (but without offering membership), have been steadily deepening and strengthening (however, not without problems). This was demonstrated by the signing in June 2014 of an Association Agreement, including an agreement on a Deep and Comprehensive Free Trade Area (DCFTA). While Moldova has been advancing its European integration, the Kremlin wants Moldova to abandon this path and align with Russia. This includes participation in Russian integration projects in the post-Soviet area, falling under the umbrella of Eurasian integration. The latest project is the Eurasian Economic Union (EAEU),

186 *Marcin Kosienkowski*

operational since 2015; previously it was the Eurasian Customs Union, launched in 2010 and was subsequently integrated into the EAEU (Całus and Kosienkowski 2018).

In the case of the competition between Russia and the West over Ukraine, it has intensified since late 2004. At this time the Western actors supported the Ukrainian Orange Revolution that called into question the initial victory in the presidential elections of the pro-Russian Viktor Yanukovych. This directly led to the election of Viktor Yushchenko, supporting Ukraine's EU and NATO memberships. The rivalry has further intensified as a result of the following Ukrainian revolution, called the Euromaidan Revolution that took place at the turn of 2013 and 2014. Most Western governments sympathized with the protesters, while Russia backed the then President Yanukovych, who refused to sign the EU-Ukraine Association Agreement and then tried to violently crush the protests triggered by this decision. The revolution ended when the Euromaidan movement, explicitly pro-EU in its origins, ousted Yanukovych and a pro-Western government took power in Ukraine. Russia framed these events as a coup d'état orchestrated by the United States and responded with the annexation of Crimea and subversion in South and Eastern Ukraine. Subsequently, this led to a separatist war in Donbas and the emergence of the Donetsk and Luhansk People's Republics (Toal 2017).

Benefits

The two Cold War superpowers strove to obtain from their clients one or more of three specific types of benefits: ideological convergence, international solidarity, and strategic advantage, which is seen as the most important. These advantages were meant to increase the United States' and Soviet Union's power vis-à-vis each other in their global competition. The ideological benefits were gained when a client aligned to its patron ideology, at least in selected spheres. Moreover, such a client could be presented to the outside world as a showplace of the patron's ideological superiority in the hope of encouraging other states to converge upon it too. The benefits of international solidarity were about a client's voting cohesion with a patron in international organizations (mainly the UN) or a client's pronouncements of support for a patron in international forums. Finally, the strategic benefits entailed gaining control over a client's strategically important territory and resources, including having a direct military presence. Furthermore, a client could be exploited by a patron as a surrogate in a regional conflict or a staging area for revolution (Shoemaker and Spanier 1984, 17–20; Carney 1989, 49–51).

As demonstrated by Eiki Berg and Kristel Vits (2018, 4), this typology can be applied to the post-Cold War relationship between patron states and client de facto states. Furthermore, it has also been employed to analyze post-Cold War relations between patrons and client microstates (Veenendaal

2017, 566–567) that share some similarities with de facto states, such as a small size, weak economies, and the need for external assistance (Comai 2017). With regard to the Russian-Transnistrian patron-client relations, ideological convergence and benefits from international solidarity are of rather limited significance, while the most important benefit that Transnistria gives to Russia is a strategic advantage (cf. Devyatkov 2017; Berg and Vits 2018, 4).

The main example of an ideological benefit is when the Transnistrian authorities declared the de facto state's Eurasian integration "national idea" in November 2012 (MID PMR 2012). Importantly, in the same month the Russian authorities established an "NGO" called Eurasian Integration, based in Moscow and headed by the Russian MP, Aleksei Zhuravlyov, with the aim of constructing or renovating public buildings (e.g. hospitals and schools) in the Transnistrian region and providing it with public vehicles (e.g. ambulances and trolleybuses), using Russian governmental money (ANO "Yevraziiskaya Integratsiya" 2013). The idea was to make Transnistria a showplace of Eurasian integration's superiority and to sway the public opinion in Moldova that was not decisively in favour of European integration. What worked in favour of Russia's plan was the tangibility of the Russian support provided to Transnistria. In contrast the EU's assistance to Moldova was, in fact, barely visible to the Moldovan population because it was mainly focussed on institution building (Ghinea, Paul, and Chirila 2013, 2).

However, the Eurasian Integration organization virtually suspended its activity in 2018 because of a corruption scandal that left many Transnistrian subcontractors without payment (Tkhorik, Tuzlova, and Zvarish 2017). Moreover, being an unrecognized entity, Transnistria cannot, in reality, pursue Eurasian integration. Instead, it can integrate with the EU via Moldova and this is what has actually started to happen in the economic sphere. While the Transnistrian de facto state refused to co-negotiate and join the DCFTA agreement between the EU and Moldova, referring, among others, to its incompatibility with Eurasian integration, it finally decided in late 2015 to be included in the DCFTA (starting 1st January 2018) due to economic reasons and having won Russia's approval (Całus 2016; Secrieru 2016). Against this backdrop, Transnistria's declarations about Eurasian integration look more and more awkward.

Transnistria quite often displays solidarity with Russia. For instance, the Transnistrian authorities supported Russia's military invasion of Georgia and praised the subsequent recognition of Abkhazia and South Ossetia in August 2008 (MID PMR 2009). They also endorsed the annexation of the Crimea by Russia in March 2014 (MID PMR 2014). In all cases it was rather exceptional behaviour, not only in the post-Soviet area but also worldwide. Furthermore, the Transnistrian government harshly criticizes Moldovan attempts to get rid of Russian soldiers from Transnistria. An example is its criticism of the Moldova-sponsored resolution adopted by the UN General Assembly in June 2018, urging Russia to unconditionally withdraw Russian troops from the region (Krasnoselskii 2018c). However, given that, as an

188   *Marcin Kosienkowski*

unrecognized entity, Transnistria is not a member of international organizations and has restricted access to international forums, these displays of solidarity yield rather little substantial benefit to Russia.

The main strategic advantage Transnistria gives to Russia is that the Transnistrian de facto state prevents Moldova from entering the EU. While in 2004 Cyprus joined the EU with the de facto state of Northern Cyprus on its territory, it is highly unlikely that the EU would be ready to repeat a similar scenario with regard to Moldova in the future. Furthermore, the breakaway region of Transnistria prevents Moldova from entering NATO, which has been Moldova's direct neighbour since 2007 when Romania became a member, is especially significant as the Transnistrian de facto state hosts Russian soldiers on its soil. To be sure, being a constitutionally neutral country, Moldova does not seek NATO membership; however, it cannot be ruled out that the Moldovan authorities will abandon neutrality some day in the future. This is a matter of great concern for Russia (Devyatkov 2014, 55).

Another strategic benefit is that Transnistria can be used by Russia to hinder the process of Moldovan integration into the EU, which has been underway since the beginning of the 21st century. First, the mere existence of the Transnistrian de facto state provides the Kremlin with advantages. For example, the fact that the Moldovan central authorities do not control all of their territory has turned out to be a serious obstacle (eventually circumvented) to the conclusion of visa liberalization and DCFTA agreements between the EU and Moldova (Kononczuk and Rodkiewicz 2012). Second, Russia can use the Transnistrian de facto state to trigger a crisis in relations between Transnistria and Moldova. The rationale is to convince the EU, including its member states, and Moldova to stop enhancing their cooperation in order to stabilize the region.[1] One such Russian-inspired provocation may have been Transnistria's attempt to install checkpoints between a Moldova-controlled village of Varnita, and a district of the Transnistria-controlled Bendery city in April 2013. As a result, a scuffle ensued between Transnistrian law enforcement officials and Moldovans, which could have turned into military hostilities (Całus 2013b). Third, according to some experts (e.g. Całus 2014), Transnistrian-based Russian and/or Transnistrian military units could have been used by the Kremlin to unfold a 2014 Crimea/Donbas-like scenario in Moldova's pro-Russian regions such as Gagauzia. This would severely hamper the process of Moldova's European integration.

At the same time, Russia also uses Transnistria as a bargaining chip, alluding to the idea that the Transnistrian region could be reunited with Moldova if the Moldovan authorities aligned with Russia. What adds credibility to the Russian offer is that the Kremlin has never officially renounced its support for Moldova's territorial integrity and is the main, if not the only actor capable of pushing Transnistria, as its client, to abandon de facto independence (as demonstrated by Transnistria's approval of the Russia-orchestrated Kozak Memorandum in 2003). Crucially, in the case of reintegration under

Russia's conditions the whole of Moldova could be anchored in Russia's sphere of exclusive influence. These provisions would legalize Russia's military presence in all of Moldova and guarantee a disproportionate degree of influence for pro-Russian Transnistria and Gagauzia in the united country, just as envisaged by the Kozak Memorandum (Hill 2012).

Another strategic advantage Transnistria gives to Russia is related to Ukraine. The Transnistrian de facto state is considered "an unsinkable aircraft carrier" on Ukraine's Western borders limiting the Ukrainian leadership's strategic options (Hensel 2006, 9). According to the Ukrainian authorities, Russia made attempts to use it directly, as a staging ground for Russian and Transnistrian subversive groups to infiltrate and destabilize the adjacent Ukrainian region of Odesa during the initial phase of Russian aggression against Ukraine in the winter and spring of 2014. Moreover, the Ukrainian government seemed to fear that the Transnistria-based Russian military units could invade Ukraine (see, e.g., DPSU 2014; MZS Ukrayiny 2014; Ukrinform 2014). The aim of these actions would have been to establish another pro-Russian separatist republic within Ukraine to be included into the separatist, pro-Russian Novorossiya together with Transnistria and other Southern and Eastern Ukrainian regions, cutting Ukraine off from the Black Sea (Całus 2014; Goble 2014).

Even if the Russian authorities did not consider sending subversive groups to Ukraine or invading it from Transnistria, by posing such a threat, Russia tied up some Ukrainian military units close to the Transnistrian de facto state, preventing their deployment in the Donbas theatre of war. It can be added that Transnistria – as a pro-Russian region with Russian troops and security service – is still identified by the Ukrainian government as a direct threat to Ukraine's security and territorial integrity (Interfaks-Ukraina 2018).

Legitimization

Stronger states point at derived benefits – that advance their interests – to justify upholding costly, patronal relations with weaker countries. In addition, they may refer to the affective factor stemming from ethnic, religious, ideological, historical, or political affinities with clients (Carney 1989, 46, 51; Bercovitch 1991, 18; Ciorciari 2015, 248). In the case of its relationship with Transnistria, Russia avoids making any reference to its instrumental gains. The point is that the Kremlin would not like to be internationally associated with deriving benefits from a de facto state, considered by the international community to be an illegitimate entity. Instead, Russia legitimizes its patronage over Transnistria with affective and normative factors, that is, its obligation to protect Russian citizens and compatriots, understood as people somehow identifying themselves with Russia or simply as members of the Russian world (*russkii mir*) living in the Transnistrian de facto state (Regnum 2009; Rossiiskaya Gazeta 2018). This is why Russian press releases on meetings between Transnistria's and Russia's representatives create the impression

190 *Marcin Kosienkowski*

that mutual relations were restricted to socio-economic and humanitarian spheres as well as the Transnistrian conflict settlement process, being of great importance for ordinary Transnistrians (see, e.g., MID RF 2016).

The number of Russia's citizens in the Transnistrian de facto state has been steadily growing (Nagashima 2017, 9–10). At present, 220 thousand Transnistrians hold Russian citizenship, which constitutes almost 50% of Transnistrian inhabitants. What is more, all of Transnistria's population – composed mainly of Russians, Moldovans, and Ukrainians – appear to be considered compatriots by the Russian authorities. The Kremlin can support such a claim, for example, by referring to the 2006 Transnistrian referendum, in which virtually all Transnistrians backed the idea of Transnistria joining Russia.

Transnistria's cliency: rationale, benefits, and legitimization

Rationale

Weaker states become clients seeking to advance their national interests this way (cf. Gasiorowski and Baek 1987; Constantin 1995, 185–186; Afoaku 2000). For example, by entering the patron-client relationship, they may want to ensure their own survival. Christopher C. Shoemaker and John W. Spanier (1984, 21–22 and 183) noted that during the Cold War many states lived in what they perceived extremely hostile security environments, being afraid of military invasion by other states that would deal them a mortal blow. In such circumstances they looked for patrons for their salvation. Israel and Kuwait were cases in point. They looked for external protection against belligerent neighbours – that is, respectively, the Arab states and, mainly, Iraq – that put their very existence at risk (Tètreault 1991, 584–587; Sorokin 1997, 63–64). In the case of microstates in the post-Cold War period Wouter P. Veenendaal (2017, 567) points mainly at their economic vulnerability, resulting from having small, weak economies. In order to avoid economic collapse and survive they tend to associate themselves with stronger patrons. Quite similarly, in the face of famine "mini-states" – that appeared in the territories of the failed Somalia at the beginning of 1990s – decided to collectively enter a patron-client relationship with the UN, seeking the provision of food and other humanitarian aid necessary for their continued existence (Bariagaber 1996, 171).

De facto states share similar risks. They believe they are facing a constant military threat from their parent states that continue to lay claim to lost territories. They also have small, weak economies. Moreover, due to their non-recognition, de facto states are far more vulnerable – both military and economically – than the above-mentioned Cold War states and post-Cold War microstates (Kolstø 2006).While, in theory, they may enjoy the protection of the prohibition of the use of force (Coppieters 2018, 350, 357), just as universally recognized states do, in practice, it does not hold true as demonstrated by the forcible eradications of the Republika Srpska Krajina in 1995, Chechnya in 1999, and Tamil Eelam in 2009. These events were met with virtually no international legal and non-legal consequences for, respectively, Croatia, Russia, and Sri Lanka. Furthermore, being unrecognized entities, de facto states are more or less economically isolated by the international community. This restricts their opportunities to obtain assistance from international financial institutions or bilateral donors, sell products abroad or attract foreign investment, making a de facto states' economic collapse and subsequent recapture by their parent state more likely.

As put by Berg and Vits (2018, 1) in reference to these vulnerabilities, de facto states face a "do or die" dilemma where they "either seek protection from external patrons ('do') or face the prospect of forceful reintegration back into their parent states ('die')". Transnistria has chosen the first option and associated itself with Russia since its outset at the beginning of the 1990s. To be sure, having failed to forcibly eradicate the Transnistrian de facto state in 1992, Moldova may not seek to retake its territories by force any longer, however, in the Transnistrian leadership's opinion such a threat has never disappeared. In addition, for some time during the Russian-Ukrainian conflict that erupted in 2014, the de facto state's authorities even seemed to believe that – as a pro-Russian entity – Transnistria could be invaded by Ukraine (Regnum 2015).

Furthermore, although when compared to the economies of other de facto states, Transnistria's highly industrialized economy is stronger and well-connected with the outside world in terms of trade (thanks to Moldova's consent). The Transnistrian de facto state is unable to function properly and simply survive by itself. The point is that Transnistria lacks enough internal resources – such as money to cover public expenses (including paying numerous public employees and pensioners) or the means of production (mainly natural gas), necessary for an economy based on heavy industry (Blakkisrud and Kolstø 2011, 188–193; Całus 2013a). For example, the de facto state will be able to cover only 36% of its budgetary expenditures in 2019 (Krudu 2018).

Benefits

According to Christopher P. Carney (1989, 48–49), by entering the patron-client relationship, the Cold War clients strove to derive security, economic, domestic, and diplomatic benefits that would help to advance their national interests (see also Gasiorowski and Baek 1987, 115; Bercovitch 1991, 17–18; Ciorciari 2015, 252–257; Veenendaal 2017, 567). With some additions this typology can be applied to the post-Cold War client de facto states that, struggling for their survival, associate themselves with stronger countries.

A client may obtain security guarantees as well as military equipment and training that enhance its position vis-à-vis its adversaries. A client country may also be provided with vital economic support by a patron, in the form

192 *Marcin Kosienkowski*

of loans, grants, in-kind aid, and favourable trade conditions or investment. Furthermore, a patron's assistance that is used to improve material and physical wellbeing of the client's population can enhance the domestic legitimacy of a client government. While this also holds true in the case of de facto states, even more important is harnessing a patron's support to strengthen the domestic legitimacy of these entities. The point is that de facto states that have little popular support may not be able to mobilize armies or avoid massive emigration and may face collapse and reintegration by a parent state (Bakke et al. 2014, 591–594). Finally, a client may also receive diplomatic protection and backing in international forums or brokerage with the outside world. This is especially important in the case of more or less internationally isolated de facto states.

With regard to Transnistria, it receives security guarantees from Russia, enhanced by the Russian military presence in the region. Russia keeps about 1,500 soldiers there within two formations – a peacekeeping contingent (within the trilateral Russian-Moldovan-Transnistrian peacekeeping operation) and an Operational Group of Russian Forces (the OGRF is a remnant of the Soviet and then Russian Fourteenth Army). While Moldova and Western actors call for the transformation of the peacekeeping operation into a civilian one and for the withdrawal of the OGRF, this permanently meets with the Kremlin's refusal. Although Russia's military presence is limited, it nevertheless serves in the eyes of the Transnistrian authorities as a deterrent against Moldova's and, more recently, Ukraine's invasion of Transnistria that is highly unlikely anyway. Moreover, a potential attack would probably meet with a military response by Russia, even if it has no common border with Transnistria. Importantly, Russia's security guarantees allow the Transnistrian leadership to focus on state- and nation-building activities that strengthen Transnistria's de facto independence. It should be added that it was the Russian Fourteenth Army that secured Transnistria's victory in the 1992 war with Moldova as well as helped to create, equip, and train Transnistrian armed forces (Blakkisrud and Kolstø 2011, 184–186; Lynch 2004, 74–79).

Undoubtedly, Transnistria gets vital economic support from Russia. First, Russia provides the Transnistrian de facto state with natural gas, although Transnistria has only paid for some of it and since 2009, has not paid at all. This has led to its astronomical debt of more than $6 billion (almost seven times more than Transnistria's GDP) owed to Gazprom at the end of 2017. The Russian gas is consumed predominantly by three large export-oriented industrial plants that are one of the main pillars of Transnistria's economy: Moldova Steel Works, the Moldavskaya GRES power plant, and the Rybnitsa Cement Plant. The next major gas consumer is Tirotex-energo – a power plant orientated to the needs of its owner, the Sheriff holding, that is another driving force of the Transnistrian economy. To be sure, the aforementioned and other corporate consumers pay Transnistria's authorities for the natural gas; however, it is bought at dumping prices, that reduces their production costs and makes their goods more competitive. This also means cheaper utilities, such as heating, improving the life of ordinary people. Furthermore, money collected from gas consumers – instead of being transferred to Gazprom – is used by the Transnistrian leadership to pay pensions and wages to public employees (Chamberlain-Creanga and Allin 2010, 336–339; Całus 2013a; Gorchakov 2016).

Second, Transnistria receives financial aid from Russia – on average $100 million annually – in the form of loans and grants that are used to cover public expenses, increase pensions, assist Transnistrian businessmen and farmers, stabilize the Transnistrian currency, and buy food for poor people. Third, Russian companies are the main foreign investors in Transnistria, all the more important as the region is hardly attractive in terms of investment opportunities due to its status of a de facto state. Fourth, Transnistria receives Russian in-kind support via the aforementioned Eurasian Integration organization. Fifth, Russia accepts economic migrants from Transnistria – their cash remittances are of great importance to the region's economy. Sixth, Russia is one of the major markets for Transnistrian goods; however, its importance has declined over the course of time. Its share in Transnistria's exports accounted for 10.20% in January–August of 2018, placing it after Moldova (28.26%), Ukraine (21.81%), and Romania (17.03%) (Całus 2013a; Blakkisrud and Kolstø 2011, 188–193; GTK PMR 2018b).

As explained above, the Transnistrian population benefits economically – both directly (e.g. getting higher pensions or new public buildings) and indirectly (e.g. paying less for utilities) – from the patron-client relationship between Russia and Transnistria. Due to Russia's economic support for the de facto state, Transnistrians perceive the region's living conditions to be better than in Moldova, a country that Transnistria seeks to detach from (O'Loughlin, Toal, and Chamberlain-Creangă 2013, 235–240). Indeed, compared to its parent state, utilities are cheaper and pensions are higher in the Transnistrian de facto state (Karaban 2017). Thus, it can be said that benefits derived by Transnistria from Russia contribute to strengthening the de facto state's domestic legitimacy, even if the Transnistrian economy is actually marked by a permanent crisis and considerable workforce emigration.

To be sure, some may say that the fact that Transnistrians' well-being largely depends on Russia undermines the internal legitimacy of the Transnistrian de facto state (Chamberlain-Creanga and Allin 2010, 339). This would be a problem, if Transnistria sought internationally recognized independence. However, since the 2006 referendum the Transnistrian de facto state has officially strived to join Russia. Moreover, the Transnistrian identity forged by Transnistria's authorities is based not only on a regional Transnistrian identity but also on a civilizational, Russian identity. As noted by Piotr Oleksy (2016, 143), "[b]eing a Transnistrian simply implies being a Russian (understood as a member of the Russian civilization) and at the same time does not interfere with being (in ethnic terms) a Bulgarian, a Ukrainian or a Moldovan".

194 *Marcin Kosienkowski*

Finally, Russia has also brought Transnistria under a protective umbrella in the international arena, such as the OSCE forum. In fact, it is the only country that provides the Transnistrian de facto state with diplomatic backing. For example, Russia praises Transnistria for progress within the Transnistrian conflict settlement process and points at Moldova as its main spoiler. Moldova is usually criticized for undertaking unilateral steps such as in May 2017, when they established a shared Moldovan-Ukrainian control post at the Transnistrian section of the Moldova-Ukraine border. The Russian point is that such actions are undertaken without consultations with the Transnistrian de facto state – that should be equal to Moldova – and undermine its de facto independence and performance. Furthermore, Russia's officials meet with Transnistrian officials, quite often addressing them with their official titles such as "the President of Transnistria" (see, e.g., MID RF 2018, 2016). This enhances the legitimacy of Transnistria's officials and the legitimacy of the entity they represent.

While Transnistria's internal resources and its leadership's state- and nation-building efforts should not be underestimated (Kolstø 2006), in fact, the Transnistrian de facto state is able to survive only thanks to Russia's comprehensive assistance. This is generally accepted in the literature (see, e.g., Popescu 2006) and has been overtly admitted by Transnistria's authorities (Gamova 2010; Sputnik 2016), even if they tend to underline that the Transnistrian de facto state is self-sufficient. This is also generally consistent with insights from literature on the patron-client relationship, saying that patrons play a crucial role in meeting their clients' demands (Bercovitch 1991, 15; Veenendaal 2017, 567).

To be sure, some may say that the Transnistrian de facto state depends on the West for survival as well, pointing out that a considerable part of Transnistria's exports go to the EU (Dembińska and Mérand 2018, 13; see also Berg and Vits 2018, 3), most recently, that is, between January and August of 2018 this is 36.18% (GTK PMR 2018b). However, the vast majority of products exported to the EU – that is steel and textiles, constituting, respectively, 77.71% and 10.43% of Transnistria's European export (GTK PMR 2018a) – were manufactured by companies (the Moldova Steel Works and the Sheriff-owned Tirotex) benefiting directly or indirectly (i.e. consuming electric energy generated using gas) from the natural gas provided by Russia to Transnistria for free. Others may say that Transnistria's survival depends also on Ukraine that provides the facto state with lines of communication and access to the international market, which is of crucial importance to its export-oriented economy (Istomin and Bolgova 2016, 182). However, it can be said it is largely due to Russia that this window to the outside world is permanently opened for Transnistria, even when Russian-Ukrainian relations are marked by hostility (cf. Istomin and Bolgova 2016, 185–187). The point is that if Ukraine closed the border with Transnistria, it would create new tensions with Russia, which is something the Ukrainian authorities would rather like to avoid.

Legitimization

The maintenance of the clientelist relationship means that weaker states expose themselves to the influence or control of stronger states (Carney 1989, 48). Because of these clients may be portrayed as "lackeys", "satellites", or "puppets" by third parties – this is what any government wants to avoid (Ciorciari 2015, 248). This is why client states deny abdicating autonomy to patrons and say that their relations with stronger countries are held on equal terms, branding these relations as a friendship or partnership. Clients also make an effort to legitimize upholding the relationship with patrons. Client de facto states are no exception to these patterns. This is especially true with respect to de facto states that strive for internationally recognized independence – the point is that the clientelist relationship reveals their non-viability and far-reaching dependencies on other states, making their claim to independent statehood less credible (Caspersen 2012, 108–109).

Clients usually point at derived benefits – that considerably advance their interests – to justify their association with stronger states. Furthermore, they may also refer to the affective factor, that bonds them to patrons, to legitimize their relationship. This affectivity stems from various similarities between parties (Ciorciari 2015, 252, 267; Carney 1989, 44–46, 51). These may be historical and linguistic affinities, like between African states and their former colonial masters such as France (Constantin 1995, 186), or normative commonalities, like between the two democracies – Israel and the United States (Bar-Siman-Tov 1998, 232). The affectivity may also be based on a clients' feeling of gratitude towards patrons for assistance, such as in the case of the South Koreans' appreciation to the United States for saving them from a possible Communist takeover and poverty in the 1950s (Kim and Lim 2007, 74; see also Veenendaal 2017). Finally, clients may point at common adversaries or threats shared with their patrons or, broadly speaking, converging interests of parties as well (Carney 1989, 51).

These patterns fit well with the relationship between Transnistria and Russia. The Transnistrian de facto state is quite often depicted in the media and scholarly works as no more than Russia's puppet (see, e.g., Robertson 2014; Ivanel 2016). While Transnistria does not ultimately seek internationally recognized independence, it nevertheless attempts to improve this poor image. Transnistrian authorities underline their independency and brand Transnistria's relations with Russia as a partnership. They also try to legitimize this relationship by pointing to the Russian security guarantees and economic support to Transnistria that are crucial for its survival. The provision of such vital assistance generates positive feelings towards Russia – which is called Transnistria's saviour and "hope for the future" – and additionally used to justify the Transnistrian de facto state's clientelist relationship with its patron (Smirnov 2007; Krasnoselskii 2018b).

The Transnistrian leadership also refers to other affective factors, stemming from historical and cultural commonalities. Indeed, the Transnistrian region has been almost persistently connected with Russia – understood not only as contemporary Russia but also the Tsarist Russia and the Soviet Union – since the end of the 18th century, when it was merged with the Russian Empire. Apart from this historical affinity, the Transnistrian de facto state's population is heavily Russified and has a deep sense of togetherness with Russia, despite the fact that Transnistria is a multi-ethnic region. This is why Transnistria is presented by its leadership as an integral part of the Russian civilization (the *russkii mir*) and even as a mirror reflection of Russia inhabited by model Russians. Furthermore, the Transnistrian authorities claim that Transnistria's and Russia's interests largely converge. For example, they point out that both parties want Russian soldiers to be stationed in the Transnistrian territory. Last but not least, the special relationship with Russia is justified by its consistency with Transnistria's officially declared goals – based on the people's will – of Eurasian integration and ultimate accession to Russia (Smirnov 2007; Krasnoselskii 2018b).

Dynamics of the patron-client relationship between Russia and Transnistria

Mutually valued relationship marked by tensions

The patron-client relationship is based on the premise that the supply of goods and services by one party to another meets with the reciprocal provision of (non-comparable) resources. In other words, both a patron and a client give and take. This instrumental, mutually valued exchange of resources sustains patron-client relations. The relationship may be further enhanced by the affective factor, originating from similarities between parties or a client's gratitude towards a patron for assistance. However, as pointed by Jacob Bercovitch (1991, 19), "[b]ehind the formal façade of loyalty, shared interests ... there is an informal reality of tensions, disagreements and shifting directions of influence" in patron-client relations. The main problem is that parties try to extract as much support as possible from each other while seeking to minimize their own concessions. Moreover, being perceived as too costly or risky, some demands may be hard to meet. There may be also red lines not to be crossed (Shoemaker and Spanier 1984, 17, 24; Bercovitch 1991, 18–19; Bariagaber 1996, 166; Heimann 2010; Ciorciari 2015, 248; Ladwig 2016, 105).

Likewise, the patron-client relationship between Russia and Transnistria is generally mutually beneficial and valued as well as marked by a strong element of affectivity based on affinities and Transnistria's appreciation of Russian assistance; however, it is not free from serious tensions. First of all, the Russian and Transnistrian authorities totally differ on such a crucial issue as the future status of Transnistria. Unlike the Transnistrian government, the Russian authorities want Transnistria to be reintegrated with Moldova (under Russian conditions that would anchor Moldova in Russia's sphere of exclusive influence). Instead, referring to the results of the 2006

Russia and Transnistria 197

referendum, the Transnistrian leadership seeks its de facto state to be incorporated into Russia, this is something the Russian authorities do not want to do (cf. Kosienkowski 2012, 16–29).

Furthermore, the Transnistrian government desires Russian financial assistance to keep flowing to the region, whereas the Kremlin tends to limit such support because of political or economic reasons. There were even cases when the financial aid was halted – as seen for the entirety of 2007 and 2017 – substantially worsening the socio-economic situation in the Transnistrian de facto state. It can also be noted that while Russia may have considered using the Russian army based in the Transnistrian region to invade Ukraine, this seemed to contradict the interests of Transnistria because it may have put the Transnistrian de facto state's performance and existence at risk (Novosti Pridnestrovya 2014; Oleksy 2014).

Achieving Transnistria's compliance

Normally patrons achieve a clients' compliance with their needs through inducement, that is, providing and increasing support to clients. The more a given client values gained benefits, the more it is responsive to a patron's demands. De facto states can be classified as clients that highly regard a patron's assistance, given that it ensures their survival. Moreover, this support is hard to replace. The point is that, due to the illegitimate status of de facto states, the number of their potential patrons is extremely limited, if not non-existent (Kolstø and Blakkisrud 2017, 506). As such, de facto states can be expected to be highly responsive to the demands of their patrons.

In the case of problems, clients can simply be reprimanded by patrons to ensure their voluntary compliance. Moreover, their behaviour can also be shaped through the threat or use of coercion. This can be about the reduction of economic aid, trade restrictions, or increased diplomatic pressure (Carney 1989, 47–48; Bercovitch 1991, 15–19, 27; Bariagaber 1996, 172–174; Ladwig 2016, 105–108). Furthermore, while patrons appreciate a client states' internal stability (Afoaku 2000), they may nevertheless try to influence domestic politics in client countries in order to replace their governments with more compliant authorities (Gasiorowski and Baek 1987).

As regards to the Russian-Transnistrian relationship, the vital and non-replaceable support provided by Russia to Transnistria makes the Transnistrian de facto state's leadership highly responsive to demands from the Russian authorities and even anticipatory to their needs.[2] Yet, sometimes the Transnistrian government has had to be reprimanded by Russia, just as in the case of Yevgenii Shevchuk who served as the second president of Transnistria between 2011 and 2016. Having come to power he pursued his own, pragmatic foreign policy for a few months but, admonished by the Kremlin, he voluntarily and smoothly started complying with Russia's needs (Całus and Oleksy 2013; see also Kosienkowski 2012). According to some accounts, he became even "more Russian than Russia".[3]

198 *Marcin Kosienkowski*

There were also cases when the Transnistrian leadership did not want to follow its patron's will – this especially concerned the first Transnistrian president, Igor Smirnov, who held his position between 1991 and 2011. As a result, the Russian authorities resorted to threats or the use of coercion. More precisely, they restricted or halted financial support (or made threats to do it), demanded the gas debt to be paid back, threatened to cut off gas deliveries, and exerted diplomatic pressure on Transnistria. As a result, the Transnistrian leadership had no choice but to comply. Russia employed such tactics primarily when the opportunity appeared – that is, when the Moldovan authorities were ready to align with Russian interests – to make Transnistria reintegrate with its parent state or simply negotiate with Moldova on the conflict settlement. Russia's successful attempt to make Transnistria approve the Kozak Memorandum – a Russian-orchestrated plan of the Transnistrian conflict settlement – is a case in point (Soloviev 2007, 2008; Hill 2012, 124, 138, 175). It can also be added that Russia restricted the provision of funds to Transnistria seeking to save money (Całus 2017) or because of money misappropriation by the Transnistrian authorities (Soloviev 2007; Soloviev and Butrin 2010).

Being afraid that internal instability in Transnistria could undermine the de facto state's existence, Russia supports subsequent Transnistrian authorities, supervises the peaceful transfer of power after elections, and helps to reconcile contending Transnistrian political groups (Devyatkov and Kosienkowski 2013, 314–316; Kolstø and Blakkisrud 2017, 519–526). However, the 2011 presidential election in Transnistria is an exception to this rule. Being dissatisfied with the then President Smirnov's non-compliance with Russia's needs and misappropriation of Russian financial aid, the Kremlin started to put pressure on Smirnov not to run for his fifth term as president. This included spreading slanderous material about Smirnov by the Russian media, which was very popular in Transnistria, and initiating a criminal case by the Russian Investigation Committee against his son, accused of embezzling money, including Russian humanitarian assistance granted to the Transnistrian de facto state. Largely due to Russia's campaign, Smirnov was expelled from the presidential run after the first round of the elections. Yet, it should be added that the Kremlin did not manage to ensure the victory of its candidate, Anatolii Kaminskii; instead, it was Yevgenii Shevchuk who won the election (Devyatkov and Kosienkowski 2013, 315–317).

Achieving Russia's compliance

Patrons comply with clientelist demands in reciprocation for the benefits provided to them by their clients. At the same time, clients can undertake additional steps to maintain (in case of problems) or achieve a higher degree of a patrons' compliance with their preferences and retain more autonomy vis-à-vis stronger states. First of all, clients can influence a patrons' behaviour by threatening to abandon them and become clients of other states or play two (or more) patrons off against each other (Bercovitch 1991, 16; Afoaku 2000, 17; Veenendaal 2017, 567). To be sure, de facto states have limited opportunities to employ these tactics, given that there are no alternative patrons in sight. However, it does not mean that such tactics cannot be used in some form.

Clients can also rely on lobbying patronal governments by friendly officials, politicians, and activists from patron states (Bercovitch 1991, 23–24; Afoaku 2000). Additionally, client countries can (over)emphasize the importance of benefits they provide (or may provide) to their patrons (Bar-Siman-Tov 1998, 244; Afoaku 2000, 18; Jourde 2007) and anticipate patronal interests, trying to satisfy them and obtain sympathy and the benevolence of patrons (Veenendaal 2017, 572). Finally, clients can make emotional appeals to a patrons' government and public opinion referring to various affinities between clients and patrons (Bercovitch 1991, 24).

The Transnistrian authorities take similar steps in order to maintain or achieve a higher degree of Russia's compliance with Transnistria's needs and the ability to retain more autonomy vis-à-vis the Russian patron. While there is no country ready to replace Russian patronage and provide Transnistria with security guarantees as well as vital economic assistance, the Transnistrian authorities pretended to seek an alternative patron exactly as the de facto state lost Russia's support. The aim of such tactics was to pressure the Kremlin to resume aid. During the Smirnov presidency, Transnistria announced its intention to enhance cooperation with Ukraine, including possibly joining this state. Moreover, the Transnistrian de facto state even expressed the intention to conduct multi-vector foreign policy or closely cooperate with the EU and the United States, instead of Russia (Kosienkowski 2012, 19, 27; Istomin and Bolgova 2016). While due to the Russian-Ukrainian conflict Transnistria cannot court Ukraine any longer, the Transnistrian leadership can still exploit (trade) links with the EU, trying to influence Russia. Perhaps, this is why – having not received the Russian financial support for the whole of 2017 – the Transnistrian President, Vadim Krasnoselskii (2018a), said that Transnistria should become a place where the (competing) interests of the EU (and generally the West) and Russia could be reconciled.

Furthermore, the Transnistrian authorities rely on Russian officials and politicians of various levels as well as military officers, willing to lobby the Russian authorities for the Transnistrian cause. These are nationalists, communists, or opportunists as well as people coming from the Transnistrian region or elected by Russian citizens living in Transnistria. These are also Russian businessmen that – encouraged by the Transnistria's authorities – invested their money in the Transnistrian de facto state (Hill 2012, 70; Kosienkowski 2012, 26). Furthermore, the Transnistrian leadership emphasizes the region's geostrategic importance to Russia, presenting it as the last Russian military stronghold in Southeastern Europe. For example, the Smirnov regime made an effort to underline this, suggesting the deployment of the medium-range Iskander missiles in Transnistria in 2010, in response

200 *Marcin Kosienkowski*

to Romania's intentions to have elements of a US anti-missile shield on its territory (Kosienkowski 2012, 26–27).

The Transnistrian authorities also claim that Russia should protect and endorse its citizens and compatriots living in Transnistria, calling it an outpost of the Russian civilization in this part of Europe. Additionally, when the de facto state lost Russia's assistance, the Smirnov regime resorted to histrionics and appealed to Russian public opinion and nationalist politicians for support (Kosienkowski 2012, 24–27; Oleksy 2016, 167–174). Overall, it can be said that all these steps help shape Russia's policy towards Transnistria in the direction desired by the Transnistrian authorities, especially during periods when the Russian government does not see the opportunity of merging Transnistria with Moldova. Referring to the period of the Smirnov regime, a senior expert of the Carnegie Moscow Center even called it a case of the tail wagging the dog.[4]

Conclusions

As demonstrated in this chapter, the relations between Russia and the de facto state of Transnistria can be analyzed by employing the patron-client concept. Such a relationship between the stronger Russian patron and the weaker Transnistrian client is essentially about the mutually beneficial exchange of non-comparable goods and services. The most important benefit that Russia derives from Transnistria is a strategic advantage. It allows Russia to increase its power in the competition with Western actors for influence in two of the former Soviet republics: mainly in Moldova, Transnistria's parent state but also in the Ukraine. While legitimizing its special relationship with Transnistria, however, Russia refers exclusively to affective and normative arguments, that it is its obligation to protect Russian citizens and compatriots living in the Transnistrian region. The reason is that it does not want to be associated with the instrumental use of a de facto state that is considered an illegitimate entity by the international community.

In return, Transnistria obtains security, economic, domestic, and diplomatic benefits from Russia. Among others, the Transnistrian de facto state is provided with guarantees of security, free natural gas, financial aid, and diplomatic protection in international forums. The economic assistance also reaches the population, strengthening Transnistria's domestic legitimacy. Crucially, the support derived from Russia is necessary for Transnistria to survive as a de facto state. Being often depicted as no more than a Russian puppet, Transnistria attempts to legitimize its clientelist relationship with Russia. It refers to the importance of instrumental benefits as well as affective factors, such as historical and cultural commonalities with the Russian patron, and converging interests of both parties.

This instrumental, mutually beneficial exchange of goods and services is what sustains relations between Russia and Transnistria. They are further enhanced by a strong element of affectivity based mainly on affinities

Russia and Transnistria 201

between parties. However, the relationship is not free from serious tensions. The fundamental divergence is that the Russian authorities want Transnistria to be reintegrated with its parent state under Russian conditions that would anchor Moldova in Russia's sphere of exclusive influence. Alternatively, the Transnistrian leadership wants Transnistria to be integrated with Russia. Facing such problems, parties undertake additional steps to achieve each other's compliance with their needs. These include Russia resorting to coercion and Transnistria lobbying the Russian government via individuals sympathizing with the Transnistrian cause. While Transnistria is neither a Russian puppet nor a powerless actor vis-à-vis its Russian patron, however, if resolutely pressed by Russia, it has no choice but to finally comply with its patron's demands. What is decisive is that Russia provides Transnistria with vital and non-replaceable support.

Notes

1 Interview with a Western diplomat to Moldova, July 2013.
2 Interviews with former senior officials in the Transnistrian Foreign Ministry, July 2013.
3 Interviews with former senior officials in the Transnistrian Foreign Ministry, July 2013.
4 Interview, November 2007.

Literature

Afoaku, Osita G. 2000. "U.S. Foreign Policy and Authoritarian Regimes: Change and Continuity in International Clientelism." *Journal of Third World Studies* 17 (2): 13–40.

ANO Yevraziiskaya Integratsiya. 2013. "O nas [About Us]." ANO Yevraziiskaya Integratsiya [Autonomous Non-Commercial Organization Eurasian Integration], May 29 http://eurasianintegration.ru/?q=node/71.

Bakke, Kristin M., John O'Loughlin, Gerard Toal, and Michael D. Ward. 2014. "Convincing State-Builders? Disaggregating Internal Legitimacy in Abkhazia." *International Studies Quarterly* 58 (3): 591–607.

Bariagaber, Assefaw. 1996. "The United Nations and Somalia: An Examination of a Collective Clientelist Relationship." *Journal of African and Asian Studies* 31 (3–4): 162–177.

Bar-Siman-Tov, Yaacov. 1998. "The United States and Israel since 1948: A 'Special Relationship'?" *Diplomatic History* 22 (2): 231–262.

Bercovitch, Jacob. 1991. "Superpowers and Client States: Analysing Relations and Patterns of Influence." In *Superpowers and Client States in the Middle East: The Imbalance of Influence*, edited by Moshe Efrat and Jacob Bercovitch, 9–32. London and New York: Routledge.

Berg, Eiki, and Kristel Vits. 2018. "The Do-or-Die Dilemma Facing Post-Soviet De Facto States." *PONARS Eurasia Policy Memo* 527. www.ponarseurasia.org/sites/default/files/policy-memos-pdf/Pepm527_Berg-Vits_May2018.pdf.

Blakkisrud, Helge, and Pål Kolstø. 2011. "From Secessionist Conflict toward a Functioning State: Processes of State- and Nation-Building in Transnistria." *Post-Soviet Affairs* 27 (2): 178–210.

Całus, Kamil. 2013a. "An Aided Economy: The Characteristics of the Transnistrian Economic Model." *OSW Commentary*, May 14. www.osw.waw.pl/sites/default/files/commentary_108.pdf.

Całus, Kamil. 2013b. "Tensions between Moldova and Transnistria pose a Threat to the Vilnius Summit." *OSW Analyses*, July 10. www.osw.waw.pl/en/publikacje/analyses/2013-07-10/tensions-between-moldova-and-transnistria-pose-a-threat-to-vilnius.

Całus, Kamil. 2014. "Crimean Gagauzia?" *New Eastern Europe*, March 13. http://neweasterneurope.eu/2014/03/13/crimean-gagauzia/.

Całus, Kamil. 2016. "The DCFTA in Transnistria: Who Gains?" *New Eastern Europe*, January 15. http://neweasterneurope.eu/old_site/articles-and-commentary/1861-the-dcfta-in-transnistria-who-gains.

Całus, Kamil. 2017. "The Transnistrian Gambit." *New Eastern Europe*, December 21. http://neweasterneurope.eu/2017/12/21/the-transnistrian-gambit/.

Całus, Kamil, and Marcin Kosienkowski. 2018. "Relations between Moldova and the European Union." In *The European Union and Its Eastern Neighbourhood: Europeanisation and Its Twenty-first-century Contradictions*, edited by Michael Mannin and Paul Flenley, 99–113. Manchester: Manchester University Press.

Całus, Kamil, and Piotr Oleksy. 2013. "Expectations and Reality Collide in Tiraspol." *New Eastern Europe*, June 9. http://neweasterneurope.eu/2013/06/09/expectations-and-reality-collide-in-tiraspol/.

Carney, Christopher P. 1989. "International Patron-Client Relationships: A Conceptual Framework." *Studies in Comparative International Development* 24 (2): 42–55.

Caspersen, Nina. 2012. *Unrecognized States: The Struggle for Sovereignty in the Modern International System*. Cambridge: Polity.

Chamberlain-Creanga, Rebecca, and Lyndon K. Allin. 2010. "Acquiring Assets, Debts and Citizens: Russia and the Micro-Foundations of Transnistria's Stalemated Conflict." *Demokratizatsiya* 18 (4): 329–356.

Ciorciari, John D. 2015. "A Chinese Model for Patron-client Relations? The Sino-Cambodian Partnership." *International Relations of the Asia-Pacific* 15 (2): 245–278.

Comai, Giorgio. 2017. "Conceptualising Post-Soviet De Facto States as Small Dependent Jurisdictions." *Ethnopolitics* 17 (2): 181–200.

Constantin, François G. 1995. "The Foreign Policy of Francophone Africa: Clientelism and After." In *State and Society in Francophone Africa since Independence*, edited by Anthony Kirk-Greene and Daniel Bach, 183–199. Basingstoke: St. Martin's Press.

Coppieters, Bruno. 2018. "'Statehood', 'De Facto Authorities' and 'Occupation': Contested Concepts and the EU's Engagement in Its European Neighbourhood." *Ethnopolitics* 17 (4): 343–361.

Dembińska, Magdalena, and Frédéric Mérand. 2018. "The Role of International Brokers in Frozen Conflicts: The Case of Transnistria." *Asia Europe Journal*, 1–16.

Devyatkov, Andrey. 2014. "Russian Policy toward Transnistria: Between Multilateralism and Marginalization." *Problems of Post-Communism* 59 (3): 53–62.

Devyatkov, Andrey. 2017. "Russia and Transnistria in a Patron-client Relationship." Laboratorul pentru Analiza Conflictului Transnistrean, April 17. www.lact.ro/2017/04/17/andrey-devyatkov-russia-and-transnistria-in-a-patron-client-relationship/.

Devyatkov, Andrey, and Marcin Kosienkowski. 2013. "Testing Pluralism: Transnistria in the Light of 2011 Presidential Elections." In *Spotkania polsko-mołdawskie: Księga poświęcona pamięci Profesora Janusza Solaka* [Polish-Moldovan Encounters: The Commemorative Book for Professor Janusz Solak], edited by Marcin Kosienkowski, 303–328. Lublin: Episteme.

DPSU. 2014. "Derzhprykordonsluzhba zdiisnyuye posylenu okhoronu derzhavnoho kordonu [The State Border Service Carries Out the Enhanced Protection of the State Border]." Derzhavna prykordonna sluzhba Ukrayiny, March 21. https://dpsu.gov.ua/ua/news/derzhprikordonslyzhba-zdijsnjuje-posileny-ohorony-derzhavnogo-kordony/.

Dunn, Elizabeth Cullen, and Michael S. Bobick. 2014. "The Empire Strikes Back: War without War and Occupation without Occupation in the Russian Sphere of Influence." *American Ethnologist* 41 (3): 405–413.

Efrat, Moshe, and Jacob Bercovitch, eds. 1991. *Superpowers and Client States in the Middle East: The Imbalance of Influence.* London and New York: Routledge.

Gamova, Svetlana. 2010. "Amerikanskaya PRO kak podarok Pridnestrovyu [American Anti-Missile Defence as a present for Transnistria]." *Nezavisimaya Gazeta*, March 3. www.ng.ru/cis/2010-03-03/1_pro.html.

Gasiorowski, Mark J., and Seung-hyun Baek. 1987. "International Cliency Relationships and Client States in East Asia." *Pacific Focus* 2 (2): 113–143.

Ghinea, Cristian, Amanda Paul, and Victor Chirila. 2013. "Helping Moldova Stay on the EU Course: Proposals for a Real 'More for More' Approach." *EPC Policy Brief*, December 11. www.epc.eu/documents/uploads/pub_4006_helping_moldova_stay_on_the_eu_course.pdf.

Goble, Paul. 2014. "Moscow Threatens Ukraine from the West." *Eurasia Daily Monitor*, March 25. https://jamestown.org/program/moscow-threatens-ukraine-from-the-west/.

Gorchakov, Sergey. 2016. "Mify o pridnestrovskom postavshchike rossiiskogo gaza [Myths about Russian Gas Supplies to Moldova]." *Novosti Pridnestrovya*, October 6. https://novostipmr.com/ru/news/16-10-06/mify-o-pridnestrovskom-postavshchike-rossiyskogo-gaza.

GTK PMR. 2018a. "Vneshnyaya torgovlya PMR po osnovnym stranam i gruppam stran v razreze tovarnykh struktur za yanvar-avgust 2018 g. [International Trade of the TMR – Major Trade Partners, Groups of Countries and Commodities, January–August 2018]." Gosudarstvennyi Tamozhennyi Komitet Pridnestrovskoi Moldavskoi Respubliki, September 14. http://customs.gospmr.org/vneshnyaya-torgovlya-pmr-po-osnovnym-stra.html.

GTK PMR. 2018b. "Vneshnyaya torgovlya PMR po osnovnym stranam i gruppam stran za yanvar–avgust 2018 g. [International Trade of the TMR – Major Trade Partners, Groups of Countries, January–August 2018]." Gosudarstvennyi Tamozhennyi Komitet Pridnestrovskoi Moldavskoi Respubliki, September 14. http://customs.gospmr.org/2014-3.html.

Heimann, Gadi. 2010. "From Friendship to Patronage: France–Israel Relations, 1958–1967." *Diplomacy & Statecraft* 21 (2): 240–258.

Hensel, Stuart. 2006. *Moldova Strategic Conflict Assessment (SCA).* London: UK Global Conflict Prevention Pool.

Hill, William H. 2012. *Russia, the Near Abroad, and the West: Lessons from the Moldova-Transdniestria Conflict.* Washington, DC: Woodrow Wilson Center Press.

204 Marcin Kosienkowski

Imai, Kunihiko, and Peggy Ann James. 1996. "Dynamics of a Trilateral Game of Influence: Interactions between Major Powers' Foreign Policy Instruments and the Behavior of Weaker States." *International Interactions* 22 (2): 165–195.

Interfaks-Ukrayina. 2018. "Poroshenko zayavlyaet o roste boegotovnosti VSU [Poroshenko on Increase in Combat Readiness of the Armed Forces of Ukraine]." *Interfaks-Ukryina*, October 11. https://interfax.com.ua/news/general/537359.html.

Istomin, Igor, and Irina Bolgova. 2016. "Transnistrian Strategy in the Context of Russian–Ukrainian Relations: The Rise and Failure of 'Dual Alignment'." *Southeast European and Black Sea Studies* 16 (1): 169–194.

Ivanel, Bogdan. 2016. "Puppet States: A Growing Trend of Covert Occupation." In *Yearbook of International Humanitarian Law 2015*, edited by Terry D. Gill, 43–65. The Hague: Asser Press and Springer.

Jourde, Cédric. 2007. "The International Relations of Small Neoauthoritarian States: Islamism, Warlordism, and the Framing of Stability." *International Studies Quarterly* 51 (2): 481–503.

Kanet, Roger E., and Matthew Sussex, eds. 2015. *Power, Politics and Confrontation in Eurasia: Foreign Policy in a Contested Region.* London: Palgrave Macmillan.

Karaban, Dmitrii. 2017. "Kak zhivut v Moldove i Pridnestrovie [Life in Moldova and Transnistria]." *2000*, October 11. www.2000.ua/v-nomere/derzhava/realii/kak-zhivut-v-moldove-i-pridnestrove.htm.

Kennedy, Ryan. 2016. "The Limits of Soft Balancing: The Frozen Conflict in Transnistria and the Challenge to EU and NATO Strategy." *Small Wars & Insurgencies* 27 (3): 512–537.

Kim, Sunhyuk, and Wonhyuk Lim. 2007. "How to Deal with South Korea." *The Washington Quarterly* 30 (2): 71–82.

Kolstø, Pål. 2006. "The Sustainability and Future of Unrecognized Quasi-States." *Journal of Peace Research* 43 (6): 723–740.

Kolstø, Pål, and Helge Blakkisrud. 2017. "Regime Development and Patron–Client Relations: The 2016 Transnistrian Presidential Elections and the 'Russia Factor'." *Demokratizatsiya* 25 (4): 503–528.

Konończuk, Wojciech, and Witold Rodkiewicz. 2012. "Could Transnistria Block Moldova's Integration with the EU?" *OSW Commentary*, October 23. www.osw.waw.pl/sites/default/files/commentary_95.pdf.

Kosienkowski, Marcin. 2012. *Continuity and Change in Transnistria's Foreign Policy after the 2011 Presidential Elections.* Lublin: The Catholic University of Lublin Publishing House.

Krasnoselskii, Vadim. 2018a. "Pridnestrovie mozhet byt priznano kak Kosovo [Transnistria can be recognized as Kosovo]." Interview with *Nezavisimaya Gazeta*, January 22. www.ng.ru/cis/2018-01-22/1_7155_pridnestrovie.html.

Krasnoselskii, Vadim. 2018b. "Pridnestrovie – sostavnaya chast Russkogo mira: Tekushchaya situatsiya i perspektivy razvitiya [Transnistria – An Integral Part of the Russian World: Current Situation and Prospects for Development]." Lecture, Mezhdunarodnyi forum rossiiskikh sootechestvennikov 'Vmeste s Rossiei', Moscow, March 5. https://bit.ly/2Nj7fQf.

Krasnoselskii, Vadim. 2018c. "Poka rossiiskii mirotvorets na Dnestre — voiny ne budet [As Long as the Russian Peacekeeper is on the Dniester – There Will Be No War]." Interview with *Izvestiya*, July 30. https://iz.ru/771442/aleksei-zabrodin-dmitrii-laru/poka-rossiiskii-mirotvoretc-na-dnestre-voiny-ne-budet.

Krudu, Igor. 2018. "Defitsit byudzheta Pridnestrovya v sleduyushchem godu sostavit 1,8 milliarda rublei [The Budget Deficit of Transnistria Will Amount

to 1.8 Billion Rubles Next Year]." *Komsomolskaya Pravda*, September 22. www. kp.md/online/news/3243863/.
Ladwig, Walter C. 2016. "Influencing Clients in Counterinsurgency: U.S. Involvement in El Salvador's Civil War, 1979–92." *International Security* 41 (1): 99–146.
Lynch, Dov. 2004. *Engaging Eurasia's Separatist States: Unresolved Conflicts and De Facto States*. Washington, DC: United States Institute of Peace Press.
MID PMR. 2009. "MID Pridnestrovya napravil soboleznovaniya MIDu Yuzhnoi Osetii [Foreign Ministry of Transnistria Sent Condolences to the Foreign Ministry of South Ossetia]." Ministerstvo inostrannykh del Pridnestrovskoi Moldavskoi Respubliki, August 7. http://mfa-pmr.org/ru/Lxt.
MID PMR. 2012. "Kontseptsiya vneshnei politiki Pridnestrovskoi Moldavskoi Respubliki [Conception of External Policy of the Transnistrian Moldovan Republic]." Ministerstvo innostrannykh del Pridnestrovskoi Moldavskoi Respubliki, November 20. http://mfa-pmr.org/ru/Qpj.
MID PMR. 2014. "Zayavlenie Ministerstva inostrannykh del PMR v svyazi s prinyatiem Kryma i Sevastopolya v sostav Rossiiskoi Federatsii [Statement of the Ministry of Foreign Affairs of Transnistria in Connection with the Accession of the Crimea and Sevastopol into the Russian Federation]." Ministerstvo inostrannykh del Pridnestrovskoi Moldavskoi Respubliki, March 19. http://mfa-pmr.org/ru/pnh.
MID RF. 2016. "O vstreche stats-sekretarya – zamestitelya Ministra inostrannykh del Rossii G. B. Karasina s Prezidentom Pridnestrovya V. N. Krasnoselskim [On the Meeting of Secretary of State – Deputy Minister of Foreign Affairs of Russia Grigory Karasin with President of Transnistria V. N. Krasnoselskii]." Ministerstvo inostrannykh del Rossiiskoi Federatsii, December 20. www.mid.ru/ foreign_policy/news/-/asset_publisher/cKNonkJE02Bw/content/id/2574860.
MID RF. 2018. "Vystuplenie postoyannogo predstavitelya Rossii pri OBSE A. K. Lukashevicha na Zasedanii postoyannogo soveta OBSE v otvet na doklad glavy Missii OBSE v Moldavii, Vena, 12 iyulya 2018 goda [Speech by Alexander Lukashevich, Permanent Representative of Russia to the OSCE, at a Meeting of the OSCE Permanent Council in Response to the Report of the Head of the OSCE Mission to Moldova, Vienna, July 12, 2018]." Ministerstvo inostrannykh del Rossiiskoi Federatsii, July 13. www.mid.ru/foreign_policy/news/-/asset_publisher/ cKNonkJE02Bw/content/id/3294212.
MZS Ukrayiny. 2014. "Bryfinh v MZS [Briefing in the Ministry of Foreign Affairs]." Ministerstvo Zakordonnykh Sprav Ukrayiny, March 20. https://mfa.gov.ua/ua/ press-center/briefing/1197-brifing-v-mzs.
Nagashima, Toru. 2017. "Russia's Passportization Policy towards Unrecognized Republics: Abkhazia, South Ossetia, and Transnistria." *Problems of Post-Communism* 12 (4): 1–14.
Novosti Pridnestrovya. 2014. "Yevgenii Shevchuk: 'Pridnestrovie za vsyu svoyu istoriyu nikogda ni na kogo ne napadalo' [Yevgenii Shevchuk: 'Transnistria Has Never Attacked Any Other Country']." *Novosti Pridnestrovya*, March 11. https://novostipmr.com/ru/news/14-03-11/evgeniy-shevchuk-pridnestrove-za-vsyu-svoyu-istoriyu-nikogda-ni-na.
Oleksy, Piotr. 2014. "Transnistria's Difficult Choice." *New Eastern Europe*, August 5. http://neweasterneurope.eu/old_site/articles-and-commentary/1286-transnistria-s-difficult-choice.
Oleksy, Piotr. 2016. *Wspólnota z przypadku: Studium tożsamości mieszkańców Naddniestrza* [Community by Chance: Study of the Identity of the Inhabitants of Transnistria]. Gniezno: Instytut Kultury Europejskiej UAM w Gnieźnie.

O'Loughlin, John, Gerard Toal, and Rebecca Chamberlain-Creangă. 2013. "Divided Space, Divided Attitudes? Comparing the Republics of Moldova and Pridnestrovie (Transnistria) Using Simultaneous Surveys." *Eurasian Geography and Economics* 54 (2): 227–258.

Popescu, Nicu. 2006. "'Outsourcing' De Facto Statehood: Russia and the Secessionist Entities in Georgia and Moldova." CEPS Policy Brief 109. www.ceps.eu/system/files/book/1361.pdf.

Ravenhill, John. 1985. *Collective Clientelism: The Lomé Conventions and North-South Relations.* New York: Columbia University Press.

Regnum. 2009. "Rossiiskii deputat: Rossiya gotova zashchishchat svoikh sootechestvennikov v Pridnestrovie [Russian MP: Russia is ready to defend its compatriots in Transnistria]." *Regnum*, August 31. https://regnum.ru/news/polit/1201278.html.

Regnum. 2015. "Tiraspol: Agressiya v otnoshenii PMR budet oznachat napadenie na Rossiyu [Tiraspol: Aggression against Transnistria will mean an attack on Russia]." *Regnum*, July 27. https://regnum.ru/news/1946454.html.

Robertson, Dylan C. 2014. "Is Transnistria the Ghost of Crimea's Future?" *The Christian Science Monitor*, March 5. www.csmonitor.com/World/Europe/2014/0305/Is-Transnistria-the-ghost-of-Crimea-s-future.

Rodkiewicz, Witold. 2012. "Russia's Strategy towards Moldova: Continuation or Change?" *OSW Commentary*, April 19. www.osw.waw.pl/sites/default/files/commentary_74.pdf.

Rogstad, Adrian. 2016. "The Next Crimea? Getting Russia's Transnistria Policy Right." *Problems of Post-Communism* 65 (1): 49–64.

Rossiiskaya Gazeta. 2018. "Rogozin: RF ne svernet mirotvorcheskuyu missiyu v Pridnestrovie [Rogozin: Russia Will Not End the Peacekeeping Mission in Transnistria]." April 13. https://rg.ru/2018/04/13/rogozin-rf-ne-svernet-mirotvorcheskuiu-missiiu-v-pridnestrove.html.

Secrieru, Stanislav. 2016. "Transnistria Zig-zagging towards a DCFTA." *PISM Policy Paper* 145 (4). www.pism.pl/files/?id_plik=21295.

Shoemaker, Christopher C., and John W. Spanier. 1984. *Patron-Client State Relationships: Multilateral Crises in the Nuclear Age.* New York: Praeger.

Smirnov, Igor. 2007. *Vmeste s Rossiei* [Together with Russia]. Tiraspol: TIPAR.

Soloviev, Vladimir. 2007. "Ruka Moskvy davat ustala: Lider Pridnestrovya zloupotrebil rossiiskoi pomoshchyu [Moscow Hand Ceased Contributing: Transnistrian Leader Abused Russian Help]." *Kommersant*, April 6. www.kommersant.ru/doc/756473.

Soloviev, Vladimir. 2008. "Pridnestrovie smirilos s Moldaviei: Rossiya vynudila Igorya Smirnova k peregovoram s Kishinevom [Transnistria Reconciled with Moldova. Russia Forced Igor Smirnov to Negotiate with Chisinau]." *Kommersant*, February 29. www.kommersant.ru/doc/858155.

Soloviev, Vladimir, and Dmitrii Butrin. 2010. "Ruka Moskvy davat ustala: Rossiya zamorozila finansovuyu pomoshch Pridnestrovyu [Moscow Hand Ceased to Contribute: Russia Froze Financial Assistance to Transnistria]." *Kommersant*, July 23. www.kommersant.ru/doc/1473776.

Sorokin, Gerald L. 1997. "Patrons, Clients, and Allies in the Arab-Israeli Conflict." *Journal of Strategic Studies* 20 (1): 46–71.

Sputnik. 2016. "Krasnoselskii: Ekonomika Pridnestrovya zhiva blagodarya Rossii [Krasnoselskii: Transnistrian Economy Lives Thanks to Russia]." *Sputnik*,

December 21. https://ru.sputnik.md/news/20161221/10445026/krasnoselskijj-ekonomika-pridnestrovje-rossia.html.

Tètreault, Mary Ann. 1991. "Autonomy, Necessity, and the Small State: Ruling Kuwait in the Twentieth Century." *International Organization* 45 (4): 565–91.

Tkhorik, Vladimir, Mariya Tuzlova, and Natalya Zvarish. 2017. "Kontrabandnaya 'gumanitarka' dlya Pridnestrovya [Contraband 'humanitarian aid' for Transnistria]." RISE Moldova, June 29. www.rise.md/rusa/контрабандная-гуманитарка-для-при/.

Toal, Gerard. 2017. *Near Abroad: Putin, the West and the Contest over Ukraine and the Caucasus*. New York: Oxford University Press.

Ukrinform. 2014. "SBU zatrymala shpyhuna z prydnistrovskoho KDB [Ukrainian Intelligence Service Arrested a Spy from Transnistrian Intelligence Office]." *Ukrinform*, March 31. www.ukrinform.ua/rubric-polytics/1640800-sbu_zatrimala_shpiguna_z_pridnistrovskogo_kdb_1923733.html.

Veenendaal, Wouter P. 2017. "Analyzing the Foreign Policy of Microstates: The Relevance of the International Patron-Client Model." *Foreign Policy Analysis* 13 (3): 561–577.

4.4 The Nagorno-Karabakh Republic and the Republic of Armenia

Who instrumentalizes whom?

Vincenc Kopeček

The NKR is a relatively distinct entity compared with other post-Soviet de facto states. Its patron state is not Russia, but Armenia – though Russia has also played (and continues to play) a role in the conflict (Shirinyan 2013). While Russia uses its "client" de facto states – and, to a certain extent, also the NKR – to further its interests in the region (see Chapter 4.2), for Armenia the NKR is not only a state under its patronage but also a kin-state (Caspersen 2008), that is, an entity to which it is bound by ethnic ties, and which it feels morally obliged to assist (Brubaker 1996, 56) – even if such assistance entails the internationalization of the separatist conflict from which the kin-state emerged (Sisk 1996, 19–20). Using the examples of Serbian Kraina, Republika Srpska, and the NKR, Caspersen (2008) demonstrates that such situations do not always involve a unilateral dependence by the separatists on their kin/patron state; in some cases the separatists are able to leverage their ethnic kinship with the patron state and thus influence internal political decision-making processes within the patron state.

This chapter presents a systematic analysis of Armenian-Karabakhi relations. First it describes the emergence of the NKR in the context of its relations with Armenia, the NKR's kin-state. The chapter then analyzes Karabakh's influence on political decision-making processes in the Republic of Armenia, as well as the Armenian influence on the Karabakhi political elite; the main focus here is on informal aspects of Karabakhi-Armenian relations. The key question addressed by this chapter is: Who instrumentalizes whom? Does the Republic of Armenia instrumentalize the NKR, or vice versa?

The Karabakh Movement: from internal irredentism to separatism

Demands for the incorporation of Nagorno-Karabakh into the Armenian SSR were voiced at regular intervals practically from 1921 onwards, when the territory became a part of the Azerbaijan SSR in the form of the Nagorno-Karabakh Autonomous Region (NKAR) (Chorbajian, Donabedian, and Mutafian 1994, 144–147; Saparov 2012) – despite the fact that

Nagorno-Karabakh and Armenia 209

the majority of the population were ethnic Armenians (Baar 2001, 249). In the late 1980s, the liberalization of Soviet society led to renewed calls for the NKAR to be incorporated into the Armenian SSR; these demands became a catalyst for modern Armenian nationalism and emancipation from the USSR (Laitin and Suny 1999, 147). The so-called Karabakh Movement (*Gharabaghyan Sharzhum*), which emerged in the Armenian SSR at the end of the 1980s and was initially represented by the informal Karabakh Committee (*Gharabagh Komite*), eventually became the basis for the Pan-Armenian National Movement (*Hayots Hamazgayin Sharzhum*) – the political party which guided Armenia to independence when the USSR disintegrated (cf. Libaridian 2004, 205–208).

The incorporation of the NKAR into the Armenian SSR was initially one of the core demands voiced by leading representatives of the Pan-Armenian National Movement. However, this stance changed when the party's chairman Levon Ter-Petrosyan became the President of the independent Republic of Armenia. Whereas in August 1990, in the run-up to the elections for the Armenian Supreme Soviet, Ter-Petrosyan demanded the incorporation of the NKAR into Armenia (Astourian 2001, 19), a year later, as the head of the newly independent Armenian state he proved to be a moderate pragmatist. He declined to support the Karabakhi irredentists (support which would have provoked a military conflict with Azerbaijan, also a newly independent state), and instead prioritized Armenia's economic development and cultivated good relations with all its neighbours – including Turkey, which had always backed Azerbaijan in the conflict over Nagorno-Karabakh (Astourian 2001, 22–27; Cornell 2001, 303–304).

The representatives of the Karabakhi Armenians, who vehemently demanded the incorporation of the NKAR into Armenia (Croissant 1998, 35; Saparov 2015, Loc. 4164), thus found themselves in an unenviable situation. In 1990 the Karabakh problem had been an internal Soviet matter, whose only potential consequence would have been a border change affecting two SSRs (Libaridian 2004, 205–207). By now, however, it had become an international separatist conflict. Ter-Petrosyan had officially renounced Armenia's claim to Nagorno-Karabakh, so instead the Karabakhis declared independence as the Nagorno-Karabakh Republic (NKR) (Balayan 2005, 308); the Karabakhi self-defence units – gradually being organized into the Karabakh Defence Army[1] – had to face the Azerbaijani military. However, this did not mean that the Republic of Armenia withdrew its support from the Karabakhi kin. Quite the opposite: units made up of volunteers (*fedayee*) arrived from Armenia itself (and to a lesser extent from the Armenian diaspora) and fought alongside the Karabakh Defence Army (de Waal 2003, 163–187, 207). Particularly in the last two years of the war, units from the regular Armenian army also became involved in the conflict. Their involvement was on an unofficial basis, without the consent of the Armenian President, though Armenia's Defence Minister and army generals were fully aware of the situation (de Waal 2003, 210–212, 227).

210 *Vincenc Kopeček*

When the Bishkek Protocol was signed in May 1994, bringing a cease-fire between the parties in the conflict, the NKR won de facto independence from Azerbaijan. However, its independence was not recognized by any other state in the world – not even by the Republic of Armenia itself. There is speculation in the literature regarding the reasons that may have led Armenia to offer only unofficial support to the Karabakhi separatists rather than granting official recognition. Two main explanations are given: First, there was a political rupture between the NKR and Armenia. While Ter-Petrosyan prioritized economic development and cultivated good relations with neighbouring states, the Karabakhi Armenians based their claims on the USSR's Law on Secession,[2] which had been passed in April 1990 at the instigation of Mikhail Gorbachev. This law (which actually contravened the Soviet constitution) enabled autonomous units, or other similar territories within the individual SSRs, to hold referenda on their status if "their" SSR seceded from the USSR (Walker 2003, 166).[3] The second explanation is that Armenia's stance was merely a smokescreen (Caspersen 2008, 358) to conceal its support for the Karabakhi separatists and for the de facto annexation of Nagorno-Karabakh by Armenia, thus enabling Armenia to take part in peace talks not as a direct participant in the conflict, but in the advantageous position of a mediator – which, though it sympathized with the Karabakhi Armenians, had only a limited influence over them (Croissant 1998, 70; Cornell 2001, 92). This is in fact the official position taken by Azerbaijan, which views the NKR as a puppet government controlled by Yerevan (e.g. President.az 2015; Makili-Aliyev 2016). The motives behind Armenia's non-recognition of the NKR may be a subject for passionate debate; however, it is far more important to seek an understanding of relations between Armenia and the NKR today, over a quarter of a century after the official declaration of Karabakhi independence and more than two decades after the end of the Nagorno-Karabakh war. Is the NKR really just a smokescreen for Armenia's annexation of part of Azerbaijan's territory, or is the situation in fact much more complex – with each of the Armenian entities (though closely interlinked) operating according to its own distinct internal logic?

The NKR instrumentalizing Armenia?

Although Azerbaijan claims that part of its territory is occupied by Armenia, for more than two decades, until the Armenian Velvet Revolution of April 2018 which brought a major political earthquake, observers have been often noting that it was in fact the NKR which controlled Armenia (Caspersen 2008, 364). The main basis for this claim was the fact that two leading representatives of the Karabakhi Armenians – Serzh Sargsyan, the Commander-in-Chief of the Karabakh Defence Army, and Robert Kocharyan, the Chairman of the Karabakhi State Defence Committee[4] and the first elected President (1994) of the NKR – left Nagorno-Karabakh either

Nagorno-Karabakh and Armenia 211

during the war or shortly after it and settled in the Republic of Armenia, where they held a series of high-ranking positions. Their political careers, however, seem to be over – and with them also the direct Karabakhi influence on Armenia's politics. This subchapter thus mostly focusses on a period of Karabakhi-Armenian relations that recently came to its end; the new period is in its very beginning and it seems that the new Armenian political elite is going to further limit NKR's influence in its internal matters.

Robert Kocharyan was called to Yerevan by the Armenian President Ter-Petrosyan in 1997 during an internal political crisis following Armenia's 1996 Presidential elections, which appear to have been manipulated in Ter-Petrosyan's favour (Dudwick 1997, 104). There is no consensus on why Ter-Petrosyan decided to appoint Kocharyan (a *de jure* citizen of Azerbaijan) as the Prime Minister (Herzig 1999, 21),[5] though the aim was evidently to strengthen Ter-Petrosyan's position. However, neither Kocharyan nor Ter-Petrosyan lasted longer than a year in their posts. In early 1998 Ter-Petrosyan was forced to resign in a "constitutional coup"; this was in response to his support for a phased solution to the Karabakhi conflict[6] – a solution that was opposed by the Karabakhis, who felt that it was against the NKR's interests. Ter-Petrosyan's opponents included not only Kocharyan but also the Defence Minister Vazgen Sargsyan and the interior minister Serzh Sargsyan (Astourian 2001, 52–58).[7]

After the resignation of Ter-Petrosyan and other leading politicians from the Pan-Armenian National Movement, Kocharyan became the acting President; several months later his position was confirmed in a presidential election (Cornell 2001, 117). In October 1999 the Prime Minister Vazgen Sargsyan and the Speaker of the Parliament (and former First Secretary of the Armenian Communist Party) Karen Demirchyan were both killed in a terrorist attack on the Armenian Parliament, enabling the duo of Robert Kocharyan and Serzh Sargsyan to become the foremost centre of power in Armenia (Stefes 2008, 78). Kocharyan remained President until 2008, while Sargsyan served as the Defence Minister (2000–2007) and subsequently the Prime Minister (2007–2008). After Kocharyan's second presidential term he was replaced by Sargsyan, who not only managed to secure re-election, but during his second term in office he pushed through a constitutional reform in direction of parliamentarism and tried to serve another term as Prime Minister. He was eventually forced to resign in April 2018 after massive popular protests (Roth 2018). Sargsyan's fall during the Armenian Velvet Revolution in fact brought the end of a direct Karabakhi influence in Republic of Armenia's politics, which was symbolized by the so-called "Karabakh clan", a grouping which was widely believed to more or less control Armenia, de facto subordinating it to Karabakhi interests (de Waal 2013; Jaksa 2015).

The idea of the "Karabakh clan" de facto controlling Armenia is attractive, yet the situation is actually somewhat more complicated; it is important to distinguish several different aspects connected with the rise and fall of

212   *Vincenc Kopeček*

the originally Karabakhi political elite in the Republic of Armenia. First, the "Karabakh clan" is not a clan in the strict sense of the word; it is made up of individuals originally from Karabakh, who proved their credentials in the struggle for Karabakhi independence and who were (and to some extent still are) protégés of Kocharyan and Sargsyan (ICG 2008, 7; Stefes 2008, 78). Of the "clan" members, the two who have risen highest on the Armenian political scene are Oleg Yesayan, the first Karabakhi Prime Minister who became Armenia's ambassador in Russia and Belarus (Badalyan 2016; Artsakh Press 2017), and Seyran Ohanyan, who for many years was the Karabakhi Defence Minister before becoming the Chief of the General Staff of the Armenian army (2007) and Armenia's Defence Minister (2008) (RFE/RL 2008). For both of them, indeed, the Velvet Revolution most likely meant the end of their political career. Whereas Oleg Yesayan was only removed from his post, Seyran Ohanyan was charged with subverting public order in Armenia during the mass anti-government protest in March 2008 and taken into custody (A1Plus 2018b; Aysor.am 2019).

Second, although Kocharyan and Sargsyan rose to the highest echelons of Armenian politics, on their arrival in Armenia they still lacked a power base, so they co-opted the support of large sections of the Armenian economic and political elite who had originally supported Ter-Petrosyan (Stefes 2008, 78; Minasyan 2011, 143). They even managed to cultivate a key alliance with the war veterans' movement *Yerkrapah* (Defenders of the Land), which had originally belonged to the power base of Vazgen Sargsyan, a political rival of Kocharyan and Serzh Sargsyan (Astourian 2001, 56). *Yerkrapah* later joined forces with the Republican Party of Armenia (*Hayastani Hanrapetakan Kusaktsutyun*), led by the experienced Prime Minister Andranik Margaryan, enabling it to become the main pro-presidential party in Armenia; after Margaryan's death the party leadership (and the office of Prime Minister) was taken over by Serzh Sargsyan. The Republicans had been the most powerful political party in Armenia until April 2018, but the "Karabakh clan" only made up a small proportion of the party[8] – and some politicians originally from Karabakh, especially Robert Kocharyan and Seyran Ohanyan, have since fallen out with Serzh Sargsyan and taken their own political paths (Hayrumyan 2010; Hovhannisyan and Musayelyan 2011; The Armenian Weekly 2016). The fall of Kocharyan continued after the Velvet Revolution, when he was, likewise Ohanyan, charged with subverting of public order in Armenia during the mass anti-government protest in March 2008 and taken into custody (Mkrtchyan, Antidze, and Lawrence 2018).

Third, Kocharyan and Sargsyan initially prioritized Karabakhi interests. Kocharyan in particular, during the first years of his presidency, felt himself to be the political leader of both Armenian entities; this paradoxically led to the exclusion of the NKR from the peace talks, as Kocharyan took it upon himself to play a leading role in the talks.[9] In fact, in 2001–2002 Robert Kocharyan and his Azerbaijani counterpart Heydar Aliyev almost succeeded in reaching a negotiated solution to the Karabakhi conflict. Their proposal was that Nagorno-Karabakh should be absorbed into Armenia, the so-called occupied territories[10] were to be returned to Azerbaijan, and there was to be a land swap between the two countries – Azerbaijan would give up the Lachin corridor (which provided a direct link between Armenia and Nagorno-Karabakh), while Armenia would give up a strip of land along the Araxes River, providing Azerbaijan with a direct connection to its Nakhchivan exclave. This solution would also have given Azerbaijan a direct land link with Turkey, while Armenia would have lost its important border with Iran (Libaridian 2004, 261–262). Although at first sight this would have been a logical solution, it never became a reality due to a number of reasons[11]; however, it is interesting that the proposed solution would have been particularly beneficial for Karabakh and Nakhchivan (the birthplaces of Robert Kocharyan and Heydar Aliyev, respectively). For Armenia and Azerbaijan themselves, the solution would have involved losses of territory. Eventually, however, both Kocharyan and (especially) Sargsyan shifted their focus away from Karabakh, instead taking a political course that prioritized their own interests and their struggle for prominence on the Armenian political scene (Hayrumyan 2012).[12] By the end of the first decade of the 21st century, Serzh Sargsyan's politics were viewed in Karabakh as highly problematic, and he had come to embody national betrayal.[13] This was due to the so-called Armenian-Turkish rapprochement, which was to lead to the opening of the Turkish-Armenian border; the border had been closed by Turkey as an expression of solidarity with Azerbaijan. Although Armenia and Turkey signed an agreement formalizing this rapprochement, it was never actually ratified – not only due to protests by the Armenian diaspora and in Karabakh itself but also because the then Turkish Prime Minister Erdogan began to ratchet up his demands, making the ratification conditional upon the solution of the Karabakh conflict (Kardas 2016).

The relocation of the Karabakhi political elite to Yerevan could therefore have been motivated (among other factors) by their desire to provide security to Nagorno-Karabakh, but it is not possible to state that the "Karabakh clan" actually controlled Armenia. In fact, it merely became one part of the Yerevan political establishment (ICG 2008, 7–9), and if the NKR is attempting to instrumentalize Armenia to its own benefit, then this process is also taking place via other channels. The current political elite in the NKR is very well aware that although the Karabakh conflict is not an everyday item on Armenia's domestic political agenda or a key issue through which Armenian politicians seek to appeal to the electorate (Minasyan 2011, 144), the status of Nagorno-Karabakh is nevertheless a matter to which the Armenian public remains highly sensitive. The end of the 1980s marked the beginning of a process which Alexander Iskandaryan terms the "Karabakhization" (*karabakhizatsya*) of Armenian historiography (Iskandaryan and Arutyunyan 2003); Nagorno-Karabakh has become the focal point around which a narrative has emerged based on the notion of a centuries-old struggle for

214 *Vincenc Kopeček*

Armenian "independence in its 'historical' territories" (Minasyan 2009, 10). The members of the Karabakhi political elite are well aware of how they can use this image of Karabakh to influence the Armenian public – and also to exert pressure on the government of the Republic of Armenia, for which it is quite difficult to be at odds with the NKR government on key issues affecting the security of Karabakh.[14] A recent example is the growing anti-Russian sentiment in Armenia in connection with Russia's continuing supply of weapons to Azerbaijan. Traditionally, the Armenian-Russian alliance was considered to represent a guarantee of security not only for the Republic of Armenia but also for Nagorno-Karabakh. However, Karabakhi politicians have successfully managed to "sell" the notion to the Armenian public that Russia is an unreliable partner that is in fact helping to arm Azerbaijan – which then uses Russian weapons in armed operations against the NKR, as in the "four-day war" of April 2016 (Mghdesyan 2016). In an attempt to improve security guarantees for itself and the NKR, Armenia pulled strings to have its own representative appointed as the General Secretary of the Collective Security Treaty Organization (CSTO) – a military alliance dominated by Russia, of which Armenia (unlike Azerbaijan) is a member. In April 2017 Armenia was successful and the former Chief of the General Staff at the Armenian army Yuri Khachaturov, who is often perceived as a member of the "Karabakh clan", took the post (Kucera 2017).

Although it is far from true to claim that the "Karabakh clan" was in charge of Armenia, it definitely used to play a dominant role in one area which is of primary importance for the NKR – defence (ICG 2012, 11). For sixteen years – since Kocharyan's consolidation of his position after the deaths of Vazgen Sargsyan and Karen Demirchyan – the Armenian army was led by Karabakhi Armenians (either in the position of the Defence Minister or as the Chief of the General Staff) who previously held similar posts in the NKR. Serzh Sargsyan was Armenia's Defence Minister from 2000 to 2007,[15] and Seyran Ohanyan held the same post from 2008 to 2016 (The Armenian Weekly 2016). Yuri Khachaturov – who, though not originally from Karabakh, nevertheless played a major role in the Karabakh war (ICG 2012, 11) – was Armenia's Deputy Defence Minister from 2000 to 2008 and the Chief of the General Staff of the Armenian army from 2008 to 2016 (Armenpress 2016). After leaving Karabakh for Armenia, Movses Hakobyan (who had been the Karabakhi Defence Minister from 2007 to 2015) was initially the Deputy Chief of the General Staff, and later the Chief of the General Staff (MoD Armenia 2016). The dominance of the "Karabakh clan" in Armenia's defence sector ended in Spring 2018, when Movses Hakobyan was dismissed from his post and Artak Davtyan became the new Chief of the General Staff (Panorama.am 2018). Moreover, in July 2018, Yuri Khachaturov was (likewise Kocharyan and Ohanyan) accused of subverting public order in connection with the crackdown on anti-government protesters in 2008, and it is thus not sure if he is going to remain in the office of the Secretary General of the CSTO (Kucera 2018).

Nagorno-Karabakh and Armenia   215

It is, however, not only Armenian politicians of Karabakh origin but also the present-day leading Karabakhi politicians, who have a say in Armenia's internal politics. A good example is the situation preceding the resignation of Prime Minister Serzh Sargsyan in April 2018. Armenia's President Armen Sargsyan called a meeting of several prominent figures, who met with Serzh Sargsyan just several hours before his resignation, and one can expect, that Serzh Sargsyan discussed his decision with them. These figures were First Deputy Prime Minister Karen Karapetyan, Speaker of the National Assembly Ara Babloyan, Chairman of Public Council Vazgen Manukyan, Catholicos of All Armenians Garegin II, and President of the NKR Bako Sahakyan (A1Plus 2018a).

The taming of the NKR

Just as the NKR has at its disposal certain mechanisms for influencing political decision-making in the Republic of Armenia, so Armenia itself also has means of influencing internal politics in the NKR. These means are mainly a consequence of the fact that – although the NKR and Armenia are in many respects more equal than other post-Soviet de facto states and their patron states – Armenia is nevertheless the stronger partner in terms of its population, economy, and military capacity. The territory under the de facto control of the NKR government is one-third of the size of the Republic of Armenia, but its population is a mere 150,000 people, compared with the 3 million inhabitants of the Republic of Armenia itself. Economically too, the NKR is by far the weaker partner, with a GDP of just 400 million USD compared with Armenia's GDP in excess of 25 billion USD (ARMSTAT 2015; STAT NKR 2015; World Bank 2015). The NKR is thus dependent on Armenia in many respects – particularly with regard to its economy, defence issues, and foreign policy.

In economic terms, the NKR is entirely dependent on Armenia in matters of international trade[16]; there are only two routes connecting the NKR with the outside world, and both of them run through Armenia. Trade with Armenia makes up 82.3% of Nagorno-Karabakh's exports and 95.9% of its imports (STAT NKR 2016, 84–85). The NKR lacks its own central bank, and its currency is the Armenian dram, leaving it entirely dependent on Armenia's monetary policy. On the other hand, Armenia (along with the diaspora) has played a decisive role in the post-war reconstruction of the NKR (Kolstø and Blakkisrud 2008, 495–496), and even today, despite the ongoing recovery of the Karabakhi economy,[17] Armenia offers direct budgetary support (officially in the form of a loan)[18] amounting to around 50% of the total receipts of the Karabakhi budget (Krüger 2010, 111). According to the interviewed representatives of the NKR, however, this budgetary support is effectively a form of bribery through which Armenia ensures that the NKR remains compliant; in return, the NKR is given absolutely free rein on how it spends the money received from Yerevan.[19]

216 *Vincenc Kopeček*

Although the Karabakh Defence Army is an autonomous and militarily capable force with its own command structure, Armenian troops still operate within the NKR, though Armenia tends to deny this fact (Schmidt 2009, 12). The stated numerical strength of the Karabakh Defence Army is around 20,000 troops (Baranec and Beskid 2016), which amounts to around 15% of the NKR's total population; it is therefore likely that around half of this number are actually troops from Armenia (Blandy 2008, 14). Despite Armenian denials, these troops can be seen daily in the streets of Stepanakert and other Karabakhi towns.[20] Armenia is also supplying weapons to the Karabakhi forces, though this process is being conducted clandestinely, and precise figures on this military aid are not known (Blandy 2008, 14; Schmidt 2009, 12). Here, however, it is important to remember that the so-called "Karabakh clan" used to control the Armenian army to a considerable degree; this to an extent used to mitigate the NKR's dependence on Armenia for its defence capabilities, as well as it used to ensure that the two armies would be well coordinated in the event of war.[21] This coordination, however, remains priority even for the new Armenian government. The newly appointed Chief of the General Staff visited Nagorno-Karabakh only a few days after his appointment (News.am 2018).

The third area in which the NKR is highly dependent on Armenia is foreign policy. As the NKR is not a party to direct talks with Azerbaijan, its interests in these talks are represented by Armenia – even though Armenia does not officially recognize the NKR. This is a highly problematic situation for the NKR because the Karabakhi political elite does not consider the Republic of Armenia to be an entirely reliable partner[22]; the attempt by President Ter-Petrosyan to solve the Karabakh conflict at the expense of the NKR, the attempt by President Serzh Sargsyan to cultivate relations with Turkey, and the verbal dispute between Prime Minister Pashinyan and some Karabakhi politicians in December 2018 (Mejlumyan 2018) met with a very negative reception in the NKR.[23] Thus, the NKR government keeps a close watch on Armenia's foreign policy and it would also prefer to be a party to the peace talks; nevertheless, there are two main reasons because of which the NKR government has so far tolerated this situation. First, there is at least one benefit of being out of the talks: if the NKR government were a direct party to the talks, any failures in the negotiations could expose it to criticism by the Karabakhi population.[24] Second, for about two decades there have been two main obstacles which simply could not be removed by the NKR government. Whereas the first obstacle is still present, the second one seems to be lifted. The first obstacle is that Azerbaijan views Nagorno-Karabakh as Armenian-occupied territory and thus refuses to negotiate with the Karabakhi Armenians. The second obstacle dwelled in Kocharyan's and Sargsyan's endeavour to monopolize talks with Azerbaijan. Not only they most likely considered themselves as the true representatives of Karabakh Armenians, but the monopolization of the peace talks was also a good tool enabling them to exercise influence over the Karabakh government.

Nagorno-Karabakh and Armenia 217

However, the role of Armenia in the peace talks seems to change. The new Armenian Prime Minister Nikol Pashinyan stressed that at the peace talks he would represent the interest of Armenia, not the NKR, which should become, in his opinion, a party in the peace talks (Abrahamyan 2018).

The NKR government likewise tolerates the fact that Armenia does not officially recognize it. This situation complicates the NKR's attempts to achieve international recognition, though Armenia has little choice in the matter[25]; if it were to recognize the NKR, not only would Armenia be disqualified from participating in the peace talks, but Azerbaijan could potentially launch a retaliatory military strike against Nagorno-Karabakh – an eventuality that both Armenia and the NKR are keen to avoid (Erőss and Tátrai 2016, 14; Markedonov 2016). The new Armenian Prime Minister Nikol Pashinyan is apparently not only going to refuse the NKR's demands for recognition, but he also publicly stated that the NKR should become part of Armenia. Relations between Pashinyan and the Karabakhi leaders, however, remain tense; whereas the Armenian political elite has changed completely, in Nagorno-Karabakh the local elite survived virtually unchanged and it apparently does not enjoy Pashinyan's trust (Abrahamyan 2018; Mejlumyan 2018).

The NKR's dependence on Armenia is also reflected in its laws, which – for purely pragmatic reasons – are largely harmonized with Armenian legislation.[26] One Karabakhi Member of Parliament described this situation as a shared legal framework; laws passed by the Armenian Parliament are often subsequently passed in some form by the Karabakhi Parliament.[27]

The NKR's above-mentioned dependence on Armenia is a result of geographical, economic, and geopolitical facts. However, the Armenian government also has at its disposal softer means of influencing Karabakhi domestic politics – primarily its ability to informally influence the election of the NKR's President and the appointment of members of the government. Armenia does not have a formal veto which would enable it to prevent a particular candidate from standing for election or which would allow it to pre-select suitable candidates. Armenia's influence lies in the preferences of the Karabakhi voters themselves; a candidate who lacks good relations with *Mayr Hayastan* (Mother Armenia), the guarantor of Karabakh's security, has no realistic chance of being elected President (Smolnik 2016, 287). Once elected, the President likewise tends to appoint ministers who have good relations with the ruling elite in Armenia.[28] This is a consequence of events that unfolded in the first half of 1992, when Arthur Mkrtchyan (President of the Karabakhi National Council and the leader of the NKR) became embroiled in a serious dispute with the Armenian President Levon Ter-Petrosyan (Hakobyan 2010, 156–157; Smolnik 2016, 287). This dispute prevented cooperation between the NKR and Armenia, and it is considered to be one reason for the series of military defeats suffered by Karabakhi forces in the summer of 1992. One Karabakhi journalist gave an apt summary of the problem: "People know that we should tread our own political

218   *Vincenc Kopeček*

path, but there is a psychological problem here: Azerbaijan is preparing for war, so why are we arguing with Armenia?"[29]

An illustrative example in this context is the debate that has taken place on potential changes to the NKR constitution. In 2015 the general consensus was that the NKR would follow the Armenian model and move from semi-presidentialism to parliamentarism.[30] However, after the four-day war with Azerbaijan in April 2016, the NKR government surprisingly changed course and announced that the constitutional reforms would introduce a presidentialist system (a form of government which, in the region, is considered more agile and effective than parliamentarism). This change of direction appears to have followed an intervention by the then Armenian President Sargsyan, who preferred dealing directly with the NKR President; as mentioned above, Armenia exercises a strong influence over the election of the Karabakhi President, whereas its influence over parliamentary elections would be much weaker (Khanumyan 2016). There is, of course, an important question, if the new Pashinyan's government would follow the same path, or if it develops its own modus operandi in Karabakh.

Conclusion

The theory of de facto statehood traditionally describes Armenia as the patron state of the NKR. However, Karabakhi-Armenian relations are somewhat different – and considerably more complex – than the typical relations between de facto states and their patrons. The relationship between the NKR and Armenia is more equal than is typically the case: while Russia uses its "client" de facto states primarily as tools for furthering its interests in the region, for Armenia the NKR is not only a state under its patronage but also a kin-state – an entity to which it is bound primarily by ethnic ties rather than foreign policy interests. This kinship – bolstered by the mythologized role of Karabakh in the Armenian national historical narrative – enables the NKR to influence public opinion within Armenia, especially when the political course taken by the Armenian government represents an existential threat to Karabakh. This influence appears to be a stronger factor in Karabakhi-Armenian relations than the (former) presence of Karabakhi politicians at the highest level of Armenian politics. Those members of the Armenian political elite originating in Karabakh (dubbed the "Karabakh clan") have become largely "assimilated" in Yerevan, and serving their own political interests became their main priority. Moreover, after the Velvet Revolution of April 2018 most of them were deposed. The only areas in which the "Karabakh clan" used to exercise direct control were the Armenian Defence Ministry and the armed forces. The Republic of Armenia is able to influence the NKR by virtue of its economic, military, and demographic dominance, though it also makes use of certain informal mechanisms through which it can influence the election of leading NKR representatives. These mechanisms do not involve threats or bribery;

Nagorno-Karabakh and Armenia 219

instead they draw on the Karabakhi population's perception of "Mother Armenia" as a protector whose will must be respected. It is therefore not possible to claim that one entity instrumentalizes the other. Although Armenia is definitely the stronger partner, the overall situation is more one of mutual dependency.

Notes

1 The Defence Army of the Nagorno-Karabakh Republic (*Lernayin Gharabaghi Hanrapetutyan pashtpanutyan banak*) was established in 1992 under the command of Serzh Sargsyan, bringing together the existing Karabakhi self-defence units with the volunteer units from the Republic of Armenia.

2 Author's interview with a Karabakhi civil society leader and politician, October 2015.

3 In view of the large number of unrealistic formal conditions that the autonomous entities had to fulfil in order to hold a referendum, it is evident that the law was not in fact designed to enable autonomous territories to secede, but rather to stop the SSRs seceding from the USSR; however, it ultimately proved ineffective in this task (Walker 2003, 166).

4 Faced with the real prospect of military defeat, in July 1992 the Karabakhis established the State Defence Committee (*Pashtpanutyan petakan komite*), an executive body based on a Stalin-era model dating back to 1941; the Committee was the exclusive holder of all decision-making powers (political, military, and economic). It mobilized the entire able-bodied population of Nagorno-Karabakh for military service, and the economy of the territory was placed on a war footing (de Waal 2003, 196–197).

5 According to Herzig (1999, 21) there are three explanations for this move. First, Ter-Petrosyan wanted to legitimize his government by appointing some new faces who had not been tainted by their association with the corrupt political scene in Armenia. Second, Kocharyan – as a representative of the NKR – was to assist in negotiating a solution to the Karabakhi conflict. Third, Kocharyan was appointed as Prime Minister as a member of the "Karabakh clan" (see below), whose influence in Armenian politics was growing; the intention was that the Karabakh clan would help bolster support for Ter-Petrosyan against his opponents (including Vazgen Manukyan and Vazgen Sargsyan).

6 The "phased approach" meant that Armenian units were first to withdraw from the so-called occupied territories outside the former NKAR (with the exception of Lachin and Kelbajar), enabling refugees to return to their homes and economic cooperation to be re-established. Only then would the decision on the final status of Nagorno-Karabakh be taken. However, the Karabakhis instead pushed for a "package approach", which they considered more beneficial to them; this involved first deciding on the status of Nagorno-Karabakh, and only then withdrawing Armenian units from the territory outside the former NKAR.

7 The two Sargsyans were not related, but they both played an important role in the Karabakh war – Serzh as the Commander-in-Chief of the Karabakh Defence Army and Vazgen as the most prominent commander of the Armenian volunteer units.

8 Interview with an Armenian journalist, October 2015, and with an Armenian political analyst, October 2015.

9 Interview with an Armenian journalist, October 2015, and interview with a Karabakhi journalist, October 2015.

220 Vincenc Kopeček

10 The term "occupied territories" refers to Azerbaijani districts (or parts of districts) controlled by Armenian forces and located outside the territory of the former NKAR – Lachin, Kelbajar, Qubadli, Fizuli, Zangilan, Jebrail, and Aghdam.
11 According to Libaridian (2004, 262), the proposed solution was supported by both Turkey and the United States, but it failed to win the support of both presidents' advisors, Iran, and (despite official support) Russia. Azerbaijan eventually rejected the proposal.
12 Interview with an Armenian journalist, October 2015, and interview with an Armenian political analyst, October 2015.
13 Group interview with representatives of Karabakhi political parties, October 2009.
14 Interview with a Karabakhi journalist, October 2015.
15 He had also held the post of Defence Minister from 1993 to 1995.
16 Interview with a representative of Armenian Ministry of Economy, October 2009.
17 For more on the NKR's economy see, for example, Baar and Baarová (2017).
18 Interview with a Karabakhi journalist, October 2015, and interview with a Karabakhi civil society leader and politician, October 2015.
19 Interview with a Karabakhi journalist, October 2015.
20 Interview with a Karabakhi official, October 2009.
21 Interview with a former Karabakhi diplomat, October 2015; cf. Schmidt (2009, 12).
22 Interview with an Armenian political analyst, October 2015.
23 Interview with a high-ranked Karabakhi politician, October 2009, and online communication with a Karabakhi politician and civil activist, December 2018.
24 Interview with a Karabakhi journalist, October 2015.
25 Interview with a Karabakhi diplomat, October 2015.
26 Interview with a Karabakhi diplomat, October 2015.
27 Interview with a Karabakhi MP, October 2015.
28 Interview with a former Karabakhi diplomat, October 2015.
29 Interview with a Karabakhi journalist, October 2015.
30 Interview with a former Karabakhi diplomat, October 2015, interview with a Karabakhi civil society leader and politician, October 2015, and interview with a Karabakhi member of parliament, October 2015.

Literature

A1Plus. 2018a. "Bako Sahakyan met Serzh Sargsyan, Ara Babloyan and others." *A1Plus*, April 23. http://en.a1plus.am/1272720.html.
A1Plus. 2018b. "Oleg Yesayan Recalled for Post of Ambassador of Armenia to Belarus." *A1Plus*, August 15. https://en.a1plus.am/1276995.html.
Abrahamyan, Eduard. 2018. "Pashinyan Stiffens Armenia's Posture toward Karabakh." *Eurasian Daily Monitor* 15 (72). https://jamestown.org/program/pashinyan-stiffens-armenias-posture-toward-karabakh/.
Armenpress. 2016. "Biography of Secretary of National Security Council Yuri Khachaturov." *Armenpress*, October 3. https://armenpress.am/eng/news/862310/biography-of-secretary-of-national-security-council-yuri-khachaturov.html.
ARMSTAT. 2015. *Statistical Yearbook of Armenia, 2015*. Yerevan: National Statistical Service of the Republic of Armenia.
Artsakh Press. 2017. "Oleg Yesayan appointed as Ambassador of Armenia to Belarus." *Artsakh Press*, March 23. https://artsakhpress.am/eng/news/63940/oleg-yesayan-appointed-as-ambassador-of-armenia-to-belarus.html.

Nagorno-Karabakh and Armenia 221

Astourian, Stepan H. 2001. *From Ter-Petrosian to Kocharian: Leadership Change in Armenia*. Berkeley Program in Soviet and Post-Soviet Studies. Berkeley: University of California.

Aysor.am. 2019. "Ex Defense Minister Seyran Ohanyan charged." *Aysor.am*, January 10. www.aysor.am/en/news/2019/01/10/seyran-ohanyan/1511047.

Baar, Vladimír. 2001. *Národy na prahu 21. století. Emancipace nebo nacionalismus?* [Nations on the Threshold of the 21st Century. Emancipation or Nationalism?]. Ostrava a Šenov: Ostravská univerzita a Tilia.

Baar, Vladimír, and Barbara Baarová. 2017. "De Facto States and Their Socio-Economic Structures in the Post-Soviet Space after the Annexation of Crimea." *Studia z Geografii Politycznej i Historycznej* 6 (3): 267–303.

Badalyan, Naira. 2016. "Armenian Ambassador to Russia Comments on Vladimir Zhirinovsky's Recent Remarks about Armenia." *Arminfo*, August 3. www.arminfo.info/full_news.php?id=21358&lang=3.

Balayan, Vahram. 2005. *Artsakh History*. Yerevan: Zangak-97 Press.

Baranec, Tomáš, and Juraj Beskid. 2016. "Nagorno-Karabakh and the Military Balance." *Central Asia – Caucasus Analyst*, May 10. www.cacianalyst.org/publications/analytical-articles/item/13362-nagorno-karabakh-and-the-military-balance.html.

Blandy, C. W. 2008. *Azerbaijan: Is War over Nagornyy Karabakh a Realistic Option?* Caucasus Series 08/17. Shrivenham: Defence Academy of the United Kingdom – Advanced Research and Assessment Group. www.files.ethz.ch/isn/87342/08_may.pdf.

Brubaker, Rogers. 1996. *Nationalism Reframed: Nationhood and the National Question in the New Europe*. Cambridge: Cambridge University Press.

Caspersen, Nina. 2008. "Between Puppets and Independent Actors: Kin-State Involvement in the Conflicts in Bosnia, Croatia and Nagorno Karabakh." *Ethnopolitics* 7 (4): 357–372.

Chorbajian, Levon, Patrick Donabedian, and Claude Mutafian. 1994. *The Caucasian Knot. The History and Geo-Politics of Nagorno-Karabagh*. London and New Jersey: Zed Books.

Cornell, Svante E. 2001. *Small Nations and Great Powers. A Study of Ethnopolitical Conflict in the Caucasus*. Richmond: Curzon Press.

Croissant, Michael P. 1998. *The Armenia-Azerbaijan Conflict. Causes and Implications*. Westport and London: Praeger.

de Waal, Thomas. 2003. *Black Garden. Armenia and Azerbaijan through Peace and War*. London and New York: New York University Press.

de Waal, Thomas. 2013. *Nagorny Karabakh: Closer to War than Peace*. Russia and Eurasia Summary. London: Chatham House. www.files.ethz.ch/isn/168157/Nagorny%20Karabakh.pdf.

Dudwick, Nora. 1997. "Political Transformations in Postcommunist Armenia: Images and Realities." In *Conflict, Cleavage, and Change in Central Asia and the Caucasus*, edited by Karen Dawisha and Bruce Parrott, 69–109. Cambridge: Cambridge University Press.

Erőss, Ágnes, and Patrik Tátrai. 2016. "When Reality Meets Power-Rhetoric. Power, Mapping and Practice in Contested Spaces: The Case of Cyprus and Karabakh." *Documenti Geografici* 5 (1): 1–30.

Hakobyan, Tatul. 2010. *Karabakh Diary: Green and Black*. Lebanon: Antelias.

Hayrumyan, Naira. 2010. "Kocharyan's Moment? Armenia's Political Situation Might Be Favorable for Ex-President's Return to Big Politics." *ArmeniaNow*, April 18. www.armenianow.com/news/politics/21791/kocharyan_return_big_politics.

222 *Vincenc Kopeček*

Hayrumyan, Naira. 2012. "Secret of 'Karabakh Clan'." *Lragir*, October 8. www. lragir.am/index.php/eng/0/comments/home/27638.

Herzig, Edmund. 1999. *The New Caucasus. Armenia, Azerbaijan and Georgia.* London: Royal Institute of International Affairs.

Hovhannisyan, Irina, and Suren Musayelyan. 2011. "Parallels Drawn in Armenia After Kremlin Reshuffle." *Azatutyun*, September 27. www.azatutyun. am/a/24341709.html.

ICG. 2008. "Armenia: Picking up the Pieces." Europe Briefing N 48. Yerevan/ Tbilisi/Brussels: International Crisis Group. www.crisisgroup.org/~/media/Files/ europe/b48_armenia_picking_up_the_pieces.

ICG. 2012. "Armenia: An Opportunity for Statemanship." Europe Report N 217. International Crisis Group. www.crisisgroup.org/~/media/Files/europe/caucasus/ armenia/217-armenia-an-opportunity-for-statesmanship.pdf.

Iskandaryan, Aleksandr, and Babken Arutyunyan. 2003. "Armenia: Karabakhizatsya natsionalnoi istorii [Armenia: Karabakhization of National History]. In *Natsionalnye istorii v sovetskom i postsovetskikh gosudarstvakh* [National Histories in Soviet and Post-Soviet States], edited by Karl Aimermakhev and Gennadii Bordyugov, 145–158. Moskva: Fond Fridrikha Naumanna.

Jaksa, Urban. 2015. *South Caucasus: Nagorno-Karabakh between a Contested Territory and a Small State.* Small State Briefs. York: University of York, Centre for Small State Studies. http://ams.hi.is/wp-content/uploads/2014/04/White-Paper-6.pdf.

Kardas, Saban. 2016. "Erdogan Reconnects Turkish-Armenian Normalization to Progress on Karabakh." *Eurasia Daily Monitor* 7 (76). www.jamestown.org/ single/?tx_ttnews%5Btt_news%5D=36288&no_cache=1.

Khanumyan, Hayk. 2016. "Konstitutsionnye reformy – sredstvo reproduktsii vlasti [Constitutional Reforms – The Way How the Power Reproduces Itself]." *Analyticon*, no. October. http://theanalyticon.com/?p=8350&lang=ru.

Kolstø, Pål, and Helge Blakkisrud. 2008. "Living with Non-Recognition: State- and Nation-Building in South Caucasian Quasi-States." *Europe-Asia Studies* 60 (3): 483–509.

Krüger, Heiko. 2010. *The Nagorno-Karabakh Conflict: A Legal Analysis.* Heidelberg, New York, Dordrecht, London: Springer.

Kucera, Joshua. 2017. "With an Armenian (Finally) in Charge, Will CSTO Alter Course?" Eurasianet, April 27. https://eurasianet.org/armenian-finally-charge-will-csto-alter-course.

Kucera, Joshua. 2018. "Armenian Investigators Charge Head of Russia-led Security Bloc with 'Subverting Public Order'." *Eurasianet*, July 30. https:// eurasianet.org/armenian-investigators-charge-head-of-russia-led-security-bloc-with-subverting-public-order.

Laitin, David D., and Ronald Grigor Suny. 1999. "Armenia and Azerbaijan: Thinking a Way out of Karabakh." *Middle East Policy* 7 (1): 145–176.

Libaridian, Gerard J. 2004. *Modern Armenia. People, Nation, State.* London and New York: Transaction Publishers.

Makili-Aliyev, Kamal. 2016. "Nagorno-Karabakh Isn't Disputed Territory—It's Occupied." *The National Interest*, May 10. http://nationalinterest.org/blog/the-buzz/ nagorno-karabakh-isnt-disputed-territory%E2%80%94its-occupied-16141.

Markedonov, Sergey. 2016. "Independence for Nagorno-Karabakh: A Hard Dilemma for Yerevan." *Russia Direct*, May 5. www.russia-direct.org/opinion/ independence-nagorno-karabakh-republic-hard-dilemma-yerevan.

Mejlumyan, Ani. 2018. "Pashinyan clashes with Nagorno-Karabakh leaders." *Eurasianet* December 3. https://eurasianet.org/pashinyan-clashes-with-nagorno-karabakh-leaders.

Mghdesyan, Arshaluis. 2016. "Karabakh Challenges Armenian-Russian Alliance." *Institute for War and Peace Reporting*, April 19. https://iwpr.net/global-voices/karabakh-challenges-armenian-russian-alliance.

Minasyan, Sergey. 2009. "Armenia's Attitude towards Its Past: History and Politics." *Caucasus Analytical Digest* 9: 10–13.

Minasyan, Sergey. 2011. "Armenia in Karabakh, Karabakh in Armenia: Living with a Conflict." In *Identities, Ideologies & Institutions*, edited by Alexander Iskandaryan, 142–152. Yerevan: The Caucasus Institute.

Mkrtchyan, Hasmik, Margarita Antidze, and Janet Lawrence. 2018. "Armenian Ex-president Kocharyan Detained after Court Ruling." *Reuters*, December 7. www.reuters.com/article/us-armenia-kocharyan/armenian-ex-president-kocharyan-detained-after-court-ruling-lawyer-idUSKBN1O623U.

MoD Armenia. 2016. "Movses Hakobyan – Chief of the RA AF GS." Ministry of Defence of the Republic of Armenia. www.mil.am/en/50/53.

News.am. 2018. "Armenia Army Chief in Karabakh, Visits Frontline." *News.am*, June 6. https://news.am/eng/news/455010.html.

Panorama.am. 2018. "Artak Davtyan Appointed New Armenian Army Chief." *Panorama.am*, May 25. www.panorama.am/en/news/2018/05/25/Armenian-army-chief/1954298.

President.az. 2015. "Karabakh." Official Web-Site of President of Azerbaijan Republic. http://en.president.az/azerbaijan/karabakh.

RFE/RL. 2008. "Sarkisian Appoints Key Ministers in Emerging Cabinet." *Radio Free Europe / Radio Liberty*, April 15. www.azatutyun.am/a/1594499.html.

Roth, Andrew. 2018. "Shock as Armenia's Prime Minister Steps down after 11 Days of Protests." *The Guardian*, April 23. www.theguardian.com/world/2018/apr/23/serzh-sargsyan-resigns-as-armenias-prime-minister-after-protests.

Saparov, Arsène. 2012. "Why Autonomy? The Making of Nagorno-Karabakh Autonomous Region 1918–1925." *Europe-Asia Studies* 64 (2): 281–323.

Saparov, Arsène. 2015. *From Conflict to Autonomy in the Caucasus: The Soviet Union and the Making of Abkhazia, South Ossetia and Nagorno Karabakh*. Kindle Edition. Abingdon and New York: Routledge.

Schmidt, Hans-Joachim. 2009. *Military Confidence Building and Arms Control in Unresolved Territorial Conflicts*. PRIF-Reports No. 89. Frankfurt am Main: Peace Research Institute Frankfurt. www.hsfk.de/fileadmin/HSFK/hsfk_downloads/prif89.pdf.

Shirinyan, Anahit. 2013. "Assessing Russia's Role in Efforts to Resolve the Nagorno-Karabakh Conflict: From Perception to Reality." *Journal of Conflict Transformation*, no. February. http://caucasusedition.net/analysis/assessing-russias-role-in-efforts-to-resolve-the-nagorno-karabakh-conflict-from-perception-to-reality/.

Sisk, Timothy D. 1996. *Power Sharing and International Mediation in Ethnic Conflicts*. Washington, DC: US Institute of Peace Press.

Smolnik, Franziska. 2016. *Secessionist Rule: Protracted Conflict and Configurations of Non-State Authority*. Frankfurt and New York: Campus Verlag.

STAT NKR. 2015. *Nakorno Karabkh in Figures 2015*. Stepanakert: National Statistical Service of NKR. http://stat-nkr.am/files/publications/2015/LXH_tverov_2015.pdf.

224 *Vincenc Kopeček*

STAT NKR. 2016. *Nagorno Karabakh in Figures*. Stepanakert: National Statistical Service of the NKR.

Stefes, Christoph H. 2008. "Governance, the State, and Systemic Corruption: Armenia and Georgia in Comparison." *Caucasian Review of International Affairs* 2 (2): 73–83.

The Armenian Weekly. 2016. "Former Armenian Defense Minister Seyran Ohanyan to Return to Politics." *The Armenian Weekly*, December 20. http://armenianweekly.com/2016/12/20/seyran-ohanyan-return/.

Walker, Edward W. 2003. *Dissolution: Sovereignty and the Breakup of the Soviet Union*. Lanham: Rowman & Littlefield.

World Bank. 2015. "World Development Indicators." *World DataBank*. http://databank.worldbank.org/data/home.aspx.

4.5 Inside a de facto state
Forming and sustaining the Abkhazian and Nagorno-Karabakh Republic polities

Vincenc Kopeček

De facto states in the post-Soviet space are sustained not only by the influence of the patron state (whether an external power or a kin-state) or the weakness of the parent state but also by the de facto state's own efforts to form, sustain, and strengthen its institutional structures. This chapter therefore focusses on the internal situation within post-Soviet de facto states, using Abkhazia and the NKR as examples. Both these entities have followed similar paths of development, yet they nevertheless differ in many respects. The following analysis of the development of political institutions in both de facto states will centre on four distinct aspects.

First, the chapter focusses on the immediate consequences of the military conflicts from which both entities emerged. The second aspect concerns the impacts of the so-called democratization-for-recognition strategy, which both Abkhazia and the NKR began to apply at the beginning of the 21st century to bolster their efforts to gain international recognition. The third aspect involves the risk of a re-ignition of the conflict and the threat to the de facto state from its parent state. The fourth aspect is the ethnic composition of the population in both de facto states – a factor which determines the nature of the Karabakhi and Abkhazian national projects.

The beginnings of de facto statehood: commanders, warlords, and presidents

In the 1990s, post-Soviet de facto states were viewed as "black holes" on the world political map – as territories under the control of warlords, with economies based on corruption and clientelism, and as hotbeds of criminal activity, with smuggling across otherwise closed borders, money-laundering and other illicit practices (Kolossov and O'Loughlin 1998, 1; King 2001; Lynch 2004, 4). It would be a mistake to view de facto states during this period solely through this lens; however, all of the above-mentioned issues were certainly more prevalent at that time than was the case ten years later. This change has been reflected in the scholarly literature, which has begun to focus more closely on the internal politics of de facto states (Caspersen

226   *Vincenc Kopeček*

2008, 117). However, this recent academic interest was preceded by significant re-configurations of political forces and structures in the de facto states – and shifts in the nature of their polities *per se*.

The victorious wars of independence swept new elites to power in both Abkhazia and the NKR. Some members of these elites had already been closely associated with the separatist movements before the conflicts began, while others were prominent military commanders. Both these groups enjoyed an almost unassailable status as national heroes (Matsuzato 2008, 96), though there were considerable differences among them in terms of the roles they played in Abkhazian and Karabakhi politics, as well as in their paths to power. The driving force behind Abkhazia's independence was Vladislav Ardzinba. An intellectual, historian, and linguist employed by the Abkhazian Academy of Sciences, Ardzinba was the *de facto* founder of the Abkhazian separatist movement. Prior to the conflict, he had been the Chairman of the Supreme Soviet of the Abkhazian ASSR. After the conflict, he became Abkhazia's first President – a position he held without any significant political rivals for two electoral terms (Matsuzato 2008, 106–107). His only opponent in the 1999 presidential election was Leonid Lakerbaia, but the Central Electoral Commission rejected Lakerbaia's candidacy on the grounds of "technical problems" (Hale 2015, 156).

The situation in the NKR was somewhat more complex. In the parliamentary elections of 1992, the first generation of Karabakhi political leaders – led by Oleg Yesayan, Karabakh's first Prime Minister – was defeated by a group led by Artur Mkrtchyan, who became the Speaker of the Parliament, and thus – under the Soviet model that was still used – also the head of state (Balayan 2005, 309; Avakian 2010, 18). Mkrtchyan and his political allies were loyal to the Dashnaks – the Armenian Revolutionary Federation (*Hay Heghapokhakhan Dashnaktsutyun*), a worldwide Armenian nationalist party. The Dashnaks were somewhat more radical and assertive than Yesayan's grouping, which had links with the relatively moderate Armenian President Levon Ter-Petrosyan. Besides creating a schism on the Karabakhi domestic political scene, this also caused a split between the Republic of Armenia and the NKR (Hakobyan 2010, 156–159). Especially in Karabakh itself, this split is regarded as having been responsible for the serious setbacks that beset the Karabakhi-Armenian side in the early phase of the Karabakh war, ultimately leading to the loss of the Shahumyan district (lying north of the original Nagorno-Karabakh Autonomous Region but also inhabited primarily by ethnic Armenians).[1] The internal political disputes in Karabakh culminated in the murder of Mkrtchyan and the formation of the State Defence Committee in response to an Azerbaijani offensive; the Committee took de facto control of Nagorno-Karabakh, under the leadership of Robert Kocharyan (Hakobyan 2010, 156–159). From the beginnings of the Karabakh Movement, Kocharyan had been involved in the so-called Krunk Committee, though during the first months of Karabakhi independence he was somewhat reluctant to hold high-ranking political positions (de

Inside a de facto state 227

Waal 2003, 56). In the end, however, it was Kocharyan who – with the assistance of regular Armenian forces – led Nagorno-Karabakh to victory in the war, and at the end of 1994 he became its first President.

Other leaders of the Karabakhi separatists besides Kocharyan included Serzh Sargsyan (Kocharyan's ally from the era of the Krunk Committee) and Samvel Babayan, a former car mechanic and petty criminal (de Waal 2003, 227) who, after Sargsyan's departure for Armenia (see Chapter 4.2) became the Commander-in-Chief of the Karabakh Defence Army (Matsuzato 2008, 102). In 1997, when Robert Kocharyan was invited to Yerevan by the Armenian President Levon Ter-Petrosyan to take up the position of Armenia's Prime Minister, the presidency of the NKR passed to Kocharyan's protégé Arkadi Ghukasyan. However, Ghukasyan – a representative of the civilian government – faced opposition from Samvel Babayan, who (as the Defence Minister and the head of the war veterans' association *Yerkrapah*) controlled an extensive clientelistic network that had been built up gradually since the war years. Contemporary observers frequently noted that Babayan was the real leader of the NKR; unlike Kocharyan and Sargsyan, who had prioritized their own careers in the Republic of Armenia, Babayan remained in Karabakh as an *eminence grise*, pulling the strings of Karabakhi politics and profiting from the black economy (Lynch 2004, 60; Matsuzato 2008, 102). He was a sort of warlord – though it must also be noted that Kocharyan and Sargsyan too were involved in the black economy; they allegedly controlled a network smuggling oil products from Azerbaijan to Armenia, and indeed this is cited by some authors as an explanation for Kocharyan's rise to power and his appointment as the Armenian Prime Minister (Herzig 1999, 21). Babayan turned out to be a nightmare for Nagorno-Karabakh. In peacetime, his control over the black market (originally based on smuggling loot from the conquered territories into Iran) grew to give him informal control over the entire economy – accompanied by extortion, kidnappings, and other forms of violent crime (de Waal 2003, 242–243; Kolstø and Blakkisrud 2008, 290–292). As Babayan's power continued to grow, President Ghukasyan eventually decided to remove him from the scene. In 1999 Babayan was dismissed from the post of Defence Minister, and in the following year he was accused of having planned an unsuccessful assassination attempt against Ghukasyan; in February 2001 he was convicted and sentenced to fourteen years' imprisonment (de Waal 2003, 241–245).[2]

While in the NKR the civilian government was crushing the warlords, in Abkhazia it was the representatives of war veterans who helped to remove power from Ardzinba's clique and achieve a victory for the opposition in the 2004 presidential elections. Ardzinba was not a warlord, and he led a civilian government. However, especially during his second electoral term he took an increasingly authoritarian stance, and his power was based on an extensive network of clientelistic and nepotistic structures; he appointed numerous protégés and relatives to leading official positions (Skakov 2005, 159; Matsuzato 2008, 107). These relatives were not family in the Western

228 *Vincenc Kopeček*

sense; they were based on the Abkhazian concept of the *azhvla*, a broad kinship encompassing all persons sharing the same surname (Smolnik 2016, 168). During Vladislav Ardzinba's second presidential term, when it became clear that the President was too ill to stand for a third term (which, in any case, was not permitted under the Abkhazian constitution), two branches of the Ardzinba *azhvla* (the *Ardzinbovtsy*) and their protégés began a power struggle (Skakov 2005, 161). First, in December 2002, the Prime Minister Anri Jergenia was dismissed from his post; he had been tipped as Vladislav Ardzinba's successor, and he was a protégé of Salibey Ardzinba, the leader of one branch of the *Ardzinbovtsy*. During the following year, both Salibey Ardzinba and Levan Ardzinba (one of the two leaders of another branch of the *azhvla*) were murdered. The other leader of Levan Ardzinba's branch of the *azhvla*, Pavel Ardzinba, became Abkhazia's *eminence grise*. Nevertheless, the situation – with the President suffering increasing health problems and the *Ardzinbovtsy* greatly weakened – emboldened critics of the corrupt political elite (Skakov 2005, 163–164; Smolnik 2016, 168–170). The most prominent opposition forces were the *Aitaira* (Revival) movement, and later also the *Amtsakhara* (Eternal Flame) organization, an association of war veterans founded by the war hero General Sergei Dbar. After Dbar's death in 2002 the *Amtsakhara* fell under the control of the *Ardzinbovtsy* for a while, though in 2003 its members again elected generals as their leaders – Vladimir Nachach-ogly and Mirab Kishmaria. Under their leadership, the *Amtsakhara* joined forces with the *Aitaira* to form the main opposition grouping (Skakov 2005, 163–165). The clash between this new opposition movement and the previously untouchable Vladislav Ardzinba brought about a lengthy political crisis which culminated in a battle for the presidency between the opposition candidate Sergei Bagapsh and Ardzinba's protégé, the Prime Minister Raul Khajimba – who was generally considered to have Russia's backing. The complex situation in the aftermath of the election eventually led to an agreement between both candidates; the repeat election in October 2004 saw Bagapsh elected as President and Khajimba as his Vice-President (Matsuzato 2008, 106–108).

Ten years after the end of the war, the first stage in Abkhazia's development – dominated by President Vladislav Ardzinba and his *azhvla* – finally came to an end, and power passed to the pro-democratic opposition. The NKR found itself in a similar situation at the turn of the new millennium, as the influence of the warlord Babayan receded and was replaced by a democratizing polity.

Building democratic institutions: to benefit citizens, or to impress the West?

The democratization of Abkhazia and the NKR during the first decade of the 21st century resulted from a combination of three factors: (1) the initial situation, (2) the motives underlying the process of democratization, and

Inside a de facto state 229

(3) synergies within society as a whole. With regard to the first factor: in the words of Lucan Way (2005), both de facto states were "failed authoritarianisms". Due to the relative weakness of both entities, no political leaders had sufficient power and resources to enable them to remove their opponents entirely from the scene. At the beginning of the 21st century, both de facto states ousted the political cliques that had prevented democratization (the *Ardzinbovtsy* in Abkhazia and the Babayan clique in the NKR), opening up a path towards a more democratic society in both cases. We use this metaphor of "opening up a path" merely to describe the emergence of a situation that potentially enabled democratization to take place; we do not mean to imply that democratization was an inevitable consequence. The fact that a path exists does not necessarily mean that individuals, groups, or entire states will follow that path.

With regard to the second factor, it is important to analyze the motives for this democratization. The literature (e.g. Broers 2005; Popescu 2006; Berg and Mölder 2012; Kolstø and Blakkisrud 2012) generally refers to the so-called "democratization-for-recognition strategy". This strategy is based on the opinion, commonly held by the political leaders of de facto states, that democratic states "have more chance of being recognized by the international community than others" (Ghukasyan cited in Caspersen 2009, 55–56). A contributing role has been played here by the Kosovo precedent. Kosovo received recognition from many states as it was considered a "unique case" (Ker-Lindsay 2013), and not as a result of a democratization-for-recognition strategy. Nevertheless, representatives of de facto states in the Caucasus argued that they were in fact more democratic than Kosovo, and should therefore receive international recognition on this basis (Popescu 2007, 18).

With regard to the third factor, it is important to take into account the synergies created by the events which appeared to act as catalysts for the entire process. Declarations by political leaders – which could easily have gone no further than the creation of nominally democratic constitutions – were in fact taken seriously by the emerging civil societies in both de facto states, which to a large extent viewed democratization as a continuation of the Abkhazian and Karabakhi national projects. According to this logic, the first essential step was to defend the de facto state's newly gained independence, and then the focus could shift to building its own statehood; democracy was viewed as the only possible path, a logical culmination of the struggle for independence. Proponents of this stance maintained that it was impossible to achieve democracy while still a part of Georgia or Azerbaijan, respectively, because the governments of these parent states had violently repressed the political aspirations of the Abkhazians and the Karabakhi Armenians.[3] Civil society organizations' determination to support democratization and to defend human and civil rights also stemmed from their disappointment at the lack of progress achieved by peace initiatives taking place as part of track II diplomacy,[4] which had achieved virtually nothing in an entire decade. Civil society organizations' refocussing of their attention on the

230   *Vincenc Kopeček*

domestic political scene within the de facto states was a logical consequence of this situation (Kopecek, Hoch, and Baar 2016, 451; Hoch, Kopeček, and Baar 2017, 338).

Both societies – Abkhazia and Nagorno-Karabakh – thus embarked upon a quite dramatic process of internal change, transforming these former "black holes" on the world map into state entities which – by the standards of the region – functioned remarkably well. It is important to note that these are not liberal democracies in the European sense, but rather hybrid regimes in which certain democratic institutions have been implanted into an essentially authoritarian reality; both societies continue to suffer from typical features of post-Soviet states, including high levels of corruption and clientelism. Nevertheless, both entities have constitutions which are based on democratic principles, political party systems which (though not ideal) are pluralistic in nature (Kolstø and Blakkisrud 2012, 145–146), elections which (though not entirely fair) do involve genuine competition (Ó Beacháin 2012, 2015), media and local government bodies which (by post-Soviet standards) enjoy a high degree of freedom, and relatively active civil societies (Kopeček 2016, 82–84; Kopecek, Hoch, and Baar 2016; Hoch, Kopeček, and Baar 2017).

The constitutions of both de facto entities crystallized over a period of time; constitutionality was not considered a priority during the phase of armed struggle, when basic legislation was put in place via various provisional means. In 1992 Abkhazia merely re-activated the constitution of the Abkhazian SSR dating from 1925, though the purpose was not to create a framework for internal political systems, but rather to demonstrate Abkhazia's status as a separate entity from Georgia; the constitution stated that Abkhazia was in fact a separate republic, loosely associated with the Georgian SSR (Cornell 2001, 170). The NKR had been an autonomous region within the Soviet Union, and so it had no similar former constitution to fall back upon. In January 1992 it therefore immediately issued its Constitutional Law on Basic Principles of the State Independence of the NKR (Avakian 2010, 18); the individual state institutions, including the presidency and the government, were created at a later date by separate acts of legislation. It was not until 2006, as part of the democratization-for-recognition strategy, that the basic principles of Karabakh's political system were finally consolidated in a constitution approved by referendum (Kopeček 2016, 77). In Abkhazia too there was a delay before a new constitution was adopted; the Abkhazian Parliament approved the new constitution in 1994, but it was not approved by referendum (after several amendments) until 1999 (Kopecek, Hoch, and Baar 2016, 93).

The approval of the Abkhazian constitution and Karabakh's Law on Presidency marked a departure from the Soviet parliamentary model, in which the Speaker of the Parliament (or the Chairman of the Supreme Soviet) was also the head of state. Abkhazia introduced a presidential system with a directly elected President and Vice-President; the President appoints

Inside a de facto state 231

the members of the government, including the Prime Minister. Up until the 2017 constitutional reform, the Karabakhi system was ostensibly closer to semi-presidentialism – though in reality (like the Abkhazian presidential system) it was actually more akin to super-presidentialism, which puts excessive competencies to the hands of President. It is likely that the new presidential model of government will behave in a similar way (Khanumyan 2016). In both cases, the President's dominance is not restricted to the appointment of the government; the President also selects candidates for (or makes direct appointments to) numerous important positions – including the chief prosecutor, judges, members of the central bank committee, and the heads of local or regional government bodies (Kopeček 2016, 76–77).

A pluralistic system of political parties has developed in both de facto states, especially during the first decade of the 21st century. Political parties did exist during the 1990s, but their influence on political decision-making was minimal. This was due to the majoritarian (plurality voting) system and (in the case of Abkhazia) the process for selecting candidates, who were nominated by citizens or civil society organizations (Krylov 2002; Ó Beacháin 2012, 168). In Abkhazia, CSOs are termed "socio-political movements", and for many years they largely took the place of political parties. Indeed, most of them eventually registered as fully fledged political parties (Kopeček 2016, 80). In the NKR the boom in political parties came after 2005, when new legislation on political parties was passed and the electoral system was changed from a plurality voting system to a mixed-member system (Smolnik 2012, 158).

Although political parties formally exist both in Abkhazia and the NKR, they are somewhat different to the political parties we know from Western democracies. Few of them are defined by their ideology or political manifesto; instead, most of them are classic one-man parties (Kopeček 2016, 80) of the type that is familiar in the post-Soviet space (cf. Miller and Klobucar 2000; Wilson 2005; Nodia and Scholtbach 2006). Especially in Abkhazia, these political parties are known as *grupirovky*.[5] The elections are genuinely competitive, but the competition is typical of hybrid regimes; it mainly involves a battle between individual strong leaders, often controlling extensive clientelistic networks (Hale 2015, 155–158), and the ruling political groupings are able to call upon various financial and administrative resources in order to ensure that the election takes place on a distinctly uneven playing-field (Kopeček 2016, 82). This, in the words of Ishiyama and Batta (2012), gives rise to dominant political party systems, in which the pro-presidential party remains in power for long periods. Nevertheless, opposition parties have managed to achieve electoral success in both Abkhazia and the NKR. In Abkhazia this occurred in 2004, when Sergei Bagapsh won the presidential election. The political camp loyal to Bagapsh (and his successor Alexander Ankvab) then remained in power for an entire decade until 2014, when a coup d'état (viewed by many Abkhazians as instigated and backed by Russia)[6] made Raul Khajimba President. In the

232   *Vincenc Kopeček*

NKR, the opposition has not been able to break the dominance of the ruling parties at a national level, but in 2004 the opposition candidate Edvard Aghabeghyan was elected Mayor of the capital city Stepanakert (Matsuzato 2008, 105). Opposition parties play a normal role in the parliamentary systems of both de facto states, with some parties leaving the opposition to become part of coalition governments or vice versa (Kolstø and Blakkisrud 2012, 145–146; Kopeček 2016, 81).

Both de facto states place a surprisingly strong emphasis on systems of local government. In Abkhazia, local government exists on two separate levels – local and regional – though the elected assemblies operate in tandem with the chairman of the executive body; the chairman has greater powers than the assembly, and is appointed directly by the President. Local government in the NKR operates only at the municipal level, but there are elections for both municipal assemblies and mayors. However, in the NKR (as in Abkhazia) central government prevents local government from gaining too much power by retaining control over the allocation of funding and by ensuring that local government powers are relatively restricted (Kopeček 2016, 82–84).

Although democratization in Abkhazia and Nagorno-Karabakh has its limitations – having in no way moved beyond a hybrid political regime and having so far failed to bring widespread international recognition – it has nevertheless played an important role in the creation of political institutions which enable both de facto entities to apply political solutions to internal issues. Both in Abkhazia and in the NKR there has been a certain regression in democratization during recent years (in Abkhazia as a result of Russian pressure, and in the NKR due to the deteriorating security situation); nevertheless, the political institutions in both entities have shown a high degree of resilience – demonstrating that both de facto states are relatively well-consolidated and stable entities. Both de facto states still retain pluralistic systems of political parties and competitive (if not entirely fair) elections (Ó Beacháin 2014, 2015). Key political reforms are discussed publicly – such as the change to a mixed-member electoral system in Abkhazia[7] or the change in the NKR constitution (Khanumyan 2016; Sargsyan 2016).[8] In Abkhazia, pressure from the opposition and civil society has meant that even the Khajimba government was not willing to accept certain Russian demands – both in the Russian-Abkhazian Agreement and in a proposed law permitting foreigners (i.e. mainly Russians) to purchase real estate in Abkhazia (DFWatch 2016).

Democracy in the shadow of war: can we afford to argue among ourselves?

As the NKR and Abkhazia are hybrid political regimes, political parties in both de facto states find themselves in a precarious situation. Keen to retain power, the ruling parties take advantage of the administrative resources at

Inside a de facto state 233

their disposal to create an uneven playing-field. However, this weakens the democratic nature of the state – an aspect that it is keen to present to the outside world. For opposition political parties, the situation is even more complicated. In order to overcome the unevenness of the playing-field, they have to attempt to undermine the current political regime – criticizing it, organizing protests and demonstrations, and so on (cf. Levitsky and Way 2010, 29–32). However, these efforts by opposition politicians are severely limited by the fact that neither Abkhazia nor the NKR are internationally recognized. For both entities, national unity is a fundamental requirement if they are to even remain in existence, let alone achieve international recognition – so political parties always have to consider whether provoking domestic political conflicts could potentially weaken the state *per se* (Kopeček 2016, 78).

Abkhazia currently benefits from Russian security guarantees which effectively exclude the possibility of Georgia attempting to annex it by force. This satisfactory security situation has enabled Abkhazia to implement a process of democratization – though at the same time the Russian influence in Abkhazia encourages political parties to seek consensus, which, in turn, strengthens Russia's hold over the territory. These somewhat contradictory tendencies co-exist alongside the traditional emphasis on Abkhazian unity. In 2003, when the opposition candidate Sergei Bagapsh won the presidential election after over a decade of rule by Vladislav Ardzinba, it was the former pro-government camp which began to organize demonstrations in support of the defeated candidate Raul Khajimba, in an attempt to overturn the election result. These attempts were ultimately unsuccessful, as (with Russian mediation) both camps eventually agreed on a compromise: the election was repeated, with Khajimba standing for election as Bagapsh's Vice-President (Matsuzato 2008, 108). National unity and the preservation of good relations with the patron state were viewed as the priority, and the political conflict was not allowed to escalate. However, Khajimba's vice-presidency proved to be merely a formal role, and in 2009 he resigned (Ó Beacháin 2012, 167). This marked the beginning of what has so far been Abkhazia's most intensely competitive period of democratic politics – brought to an end by a coup d'état in which the previously unsuccessful opposition leader Raul Khajimba (with evident Russian backing)[9] toppled Bagapsh's successor Alexander Ankvab.

Since the coup, the above-described tendencies have remained present within Abkhazian society: the emphasis on national unity and a consensus acceptable to Russia, combined with confident opposition to government policy (and especially the strongly pro-Russian President Khajimba). Thus, while *Amtsakhara* identifies itself as an opposition party, which at the end of 2016 actually called for Khajimba's resignation (Abkhaziya-Inform 2016a), United Abkhazia (*Apsny Akzaara*) is a typical example of a compromise-oriented political party, neither part of the opposition nor a member of the government camp. In their attempts to mediate a reconciliation between

234   *Vincenc Kopeček*

the opposition and the pro-government camp, representatives of United Abkhazia have explicitly referred to Sergei Bagapsh's 2004 agreement with Khajimba, which in their opinion prevented the outbreak of civil war (Abkhaziya-Inform 2016b).

The situation in the NKR is rather more complicated than in Abkhazia, as the security guarantees given by Armenia (and, by extension, Russia) may not be enough to protect the territory from a future Azerbaijani offensive. In the NKR, the tendency towards political consensus in order to ensure stability is even stronger than in Abkhazia; in the words of Laurence Broers (2005, 78) the NKR is essentially a "single-issue regime", which still – despite the process of democratization that it has undergone over the past decade – has to face the question of its very survival on a daily basis. This situation in fact suits a large section of the Karabakhi political elite; its members have become accustomed to the situation, and they know how to use these circumstances to their advantage, in order to retain power (Smolnik 2016, 286). A good example of this is the 2007 presidential election, in which the incumbent President Ghukasyan was not constitutionally permitted to stand for a third term. As his successor he recommended his close associate Bako Sahakyan – whose candidacy was surprisingly supported not only by the two government parties – the Democratic Party of Artsakh (*Artsakhi Demokratakan Kusaktsutyun*) and Free Motherland (*Azat Hayrenik*) – but also by the opposition Dashnaks and Movement-88 (*Sharzhum-88*). At the time, the leader of the latter party was Artur Aghabeghyan, who as the Mayor of Stepanakert was out of favour with the central authorities,[10] and even he declared that "we should not forget that with these elections we at once tackle the question of our security" (Smolnik 2016, 285).

The entire election campaign was thus essentially based on the notion that Sahakyan represented a guarantee of the NKR's security, while his only realistic opponent – the liberal candidate and former deputy to the Karabakhi Minister of Foreign Affairs Masis Mayilyan (Owen 2007) – was presented as a security threat (Smolnik 2016, 285). A number of factors contributed to this public perception of the candidates. In Armenia, the second term of Robert Kocharyan's presidency was to come to an end in the following year, and during the Karabakhi presidential election it was still not clear who would be elected as his successor – and what stance his successor would take towards the NKR. It is also frequently pointed out that in 2007 the NKR feared that if Kocharyan were to reach an agreement with his Azerbaijani counterpart on a solution to the Karabakh conflict (Braxatoris 2007) – an outcome which was imminent, according to some sources (Kavkazskii Uzel 2007) – the NKR would have to be led by somebody who had good relations with the Armenian President; this (according to several sources) remains an essential requirement for any Karabakhi President to be elected (Danielyan 2009; Kopeček 2016, 88; Smolnik 2016, 287). Paradoxically, although the Karabakhi political mainstream sidelined its

Inside a de facto state 235

democratization-for-recognition strategy by joining forces to support just one of the candidates in the presidential election, Masis Mayilyan himself was motivated to stand for the presidency by a desire to preserve the NKR's democratic image:

> In 2005 the Democratic Party and Free Motherland formed a coalition, and then they reached an agreement with the opposition Dashnaks and Movement-88 to jointly support one presidential candidate, Bako Sahakyan. (...) For me this was unacceptable, abnormal – and moreover it damaged the democratic image of the NKR, which I had worked hard to build up while at the Ministry of Foreign Affairs. That was the first reason why I decided to stand for President; when there is only one candidate (the other three candidates were very weak, with only minimal numbers of votes), then there is no election, merely an appointment. If I had not stood for President, Sahakyan would have gained 99% of the votes – and that doesn't happen even in Azerbaijan.[11]

As was the case in the presidential campaign of 2007, the debate on the proposed change to Karabakh's constitution and the subsequent campaign before the February 2017 referendum focussed strongly on issues of security. In the autumn of 2015 there were still discussions on the possibility of moving away from a semi-presidentialist system to an Armenian-style parliamentary system,[12] but following the four-day war with Azerbaijan in April 2016, a reform proposal to introduce a fully presidential system in the NKR was presented.[13] There was a heated debate between the supporters and opponents of parliamentarism; opponents suspected President Sahakyan of attempting to prolong his career as the holder of the NKR's highest political office by creating a prime ministerial position for himself, and they emphasized the advantages of (semi)presidentialism if Nagorno-Karabakh were to come under threat.[14] Initially, the supporters of parliamentarism claimed that it was a more democratic system and emphasized the need to reach a broad consensus[15]; however, during the course of 2016 support for parliamentarism waned to such an extent that presidentialism eventually enjoyed almost unopposed backing. The final proposal for the constitutional change was approved by the President and by Parliament, and later also by 87% of voters in a referendum (Aravot 2017); its only opponents were the smallest parliamentary political party National Revival (*Azgayin Veratsnund*) (Kavkazskii Uzel 2017).

Besides the issue of security (or at least appeals to public concerns about security), another factor in the relatively consensual nature of politics in the NKR is the inclusive stance taken by the current government, and especially by President Bako Sahakyan. One Karabakhi journalist describes Sahakyan as "a very consensual person", who "can get on with almost everyone", and under whose presidency "the ruling regime is very soft and open to incorporate anybody".[16] This approach is particularly effective in a situation

236 *Vincenc Kopeček*

when there are only minimal ideological differences among the individual parties, with fault-lines drawn on a personal basis.[17] Of course, this does not mean that there are no conflicts among the different political groupings in the NKR, or that there is broad consensus on all political matters – as has already been shown above when discussing the debate on the change to the constitution. One Member of Parliament, declaring himself to be a member of the opposition, described the situation as follows:

> All the parties agree on the basic principles of Karabakh's foreign policy. There are, of course, some differences in the domestic politics. Nevertheless, when we meet over a glass of brandy or *chacha*, we can overcome our disputes. After all, we all have fought together.[18]

A similar approach can be seen in the actions of one Karabakhi civil society activist and opposition politician, who originally supported the retention of the semi-presidential constitution and in 2015 (in an interview with the author) gave a detailed account of the corruption and clientelistic practices of Bako Sahakyan's presidency; he considered himself partly guilty of having helped Sahakyan become the head of state.[19] A year later, however, after the four-day war of April 2016, the same activist and politician appeared publicly alongside Sahakyan at various events (e.g. when the President visited the village of Talish, which had sustained serious damage in the fighting); he expressed his support for the President, and he eventually became one of the main proponents of the new draft constitution.[20] It is unlikely that the respondent had suddenly changed his opinion of Sahakyan – rather that personal disputes had been put aside as a result of the deteriorating security situation.

A mono- or multi-ethnic state?

In terms of the ethnic makeup of their populations, the NKR and Abkhazia differ greatly. Before the war, the NKAR had an ethnic Armenian majority, making up 77% of its population (Goskomstat 1993). However, the territory lying outside the former NKAR that was seized by Karabakhi Armenian units (now known as either the occupied territories or the "security belt", depending on the speaker) was primarily inhabited by ethnic Azeris and Kurds. These sections of the population either fled or were expelled as a result of the war, as was also the case with ethnic Azeris from Nagorno-Karabakh itself. Around 550,000 people thus left the territories that are de facto controlled by the NKR (Laitin and Suny 1999, 153), including around 85,000 Kurds (McDowall 2004, 493). The territory between the former NKAR and the Republic of Armenia or Iran is now very sparsely populated; only 12,000 people live in the Kashatagh/Lachin and Karvachar/Kelbajar districts (STAT NKR 2015, 12). Although the 2006 census found that ethnic Armenians made up 99.74% of

Inside a de facto state 237

the NKR's population (STAT NKR 2006, 197), in reality the situation is somewhat more complex. The Karabakhi Armenians speak a dialect of Eastern Armenian which differs considerably from the Eastern Armenian spoken in Armenia itself (though the two dialects are mutually intelligible). Moreover, a small proportion of the Karabakhi population consists of refugees from Azerbaijan, whom the Karabakhi Armenians label *galma* (newcomers) or *shrurtvatz hayer* (not-quite-Armenians) as they speak a different Eastern Armenian dialect, incorporating numerous loanwords from Russian – indeed, for some of these refugees Russian is their mother tongue. Many of them have always rejected the goals of the Karabakh Movement, as from their perspective it brought an end to their relatively comfortable urban life in multicultural Baku and other Azerbaijani cities. As a result, they are sometimes known as *azgi davatchan* (traitors to the nation) (Shahnazarian and Ziemer 2014, 31–33). The author's field research revealed that a large percentage of these refugees are concentrated – not by choice, but by force of circumstance – in those areas of the NKR that used to be home to a non-Armenian population, such as the city of Shushi/Shusha or the Karvachar/Kelbajar district.[21]

Unlike the NKR, Abkhazia remains a multi-ethnic territory lacking a single dominant ethnic majority group – despite the fact that around 280,000 people left Abkhazia during the war, mainly ethnic Georgians (Hoch 2011, 68). The ethnic makeup of Abkhazia's pre-war population (according to the 1989 Soviet census) was 46% Georgians, 18% Abkhazians, 15% Armenians,[22] and 14% Russians (Ó Beacháin 2015, 241). According to official data from the Abkhazian Statistical Office, in 2014 ethnic Abkhazians made up 51% of the population, ethnic Georgians 19%, ethnic Armenians 17.2%, and ethnic Russians 9% (UGS RA 2016, 28). However, these figures have probably been amended, boosting the number of ethnic Abkhazians at the expense of ethnic Armenians in order to give the impression that Abkhazians are the ethnic majority population (Ó Beacháin 2015, 241). The situation is made more complicated by the fact that the ethnic category of Georgians in fact subsumes three distinct groups – not only Georgians in the strict sense of the word (who lived mainly in Sukhum/-i and other large cities and who mostly left Abkhazia during the war) but also Megrelians and Svans, whose languages are related to Georgian; these subgroups consider themselves to be a part of the Georgian political nation, and they have traditionally used Georgian as their literary language (Kopečková 2012, 113). The Svans made up the majority of the population in the Upper Kodori Gorge, which from 1994 to 2006 was under the de facto control of the *monadire* militia ("Hunters"), who were loyal to the local warlord Emzar Kvitsiani; after the five-day war in August 2008, most Svans fled to Georgia (Marten 2012, 86–98). The Megrelians, however, continue to live in their traditional homeland, the southern Abkhazian districts of Gal/-i and Tkvarchal/Tkvarcheli (see map 5), where they make up 98% and 55% of the population, respectively (UGS RA 2016, 24).

238   *Vincenc Kopeček*

In terms of the building of a national project, the two analyzed de facto states are in notably different situations – despite the fact that both entities define themselves as nation states (of Armenians and Abkhazians, respectively). In the NKR the ethnic majority population is clear, and the key question is whether the NKR should be a second Armenian nation state or an integral part of the Republic of Armenia (as well as the issue of whether and how to integrate several thousand Baku Armenians). Abkhazia, however, faces a different problem: how to politically include other ethnic groups in a national project that is exclusively Abkhazian. According to the Abkhazian constitution, the position of President can only be held by an ethnic Abkhazian who is a fluent speaker of the Abkhaz language, and although the constitution does permit the position of Vice-President to be held by a member of a different ethnic group, in practice the Vice-President has always been of Abkhazian ethnicity, as have all candidates for the highest political positions (Ó Beacháin 2012, 167). Non-Abkhazians participate in national politics as Members of Parliament; MPs have traditionally included representatives of the Armenian and Russian communities, and – particularly since around 2005 – also Georgians (Megrelians). Despite the fact that official figures list Armenians as the largest ethnic group in the Gagra district, Russians as the second largest group in the capital Sukhum/-i, and Megrelians as overwhelmingly dominant in Gal/-i (UGS RA 2016, 24) – and despite Abkhazia's majoritarian (plurality voting) electoral system – representatives of the Russian, Megrelian, and Armenian communities have not been elected as MPs due to the concentration of these ethnic groups in individual districts or constituencies; instead this has been a result of mutual agreements among the leaders of the individual ethnic groups. In constituencies where Armenians, Megrelians, and Russians make up a large proportion of the population, the Abkhazians have agreed not to put up their own candidate, allowing the representatives of the other ethnic groups to stand for election unopposed (Ó Beacháin 2012, 172). However, according to Abkhazian respondents, these "gentlemen's agreements" have largely broken down in recent years, as parliamentary seats come to represent lucrative opportunities for various clientelistic groups; this has increased electoral competition (though the competition is far from fair) and it has put an end to such informal consociational mechanisms.[23]

As a result, the only ethnic minority still represented in the Abkhazian Parliament are the Armenians, who appear to be well-organized and give their backing to a single candidate in a given constituency (especially in Gagra), ensuring that the candidate is elected. The Russian population is less geographically concentrated than the Armenian population, and the Russian community is less organized; as a result, Russians have lost their representation in Parliament.[24] The situation is different in the case of the Megrelians; here the problem is the fact that most Megrelians do not have the right to vote. Until the Bagapsh administration and the passing of the 2005 Law on Citizenship, the Megrelians were effectively excluded

Inside a de facto state 239

from Abkhazian economic and political life, as they did not hold Abkhazian citizenship. Inhabiting the east of the country, they were viewed as a potential Georgian fifth column – indeed, the Georgian paramilitary units *tetri legioni* (White Legion) and *tqis dzmebi* (Forest Brothers) were active in the Megrelians' home region (until the Saakashvili administration in Georgia disbanded them or integrated them into the regular Georgian armed forces). Moreover, the district of Gal/-i and partly the neighbouring districts of Ochamchira and Tkvarchal/Tkvarcheli were effectively cut off from the rest of Abkhazia due to a lack of infrastructure. This situation only changed after the Russian-Georgian war of 2008, when Russian border guards took control of the Abkhazian-Georgian administrative border line; the Abkhazian government began to take an interest in integrating Gal/-i into the rest of Abkhazia, and the Megrelians themselves increasingly began to take Abkhazian citizenship. By 2013, around 13,000 Megrelians were Abkhazian citizens – around 30% of the entire Georgian (Megrelian) population of Abkhazia (Prelz Oltramonti 2016, 252–257).

For Bagapsh and Ankvab (both moderate Abkhazian nationalists who maintained a certain distance from Russia), the Megrelian population was very important; Megrelians represented a new reservoir of votes which enabled them to defeat Raul Khajimba's pro-Russian opposition in the elections. However, after President Ankvab was ousted in May 2014, the new Khajimba administration began to revoke the Megrelians' citizenship – thus depriving them of their right to vote. This was possible mainly because the majority of Megrelians who had obtained Abkhazian citizenship had not renounced their Georgian citizenship (either for pragmatic reasons or because it was not technically possible); under Abkhazian law, such dual citizenship is illegal (Prelz Oltramonti 2016, 256). The removal of many Megrelians from the electorate evidently helped Khajimba to achieve a narrow victory in the first round of the presidential elections in August 2014 (Ó Beacháin 2014).

The political dominance of ethnic Abkhazians – though they currently make up no more than half of the entire country's population – is rooted in three main factors. The first is the tradition of political dominance by the Abkhazians, as the titular nation during the Soviet era and during the first year of Georgian independence, when the Gamsakhurdia administration attempted to reach a peaceful solution to the Abkhazian conflict by reducing the number of ethnic Georgian deputies and increasing the number of ethnic Abkhazian deputies in the Supreme Soviet of autonomous Abkhazia (Ó Beacháin 2012, 172). The current constitutional bias in favour of ethnic Abkhazians thus represents a logical continuation of a long-established trend. The second factor is the non-Abkhazian population's general inability to speak or understand Abkhaz (the official language) – combined, in the case of the Megrelians and some Armenians, with low levels of education and high levels of poverty.[25] The third factor is that ethnic Abkhazians sustained the greatest loss of life during the war, and are thus seen as having

240 *Vincenc Kopeček*

earned their current political dominance through this sacrifice. It appears that the other ethnic groups accept this perception (Ó Beacháin 2012, 167), though it is debatable to what extent this acceptance is merely an outward pretence which may merely mask the potential for future conflict between the Abkhazians and other ethnic groups.

While the political scene is dominated by ethnic Abkhazians, ethnic Russians and Armenians play a more prominent role in Abkhazia's economic life (O'Loughlin, Kolossov, and Toal 2014, 449). In view of this fact, it is perhaps not surprising that the author of this chapter noticed a distinctly negative image of the ethnic Abkhazians particularly among members of the Armenian community, who frequently disparaged Abkhazians for being lazy, incompetent, disorganized, and interested mainly in protecting their own traditions and language. Support for Abkhazia's incorporation into Russia is higher among ethnic Armenians (over 50%) and Russians (40%) than among ethnic Abkhazians (20%) and Megrelians (less than 10%) (O'Loughlin, Kolossov, and Toal 2014, 448). While practically the entire population (including a significant proportion of the Megrelians) view Russian security guarantees as important and desirable (O'Loughlin, Kolossov, and Toal 2014, 438), some Abkhazians (and probably a majority of the Megrelian population) have rather more reservations about close cooperation with Russia in other areas, suspecting Russia of abusing its position (O'Loughlin, Kolossov, and Toal 2014, 449). By contrast, other Abkhazians, along with ethnic Armenians and Russians, would largely welcome closer links with Russia as they believe that this would boost the development of the economy.[26] The Abkhazian authorities are promoting Abkhaz (the official language) at the expense of the Russian language, and Abkhaz is starting to become dominant in the media; as a result, the non-Abkhazian population (who use Russian as a *lingua franca*) are increasingly turning to Russian media, and thus losing touch with internal political developments in Abkhazia itself.[27] Ethnic coexistence in Abkhazia may thus be somewhat more fragile than it appears at first sight; in particular, the integration of the Megrelians and the political representation of the self-confident Armenian community are issues which the exclusively Abkhazian national project will – like it or not – have to confront and deal with at some point in the future.

Conclusions

The examples of the NKR and Abkhazia have demonstrated that internal systemic support and the building of functioning political institutions are important factors enabling the existence of de facto states to be maintained. However, the first decade of Abkhazian and Karabakhi de facto independence was dominated by clientelism, nepotism, warlordism, and strong links between politics and criminal activity – all leading to a negative image of de facto states as "black holes" on the world map. However, the Karabakhi civilian government and the Abkhazian political opposition eventually

Inside a de facto state 241

managed to wrest power away from the cliques that had informally controlled political and economic life during the 1990s (and, in some cases, well into the first decade of the 21st century), and both de facto states embarked on a process of (at least partial) democratization. The political elites viewed democratization as a means to achieve international recognition – but it was also supported by civil society, which saw democratization as a continuation of the struggle for national independence. Neither the NKR nor Abkhazia have developed into Western-style liberal democracies; they remain hybrid regimes with poorly developed party systems, high levels of corruption, and a prevalence of clientelistic structures. Nevertheless, despite having failed to achieve widespread international recognition, they have managed to develop along the same lines as other post-Soviet states such as Armenia, Georgia, Ukraine, Kyrgyzstan, and Moldova, which Freedom House (2016) likewise classifies as "partly free countries".

However, unlike internationally recognized states with hybrid political regimes, the development of democratic political institutions in the NKR and Abkhazia is hindered by their lack of widespread international recognition, and – in the case of the NKR – by the constant threat of military conflict with Azerbaijan. This situation motivates both government and opposition forces to reach a political consensus, which is seen as an essential precondition for the de facto state's continuing existence or future international recognition. Elections thus tend (with only a few exceptions) to reproduce existing governments rather than to bring genuine changes at the highest levels of power. Nevertheless, despite these limitations (and various shocks such as the coup in Abkhazia or the four-day war in the NKR), these de facto states' political institutions have proved to be quite resilient, playing a crucial role in the functioning of both entities.

In the near future, however, the institutional structures of Abkhazia and the NKR will face two major challenges. In the case of Abkhazia, the country will have to reconcile the exclusively Abkhazian nature of the national project with the multi-ethnic nature of the country itself. In the case of the NKR, the challenge will be to implement the new state constitution against the background of the deteriorating security situation and the real threat of a full-scale war with Azerbaijan.

Notes

1 Interview with a Karabakhi journalist and civil society leader, October 2015.
2 Babayan was eventually released from prison after serving four years of his sentence. He spent the next seven years mainly in Russia, and then settled in the Republic of Armenia. There he founded the political party *Dashink* (Alliance), which failed to make an electoral impact. He returned to the public spotlight in connection with the four-day war in 2016, as an open supporter of a new political project founded by Armenia's former Foreign Minister (and close associate of Kocharyan) Vartan Oskanyan (ArmeniaNow 2016).
3 Interview with a Karabakhi civil society leader, October 2009, and interview with an Abkhazian NGO representative, October 2009.

242   *Vincenc Kopeček*

4 Whereas track I diplomacy refers to the official diplomatic talks, track II diplomacy is the practice of "non-governmental, informal, and unofficial contacts and activities between private citizens or groups of individuals, sometimes called non-state actors" (Diamond and McDonald 1991, 1).
5 Interview with an Abkhazian politician, October 2015, interview with an Abkhazian journalist, October 2015, and interview with an Abkhazian civil society leader, October 2015.
6 Interview with an Abkhazian journalist, October 2015.
7 Interview with an Abkhazian NGO representative, October 2015 and interview with an Abkhazian journalist, October 2015.
8 Interview with a former Karabakhi diplomat, October 2015.
9 Interview with an Abkhazian journalist, October 2015.
10 Interview with a representative of the Movement-88 political party, October 2015.
11 Interview with Masis Mayilyan, October 2015.
12 Following a referendum in December 2015, the Republic of Armenia changed from a presidential system to a parliamentary system (Grigoryan 2015).
13 The only major difference from a classic presidential form of government is that the Parliament (the National Assembly) and the President are elected at the same time, and for concurrent five-year terms. This means that if Parliament exercises its right to dismiss the President, or if the President dissolves Parliament, both the presidential and parliamentary elections are held at the same time ("Draft Constitution of the Republic of Artsakh" 2017).
14 Interview with a former Karabakhi diplomat, October 2015 and interview with a Karabakhi opposition MP, October 2015.
15 Interview with a Karabakhi journalist, October 2015, interview with a representative of the Karabakhi branch of the *Dashnaktsutyun* party, October 2015, and interview with a Karabakhi NGO representative and journalist, October 2015.
16 Interview with a Karabakhi NGO representative and journalist, October 2015.
17 Interview with a Karabakhi NGO representative and journalist, October 2015 and interview with a Karabakhi journalist, October 2015.
18 Interview with a Karabakhi MP, October 2015.
19 Interview with a Karabakhi civil society leader and politician, October 2015.
20 Facebook profile of a Karabakhi civil society leader and politician and author's Facebook communication with the same respondent, October 2016 – February 2017.
21 Interview with a Karabakhi official, October 2009 and interview with a refugee from Baku, teacher, October 2015. See also Shahnazarian and Ziemer (2014, 31).
22 A small number of ethnic Armenians came to Abkhazia as refugees from the conflict in Nagorno-Karabakh. Interview with an ethnic Armenian refugee from Karabakh, doctor, October 2009.
23 Interview with an Abkhazian NGO representative, October 2015 and interview with a representative of the Armenian community in Abkhazia, October 2015.
24 Interview with a representative of the Armenian community in Abkhazia, October 2015 and interview with a former Abkhazian politician and diplomat, October 2015.
25 Interview with a representative of the Armenian community in Abkhazia, October 2015.
26 Interview with a representative of the Armenian community in Abkhazia, October 2015 and interview with a representative of the Russian community in Abkhazia, October 2015.
27 Interview with a representative of the Armenian community in Abkhazia, October 2015.

Literature

Abkhaziya-Inform. 2016a. "Politicheskaya partiya 'Amtsakhara' prizyvaet Prezidenta Raulya Khadzimba dosrochno slozhit polnomochya [Political party 'Amtsakhara' calls President Raul Khadjimba to Step Down Soon]." *Abkhaziya-Inform*, November 30. http://abkhazinform.com/item/4954-politicheskaya-partiya-amtskhara-prizyvaet-prezidenta-raulya-khadzhimba-dosrochno-slozhit-svoi-polnomochiya.

Abkhaziya-Inform. 2016b. "V politicheskoi partii 'Edinaya Abkhaziya' po-raznomu otnosyatsya k trebovaniyu Bloka oppozitsionnykh sil o dosrochnoy otstavke prezidenta Raulya Khadzimba [In the 'United Abkhazia' Political Party there are Differing Opinions on the Call of the Opposition Forces Block Demanding the Early Resignation of President Raul Khadzhimba]. *Abkhaziya-Inform*, December 5. http://abkhazinform.com/item/4987-v-politicheskoj-partii-edinaya-abkhaziya-po-raznomu-otnosyatsya-k-trebovaniyu-bloka-oppozitsionnykh-sil-o-dosrochnoj-otstavke-prezidenta-raulya-khadzhimba.

Aravot. 2017. "87.6% Vote in Favor of Constitutional Reforms in Nagorno Karabakh." *Aravot*, February 21. http://en.aravot.am/2017/02/21/190436/.

ArmeniaNow. 2016. "Babayan's Back: Former Karabakh Strongman Returns to Armenia after Four-Day War." *ArmeniaNow*, May 26. www.armenianow.com/en/news/politics/2016/05/26/armenia-samvel-babayan-karabakh-return-politics-security/3893/.

Avakian, Shaken. 2010. *Nagorno-Karabakh: Legal Aspects*. Yerevan: Tigran Mets Publishing House.

Balayan, Vahram. 2005. *Artsakh History*. Yerevan: Zangak-97 Press.

Berg, Eiki, and Martin Mölder. 2012. "Who is Entitled to 'Earn Sovereignty'? Legitimacy and Regime Support in Abkhazia and Nagorno-Karabakh." *Nations and Nationalism* 18 (3): 527–545.

Braxatoris, Martin. 2007. "Presidential Elections in Nagorno-Karabakh." *Despite-Borders*, July 5. http://i.despiteborders.com/presidential-elections-in-nagorno-karabakh/.

Broers, Laurence. 2005. "The Politics of Non-recognition and Democratisation." *Accord* 17: 68–71.

Caspersen, Nina. 2008. "Separatism and the Democracy in the Caucasus." *Survival* 50 (4): 113–136.

Caspersen, Nina. 2009. "Playing the Recognition Game: External Actors and De Facto States." *The International Spectator* 44 (4): 47–60.

Cornell, Svante E. 2001. *Small Nations and Great Powers. A Study of Ethnopolitical Conflict in the Caucasus*. Richmond: Curzon Press.

Danielyan, Anahit. 2009. "Karabakh Government Faces Little Competition." *Caucasus Reporting Service*, 517 (October). https://iwpr.net/global-voices/karabakh-government-faces-little-competition.

de Waal, Thomas. 2003. *Black Garden. Armenia and Azerbaijan through Peace and War*. London and New York: New York University Press.

DFWatch. 2016. "Abkhazia Shelves Proposal to Allow Sale of Real Estate to Foreigners." *Democracy & Freedom Watch*, April 22. http://dfwatch.net/abkhazia-shelves-proposal-to-allow-sale-of-real-estate-to-foreigners-41968.

Diamond, Louise, and John McDonald. 1991. *Multi-Track Diplomacy: A Systems Guide and Analysis*. Iowa City: Iowa Peace Institute.

244   Vincenc Kopeček

"Draft Constitution of the Republic of Artsakh." 2017. *National Assembly of the Nagorno Karabakh Republic*. www.nankr.am/en/1838.

Freedom House. 2016. *Freedom in the World Comparative and Historical Data. Individual Territory Ratings and Status, FIW 1972–2016*. Washington: Freedom House. https://freedomhouse.org/sites/default/files/FH_Country_and_Territory_Ratings_and_Statuses_1972-2016.xls.

Grigoryan, Armen. 2015. "Armenia's Constitutional Referendum." *Central Asia – Caucasus Analyst*, December 29. www.cacianalyst.org/publications/analytical-articles/item/13317-armenias-constitutional-referendum.html.

Goskomstat. 1993. *Itogi vsesoyuznoi perepisi naseleniya 1989 goda: natsionalnyi sostav naseleniya SSSR* [Results of the All-Union Population Census of 1989: National Structure of the USSR]. Moskva: Goskomstat.

Hakobyan, Tatul. 2010. *Karabakh Diary: Green and Black*. Antelias.

Hale, Henry E. 2015. *Patronal Politics*. New York: Cambridge University Press.

Herzig, Edmund. 1999. *The New Caucasus. Armenia, Azerbaijan and Georgia*. London: Royal Institute of International Affairs.

Hoch, Tomáš. 2011. *Možnosti rozvoje de facto států prostřednictvím humanitární pomoci, rozvojové spolupráce a aktivit organizací občanské společnosti: případová studie Abcházie* [Options for the Development of De Facto States through Humanitarian Aid, Development Cooperation and the Activities of Civil Society Organization: A Case Study of Abkhazia]. Prague: European Science and Art Publishing.

Hoch, Tomáš, Vincenc Kopeček, and Vladimír Baar. 2017. "Civil Society and Conflict Transformation in De Facto States: The Case of Abkhazia." *Problems of Post-Communism* 64 (6): 329–341.

Ishiyama, John, and Anna Batta. 2012. "The Emergence of Dominant Political Party Systems in Unrecognized States." *Communist and Post-Communist Studies*, In Search of Legitimacy: Post-Soviet De Facto States Between Institutional Stabilization and Political Transformation, 45 (1–2): 123–130.

Kavkazskii uzel. 2007. "OBSE: Situatsiya vokrug Nagornogo Karabakha blizka k razresheniyu [OSCE: The Nagorno-Karabakh Conflict is Close to Solution]." *Kavkazskii uzel*, June 5. www.kavkaz-uzel.eu/articles/115807/.

Kavkazskii uzel. 2017. "Dve partii otkazalis ot agitatsii pered referendumom v Nagornom Karabakhe [Two Parties Refused to Campaign before the Referendum in Nagorno-Karabakh]." *Kavkazskii uzel*, February 9. www.kavkaz-uzel.eu/articles/297457/.

Ker-Lindsay, James. 2013. "Preventing the Emergence of Self-Determination as a Norm of Secession: An Assessment of the Kosovo 'Unique Case' Argument." *Europe-Asia Studies* 65 (5): 837–856.

Khanumyan, Hayk. 2016. "Konstitutsionnye reformy – sredstvo reproduktsii vlasti [Constitutional Reforms – The Way How the Power Reproduces Itself]." *Analyticon*, October. http://theanalyticon.com/?p=8350&lang=ru.

King, Charles. 2001. "The Benefits of Ethnic War: Understanding Eurasia's Unrecognized States." *World Politics* 53 (4): 524–552.

Kolossov, Vladimir, and John O'Loughlin. 1998. "Pseudo-States as Harbingers of a New Geopolitics: The Example of the Trans-Dniester Moldovan Republic (TMR)." *Geopolitics* 3 (1): 151–176.

Kolstø, Pål, and Helge Blakkisrud. 2008. "Living with Non-Recognition: State- and Nation-Building in South Caucasian Quasi-States." *Europe-Asia Studies* 60 (3): 483–509.

Kolstø, Pål, and Helge Blakkisrud. 2012. "De Facto States and Democracy: The Case of Nagorno-Karabakh." *Communist and Post-Communist Studies* 45 (1–2): 141–151.

Kopeček, Vincenc. 2016. "Political Institutions in the Post-Soviet de Facto States in Comparison: Abkhazia and Nagorno-Karabakh." *Annual of Language & Politics and Politics of Identity* 10 (Special Issue): 73–99.

Kopecek, Vincenc, Tomas Hoch, and Vladimir Baar. 2016. "Conflict Transformation and Civil Society: The Case of Nagorno-Karabakh." *Europe-Asia Studies* 68 (3): 441–459.

Kopečková, Lenka. 2012. "Language Policy in Georgia with Focus on Non-Georgian Minorities." *The Annual of Language & Politics and Politics of Identity* 6 (1): 111–127.

Krylov, Alexander. 2002. "The Special Features of Forming a Multiparty System in Abkhazia." *Central Asia and the Caucasus* 3 (2). www.ca-c.org/journal/2002/journal_eng/cac-02/07.krien.shtml

Laitin, David D., and Ronald Grigor Suny. 1999. "Armenia and Azerbaijan: Thinking a Way out of Karabakh." *Middle East Policy* 7 (1): 145–176.

Levitsky, Steven, and Lucan A. Way. 2010. *Competitive Authoritarianism: Hybrid Regimes after the Cold War*. Cambridge: Cambridge University Press.

Lynch, Dov. 2004. *Engaging Eurasia's Separatist States*. Washington: United States Institute of Peace.

Marten, Kimberly. 2012. *Warlords: Strong-Arm Brokers in Weak States*. Ithaca and London: Cornell University Press.

Matsuzato, Kimitaka. 2008. "From Belligerent to Multi-Ethnic Democracy: Domestic Politics in Unrecognized States after Ceasefires." *Eurasian Review* 1: 95–119.

McDowall, David. 2004. *A Modern History of the Kurds: Third Edition*. London and New York: I. B. Tauris.

Miller, Arthur H., and Thomas F. Klobucar. 2000. "The Development of Party Identification in Post-Soviet Societies." *American Journal of Political Science* 44 (4): 667–686.

Nodia, Ghia, and Álvaro Pinto Scholtbach, eds. 2006. *The Political Landscape of Georgia. Political Parties: Achievements, Challenges and Prospects*. Delft: Eburon Academic Publishers.

Ó Beacháin, Donnacha. 2012. "The Dynamics of Electoral Politics in Abkhazia." *Communist and Post-Communist Studies* 45 (1): 165–174.

Ó Beacháin, Donnacha. 2014. "Dubious Election Produces a Divisive New President in Abkhazia." *IPI Global Observatory*, September 3. https://theglobalobservatory.org/2014/09/dubious-election-divisive-new-president-abkhazia/.

Ó Beacháin, Donnacha. 2015. "Elections without Recognition: Presidential and Parliamentary Contests in Abkhazia and Nagorny Karabakh." *Caucasus Survey* 3 (3): 239–257.

O'Loughlin, John, Vladimir Kolossov, and Gerard Toal. 2014. "Inside the Post-Soviet De Facto States: A Comparison of Attitudes in Abkhazia, Nagorny Karabakh, South Ossetia, and Transnistria." *Eurasian Geography and Economics* 55 (5): 423–456.

Owen, Elizabeth. 2007. "Domestic Debate Marks Karabakh Presidential Vote." *Eurasianet*, July 18.

Popescu, Nicu. 2006. *Democracy in Secessionism: Transnistria and Abkhazia's Domestic Policies*. International Policy Fellowship – Policy Studies. Budapest: Open

246 *Vincenc Kopeček*

Society Institute and Central European University. www.policy.hu/npopescu/
ipf%20info/IPF%204%20democracy%20in%20secessionism.pdf.

Popescu, Nicu. 2007. "Europe's Unrecognised Neighbours: The EU in Abkhazia and South Ossetia." CEPS Working Document No. 260. Brussels: Centre for European Policy Studies. http://kms2.isn.ethz.ch/serviceengine/Files/RESSpecNet/31284/ipublicationdocument_singledocument/652FEB09-0EAC-4A34-A83A-C54ACF4 77D57/en/260_Europe%19s+Unrecognised+Neighbours.pdf.

Prelz Oltramonti, Giulia. 2016. "Securing Disenfranchisement through Violence and Isolation: The Case of Georgians/Mingrelians in the District of Gali." *Conflict, Security & Development* 16 (3): 245–262.

Sargsyan, Alvard. 2016. *An Assessment of Proposed Constitutional Changes in Nagorno-Karabakh*. RSC Guest Analysis No. 5. Yerevan: Regional Studies Center. http://regional-studies.org/images/pr/2016/august/23/RSC_Guest_Analysis_5_Alvard_Sargsyan_8.16.pdf.

Shahnazarian, Nona, and Ulrike Ziemer. 2014. "Emotions, Loss and Change: Armenian Women and Post-Socialist Transformations in Nagorny Karabakh." *Caucasus Survey* 2 (1–2): 27–40.

Skakov, Alexander. 2005. "Abkhazia at a Crossroads: On the Domestic Political Situation in the Republic of Abkhazia." *Iran & the Caucasus* 9 (1): 159–185.

Smolnik, Franziska. 2012. "Political Rule and Violent Conflict: Elections as 'Institutional Mutation' in Nagorno-Karabakh." *Communist and Post-Communist Studies* 45 (1–2): 153–163.

Smolnik, Franziska. 2016. *Secessionist Rule: Protracted Conflict and Configurations of Non-State Authority*. Frankfurt and New York: Campus Verlag.

STAT NKR. 2006. *The Results of 2005 Census of the Nagorno-Karabakh Republic*. Stepanakert: National Statistical Service of NKR. http://census.stat-nkr.am/.

STAT NKR. 2015. *Nakorno Karabkh in Figures 2015*. Stepanakert: National Statistical Service of NKR. http://stat-nkr.am/files/publications/2015/LXH_tverov_2015.pdf.

UGS RA. 2016. *Abkhazia v tsifrakh 2015 goda [Abkhazia in Numbers in 2015]*. Sukhum: Upravlenie gosudarstvennoi statistiki Respubliki Abkhaziya. http://ugsra.org/abkhaziya-v-tsifrakh/2015-0.pdf.

Way, Lucan. 2005. "Kuchma's Failed Authoritarianism." *Journal of Democracy* 16 (2): 131–145.

Wilson, Andrew. 2005. *Virtual Politics. Faking Democracy in the Post-Soviet World*. New Haven and London: Yale University Press.

Section 5

Why de facto states fail

5.1 Possible ends of de facto states

Vincenc Kopeček

There is a real possibility that present-day post-Soviet de facto states could survive without international recognition for an unspecified period, possibly even for several decades; nevertheless, there are only three logical trajectories which individual de facto states can take. First, they can achieve what they have officially strived for – they can be recognized by a number of other states and become *de jure* states. Out of the post-Soviet area, this was the case of Eritrea and Kosovo, nevertheless, none of the de facto states which emerged after the collapse of the Soviet Union have so far, reached this ultimate goal. In fact, some post-Soviet de facto states, did not, or have not, seriously attempted to become internationally recognized states – as was the case of Gagauzia (see Chapter 5.4), which finally accepted the autonomous status offered by its parent state, and as is, more or less, the case of South Ossetia and Transnistria, whose populations would prefer integration with Russia, their patron state. Even in the NKR, the population is divided on whether to become part of Armenia, or to strive for independence (see Chapter 4.1). There was, however, the historical case of Mongolia, which resembled present-day de facto states in many regards, and in 1961 almost half a century after its emergence finally gained international recognition and became a UN Member State. In a way, the Bukharan People's Republic, which later transformed into the Uzbek SSR, also became an independent state after the dissolution of the Soviet Union in 1991 (see Chapter 2.2). As was already discussed in Chapter 2.3, the historical experience suggests that this may eventually happen again in the future and thus it is not ruled out that Abkhazia or even the NKR could become internationally recognized states in the long run.

Second, de facto states can be absorbed by their patron states. This trajectory, however, seems to be relatively rare (Florea 2014, 793; Riegl 2014, 22–25), and we do not have such an example in the post-Soviet area after 1991; nevertheless, the historical cases of the Bukharan People's Republic and, most importantly, Tuva, show that this is a viable solution for cases such as South Ossetia, the NKR, and possibly also Transnistria. Even recent history shows us that Russia, the patron state of South Ossetia and Transnistria, does not hesitate in annexing a territory claimed by another sovereign state – as was the case of the Crimea in 2014.

250 *Vincenc Kopeček*

Third, de facto states can be reintegrated into their parent states. This was a relatively frequent fate of many recent de facto states, such as Tamil Eelam, Biafra, or Katanga (Florea 2014, 793; Riegl 2014, 22–25). In the post-Soviet area, there were two such examples, the cases of Gagauzia and the Chechen Republic of Ichkeria. The case of Gagauzia is analyzed in Chapter 5.4, which focusses not only on Gagauzia's reintegration with Moldova but also on its emergence as a de facto state. In fact, given the relatively short period of Gagauzia as a de facto state, these two processes can hardly be analyzed separately. Whereas Gagauzia was reintegrated by peaceful means, the Chechen Republic of Ichkeria was conquered by the Russian army and remains the only post-Soviet de facto state, so far, which was reintegrated by the use of force – although there are other de facto states, most specifically, the NKR, which have to seriously take into account such a scenario.

As so far, there are just two cases of a de facto state's demise in the post-Soviet area, we turn our attention to the cases of the Chechen Republic of Ichkeria and Gagauzia. The infamous and bloody end of the Chechen de facto statehood has already been sufficiently analyzed by several authors (e.g. Tishkov 2004; Sakwa 2005; Souleimanov 2006; Hughes 2008); however, what remains somewhat understudied is the internal political development of the Chechen Republic of Ichkeria, which eventually led to the failure of the Chechen de facto state even before the Russian military campaign.

In Chapter 5.2, Huseyn Aliyev focusses on the phenomenon of state failure and claims that it is not only *de jure* states, which can fail, but it is also de facto states, who are no more prone to this phenomenon. Moreover, their de facto status makes them even more receptive to the general causes of state failure. Thus, Huseyn Aliyev identifies five causes which can contribute to a de facto states failure. In Chapter 5.3, Emil Aslan Souleimanov applies Huseyn Aliyev's criteria to the case of the Chechen Republic of Ichkeria and convincingly demonstrates that internal fractures within the Chechen de facto state played no less a decisive role in the demise of the republic, than the Russian invasion.

In Chapter 5.4, Slavomír Horák deals with the formation and failure of the Gagauz de facto state. He draws from the theoretical arguments made in Chapter 5.2; however, he also pays attention to the emergence of Gagauzia's formation. He claims that from its very beginnings it contained the germs of its own failure, which resulted in a peaceful reintegration into its parent state.

Literature

Florea, Adrian. 2014. "De Facto States in International Politics (1945–2011): A New Data Set." *International Interactions* 40 (5): 788–811.

Hughes, James. 2008. *Chechnya: From Nationalism to Jihad.* Philadelphia: University of Pennsylvania Press.

Riegl, Martin. 2014. "Prospects and Limits of Economic Development of Unrecognized States: Between Organized Hypocracy and Private Interests." *European Scientific Journal* 10 (4): 17–35.

Sakwa, Richard, ed. 2005. *Chechnya: From Past to Future.* London: Anthem Press.

Souleimanov, Emil. 2006. *An Endless War: The Russian-Chechen Conflict in Perspective.* Frankfurt: Peter Lang.

Tishkov, Valery. 2004. *Chechnya: Life in a War-torn Society.* Berkeley: University of California Press.

5.2 Explaining de facto states' failure

Huseyn Aliyev

This chapter examines how and why de facto states fail. It focusses on a number of potential causes of de facto state failure. Along with more conventional approaches – such as the focus on reintegration with the parent state, and the lack of good governance and economic problems – this study emphasizes less well-known causes of de facto state failure. These include tribalism, factionalism, and ideological fragmentation. This chapter emphasizes that de facto political entities often tend to follow similar paths to failure as recognized nation-states. Similarly to recognized states, de facto states may fail well before their loss of sovereignty and territorial control.

There are more definitions of de facto state (Pegg 2017), stretching from relatively narrow (Caspersen 2012; Kolstø and Paukovic 2014; Toomla 2016) to relatively broad ones (Florea 2014). Although the authors of the book generally stick to the rather narrow concept of de facto state, in the case of de facto state failure we will take into account also borderline cases or cases from Florea's (2014, 791) list of thirty-four entities which between 1945 and 2011 enjoyed "some degree of separation" and exerted "military control over (...) portions of territory". In fact, the structural causes such as tribalism, factionalism, and ideological fragmentation can even prevent the separatist movement from being able to transform into a de facto state.

Current research on sovereign state failure[1] closely connects the weakness, or the collapse, of a nation-state with the emergence of unrecognized polities (Rotberg 2010). The appearance of internal actors willing to split the state along ethnic, religious, or political lines is often associated with the inability of nation-states to control their territory and due to their military deficiencies (Kraxberger 2007). States with federal systems, and with more than one ethnic group, and countries affected by political crises, are considered most vulnerable to de facto secessionism during episodes of weakness and political turmoil.

The bulk of studies on state failure focusses on two relatively closely related factors explaining the state failure. First, armed conflict is depicted as the key factor of state weakness and failure because it weakens political institutions, affects economic performance, and is often associated with separatism (Vinci 2008; Rotberg 2010). For example, Rotberg (2004, 5) in his major work on failed states drew close links between civil war violence and state failure, presenting intrastate armed conflict as an inseparable part of most failed states. This claim is not hard to substantiate: many failed states around the world are currently affected by civil wars. Syria, Iraq, Afghanistan, Yemen, and Somalia are some of the most well-publicized examples. Indeed, all states included into the State Fragility Index[2] under classification of highly fragile (or failed) are engulfed by intrastate violence. Amongst these countries, Sudan, South Sudan, Somalia, and Ethiopia, at different periods of their recent history have either had de facto entities within their territories or themselves separated from their parent states.

Second, economic challenges are emphasized as one of the main causes of state failure, which, in many cases, is associated – either as its cause or as its consequence – with civil war violence. In some failed states, economic problems appeared following the emergence of civil war, destruction of infrastructure, and disruption of trade and foreign investments. In other failed states, economic weaknesses were inherent to the state system and were behind the emergence of civil violence (Iqbal and Starr 2015). Economic weaknesses are often closely interconnected with corruption, nepotism, and other governance problems intrinsic to many developing states. Another aspect of economic development pertinent to state failure is the disparities in the distribution of revenues from natural resources in states rich with mineral deposits. Conflicts over unequal distribution of resources are common causes behind secessionist conflicts and state failure in countries with resource-rich ethnic regions. Such de facto states as Biafra in Nigeria and Katanga in the Democratic Republic of Congo (DRC) or entities which used to enjoy some degree of separation, such as South Sudan (prior to independence), have emerged to a significant extent due to conflicts related to poor natural resources management by the parent state. The lack of good governance, political favouritism, and the failure of development are amongst other causes of state failure that are interrelated with both armed conflict and economic deficiencies (Iqbal and Starr 2015).

The above causes create conditions beneficial for and conducive not only to state failure but also for successful secessionism and the establishment of a durable de facto polity. The cases of effective de facto statehood in the absence of parent state's fragility are few. For example, the list compiled by Florea (2014, 793) entirely consists of parent states, which had been either fragile or highly fragile through significant periods of their modern history. This draws an inseparable link between state weakness, or failure, and the emergence of de facto states. However, the relationship between state failure and de facto statehood is not only crucial for the birth of de facto entities but is also engraved in their own demise.

It must be noted, however, that de facto state's failure is not always and not necessarily synonymous with their disappearance and demise. Therefore, this chapter does not causally connect the failure of unrecognized states with the end of their existence. Rather, the key theoretical goal of this chapter is to examine which factors are likely to precipitate de facto entities' weakness and failure.

254 *Huseyn Aliyev*

When de facto states fail

De facto states differ from recognized polities in many aspects, but they also share numerous similarities with nation-states. One of these analogies is that de facto entities are just as likely (if not more) to experience weakness, failure, and collapse as recognized states. We understand the failure of de facto states in the same terms as the failure of sovereign states (Iqbal and Starr 2015, 12). The failure of de facto states' attempt to achieve political independence does not equal to state failure and the loss by de facto entities of their capacity to control the territory and to provide their population with public goods does not mean that these states will cease to exist. As is the case with many de facto states, weakness and the failure of a parent state are conducive and beneficial towards the emergence of de facto statehood. However, many if not all de facto polities and other similar entities are doomed to inherit most of the weaknesses of their parent state. The lack of international recognition, absent or destroyed by war industries, often land-locked location, lack of experienced administrations, and numerous other malaises make their plight even more precarious. The most logical assumption to be extracted from the literature on state failure is that armed conflict, economic deficiencies, and poor governance should undermine de facto states as fast, or even faster, as recognized polities. Other factors that influence survival of de facto states include support from patrons, other countries, or stakeholders, relations between the leadership and other actors of the parent state and the breakaway region. Bearing in mind that existing literature on de facto statehood has already explored external factors in sufficient depth (Rotberg 2004, 2010; Kolstø 2006; Iqbal and Starr 2015), detailed discussion of these factors is beyond the scope of this chapter.

Nevertheless, remarkable endurance of de facto entities in the face of all these challenges had been detailed by a large and growing body of empirical literature on de facto statehood, particularly in the former Soviet Union (Baev 1998; Kolossov and O'Loughlin 1998; Beissinger and Young 2002). One noteworthy difference between the nation-state and the de facto state failure is that the latter is very likely to culminate in the disappearance of the de facto entity and its reintegration with a parent state. This makes it even more imperative for de facto states to avoid failure at all costs. Whilst failure of a de facto state significantly increases the likelihood of its disappearance, failed de facto state may still continue to exist for as long as it is capable to ward off the attempts by parent state to absorb it.

Despite the looming threat of military invasion from a parent state, stagnant economic performance that many currently existing de facto states share, and chronically poor governance, a surprisingly high percentage of de facto entities manage to survive. Moreover, the emergence of the east Ukraine's DPR and LPR in 2014, and the imminent possibility of a Kurdish de facto entity in Syria suggest that the numbers of de facto states continue growing. The de facto states' durability further increases the importance of understanding how and why these entities meet their end.

Explaining de facto states' failure 255

Research on de facto statehood maintains that effective nation-building, strong military, weakness of parent state, and the existence of a strong patron enable de facto states to survive irrespectively of their deficiencies (Kolstø 2006, 729). Most studies, however, consider the above factors as static and make few efforts to explain what happens if de facto states fail at nation-building. Are their military forces always strong? What happens when a parent state manages to overcome its weaknesses? What happens when a patron either decides to stop supporting a de facto entity (Serbian Kraina in Croatia) or when a de facto state does not have a patron (Tamil Eelam, Chechnya)?

The main theoretical argument of this chapter is that de facto states fail due to a combination of factors, most of which are associated with armed violence, socio-political cleavages, and economic collapse. The de facto state failure is a far more complex phenomenon than it is often portrayed in the literature. Conflict violence and economic deficiencies are often embedded into a patchwork of intervening factors. With that in mind, this chapter outlines – alongside armed conflicts and economic deficiencies – tribalism, warlordism, and ideological fractionalization as significant determinants of de facto failure traceable in a number of other "failed" de facto entities. This chapter does not attempt to underrate the significance of other factors of de facto states' failure, and therefore the main objective here is to analyze the above detailed set of factors not as exclusive but as complimentary to other scenarios of de facto state collapse.

Armed conflict

Reabsorption in the parent state as the result of an armed conflict is one of the possible, and most widely cited in the literature (Kolstø 2006, 737; Florea 2014; Iqbal and Starr 2015), causes of de facto states' failure. In the absence of a patron or due to their military weakness, de facto entities may be vulnerable to armed conflict with a parent state. Katanga, Biafra, Serbian Kraina, and the Chechen Republic of Ichkeria are amongst the examples of de facto states, which have failed due to armed conflict with a parent state, and were subsequently absorbed. In contrast to the inclusion of a de facto independent territory into the parent state as a separate entity (e.g. with extended autonomy), forceful incorporation of a de facto entity into parent state results in the loss of de facto state's control over its territory and governance (Kolstø 2006, 738), and therefore, equals to its failure.

Since many unrecognized states are often born out of secessionist conflicts, civil war is an inseparable part of de facto states' existence. However, unrecognized entities fail as a result of armed conflict not only when they are absorbed into the parent state – and thus lose their de facto independence – but also when civil war violence cripples socioeconomic development of a de facto state and precipitates its failure. The most obvious examples of separatist entities failing in their development as a result of armed violence are

256 *Huseyn Aliyev*

Tamil Eelam, East Timor, Muslim Mindanao, South Sudan, and Chechnya. Not all of these entities are de facto states *sensu stricto* and not all of them were incorporated in their respective parent states owing to conflict-incurred weaknesses, but all had been weakened by armed conflict with the parent states, which was one of the key causes of their failure.

Along with conflicts that de facto states fight with parent states, separatist entities might engage in internal conflicts within their own territories. In-fighting in South Sudan, Chechnya, as well as in Katanga have weakened these entities as much or even more than confrontations with their parent states. Weakened by internal armed conflicts, de facto states might either succumb to an invasion by parent state or fail in governance and economic development.

Although the majority of de facto entities tend to experience armed conflicts at different (mostly early) periods of their existence, conflict violence alone is rarely the cause of de facto statehood failure. Rather, there is an interplay of factors which might be held accountable for the failure, which occur alongside armed violence or before and after.

Economic deficiencies

Few cases of state failure occur without economic collapse. Whilst some states tend to fail exclusively due to conflict-related causes, in the majority of cases, economic deficiencies either accompany failure or precede it (Iqbal and Starr 2015, 52–54). Bearing in mind that in contrast to sovereign states, de facto states and separatist entities in general usually tend to lack developed industrial bases and have little or no experience of economic production, they are even more vulnerable to economic collapse than recognized states. Even for resource-rich secessionist territories, such as Biafra, Katanga, South Sudan, and many others, access to rich mineral resources did not guarantee economic security. Since many resource-rich provinces are used as mere sites of resource extraction, they rarely have appropriate industrial facilities needed to process and store fossil fuels and other natural resources.

Absence of a patron state willing to subsidize a territory under the actual control of rebel or separatist forces presents an insurmountable challenge for newly minted separatist entities. Lacking constant funding from a patron state, such as that provided by Russia to South Ossetia, Abkhazia, and the eastern Ukrainian de facto entities, many polities of this kind transform into hubs of drug trade, smuggling, poaching, trade in illicit goods and items (e.g. endangered wildlife), and human trafficking. Whilst the territory under the control of the United Wa State Army (Myanmar) is renowned for its trade in protected wildlife (BBC 2016), two other of Myanmar's separatist entities – Karen and Kachin states – are notorious for drug production and illicit trade in gems and timber. Tamil Eelam procured significant portion of its funding from the extortion of taxes from Tamil Diasporas abroad (Wayland 2004).

Explaining de facto states' failure 257

The lack of international recognition further limits the de facto states' opportunities to receive economic aid from abroad and reduces their legal financial interactions with the rest of the world. As unrecognized territories, de facto states are not entitled to economic assistance from international financial institutions, such as the World Bank or International Monetary Fund. Most international banks, companies, and organizations tend to avoid dealing with de facto states and normally maintain no presence on their territory. Not only de facto states are deprived of opportunities to trade internationally, but, often due to the pressure from the parent state, are unable to even trade with their neighbours. Whilst most de facto territories lack industrial bases, limited opportunities to export their production legally further decrease the de facto states' chances to develop their industries.

All of the above suggests that from the moment of their inception, many de facto states remain highly vulnerable to economic downfall. Faced with economic collapse, de facto entities would be unable to provide basic public goods to the population and might find their military disintegrate into factions along tribal, sectarian, or ethnic divisions. Economic collapse would also enable the parent state to wage effective financial and trade blockade of its breakaway regions. Above all, the inability of the de facto states' leadership to demonstrate to the population that their nation-building project is not sustainable is a precursor of state failure.

Tribalism

In many secessionist conflicts, clan and/or tribal identities are amongst the key sub-ethnic forms of fractionalization (Cederman, Wimmer, and Min 2010) and violent conflict mobilization (Souleimanov and Aliyev 2015). Whilst for some de facto entities – particularly in post-communist Eastern Europe – clan divisions persist along oligarchic interests or geographical origins of individuals (Donetsk clan) (Kuzio 2014; Aliyev 2017), for many other societies, clans are embedded in tribal and ethnic structures. Given that both clan- and tribe-based divisions entail fractionalization into relatively small groups of individuals – as opposed to ethnicity-centred factionalism – it is potentially detrimental to both nation- and state-building processes. As soon as the de facto state's nation-building project becomes hijacked by clan and tribal interests, popular mobilization and nationalist awareness may easily turn into clan in-fighting. Inter-clan and tribal tensions may not only undermine nation-building but might also weaken de facto state's armed forces and scare off external patrons.

Some de facto states (e.g. Somaliland) have managed to avoid clan and tribal fractionalization due to effective inter-clan consensus building. However, even in this Somalian polity, nation-building processes have not succeeded in overcoming clan and tribal identities in politics (Ahmed 1999). For other de facto states, clan and tribal divisions have proven deadly.

258 *Huseyn Aliyev*

The Katanga state in eastern Congo, as well as Nigeria's Biafra, is amongst the examples of de facto states weakened by tribal divisions. In both cases, clannish and tribal disputes heavily contributed to the collapse of these entities and their forceful incorporation into the respective parent state. Tribalism has proven dangerous even for those separatist entities, which have, after a period of civil and ethnic warfare, successfully achieved international recognition. The ongoing civil war between Dinka and Nuer tribes in the newly minted state of South Sudan is an example of tribalism's impact on secessionist entities. Kosovo is yet another case of a recently recognized state with a deeply rooted clan conflict (Kaltcheva 2009; Frahm 2014).

Warlordism

The rise and competition for power of influential warlords, although often closely intertwined with tribalism, might prove even more deadly for de facto states. Conflicts amongst rebel commanders and various rebel factions are a well-known phenomenon in civil war studies (Fjelde and Nilsson 2012). Whilst research on warlordism in de facto states is limited, conflict amongst warlords following an effective secessionist campaign are very likely to occur. Conflicts between warlords belonging to the same rebel organization become particularly acute when external threat either disappears or becomes less imminent. In-fighting within Sudan People's Liberation Army (SPLA) followed in 2013, just two years after South Sudan's independence, and rapidly developed in a full-scale civil war between two prominent ex-warlords, President Salva Kiir and his deputy Riek Machar. Although South Sudan's civil conflict is fought over tribal divisions, power struggle of influential warlords had been instrumental towards the split within SPLA. In the same vein, warlordism has had a significant divisive effect on the collapse of Tamil Eelam (Stokke 2006).

The threat of warlordism is particularly destructive for newly emerged de facto states, with a recent history of civil war and the lack of economic prospects for rebel fighters. The inability of de facto states' leadership to provide employment opportunities for former rebels, either in security forces or beyond, enables warlords to keep their private armed forces and to rely on them in power struggles. Due to the potentially divisive role of power-seeking warlords in weak and fragile states, literature on state failure tends to closely associate warlordism with state failure (Rotberg 2010; Malejacq 2016).

Ideological fractionalization

The emergence of splinter groups with more radical ideology than the parent organization has been a feature of many insurgent organizations (O'Ballance 1981; Silke 1998). Governments of newly emerged de facto entities are often composed of a wide diversity of former rebel groups, characterized

Explaining de facto states' failure   259

not only by ethnic-, tribal-, and clan-based divisions but also by ideological boundaries. Although ideological rifts within de facto states might be embedded in ethnic divisions, tribalism, and warlordism, this form of fractionalization is best characterized by divisions along religious-sectarian or political lines. Bearing in mind that state ideology is crucial for the effective nation-building, failure of de facto leadership to reconcile ideological differences may endanger the entire state-building project. Simply because ideological conflicts may involve larger numbers of participants and develop higher degrees of radicalization, these conflicts might prove far more serious and consequential than tribal in-fighting, or warlord disagreements. Resolving ideological conflicts might also prove a much harder task than settling tribal or individual disagreements. Ideological rifts had been instrumental towards state fragility and failure in many parts of the world. Sectarian conflicts in Iraq, Syria, Yemen, religion-fuelled civil wars in Central African Republic and northern Nigeria, as well as south Thailand and Myanmar's Rohingya insurgencies, are amongst the examples of state failure cases induced by ideological fractionalization.

Similarly to sovereign states, separatist polities are susceptible to ideological conflicts. Split within Moro National Liberation Front (MNLF) – an organization controlling the de facto independent Autonomous Region of Muslim Mindanao, or ARMM, in the Philippines – contributed to the emergence of more ideologically centred Moro Islamic Liberation Front (MILF), as well as the al-Qaeda affiliated Abu Sayyaf group. The emergence of MILF, and particularly, of the radical Islamist Abu Sayyaf group, had been detrimental for the ARMM's autonomy and significantly limited its chances of either international recognition or cessation from the Philippines.

Conclusion

This chapter provided theoretically grounded analysis of de facto states' failure, which along with broadly studied, also includes a number of several least explored causes of de facto state failure. The emphasis on tribal, ideological, and factional divisions, along with economic challenges and armed conflicts, is highly relevant for developing states, many of which have colonial legacy. Bearing in mind that addressing the above challenges is crucial for the effective functioning of sovereign states, internal divisions and weaknesses might be expected to have even stronger impact on unrecognized polities. Despite various factors enabling them to survive pressure from the parent state, and, in some cases from the international community, many de facto states remain vulnerable to internally generated shocks. Divisions and conflicts within de facto states may prove to be as damaging to their survival as direct military invasion by a parent state. Similarly to recognized states, for de facto entities failure does not equal disappearance. However, internal cleavages are likely to weaken a de facto state and to precipitate its incorporation into the parent state. Further research is

260 *Huseyn Aliyev*

needed in order to understand the role of internal factors in de facto statehood failure. Explaining how domestic challenges affect the survival and persistence of de facto entities and how these factors interact with external shocks might shed more light on relatively under-explored process of de facto state failure.

Notes

1 This chapter relies on Iqbal and Starr's (2015, 12) general definition of state failure, which is "focused on the complete collapse of state authority."
2 See http://fsi.fundforpeace.org/.

Literature

Ahmed, Ismail I. 1999. "The Heritage of War and State Collapse in Somalia and Somaliland: Local-level Effects, External Interventions and Reconstruction." *Third World Quarterly* 20 (1): 113–127.

Aliyev, Huseyn. 2017. *When Informal Institutions Change. Institutional Reforms and Informal Practices in the Former Soviet Union.* Ann Arbor: Michigan University Press.

Baev, Pavel. 1998. *Russia's Policies in Secessionist Conflicts in Europe in the 1990s.* Oslo: Norwegian Atlantic Committee.

BBC. 2016. "Myanmar's Free-Wheeling Wa State." *BBC News*, November 17. www.bbc.com/news/world-asia-37996473.

Beissinger, Mark, and M. Crawford Young. 2002. *Beyond State Crisis? Post-colonial Africa and Post-Soviet Eurasia in Comparative Perspective.* Washington: Woodrow Wilson Center Press.

Caspersen, Nina. 2012. *Unrecognized States. The Struggle for Sovereignty in the Modern International System.* Cambridge: Polity Press.

Cederman, Lars-Erik, Andreas Wimmer, and Brian Min. 2010. "Why Do Ethnic Groups Rebel? New Data and Analysis." *World Politics* 62 (1): 87–119.

Fjelde, Hanne, and Desirée Nilsson. 2012. "Rebels against Rebels: Explaining Violence between Rebel Groups." *Journal of Conflict Resolution* 56 (4): 604–628.

Florea, Adrian. 2014. "De Facto States in International Politics (1945–2011): A New Data Set." *International Interactions* 40 (5): 788–811.

Frahm, Ole. 2015. "Making Borders and Identities in South Sudan." *Journal of Contemporary African Studies* 33 (2): 251–267.

Iqbal, Zaryab, and Harvey Starr. 2015. *State Failure in the Modern World.* Stanford: Stanford University Press.

Kaltcheva, Tzvetomira. 2009. "Kosovo's Post-independence Inter-clan Conflict." *Human Security Journal* 2: 113–124.

Kolossov, Vladimir, and John O'Loughlin. 1998. "Pseudo-States as Harbingers of a New Geopolitics: The Example of the Trans-Dniester Moldovan republic (TMR)." *Geopolitics* 3 (1): 151–176.

Kolstø, Pål. 2006. "The Sustainability and Future of Unrecognized Quasi-States." *Journal of Peace Research* 43 (6): 723–740.

Kolstø, Pål, and Davor Paukovic. 2014. "The Short and Brutish Life of Republika Srpska Kraina: Failure of a De Facto State." *Ethnopolitics* 13 (4): 309–327.

Kraxberger, Brennan M. 2007. "Failed States: Temporary Obstacles to Democratic Diffusion or Fundamental Holes in the World Political Map?" *Third world Quarterly* 28 (6): 1055–1071.

Kuzio, Taras. 2014. "Crime, Politics and Business in 1990s Ukraine." *Communist and Post-Communist Studies* 47 (2): 195–210.

Malejacq, Romain. 2016. "Warlords, Intervention, and State Consolidation: A Typology of Political Orders in Weak and Failed States." *Security Studies* 25 (1): 85–110.

O'Ballance, Edgar. 1981. "IRA Leadership Problems." *Studies in Conflict & Terrorism* 5 (1–2): 73–82.

Pegg, Scott. 2017. "Twenty Years of De Facto State Studies: Progress, Problems, and Prospects." In: *The Oxford Encyclopedia of Empirical International Relations Theory*, edited by W. R. Thompson et al. Oxford: Oxford University Press. http://politics.oxfordre.com/view/10.1093/acrefore/9780190228637.001.0001/acrefore-9780190228637-e-516.

Rotberg, Robert I., ed. 2004. *State Failure and State Weakness in a Time of Terror.* Washington: Brookings Institution Press.

Rotberg, Robert I., ed. 2010. *When States Fail: Causes and Consequences.* Princeton: Princeton University Press.

Silke, Andrew. 1998. "In Defense of the Realm: Financing Loyalist Terrorism in Northern Ireland—Part One: Extortion and Blackmail." *Studies in Conflict & Terrorism* 21 (4): 331–361.

Souleimanov, Emil Aslan, and Huseyn Aliyev. 2015. "Blood Revenge and Violent Mobilization: Evidence from the Chechen Wars." *International Security* 40 (2): 158–180.

Stokke, Kristian. 2006. "Building the Tamil Eelam State: Emerging State Institutions and Forms of Governance in LTTE-controlled Areas in Sri Lanka." *Third World Quarterly* 27 (6): 1021–1040.

Toomla, Raul. 2016. Charting Informal Engagement between De Facto States: A Quantitative Analysis. *Space and Polity* 20 (3): 330–345.

Vinci, Anthony. 2008. "Anarchy, Failed States, and Armed Groups: Reconsidering Conventional Analysis." *International Studies Quarterly* 52 (2): 295–314.

Wayland, Sarah. 2004. "Ethnonationalist Networks and Transnational Opportunities: The Sri Lankan Tamil Diaspora." *Review of International Studies* 30 (3): 405–426.

5.3 Why de facto states fail. Lessons from the Chechen Republic of Ichkeria

Emil Aslan Souleimanov

This chapter seeks to provide an empirically rich account of de facto statehood's failure. Drawing the empirical case study from interwar Chechnya (1996–1999), we demonstrate that the failure of de facto states is a complex phenomenon that combines common factors of nation-state failure and the processes specific to de facto entities. We argue that phenomena outlined in the Chapter 5.2 – tribalism, warlordism, ideological fractionalization, and economic deficiencies – emerge as significant determinants of the de facto states' failure or even demise. We seek to show that the key factors identified in the literature behind the success of de facto states – such as nation-building, strong military, and weak parent state – are not static indicators. Rather, these factors of the de facto statehood's success are susceptible to change that might as well lead to the collapse of the entities. We argue that although many aspects of the de facto states' failure are comparable to the collapse and failure of sovereign states, failure processes in unrecognized states tend to follow their own pathways, which remain distinguishable from nation-state failure.

De facto state failure: Chechnya (1996–1999)

Following the failed hardcore-Communist coup d'état of August 1991 in Moscow, Chechnya's separatist elites declared independence from Russia in mid-September, which led to three years of semi-independent statehood. In December 1994, expecting a *Blitzkrieg*, Russian Army marched into the breakaway republic situated in the eastern part of the Muslim-majority North Caucasus. A full-fledged war followed, with Russian military deploying largely indiscriminate violence and thousands of Chechens mobilizing into insurgent groups, exponential mobilization facilitated by the persistence in Chechen society of the clan organization and the custom of blood revenge (Souleimanov and Aliyev 2015). The war cost the lives of dozens of thousands of Chechens, predominantly civilians (Cichocki 1997, 11–12). Local insurgent groups mushroomed in the course of the war, most of them driven by the idea of Chechen ethno-nationalism, managing to inflict sensitive blows to the superior invading force. As a result of its incapacity to break the backbone of the popular resistance movement, Russian army

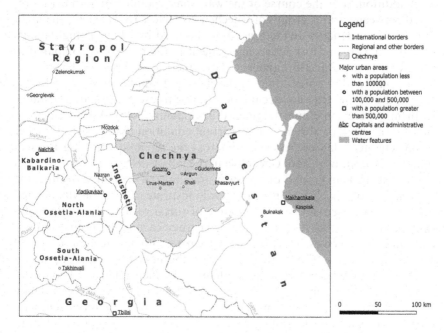

Map 8 Chechnya.
Source: Authors.

pulled out of the rebellious republic in autumn 1996 (Dunlop 1998). This move was widely considered as Moscow's humiliating defeat to the improvised military force of a country slightly more than one million inhabitants (Oliker 2001) (Map 8).

Tribalism

Interwar Chechnya (1996–1999) was a de facto state but also a country in ruins. Following an all-out war that lasted twenty-one months, most cities and villages – with the exception of the country's pro-Russian northern areas that evaded warfare – were decimated, with hundreds of thousands of civilians having become internal refugees or left Chechnya. According to some estimates, by late 1996, up to 70% of Chechnya's housing stock had been either destroyed completely or severely damaged (Souleimanov 2006). The war annihilated Chechnya's infrastructure. Factories and processing plants were thoroughly bombarded. Roads barely existed. Healthcare, education facilities, and jobs were nearly missing, with unemployment rates reaching as high as 80% and close to 100% in young people (Nezavisimaya gazeta 1997). Mines lay under roughly 5,000 hectares of Chechnya's territory, which made 15% of the republic's cultivable soil. This caused frequent deaths and injuries, complicating communication, and hampering farming work (Blandy 2003).

264 *Emil Aslan Souleimanov*

In addition, over the course of the war, some established animosities revived between various groups of Chechen populace. To an extent, the highlanders vs. lowlanders divide braced up, boosted by what the highlanders considered as their most active engagement in the war effort compared to the urban dwellers' and lowlanders' relative inertia. Members of the "treacherous" clans and families – that is, the clans and families that allegedly cooperated with the Russian occupiers or failed to exert adequate resistance to them – were sometimes targeted (Souleimanov 2015). As Grozny's authority was weak or absent – an important condition that we detail further in this chapter – lawlessness spread across the republic following Russian military's withdrawal from Chechnya in the fall of 1996.

Against the background of post-war anarchy and economic decline, the societal role of Chechen clan – the age-old institute of patrilineally defined kinship – increased as the single source of social security for the population. To survive, relatives took increased care of each other, both economically and as protectors. Thousands of Chechens with damaged or destroyed houses, particularly those stemming from the heavily bombarded urban areas, sought refuge in the villages inhabited by their relatives. Those who lacked financial resources were supported by their relatives who were lucky enough to live off their undamaged livestock. In the situation of self-help, relatives sought to stick with each other in order to survive attacks by antagonized clans or simply defend their interests and honour.[1] All in all, this contributed to the upswing of clan-based solidarity networks or, as this phenomenon has been widely termed, tribalism.[2]

The post-war rise of Chechen clan was an important factor undermining the authority of the central government in Grozny. On the one hand, the persistence of Chechen clan was crucial for the survival of the entire post-war generation. On the other hand, Chechen clan and the related mindset of clan-based in-group favouritism and out-group mistrust and discrimination implied that those in the leading positions in Grozny and elsewhere sought to assert their relatives' interests at the expense of the abstract idea of the Chechen people's or Chechen nation-state's shared interest. Formal and informal positions in the republic were held by the relatives of local chiefs, with professional merit playing minimal or no role in their (informal) appointments. Clan-based particularism led to the frequent embezzlement of thin funds allocated from Grozny to the provinces. Overall, attributing a strong personal element to republican and local politics, clan-based particularism generated immense tension in Chechen society while paralyzing the institutions of Chechen state and reducing popular trust in it. Intriguingly, Chechen president Aslan Maskhadov[3] himself, albeit being initially opposed to clan particularism, soon came to appoint the members of his clan in the leading governmental positions in order to ensure the integrity and continuity of his office's policies (Souleimanov 2006, 130).

This having been said, for most Chechens struggling for everyday survival, what mattered was the effective institute of clan solidarity. Kinship

The Chechen Republic of Ichkeria 265

networks, unlike the ill-functioning or absent central government, enabled most Chechen families to make the ends meet; it was their relatives who were capable and willing to provide support to them, not the ephemeral Chechen state.

Warlordism

Related to Chechen clan-based particularism was the persistence of strong warlord elite in post-war Chechnya. At the beginning of his term in office in early 1997, Maskhadov

> was already confronted with the necessity of finding arrangements with various war chiefs [warlords] who strengthened their fiefs during the war and did not intend to submit themselves to a man who was nevertheless the leader of the Chechen army.
>
> (Merlin 2012)

In early 1997, Maskhadov indeed gave important positions in the government to leading "brigadier generals", including Shamil Basaev,[4] who was appointed the country's first vice-premier, as well as to Aslan Ismailov, Aslanbek Abdulkhajiev, and Ruslan Gilaev (Tarasov 1997, 3). Maskhadov's initiative was to win over the key warlords, cementing their loyalty to the central government in Grozny.

Others were less successful though. In fact, soon thereafter, many leading war veterans, particularly warlords, saw the collapse of their ambitious expectations to attain power and prestige in the newly established state institutions. Post-war Chechnya's resources were simply too limited to accommodate all aspirants and their far-reaching expectations. Many warlords who saw themselves unjustly deprived of the fair share of the republic's economic and political pie soon took an immense dislike in the central authority in Grozny. Instead of disarming their units – or acknowledging the superiority of the central government in Grozny – dozens of warlords thus sought to strengthen control over their respective "spheres of influence", usually native villages, while recognizing Grozny's central authority only symbolically or refusing to recognize it whatsoever.

Claiming that they only recognized "Allah's supremacy" – and questioning the legitimacy of the Grozny government – the warlords solidified their military and political power, often at the expense of the competing clans. This, too, contributed to the strengthening of clan solidarity. In some occasions, heated confrontation led to armed clashes, with which Grozny usually hesitated to interfere. As warlords usually led their respective units, made up of their neighbours or clan relatives, the difficulty in the warlords' return to peaceful life complicated the reintegration of ordinary war veterans as well (Merlin 2012). To address this pressing challenge, Maskhadov famously declared in his 1998 appeal to the nation that

266　*Emil Aslan Souleimanov*

> [w]e spent many long years walking along the path of war with certainty and dignity: However, now we have suddenly changed entirely. Yesterday's comrades-in-arms look at one another with mistrust because the seed of discord has been sown amongst them and its name is ambition for power.
>
> (Tishkov 2001, 447)

Under these circumstances, for Maskhadov to claim back control over the rebellious warlords-controlled areas could lead to a full-fledged military confrontation and civil war. To avoid the latter, the Chechen president choose to tolerate the existence of warlord-dominated "fiefdoms", which further weakened Chechen state institutions.

The situation was exacerbated by some warlords' involvement in criminal activities both in Chechnya and in Russia. By the late 1990s, kidnappings in order to exert ransom, confiscation of property, illegal exploitation of Chechen oil wells, and business with stolen cars became a daily norm (Lo and Kwok 2012, 38). Grozny's lack of ability to put an end to these activities further weakened the idea of Chechen statehood in general and Maskhadov's reputation in particular, while boosting kin solidarity.

Ideological fractionalization

Intertwined with the above two factors were the ideological frictions that afflicted Chechen elites and population in the interwar period. In fact, drawing on ideological considerations, an influential segment of Chechen "brigadier generals", led by the infamous warlord Shamil Basaev, soon challenged the authority of the central government in Grozny in general and of president Maskhadov in particular. Inspired by Salafi-jihadism, an ideology imported in the country in the early 1990s by the Middle Eastern missionaries and particularly ethnic-Arab foreign fighters, Basaev and his associates grew increasingly opposed to the secularist rule of president Maskhadov.[5]

Against the background of the jihadists' increasingly strong standing in the republic, two warring camps soon crystallized. One camp was made up of the nationalists or Ichkerians who adhered to the traditional Sufi *virds* (brotherhoods). Albeit the Ichkerians' attitude towards the central authority in Grozny was ambivalent, with many leading Ichkerians holding sceptical or autonomist stance towards Maskhadov's regime and others refusing to acknowledge Grozny's authority on the ground, they generally supported the idea of secular Chechen state, albeit with religious elements. The opposing camp was represented by Salafi-jihadists, a highly disciplined and tight-knit community of ethnic-Chechens and foreign fighters. Salafi-jihadists, who had acquired fame for military successes in the 1994–1996 war, disputed the very legitimacy of Chechen nation-state, which they considered un-Islamic, calling for the establishment of a Salafi theocracy instead (Wilhelmsen 2005; Rich and Conduit 2015).

The Chechen Republic of Ichkeria 267

While Maskhadov initially sought to achieve social consensus, for instance calling in 1998 for the incorporation of sharia-based legal principles into Chechnya's jurisdiction, his efforts fell short of accommodating the increasingly self-confident Salafi community. Maskhadov's efforts to win Basaev over eventually failed, as well. In 1998, Basaev (who earlier resigned from the position of deputy prime minister) was again given the post of prime minister, while Basaev's younger brother Shirwani was appointed to the lucrative position of the Director of the State Committee for Energy Resources. Yet in mid-1998, Basaev again resigned, allegedly because of the Chechen president's incapacity to execute his plans. Upon his resignation, Basaev further strengthened his alliance with the jihadists.

In June 1998, the tension between Sufi and Salafi elites reached their peak during the armed clashes in Chechnya's second largest city of Gudermes, in which around 50 gunmen, predominantly Salafis, were killed by Maskhadov loyalists. Soon thereafter, Maskhadov dismissed Salafi ministers and sympathizers and urged Chechens to expel "Wahhabis", as Salafis were pejoratively named, from their neighbourhoods and villages. In fall 1998, a congress of Chechen Muslim clergy took place in Grozny, which formally outlawed Salafis, accusing them of extremism, heresy, and plans to topple the legitimate government (Souleimanov 2006, 142). Still, Grozny sought to eschew massive armed confrontation with the Salafis, with numerically superior Maskhadov loyalists refraining from targeting the Salafi groups.

Nevertheless, in early 1999, in an effort to strengthen the legitimacy of his government and to scupper the Salafis' plans to declare an Islamic theocracy, Maskhadov announced the establishment of a full-fledged sharia government. While this move was welcomed reservedly by Ichkerian elites and secularly minded stratum of Chechen populace, the Salafis sought to capitalize on it to the fullest. In Basaev's words, "our president has finally accepted Islam. He is no longer the president; hence we should elect an imam" (Souleimanov 2006, 142). Hence, this initiative to bridge the warring camps of Chechen society, it soon proved counterproductive.

In a similar vein, the Sufi-Salafi sectarian face-off spread across the country affecting the lives of ordinary people. In line with their religious dogma, Salafis considered heretical the veneration of Sufi saints along with some "pagan" practices associated with Chechen "folk Islam" (Meijer 2009). Sometimes, they deliberately destroyed the sites of pilgrimage of Sufi saints (*murshids* and *ustadhs*) and showed utmost disrespect towards what they saw as customs unrelated to the "true" Islam. Salafis also questioned the notion of clan solidarity along with the norms of the *adat*, Chechen customary law, enshrined in the socio-cultural foundations of Chechen society. The Salafis' explicit lack of respect towards clan elderly (*vokkhstag*), unheard of in the deeply patriarchal Chechnya, frequently led to the split of Chechen clans, from which the "Arabised youth" was expelled.[6]

Oftentimes, theological discord penetrated not only the social fabric of Chechen clans. It also led to violent confrontation between members of

268 *Emil Aslan Souleimanov*

neighbouring – Sufi and Salafi-majority – villages. Sectarian violence driven by ideological fractionalization further impaired the idea of Chechen nation-state, undermining its social and ideo-political foundations. The majority of those supporting the Salafis or self-identifying as Salafis increasingly resented Maskhadov's alien and presumably non-Islamic government in Grozny, refusing to acknowledge his authority. At the same time, many Sufi nationalists grew increasingly sceptical towards Maskhadov's regime, accusing him of his incapacity to adequately cope with the "Wahhabi" threat (Bedford and Souleimanov 2016). As a result, towards 1998–1999, Chechnya effectively turned into a failed state as the government grew increasingly incapable of policing the territory.

Economic deficiency

By 1996, Chechnya's formal economy, infrastructure, and industry had been completely destroyed. Following the war, chemical industry, an important segment of the republic's economy in the Soviet decades, already dramatically weakened in the early 1990s, was defunct. Most oil wells, scattered across the republic's central areas, were controlled by warlords who were involved in its illegal exploitation and exports. By 1998, around 843,000 tons of oil had been produced – and sold out – illegally in Chechnya, without Grozny's control (Zurcher 2007, 104). Thus, the Grozny authorities had no sufficient income from the republic's relatively significant oil reserves; nor were they capable of extorting taxes from the illegal exploitation of Chechnya's oil reserves (Zurcher 2007, 104).

This having been said, interwar Chechnya's shadow economy – involving ransom money acquired from kidnappings, robberies, illegal seizure of property, illegal trade – was sizeable. According to some estimates, kidnappers alone procured around 200 million dollars in the three-year period of Chechnya's de facto independence (Tishkov 2004, 114). Maskhadov's episodic efforts to consolidate control over the republic's oil exploitation failed, and "Maskhadov was thus robbed of the possibility of stabilizing his regime by means of a patron-client network redistributing oil revenues" (Zurcher 2007, 104). In the interwar period, only about 10% of Chechnya's population was legally employed (Moskalev 1996).

In the early years of interwar Chechnya, Maskhadov's government sought to pressure Moscow to invest in the rebuilding of the devastated country. Russian and Chechen authorities were engaged in talks on making Chechnya a free-trade zone with special tax concessions. There was general consensus that Chechnya would remain in the rouble zone, likely remaining part of the Commonwealth of Independent States (CIS) economically, financially, and politically. Importantly, even Chechen radicals, for instance, Basaev, admitted Chechnya should remain in Russia's economic and energy spheres (Batuev 1997, 8). However, reaching an agreement on the size and conditions of economic support for Chechnya proved eventually impossible.

The Chechen Republic of Ichkeria 269

On the one hand, Grozny insisted on acquiring Russian economic support – or even war reparations – regardless of discussion of Chechnya's legal status. On the other hand, Moscow conditioned its economic support for Chechnya by cementing the breakaway republic's subordinate standing towards the federal centre. Russian authorities also prompted Chechen authorities' efforts to crack down on illegal businesses run from Chechnya-based warlords, which posed a serious threat to the socio-economic security of Russia's southern provinces. In fact,

> Russian politicians feared that the Chechens would take the most advantageous way: in terms of the economy, to stay in Russia, while politically pursuing independence. [...] Moscow has been unwilling to render Chechnya large-scale economic assistance, unless the Chechen leadership agrees to power sharing between the federal centre and Chechnya as a "member" of the federation.
>
> (Oğuz 1997, 4)

In early 1997, Moscow made clear to the newly elected Maskhadov government that it could only allocate around 757 billion roubles to Chechnya in the 1997, a promise that eventually failed to materialize due to Moscow's and Groznys' critically opposing views. At the same time, Moscow dismissed Chechnya's demands for paying war reparations (Katin 1997). Moreover, Grozny dismissed the so-called Tatarstan model. This model, advocated by Moscow, sought to render Chechnya considerable fiscal autonomy within Russia's political and economic spheres.

Conclusion

In August 1999, a joint Chechen-Dagestani Salafi-jihadist force invaded the westernmost areas of the neighbouring republic of Dagestan. Led by Basaev and his ethnically diverse jihadist *entourage*, the invasion's declared goal was to aid a group of Salafi-dominated villages in central Dagestan, a multi-ethnic Sunni-majority autonomous republic to the east of Chechnya. The Chechen-Dagestani invaders, supported by dozens of foreign fighters, apparently sought to instigate a large anti-Russian rebellion first in Dagestan and then across the whole of the Russian-dominated North Caucasus. Basaev himself used the invasion to declare himself the imam of a united theocracy of Chechnya and Dagestan – and oust Maskhadov as head of the Chechen nation-state that was now seen as out-to-date. While the attack soon proved to a be complete disaster, with Dagestanis mobilizing to resist the Salafi invaders, the invasion, alongside the bomb blasts in apartment buildings in Russian cities itself, were used by Moscow as a pretext to relaunch war on Chechnya.[7] Maskhadov's feverish efforts to regain control over the Basaev group – or strike a compromise deal with Moscow in order to pull back an evolving military confrontation with Russia – ultimately failed

270   *Emil Aslan Souleimanov*

as neither Basaev nor Kremlin showed interest in negotiating with Grozny (Williams 1999). Having reorganized military considerably, Russian army regained control over Chechnya by the early 2000, leading to a protracted insurgency and counterinsurgency that has been underway since (Kramer 2005; Dannreuther and March 2008; Souleimanov 2014; Souleimanov and Aliyev 2015; Ratelle and Souleimanov 2016). While the Russian invasion of 1999–2000 was the main factor leading to the ultimate fall of Chechen statehood, we show in this chapter that four under-researched in the literature on de facto state failure causes, tribalism, economic deficiency, warlordism, and ideological fractionalization, had prior to the beginning of the Second Russian-Chechen War led to the collapse/failure of Chechnya's de facto statehood.

The Chechen de facto state was born out of civil war similarly to many other de facto polities. It was not economically self-sustainable and lacked external patron who would provide it with economic aid and some form of protection. However, the economic deficiency was accompanied by deeply rooted disagreements within the separatist movement. Clan divisions, warlord politics, and sectarian rifts had undermined Chechen nation-building processes at their early stages. A combination of the above detailed causes contributed to state failure in Chechnya well before the 1999 Russian invasion. Whilst the international community remained sympathetic to the plight of Chechens, few international actors favoured the idea of Chechen independence and were willing to openly support the Chechen de facto state. Internal weaknesses shattered Chechen armed forces transforming military into a patchwork of warlord bands, making the de facto entity vulnerable to external aggression. The weakness of the parent state – Russian Federation – which it had demonstrated during the First Chechnya War, was not a static condition. As a matter of fact, the failure of Chechen nation- and state-building was accompanied by the strengthening of these processes in the Russian Federation.

Similarly to fragile and failing sovereign states, de facto entities are likely to be affected by analogous failure factors, most of which are related to civil violence and the economic collapse. The Chechen case demonstrates that these failure factors become even more acute in de facto entities, which usually lack the experience of statehood. In the 1990s Chechnya, high levels of national self-consciousness contributed to the rise of Chechen nationalism, which in its turn enabled Chechen separatists to succeed during the First Chechnya War. However, the failure of independent Chechen nation-building in the inter-war period demonstrated that nationalism does not ensure the success of de facto statehood and that nation-building is vulnerable to internal cleavages.

Deep divisions within the separatist camp, economic crisis, which was both a result and cause of Chechen society's internal divisions, along with the ability of the parent state to overcome its weaknesses had to various degrees contributed to the collapse of Chechen statehood. Since all of these

The Chechen Republic of Ichkeria 271

deficiencies are not specific to the Chechen case, but notable in many other de facto states, including the failed cases (Serbian Kraina, Tamil Eelam, Biafra, Katanga), de facto states are likely to suffer from similar failure factors. That said, this chapter opens avenues for future research on the topic of de facto states' failure, emphasizing the need to examine not only the rise but also fall of de facto statehood. The most obvious observation to emerge from this analysis is that de facto states are not immune to failure, and that failure occurs not simply as a result of failed nation-building, military weakness, and the strength of a parent state, but due to a complex synthesis of internal divisions and economic crises.

Notes

1 Discussions with dozens of Chechen survivors of the First (and Second) Russian-Chechen wars.
2 Distinct terms are used to refer to clans (*nekye*) and tribes (*teip*) in Chechen society. For the purpose of this chapter and to integrate its findings into general literature, a broader term tribe is used.
3 Aslan Maskhadov was the third president of the Chechen Republic of Ichkeria, following the legendary Jokhar Dudaev (1991–1996) and Zelimkhan Yandarbiev (1996–1997). A former Soviet military officer, Maskhadov was initially sympathetic to Dudaev's idea of establishing strong and unified secular statehood.
4 Shamil Basaev was a key Chechen warlord. Considered by many Chechens a hero and a traitor, he played an important role in shaping Chechen resistance during the First Russo-Chechen War, in aligning Chechen insurgent groups with jihadist foreign fighters in the interwar period, and ultimately in contributing to the relaunch of the Second Russian-Chechen War.
5 Rumours had it that Basaev grew increasingly antagonistic towards Maskhadov having lost elections to him in late 1996, a fact that Basaev never made peace with.
6 Authors' numerous discussions with Chechen eyewitnesses, 2002–2015.
7 In late August and September 1999, a series of terrorist attacks hit apartment buildings in the Russian cities of Buynaksk, Volgodonsk, and Moscow, killing around 300 people. The attacks were widely attributed to the alleged Chechen terrorists' frustration with their failed invasion to Dagestan, which galvanized Russian public opinion preparing it for the relaunch of an unpopular war against Chechnya. According to some analysts, these attacks were staged by Russian secret services to pave the ground for an invasion, which would help then-prime minister Vladimir Putin acquire power in the country. For a detailed analysis of this critical episode of Russia's post-Soviet history, see Dunlop (2014).

Literature

Batuev, V. 1997. "Shamil Basaev: Skoro poedem v Buddyonovsk s pokayaniem [Shamil Basaev: Soon We Will Go to Buddyonovsk with Repentance]." *Argumenty i fakty* 3 (848): 8.
Bedford, Sofie, and Emil Aslan Souleimanov. 2016. "Under Construction and Highly Contested: Islam in the Post-Soviet Caucasus." *Third World Quarterly* 37 (9): 1559–1580.

272 *Emil Aslan Souleimanov*

Blandy, C. W. 2003. *The Federal Response to Chechen Independence: Occupy, Liberate, Obliterate.* Cambridge: Conflict Studies Research Centre.

Cichocki, Jacek. 1997. *Konflikt rosyjsko-czeczenski, dzieje konfliktu, wojna rosyjskoczeczenska 1994–1996 i obecna sytuacja w Republice Czeczenskiej-Iczkerii* [The Russian-Chechen Conflict, Its History, the Russian-Chechen War of 1994–1996 and the Overall Situation in the Chechen Republic of Ichkeriya]. Warsaw: OSW.

Dannreuther, Roland, and Luke March. 2008. "Chechnya: Has Moscow Won?" *Survival* 50 (4): 97–112.

Dunlop, John B. 1998. *Russia Confronts Chechnya: Roots of a Separatist Conflict.* Cambridge: Cambridge University Press.

Dunlop, John. B. 2014. *The Moscow Bombings of September 1999: Examinations of Russian Terrorist Attacks at the Onset of Vladimir Putin's Rule.* Stuttgart: Ibidem-Verlag.

Katin, V. 1997. "Moskva prodalzhaet schitat Chechnyu subektom federatsii [Moscow continues to consider Chechnya as a subject of federation]." *Nezavsimaya gazeta*, 30 January, 1 and 3.

Kramer, Mark. 2005. "Guerrilla Warfare, Counterinsurgency and Terrorism in the North Caucasus: The Military Dimension of the Russian–Chechen Conflict." *Europe-Asia Studies* 57 (2): 209–290.

Lo, T. Wing, and Sharon Ingrid Kwok. 2012. "Traditional Organized Crime in the Modern World: How Triad Societies Respond to Socioeconomic Change." In *Traditional Organized Crime in the Modern World*, edited by Dina Siegel and Henk van de Bunt, 67–89. New York: Springer US.

Meijer, R. 2009. *Global Salafism: Islam's New Religious Movement.* London: Hurst & Co.

Merlin, Aude. 2012. "The Postwar Period in Chechnya: When Spoilers Jeopardize the Emerging Chechen State (1996–1999)." In *War Veterans in Postwar Situations*, edited by Natalie Duclos, 219–239. New York: Palgrave Macmillan US.

Moskalev, Boris. 1996. "The Anatomy of the Chechen Conflict." *Mediterranean Quarterly* 7 (1): 99–117.

Nezavisimaya gazeta. 1997. "Ekonomika Chechni posle voiny [Chechnya's Economy after the War]." *Nezavisimaya gazeta*, October 28, 3.

Oğuz, C. Cem. 1997. *The Relations between Chechnya and Russia since the Election of A. Maskhadov (January–May 1997).* Ankara: Center for Strategic Research. http://sam.gov.tr/wp-content/uploads/2012/02/CemOguz1.pdf.

Oliker, Olga. 2001. *Russia's Chechen wars 1994–2000: Lessons from Urban Combat.* Santa Monica, Arlington and Pittsburg: Rand Corporation.

Ratelle, Jean-François, and Emil Aslan Souleimanov. 2016. "A Perfect Counterinsurgency? Making Sense of Moscow's Policy of Chechenisation." *Europe-Asia Studies* 68 (8): 1287–1314.

Rich, Ben, and Dara Conduit. 2015. "The Impact of Jihadist Foreign Fighters on Indigenous Secular-nationalist Causes: Contrasting Chechnya and Syria." *Studies in Conflict & Terrorism* 38 (2): 113–131.

Souleimanov, Emil. 2006. *An Endless War: The Russian-Chechen Conflict in Perspective.* Frankfurt: Peter Lang.

Souleimanov, Emil A. 2014. "Jihad or Security? Understanding the Jihadization of Chechen Insurgency through Recruitment into Jihadist Units." *Journal of Balkan and Near Eastern Studies* 17 (1): 86–105.

The Chechen Republic of Ichkeria 273

Souleimanov, Emil. 2015. "An Ethnography of Counterinsurgency: Kadyrovtsy and Russia's Policy of Chechenization." *Post-Soviet Affairs* 31 (2): 91–114.

Souleimanov, Emil A., and Huseyn Aliyev. 2015. "Asymmetry of Values, Indigenous Forces, and Incumbent Success in Counterinsurgency: Evidence from Chechnya." *Journal of Strategic Studies* 38 (5): 678–703.

Tarasov, S. 1997. "Shamil Basaev eshche ne navoevalsya [Shamil Basaev Has Not Enough Fighting]." *Segodnya*, 3 April, 3.

Tishkov, Valerii. 2001. *Obshchestvo v vooruzennom konflikte (etnografiya chechenskoi voiny)* [Society in the Armed Conflict (Chechen War's Ethnography)]. Moscow: Nauka.

Tishkov, Valery. 2004. *Chechnya: Life in a War-torn Society.* Berkeley: University of California Press.

Wilhelmsen, Julie. 2005. "Between a Rock and a Hard Place: The Islamisation of the Chechen Separatist Movement." *Europe-Asia Studies* 57 (1): 35–59.

Williams, Daniel. 1999. "Peace Pleas Unanswered, Chechens Say." *The Washington Post*, 19 October, A19.

Zurcher, Christoph. 2007. *The Post-Soviet Wars: Rebellion, Ethnic Conflict, and Nationhood in the Caucasus.* New York: NYU Press.

5.4 The emergence and failure of the Gagauz Republic (1989–1995)

Slavomír Horák

Gagauzia is frequently dealt with by scholars as a case of nonviolent conflict (Tishkov 2013, 576) and an exemplar of internal disputes that have achieved a peaceful resolution (Socor 1994; King 1997; Chinn and Roper 1998), something which is often stressed by Moldovan and Gagauz representatives themselves (Radova 2015, 174). Gagauzia is also pointed to as a marginal case of federalism (Batt 1997). Most of what has been written about the country, primarily deals with the formation of the autonomous area, the implementation of autonomy and the relationship between the autonomous area and the central government, and the relationship between the parent and de facto state (Protsyk and Rigamonti 2007). A limited number of studies also concentrate on the 1989–1991 process of separation from the parent state and its subsequent reintegration in 1992–1994 (Zabarah 2012).

Although not entirely ignored, the process of the internal failure of Gagauzia as a de facto state have so far remained under-researched. However, in order to analyze the failure of the Gagauz de facto state, it is essential to also explain its formative phase, which is in fact a prelude to Gagauzia's failure. The processes which led to the ultimate failure of the Republic of Gagauzia have their roots in the formative period of Gagauzian statehood. Moreover, the formative period is also relatively understudied. No more than a handful of studies have provided a thorough insight into the interior situation in the de facto independent Gagauz Republic that existed from 1991 to 1995 (Sato 2009; Kosienkowski 2017a, 2017b). The case is hardly mentioned in the basic theoretical literature on the issue (Caspersen 2012, 13). It was thus left to Gagauz scholars or direct participants in the events of the era to research the domestic issues (Marunevich 1993; Angeli 2006, 2007, 514–574; Bulgar 2006; Dobrov 2007; Kendigelyan 2009; Topal 2013). Their writings, unsurprisingly, frequently consist of subjective descriptions or commentaries on the events.

The internal viability of de facto states is particularly tied to their ability to create a functional and sustainable political, economic, and security unit (Kolstø and Blakkisrud 2008, 484). In the case of Gagauzia, however, the formation process was incomplete. The emerging de facto state was reintegrated peacefully into Moldova as an autonomous unit, sooner than it was able to fully develop and stabilize its state structures.

The Gagauz Republic 275

This chapter focusses on the internal situation in Gagauzia from 1989 until 1994/1995 and analyzes the reasons for Gagauzia's failure as a viable de facto entity. It shows why Gagauzia has not developed into a typical de facto state within the post-Soviet area, and ended up as part of its parent state. As noted by Huseyn Aliyev in Chapter 5.2, the failure of a de facto state is a combination of several factors among which he counts: armed conflict, economic deficiencies, tribalism, warlordism, and ideological fractionalization. In the case of Gagauzia, the conflict was essentially nonviolent, and thus the factors of armed conflict and warlordism will not be analyzed in this chapter. It is also worth mentioning that the tribalism and ideological fractionalization took a rather different form than in Chechnya. In the case of Gagauzia, it was essentially a conflict between the central Gagauzian authorities and regional bodies, which resulted in an ideological dispute over the character of Gagauzian statehood. Finally, economic deficiencies played an important if not decisive role in the failure of the Republic of Gagauzia.

The contrast between the relatively unified attitudes displayed during decision-making on independence from Moldova vs. the lack of cohesion in evidence on questions of governance, was a key factor in the disintegration of Gagauzia, leading to its reintegration into Moldova as an autonomous unit. In addition, the absence of an external patron (Caspersen 2012, 54–58) became another important determinant for the failure of Gagauzia as de facto state. In light of this, this text is divided into five subchapters

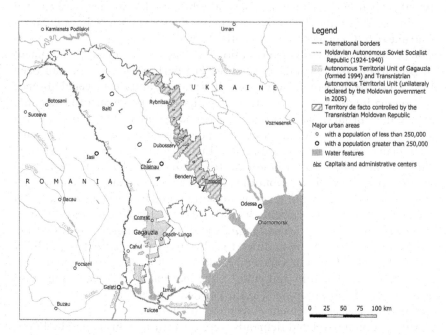

Map 9 Gagauzia and Transnistria.
Source: Authors.

276 *Slavomír Horák*

addressing the revival of Gagauzian ethnicity, the formation of the Gagauzian de facto state, and the three main reasons for its failure: internal political conflicts, economic deficiencies, and the absence of a patron state (Map 9).

Revival of Gagauzian ethnicity: from cultural to political autonomy

The thaw under Khrushchev that took place in the 1950s and the 1960s opened the door to a revival of small Soviet nations. For a time, Gagauzia experienced renewed interest in its local language, history, and culture. In the 1950s, the fight to eliminate illiteracy got underway, and the Gagauz language began to be used on a limited basis in schools. In 1958, Dionis Tanasoglu created the first alphabet and, in the late 1950s and early 1960s, published the first textbooks of Gagauz, including a primer. This period lasted until 1962, when Gagauz ceased to be taught and was replaced by Russian. Brief though it was, this era had planted the seeds for a new generation of Gagauz intellectuals that would grow up under Gorbachev's *perestroika*. Over time, their initial emphasis on the revival of Gagauz culture morphed into political demands (Bulgar 2006) in a process not too dissimilar to what also happened in other small nations within the Soviet Union. In the 1980s, informal discussion clubs were established around Gagauz tradition and folklore, with the key initiators of the Gagauz national revival being academics. Several ethnographic studies were carried out in the 1970s and 1980s, led especially by Stepan Kuroglo and Maria Marunevich (Guboglo 2012, 240–241). They drew attention to the suppression of the rights of the Gagauz nation, the way the economic development of Bulgarians and Gagauzs in the southern part of the republic had been held back, the inadequate levels of redistribution, and the targeted absence of Gagauz intellectuals in academic positions and positions of leadership. Hence in February 1988, both academic and economic elites in Gagauzia stood behind the newly established movement *Gagauz Halky* (Gagauz People) in Comrat, the Gagauz capital. In its beginnings, it was a discussion club that met in a Comrat building (Topal 2013, 35). New movements also sprang up in other towns. Obtaining autonomy for Gagauzia gradually became a central objective of these organizations and by the beginning of 1989 the cultural/revival movements had morphed into political ones. Most of them were absorbed into *Gagauz Halky* at the First Congress of the Gagauz Nation on 21 May 1989. In addition to cultural events – the *Hederlez* holiday and St. George's Day (Guboglo and Kvilinkova 2011, 362–363) – and discussions on Gagauz history and culture, the movement was institutionalized and it was also self-proclaimed as the political representative of the Gagauz nation, with a clear statement of demand for autonomy.

Most autonomy-related demands were rejected by Chisinau. The Popular Front of Moldova (*Frontul Popular din Moldova*) based on the previous Democratic Movement of Moldova (*Miscarea Democratica din Moldova*)

The Gagauz Republic 277

came into being as nationalist formation with political ambitions in May 1989. It promoted a reorientation towards Romania, with the objective being a complete merger with the former "mother country". Representatives of national minorities including Gagauzia and Transnistria strongly rejected these suggestions. Debate over the controversial Language Act requiring the Moldovan (Romanian) language to be the country's sole language, as well as proclamations about the overall threat of the Romanianization of Moldova, became a key catalyst in both the Transnistria and Gagauzia conflicts. The language issue also became a central theme at the aforementioned First Congress of Gagauz Nation. In addition to respect for the Moldovan language, both the final declaration and telegrams sent to the Congress of People's Deputies of the USSR formally requested that the Gagauz language be institutionalized (Kendigelyan 2009, 34–40); further, a request that Gagauzia be declared autonomous within the Moldavian SSR was sent to the Supreme Soviet of the USSR and to the leadership of the Communist Party of Moldova (Ana Sözü 1989).

The final text of the Language Act noted above introduced Romanian/Moldovan as the sole official language, with Russian to be used as the language of interethnic communication; Gagauz was to be given the status of a protected language to be developed within the Moldavian SSR (Law of the Republic of Moldova on the Functioning of the Languages Spoken in the Moldovan Soviet Socialist Republic). The predictable outcome from Gagauz representatives was the unilateral declaration of the Gagauz Autonomous Soviet Socialist Republic (ASSR) within the Moldavian SSR at the Second Extraordinary Congress of the Gagauz Nation on 12 November 1989.

The language issue thus gave a significant push to efforts for autonomy and, later, to movements that promoted the autonomy and independence of Gagauzia. The ethnic and linguistic nationalism present within Moldova, generated a reactive process. Efforts to revive the Gagauz language and culture transformed into a political movement under advancing Romanianization. In contradiction to Kolstø's argument (2006, 730), state-building in Gagauzia followed very soon after nation-building, not in reaction to the armed conflict which was still two years away.

Formation of the Gagauz Republic

In February and March of 1990, in a tumult of demonstrations and meetings, local elections took place. The movement's representatives also received mandates to the Supreme Soviet of the Moldavian SSR. These newly elected deputies faced discord at the national level from the nationalist parliament under formation and from the Council of Ministers of the Moldavian SSR. In spite of this, a committee to address the Gagauz issue was successfully created. Unofficially, this committee opted for the creation of Gagauz autonomy as an autonomous territory or an autonomous republic, although at sessions of the Supreme Soviet, information was given on other forms of

278   *Slavomír Horák*

autonomy such as the establishment of cultural and national districts; this was, however, rejected by Gagauz deputies as not amenable to legal codification (Leninskoe slovo 1990).

During the spring of 1990, the concrete points of Gagauz autonomy began to be negotiated. Among key moments in the rise of the Gagauz Republic was a declaration on the sovereignty of the Soviet Socialist Republic of Moldova[1] and denunciation of the conclusions of the Molotov-Ribbentrop Pact on 23 June 1990. In late June and early July 1990, following this decision, the congress of the Moldova National Front declared a programme for the reintegration of Moldova into Romania while respecting the pre-war borders (Kendigelyan 2009, 180–181). Gagauz representatives, however, had refused this step, and – in keeping with their convictions – were forced to adopt this step to forestall what they believed to be a repetition of moves in the direction of Romanianization as had occurred during the interwar period and during the Second World War (Leninskoe slovo 1990; Shornikov 2011, 104–111). Furthermore, according to interpretations of some Gagauz representatives, by this act the Soviet Socialist Republic of Moldova remained outside any legal framework, and, under the new arrangement, Gagauzs had the full right to self-determination (Topal 2013, 67). After unsuccessful attempts to present the Gagauz point of view at the sessions of the Supreme Soviet they finally ceased their activities there (Kendigelyan 2009, 187). The opportunities for dialogue were thus exhausted by the continuously escalating rhetoric emanating from both sides. As a reaction, the Gagauz Temporary Committee led by Stepan Topal was established on December 1989, and in July 1990 the Third Congress of the Gagauz Nation adopted cultural symbols of the Gagauz Autonomous Soviet Socialist Republic (the national anthem, flag, and state seal). Mircea Snegur, the Chairman of the Moldavian Supreme Soviet, vitiated the conclusions of all prior congresses, but Comrat did not accept the decision. Meanwhile, meetings in Comrat to support Gagauz deputies working at the Supreme Soviet of the Soviet Socialist Republic of Moldova voiced their demands in an increasingly confrontational tone (Popozoglo 1990).

As a reaction a Congress of the elected representatives of Gagauzia at all levels, ranging from the village Soviets up to the two People's Deputies of the USSR for Gagauzia (M. K. Pashaly and S. V. Grozdiev) was called by *Gagauz Halky* leaders for the 19th of August 1990. On the eve of the congress, Ilya Karakash, Ukrainian Gagauz and a Doctor of Law from Odessa University and a consultant of the Temporary Committee of the Gagauz Republic, drew up a key document: The Declaration on Freedom and the Independence of the Gagauz People from the Republic of Moldova (Karakash 1990; Kendigelyan 2009, 188–189). After a short period of hesitation, Gagauz leaders accepted the document and presented it on the first day of the session. It declared the Gagauz Republic as a part of the future revived Soviet Union and elections to the Supreme Soviet of the Gagauz Republic were decided to be held on 28th of October 1990 (Kendigelyan

2009, 192). Thus, since August 1990, Gagauzia was as a specific entity within the Soviet Union, whose status remained ambiguous. The Gagauzia delegation, in accordance with the declaration of sovereignty, strove to become one of the parties participating in the preparation of the New Union Treaty.

Moldovan authorities, on the contrary, refused to participate in the preparation of the New Union Treaty and took several measures in order to preserve the territorial integrity of their republic. They suspended mandates of the Gagauz and Transnistrian deputies in the Supreme Soviet of Moldova and officially dissolved *Gagauz Halky* (Sovetskaya Moldaviya 1990). At this time, however, this organ played virtually no role because its functions were transferred to the Temporary Committee. Thus, as of 19 August 1990, Gagauzia and Moldova considered themselves to be under different jurisdictions – Soviet and Moldovan, respectively. This gave rise to the first practical consequences, which continued to worsen the interpretation of the key event on both the Moldovan and Gagauz sides. The Temporary Committee of the Gagauz Republic, for instance, refused to accept an investigative group which was sent from Chisinau to look into events of the 19th of August because its acceptance would have meant acknowledging the sovereignty of the Moldovan Republic over Gagauzia.

The critical moment in the life of the newly formed entity, however, came with the elections to the Supreme Soviet of the Gagauz Republic announced by the Temporary Committee for the 28th of October 1990. The elections unfolded in a tense atmosphere, in which the Moldovan government attempted to resolve the conflict with Gagauzia by force and sent volunteer troops to the south. This was probably the closest moment to an open armed conflict between Chisinau and Comrat (Marunevich 2003, 156–157) as Moldovan volunteers, police, and Moldovan Ministry of the Interior troops stood against Gagauz volunteers who received support from the Bolgrad division, a Soviet army unit stationed in the Ukrainian SSR, just south of Gagauzia. In Transnistria, volunteer troops had been rapidly formed under the command of Igor Smirnov, the Transnistrian leader. Several clashes took place from the 26th to 30th of October 1990, resulting in damage to a number of cars caused by shooting on both sides, as well as the death of several people in the gunfire. Further bloodshed was averted because of the interplay between several factors.

The Temporary Committee of Gagauzia shifted the Election Day forward by two days, ensuring that polling stations were already open by midnight of the 25/26th of October. According to a number of testimonials and official results, most people cast their votes before the morning of the 26th October (Kretsu 2008). The elections were concluded by the evening of the 26th of October. Although the legitimacy of the election might be open to question, Gagauz representatives considered it successfully accomplished.[2] Moldovan leaders were caught off guard by the fact that Gagauz volunteers put up any resistance at all, the more so given that they were armed. This moment was probably decisive in convincing the ranks of Moldovan volunteers not to

280   *Slavomír Horák*

move *en masse* towards Gagauz cities. The involvement of the Bolgrad division as well as Transnistrian volunteers advancing forward also forced the Moldovans to abandon their original position to pacify Gagauzia by force.

Meanwhile, key representatives of the Gagauz nation, continued to think of Gagauzia as autonomous or as some other form of national-territorial unit within Moldova, and would keep doing so as long as the Chisinau government remained willing to negotiate Gagauzia's – and therefore Transnistria's – future status within the Soviet Socialist Republic of Moldova (Shastalov 1990; Topal 1990). For the same reason, the formation of governmental bodies of the future de facto state was suspended and the Supreme Soviet of the Gagauz Republic thus remained the chief executive authority. Laws and regulations of the Soviet Socialist Republic of Moldova continued to go through Gagauzia's Supreme Soviet, and most were adopted as part of Gagauz law (Topal 2013, 98). In this phase Gagauzia, on the one hand, operated formally as a distinct and potentially independent entity but, on the other hand, mostly subordinated itself to the parent state.

A substantial split with the parent state occurred only in late 1990 and early 1991, as a result of both internal and external factors. The formation of the Gagauz Republic was confirmed by a declaration of sovereignty adopted on the 8th of December 1990. While the Moldovan SSR legally left the Soviet Union (Moldovan law superseded the Soviet law) and declared its reunification plans with Romania, the Gagauzs continued to consider themselves as a part of the Soviet Union. A decree issued by Soviet President Gorbachev entitled "On Measures to Normalize the Situation in the Soviet Socialist Republic of Moldova", dated 22nd of December 1990, highlighted a re-evaluation of some regulations and laws by the Supreme Soviet of the Soviet Socialist Republic of Moldova (particularly the act on language, regulation on the conclusions arrived at by the Supreme Soviet Committee concerning the Gagauz issue, as well as a regulation on interpreting the Molotov-Ribbentrop Pact). The Decree also demanded that all legal norms adopted after August 1990 should be abolished. This placed the Supreme Soviet of the Gagauz Republic and all its subsequent decisions outside the law (Ukaz prezidenta 1990). Contrary to its intention, Gorbachev's act of external interference led to a new split between the two parties and once again stirred up a spiral of mutual accusations. The Supreme Soviet of the Gagauz Republic declared the further establishment of Gagauz state organs regardless of Moscow's opinion (Topal 1991a).

Within Gagauzia's elite, however, discrepancies arose between several groups of representatives. Although leading representatives of *Gagauz Halky* held a principal influence, some of its representatives began to distance themselves. At the regional level an ever-widening split occurred between Comrat and other regional centres, particularly Ceadir-Lunga. There, in October 1991, a power crisis flared up that almost led to the disintegration of the regional Soviet (Komratskie vesti 1991). Furthermore, Ceadir-Lunga representatives refused to take part in preparing the Gagauz budget creating the principal internal split within Gagauzia (Topal 2013, 113–115). This was also related to the issue of the Gagauz-Bulgarian relationship, which was initially based on collaboration (the possible formation of a Gagauz-Bulgarian Republic had been under consideration), but began to fall apart in 1991 when a number of Bulgarian representatives – very likely under the influence of Chisinau – became anxious about Gagauz nationalism (Zabarah 2012, 185). The split between these two key nationalities in the south of Moldova substantially reduced regional unity towards Chisinau.

The August 1991 coup attempt in Moscow and the subsequent declaration of an independent Republic of Moldova (27 August 1991) further complicated the relationship between Moldova and Gagauzia. In an effort to eliminate the locus of instability, Moldovan authorities took into custody the leading Gagauz representatives, as well as Stepan Topal and Mikhail Kendigelyan, representatives to the Moldovan Parliament. After several weeks of protests, the leaders of the Gagauz Republic were released (Topal 2013, 128–134). This action reunited the main forces within Gagauz society and politics. The elections for President of Gagauzia and a referendum on the independence of the Gagauz Republic were announced for the 1st of December 1991. In the first reading, the Constitution of the Gagauz Republic was also discussed (Shastalov 1991c). The elections turned out as expected; 95.4% of votes were for Gagauz independence with a turnout of 85.1%. As expected, Stepan Topal, the sole candidate, was elected President with 96.8% of the vote (Dunaev 1991). Despite his election and the approval of the independence of the Gagauz Republic, in December 1991 the Supreme Soviet of the Gagauz Republic still continued attempts to compromise with the Moldovan central government; it also issued a declaration on a potential federal arrangement with the Republic of Moldova.

Gagauzia's domestic politics in 1989–1991 were characterized by deepening independence, the creation of de facto institutions including an attempt to subjugate the police force under the control of the Ministry of Interior of the Soviet Social Republic of Moldova and, later, the Republic of Moldova (Komratskie vesti 1991). The process continued until 1993 when it came to a halt with the adoption of a decision by Gagauzia's Supreme Soviet (Komratskie vesti 1993a). The existence of an independent military force called *Budjak* met with – both theoretically and in practice – one condition for a sustainable state: being able to control its own territory (Kolstø and Blakkisrud 2008, 484–485).

The ever-widening gap between Chisinau and Comrat and the impact of radical elements on both sides, which required the maximum response from the other party, erected a barrier that stood in the way of talks. On the other hand, Gagauzia's political leaders were very much aware of the difficulty in sustaining the Gagauz Republic itself if the Soviet Union was not to continue in existence. These efforts at constant contact with Chisinau paradoxically led to the weakening of the Gagauz de facto state. As Richards and Smith (2015, 1717–1721) highlight, the state-building process of a de

282 *Slavomír Horák*

facto state which is nevertheless headed towards independence is, in many respects, more successful than when the effort is made to maintain contact with the parent state. This is clearly visible in the difference between Transnistria, whose leadership was evidently embarked on a path of independent existence, and Gagauzia, whose leadership never lost contact with the parent state, despite any differences between them.

At the end of the existence of the Soviet Union, Gagauzia found itself pressed in from two sides. First, they were unable to gain recognition for the Gagauzia issue at the level of the Soviet central government. It forced Gagauzia to maintain its relationship with Chisinau. Second, the Moldovan leadership, too, did not react to Gagauzia's demands for greater autonomy in the south of the republic. Moldovan leaders, particularly Mircea Snegur and Mircea Druc, tried to use force – marches of volunteers to Comrat or the apprehension of Gagauz leaders – and backstage intrigues – the support of the Gagauz-Bulgarian split – to stamp out any incipient Gagauz separatism.

The referendum on the independence of the Gagauz Republic within the reformed Soviet Union was approved on the 1st of December 1991, confirming the intent to create an independent entity, although within a commonwealth of the Soviet Union's successor states in whatever form. The question on the ballot was "Are you in favour of the independence of the Gagauz Republic in the political and economic Union of Sovereign Republics?" But just one week later, when the Belovezh Accords were signed and the Commonwealth of Independent States came into being, that question became pointless.

Thus, from late 1991 and early 1992, the Gagauz Republic can be considered as a de facto state, or at least a borderline case, because some of the attributes of de facto statehood are questionable. Gagauzia indeed declared independence, controlled territories inhabited by the Gagauz, and existed for about three years – and thus it would fulfil the definition criteria of a de facto state as used in this book. However, none of the above-mentioned criteria were fulfilled completely. First, Gagauzia's primary goal was not independence, but the formation of a separate entity within the reformed Soviet Union. When it became apparent that this was not going to happen, Gagauzia had no other choice than to declare independence. Unlike Nagorno-Karabakh (see Chapter 3.3) or Transnistria, which found themselves in a similar situation, Gagauzia, which lacked the support of a patron state, did not sever its contact with its parent state and managed to avoid an armed conflict. Second, whereas Gagauzia had its own government which controlled territories inhabited by the Gagauz, the republic, in fact, lacked clear territorial delimitation, which is one of the key pre-conditions for sustainable state entity (cf. Kolstø 2006). Third, although Gagauzia as a distinct entity existed for about three years, the very fact that it did not sever relations with Chisinau and was able to negotiate its peaceful reintegration, leads to the question, whether the Comrat government was really de facto

The Gagauz Republic 283

independent of Chisinau, or whether these two governments simply decided to tolerate each other until a mutually acceptable solution had been found.

The following subchapters are devoted to the individual criteria which contributed to the failure of the Gagauzian de facto state and thus to its reintegration into Moldova. They are: (1) internal political disputes leading to the fractionalization of elites, (2) economic deficiencies, and (3) the absence of patron state.

Internal politics as a factor of de facto state's failure

Whereas in Chechnya it was tribalism and ideological fractionalization, which caused the main disputes in Chechnya's internal politics, in Gagauzia, it was a conflict between the central Gagauz leadership in Comrat and the Ceadir-Lunga region led by Dmitriy Kroytor. The Gagauz leadership blamed Kroytor for collaborating with Chisinau behind Comrat's back.[3] Ceadir-Lunga did not join the other regions in drawing up the Gagauz budget and, in the autumn of 1993, the Ceadir-Lunga District Council ceased to respect the authority of the leadership of the Gagauz Republic. In the end, President Topal attempted to abolish the Councils of People's Deputies (Komratskie vesti 1993e), but municipal Soviets in Comrat as well as Ceadir-Lunga rejected this decision (Petku 1993).

In these circumstances, President Topal expressed his readiness to remain in a relationship with Moldova as an autonomous entity (Shastalov 1992b) with support at all levels of the Congress of People's Deputies, and by the Comrat Soviet led by Dobrov. The latter declared an initiative to be called the Gagauzia National-Territorial Formation (Shastalov 1992a). The Gagauz political elite was thus on a course for autonomy within Moldova, amounting to the liquidation of the de facto state.

However, several political parties and movements expressed disagreement with the state's political course agitating for the country's clear sovereignty (Komratskie vesti 1992b). A particular example is the National Revival Party, led by Dmitriy Savastin, the painter and former *Gagauz Halky* leader (Popozoglo 1992b). But none of these parties survived long after their founding. The *Vatan* (Homeland) movement founded in 1994 was the only political party which persisted for an extended period of time (Popozoglo 1994). *Vatan's* program, however, included autonomy as the basis of the Gagauz Constitution and it wound up supporting the moderate Mikhail Kendigelyan, the Chairman of the Gagauz Parliament, in elections for *Bashkan* (the head of the Gagauz autonomy) in 1995.

The epilogue for Gagauzia as a de facto state came with the adoption of the Act on Gagauz Autonomy (*Gagauz Eri*) in December 1994 and in particular with the elections for *Bashkan* of May and June 1995. Four registered candidates participated in the first round, among them the current president, Stepan Topal, and the Chairman of Parliament, Mikhail Kendigelyan. Topal's chances, however, were not promising. He was blamed

284 *Slavomír Horák*

by voters for a failure to address social and economic issues prior to and following the disintegration of the Soviet Union. As such, he seems to have become a symbol of everything unwanted in the Gagauz issue in 1992–1995. Kendigelyan by contrast did not suffer this fate and in addition, was backed by the sole viable regional political party – *Vatan*. Dmitriy Kroytor was also running, and as one would expect dominated "his" region, the town of Ceadir-Lunga and its surroundings (Komratskie vesti 1995a). The first round was won by Georgiy Tabunshchik, who was supported by Chisinau and people tired of Gagauz "independence". As expected, Mikhail Kendigelyan, the most popular of the former *Gagauz Halky* candidates, proceeded to the second round (Komratskie vesti 1995b), but even the threat that someone supported by Chisinau could win the second round in June 1995 was not enough to unite the Gagauz elites (Kendigelyan 2009, 437–438). Voters' frustration with the politics of an independent Gagauzia and massive support from Chisinau meant that Georgiy Tabunshchik dominated the election. Once it was over, the administrative entities of the de facto Gagauzia were dismantled.

Economy as a factor of de facto state's failure

Since the 19th century, the Budjak Steppe has been cultivated, and grains and winemaking have thrived there. In the late 1980s, issues related to Gagauz agriculture came fully to the fore at a time when independence remained difficult to envision. Water, especially potable water, was also in short supply (Marinov 1990). But these shortcomings aside, the feeling was general that Gagauzia provided the rest of Moldova with more than it got in return, and the southern region of Moldova had lacked adequate funding from the central government for a long period of time (Stoikov 1990).

Since sovereignty was declared in 1990, Gagauz leaders had tried to create their own economy, one which could keep production high enough that shops need not contend with an overall lack of goods. Products at subsidized prices were frequently resold to other markets in Moldova, Ukraine, and Belarus at market prices, whence they headed to the black market that thrived throughout the Soviet Union. The Gagauz agrarian region thus lost significant income from its otherwise scarce agricultural products, with profits going into the pockets of speculators. The level of speculation prompted the Supreme Soviet of the Gagauz Republic to reject the initial decision of the Moldovan leadership on introducing food vouchers (Topal 1991b). Meantime, the lack of a functional processing industry meant that most of what was for sale consisted of unprocessed goods such as raw wool, fruits, vegetables, and wine. There were in fact more than 70 manufacturing facilities (co-ops) in existence as of May 1991, but they functioned ineffectively. They were supposed to pay tax into local coffers, but the revenue resulted in tax losses in many local budgets in the hundreds of thousands of Soviet roubles (Shastalov 1991b).

The Gagauz Republic 285

Price liberalization became the central issue after New Year's Day 1992. The Gagauz region was characterized by several phenomena typical for the time: inflation, liberalization of prices, inadequate compensation, and growing unemployment (particularly in village agricultural facilities) that resulted in a decisively lower output for all types of production. It led to multiple price increases in the grocery sector right from the first days of January. The Gagauz leadership, therefore, turned its focus to at least partial compensation for basic product prices (Popozoglo 1992a). The Gagauz president decreed the introduction of differential pricing for products sold on the Gagauz market, as well as products marked for export, in an effort to fill state coffers and allow for at least partial compensation for the price liberalization (Komratskie vesti 1992a). The decree, however, did not have the desired outcome: the distribution of groceries within Gagauzia became unreliable as a result of continued subsidies and fixed pricing, which made products sold at the local market unprofitable. Regulating and subsidizing the prices of basic groceries, up to the half the product manufacturing price, cost the Gagauz government a significant part of its budget (Komratskie vesti 1993d).

Gagauzia's issues with the conversion to market mechanisms in the continuing subsidy pricing policy were exacerbated by the absence of capable economic leaders, and the lack of a unified conceptualization of how the Gagauz economy was to develop. Only the Comrat leadership focussed on such a systematic approach by drawing up a plan for the privatization of state assets, conversion to a market economy, and permitting the existence of private agriculture and businesses. Economic reality, meanwhile, continued to bind Gagauzia to Moldova, since a great majority of the agricultural products grown in the south of the republic ended up in Chisinau, although, as of 1991, agriculture products were successfully exported to other Soviet republics, mostly within the black market (Taushanzhi 1991).

The amount of tax levies was a point of ambiguity. Moldova changed the tax rate for both Gagauz producers and other entities several times during the course of 1991. For instance, this was an issue for the Comrat Wine Making Facility, which counted on keeping 80% of the revenues from its wine sales, but in the middle of the year (i.e. in the middle of the season), the Moldovan government cut its revenues down to 50%. As a result, the Presidium of the Supreme Soviet of the Gagauz Republic decided all wine production was to be directly sold to Russia, Ukraine, and Belarus, maintaining revenues at the 80% level for the winemaking facility, with almost 20% going to the Gagauz Republic (Leninskoe slovo 1991b). In this way, the independence of Gagauzia's economy was supported. Gagauz representatives in Chisinau also pointed out the unfair (i.e. higher) amount of taxes levied for the Moldovan state budget from Gagauzia (Shastalov 1991d). At the same time, the Moldovan budget provided much lower state expenditure for Gagauzia than taxes collected in the region, which particularly affected employees involved in budgeting – in 1993, the amount concerned was 1.138 billion roubles (Kelesh 1994).

286   Slavomír Horák

The growing tax barriers between Moldova and other countries of the former Soviet Union prevented traditional exports of agricultural products from Gagauzia. The high tax burden turned out to be a substantial obstacle to the development of entrepreneurship and, to a significant extent, taxes were under Chisinau's control (Bovyr 1992; Shastalov 1992).

In 1992, however, a significant drop in the economy and disintegration throughout the Soviet Union particularly hit agricultural production, and this drove a lack of availability for basic products in the Gagauz market-place. Furthermore, regional production was exported outside the region to Moldova, Romania, and Ukraine, where it commanded higher prices. The region was in sore need of the basics – coal and gas – supplies of which were resumed – at least partially, on a barter basis – as late as 1993. The tax burden also rose, bankrupting several *kolkhozes* (Shastalov 1992c). As a result, production fell in all key indicators: industry by 30% and agriculture by 39% (Komratskie vesti 1993b).

One of the first matters to be dealt with in forming an independent Gagauz economy was the creation of a central bank. As elsewhere in the Soviet Union, a branch of Sberank operated in Comrat. Thanks to help received from D. Sarov, a financial advisor, Oguz Bank was successfully opened, and within six months many industrial and agricultural facilities made transfers to the new bank, in spite of the highly negative reaction of Chisinau. An act in May 1991 adopted a budgeting system for the Gagauz Republic and adapted the Soviet Union's banking system for the Gagauz economy (Shastalov 1991a). Having been rejected by the Moldovan Republic, Gagauzia intended to pay money into the Union stabilization fund independently, but the act never took effect and, with the disintegration of the Soviet Union in late 1991, the issue in any event became moot. After Stepan Topal and Mikhail Kendigelyan were taken into custody after August 1991, the Moldovan central government ordered the bank to be closed. Sarov hid in Moscow to avoid arrest (Topal 2013, 112–113). Only after Topal and Kendigelyan's release were the Oguz Bank's operations reinstated, but this time it had to compete on the newly established banking market in independent Moldova. In 1992–1993, new banks such as Gagauzekonombank appeared on the market.

In addition to forming an independent bank, the issue arose as to whether the Gagauz Republic's budget was to be based upon the above noted act of May 1991 on the republic's budgeting system. In autumn of that year, the budget was negotiated by deputies from the Comrat and Ceadir-Lunga districts. At that time, the economic situation in Gagauzia had stabilized to a certain extent, and there was a shorter delay in the payment of wages than in Moldova (Topal 2013, 113). The centre in Chisinau, however, exerted pressure on the Ceadir-Lunga district leadership in which members of the Bulgarian minority played a significant role, along with a group around the chairman of the regional committee, Dmitriy Kroytor. Subsequently, the Ceadir-Lunga region gave up on the idea of a joint Gagauz budget.

The absence of a joint budget for the Gagauz regions was a significant obstacle to any integration of Gagauz territory. Economically, close ties were maintained with Moldova and, due to the customs policies of neighbouring countries, even further deepened. Political proclamations aside, the development of an independent Gagauz state was chiefly rendered impossible because of economic circumstances. Politically, Gagauzia might indeed have become independent of Moldova, but their economic ties would have deepened further.

A truly territory-wide budget within the republic came into being only in 1993 and 1994. However, at the end of the fiscal year 1993, the leadership of Ceadir-Lunga decided its contributions to the Gagauz budget would be cancelled and levies to the Moldovan budget renewed, along with the creation of a regional budget (Kelesh 1994). The new Gagauz budget for 1994 was approved only after long negotiations in which the amount of levies for the Moldovan and Gagauz budgets from Ceadir-Lunga district were set (Komratskie vesti 1994).

In addition to the disagreement inside Gagauzia, the adoption of the Moldovan Lei in 1993 further attached the Gagauz economy to Moldova. Although the leadership of the Gagauz Republic was initially interested in staying in the rouble zone (Kendigelyan 2009, 380), it was forced to accommodate the situation at hand and create a Leu-based budget.

The Gagauz economy proved to be incapable of developing independently of Moldova. Gagauzia, unlike Nagorno-Karabakh, Transnistria, or Abkhazia, had experienced no armed conflict prior to its birth and the politics of independence outranked economic issues there (Lynch 2004, 63–64). In general, living conditions in Gagauzia were worse compared to the parent state. It also could not take advantage of its geographic location for transit trading, as South Ossetia was able to do, until 2008 (Broers 2015, 278–280). In addition to the regional rivalry, the absence of a joint budget within the republic, separate from Chisinau, played a key role in the failure of the independent Gagauz state (Sato 2009, 156).

Absence of a patron state as a factor of de facto state's failure

Initially, the Gagauz search for allies outside of the Republic of Moldova resulted in the collaboration with other Soviet republics as well as Soviet centre. Several Gagauz delegations left for Moscow to negotiate the status of the Gagauz Republic as an autonomous part of the Moldavian Soviet Socialist Republic. In February 1989, the Gagauz delegation was received by the Central Committee of the Communist Party of the Soviet Union at the Presidium of the Supreme Soviet (Bulgar 2006, 165). A Committee for the Gagauz Issue was created under the Supreme Soviet. At the Conference of People's Deputies, Gagauz representatives were supported by Deputy Gennadii Anufriev. During the conference, in addition to the creation of contacts inside the central government of the Soviet Union, meetings with

288   *Slavomír Horák*

other republics took place, among them the Baltic countries (Kendigelyan 2009, 44). Despite this minor progress, decisive people in Moscow did not favour any attempt of Gagauz separatism from Moldova and their support remained rhetorical only. Although the idea of a Gagauz SSR within the USSR was also positively received at the Congress of the USSR Autonomous Republics in Moscow (Kalchu 1990), on the level of the USSR Central Committee and the USSR People's Deputy Congress, Gagauzia's demands received no support as requirements of other small nations similar to the Gagauzs could escalate already existing ethnic tensions within all of the USSR. The declaration of a sovereign Gagauz Republic in August 1990 first resulted in expanded contacts with other Soviet Republics, especially the neighbouring Ukrainian Soviet Socialist Republic. During the time of greatest tension between the Gagauz Republic and the Moldovan Republic, Odessa and Kiev became the first destinations for Gagauz politicians in their attempt to find an external help. There, Gagauz representatives were received by the Supreme Soviet of the Ukrainian Soviet Socialist Republic and their requests were met (Marunevich 2003, 154–155); however, the practical results of these visits remained invisible.

With the disintegration of the Soviet Union and the creation of the de facto Gagauz state, the key foreign-policy vectors for the new republic were Russia and Turkey. Russia is considered to have been a significant player particularly around the time the Gagauz Republic was established. The intervention of the so-called Bolgrad Division in October 1990 in Comrat, along with the creation of a peacemaking mission in Transnistria, where Russia played a major role, is considered a significant factor in the maintenance of Gagauz statehood. However, at the time of the de facto Gagauz state in 1991–1994, Russia served particularly as its business partner and a market for Gagauz agricultural products, albeit with no preferential treatment *vis-a-vis* Moldovan farmers. In contrast to Russia's political and military engagement in Transnistria, in the 1990s, Gagauzia could no longer rely on direct military or financial support from Russia. Russia thus served as a cultural model and commercial partner rather than the patron state. In that capacity, Russia's role was more rhetorical or psychological and contributed to a significant pro-Russian position of the Gagauz people (Okunev et al. 2016).

Turkey – specifically the President of Turkey Süleyman Demirel – began to show interest in Gagauzia in the early 1990s. Demirel visited Comrat in 1994 and his personal input into the agreement between Comrat and Chisinau is generally considered to have been crucial (Topal 2013, 104–105). In Gagauzia itself, Turkey applied a "soft power" policy, and its input in the development of the economy and culture in the 1990s was invaluable. Turkey was the first country to provide scholarships for Gagauz students. Many Gagauz intellectuals and artists left for Istanbul and other cities in Turkey, and Gagauzs got the opportunity to trade and work in Turkey. The Atatürk Turkish library was opened in Comrat and at present it serves as an important source of information on Gagauzia. In the 1990s, Turkey allocated several grants to fund irrigation systems on the Budjak Steppe, provided potable water for several Gagauz villages, and supported Gagauz and Turkish language courses in Comrat and Ceadir-Lunga. Thanks to support from Turkish foundations, folklore groups from Gagauzia were able to take part in festivals in Turkey. Negotiations on restoring the Ceadir-Lunga airport also took place, with the intention of making it Gagauzia's international airport. The Gagauz administration's ability to take up the offers made was, however, not always in step. The great majority of students remained in Turkey, the irrigation project fund has not been completely spent, and the plans for construction of the airport have never been implemented. At the political level, the Turkish government and Demirel presented Gagauzia as the "bridge between Turkey and Moldova". But this appellation has remained strictly rhetorical to date (Gagauzmedia 2016).

As one might expect, Transnistrian Moldovan Republic (declared independence from Moldova in September 1990), was from the beginning, among the key allies of Gagauzia. In addition to military help in the critical year of 1990, there were frequent exchanges of delegations and the mutual coordination of positions by both entities. Their relationship culminated in 1993 with the ratification of an agreement on friendship and cooperation. The highest Gagauz authorities, including the Congress of Gagauz People's Deputies, however, drew attention to the absence of concrete collaboration based on the agreements adopted (Komratskie vesti 1993c). The Republic of Abkhazia became another de facto state with which the Gagauz leadership contractually formalized relations within the agreement of friendship and cooperation (Komratskie vesti 1993a).

In sum, no patron state stood behind Gagauzia's implementation of its independent foreign policy as the source of external support (Caspersen 2009, 58). The country received real political and, when necessary, military support only from the Transnistrian Republic (itself fighting for international recognition) and some units of the Soviet army. Turkey was engaged in the legitimization of Gagauzia, but only on the autonomy level, and it did not support the formation of an independent state. Nor could Gagauzia rely on an influential diaspora, which would have been helpful for both the domestic economy and for gathering contacts abroad as in the case of Nagorno-Karabakh (Caspersen 2012, 59).

Conclusion

From the outset, then, Gagauz independence was tentative: although the Gagauz leadership created its own administrative entities and state structures (or repurposed existing Moldovan or Soviet structures), the Gagauzs did not rush headlong into a completely independent existence. As early as spring 1992, calls began to be heard to exchange the label "republic" for a term referring to a lower political status (Shastalov 1992d). Instead of

290 *Slavomír Horák*

talking outright independence, the Gagauz leadership widened its focus to explore what form Gagauzia's status should take. This situation in fact led to the self-dissolution of a de facto independent entity and return back to the parent state as an autonomous unit. This is a unique case not only in the post-Soviet area but also in the whole history of de facto states.

The internal disputes that took place after 1992 and a worsening economy led to a deepening lack of confidence in Gagauzia. Culpability was attributed to the Gagauz government, headed by Stepan Topal. The election of Georgiy Tabunshchik as *Bashkan* for Gagauz autonomy in 1995 was the epilogue for the period of the country's de facto independence. Considered a "Chisinau man", he won the elections convincingly, leaving behind Stepan Topal and Mikhail Kendigelyan, the two key actors in the fight for independence.

The analysis of the building of the de facto state in Gagauzia in 1991–1994 (or 1995) shows that in none of the areas examined – internal policy, economics, or foreign policy – was the independent Gagauz de facto state viable. Looking at internal political developments in the early 1990s, Gagauzia successfully created its own political institutions, which were to a great extent independent of the parent state, and did so even during the negotiations for Gagauz's autonomous status within Moldova. However, despite significant efforts at nation-building processes, internal policies failed to unite the country's elites at the national level when it came to the common project of de facto statehood. Under such circumstances, the government headed by Stepan Topal had but one path to at least partially safeguard Gagauz statehood: autonomy within Moldova. This attitude has become the basis of Gagauzia's relationship with the parent state since 1992.

The economy is probably the best indicator that Gagauzia could not have been sustained as a de facto state. Broers (2015) points out that the economic viability of other de facto states within the post-Soviet area does not necessarily differ from that of Gagauzia in the 1990s. Compared to other de facto states in the region, Gagauzia lacked a proper patron that would eventually support its weak and dysfunctional economy. The featured patron states – Russia or Turkey – were not willing to provide partial financial subsidies (typical for Transnistria and also Abkhazia) or even turn the economy of the de facto state into a totally rentier form, as in the case of the de facto independent South Ossetia after 2008 (see the Chapter 3.2). Gagauzia, however, lacked a strong enough external patron or sponsor to protect its own economic existence. The Gagauz leadership, too, lacked the courage to cut economic ties with Moldova and to introduce (unlike Transnistria) its own currency, or accept a currency different from that of the parent (as did Abkhazia, Nagorno-Karabakh and later South Ossetia or Luhansk and Donetsk People's Republics). Furthermore, the discrepancies among the individual Gagauz regions noted above undermined a common internal economy.

When the Soviet Union ceased to exist, Gagauzia, like other post-Soviet de facto states, sought international recognition. However, the foreign-policy

The Gagauz Republic 291

component of the Gagauz Republic suffered because there was no obvious and strong ally backing its independence. None of Gagauzia's key allies of the time – newly independent Russia, Ukraine, or ethnically allied Turkey – may be considered to have been a patron state in the true sense of the word (Caspersen 2009). Selective support from Turkey did play an important role in some areas of Gagauzia's development both economically and socially, but not when it came to political development. Selective contacts with other de facto states in the post-Soviet space (particularly Transnistria or partly Abkhazia) were not enough to maintain its de facto statehood.

Gagauzia of 1991–1994 is a borderline case of a de facto state (cf. Caspersen 2012, 13). The final form of the Gagauz political entity – Autonomous Territorial Unit of Gagauzia (*Avtonom Territorial Bölümlüü Gagauziya*) – is less than what the Gagauz elite hoped for, but taking into account the context in which the Gagauz Republic functioned, autonomy was probably the point of greatest viability of Gagauz statehood. After all, in the early phase of the attempt to gain independence from Moldova, Gagauz aimed not at the creation of an independent state, but a republic within the Soviet Union.

Notes

1 In June 1990 the official name of the entity changed from the Moldavian SSR to the Soviet Socialist Republic of Moldova. It remained in use until 23 May 1991. From that day until the declaration of independence on 27 August 1991, it was renamed the Republic of Moldova whilst remaining a constituent republic of the USSR.
2 Interview with a high-ranking Gagauz politician, Comrat, Moldova, November 2015.
3 Interview with a high-ranking Gagauz politician, Comrat, Moldova, November 2015.

Literature

Ana Sözü. 1989. Halkymyzyn birinji syezdi [The First Congress of Our Nation]. *Ana Sözü*, June 4.
Angeli, Fedor A. 2006. *Gagauzskaya avtonomiya. Lyudi i fakty (1989–2005 gg.)* [Gagauzian Autonomy: People and Facts (1989–2005)]. Chisinau: Universul.
Angeli, Fedor A. 2007. *Ocherki Istorii Gagauzov, potomkov Oguzov (seredina VIII – nachalo XXI vv.)* [Essays on the History of the Gagauz – Descendants of the Oguz (the Middle of the VIII – Beginning of the XXI Centuries)]. Chisinau: Tip. Centrala.
Batt, Judy. 1997. "Federalism versus Nationalism in Post-communist State-building: The Case of Moldova." *Regional & Federal Studies* 7 (3): 25–48.
Bovyr, Yurii. 1992. "Udruchenie nalogami [Oppressing by the Taxes]." *Komratskie vesti*, April 2.
Broers, Laurence. 2015. Resourcing De Facto Jurisdictions: A Theoretical Perspective on Cases in the South Caucasus. *Caucasus Survey* 3 (3): 269–290.
Bulgar, Stepan. 2006. "Narodnoe dvizhenie 'Gagauz Khalky' (1989–1994 gg.) [National Movement 'Gagauz Khalky' (1989–1994)]." *Rusin* 2 (4): 163–173.

292   Slavomír Horák

Caspersen, Nina. 2009. "Playing the Recognition Game: External Actors and De Facto States." *The International Spectator* 44 (4): 47–60.

Caspersen, Nina. 2012. *Unrecognized States.* Cambridge and Malden: Polity Press.

Chinn, Jeff, and Steven D. Roper. 1998. "Territorial Autonomy in Gagauzia." *Nationalities Papers* 26 (1): 87–101.

Dobrov, Leonid. 2007. *Pamyatnik Gagauz Yeri ili KGB protiv SSSR* [Monument of Gagauz Eri or the KGB against the USSR]. Komrat, 2007.

Dunaev, A. 1991. "Vesti iz izbiratelnykh uchastkov [News from Polling Stations]." *Komratskie vesti*, December 3.

Gagauzmedia. 2016. "Gagauziya – Most druzhby mezhdu narodami Moldovy i Turtsii [Gagauzia – Bridge of Friendship between the Nations of Moldova and Turkey]." *Gagauzmedia*, August 23. http://gagauzmedia.md/index.php?newsid=8194.

Guboglo, Mikhail N. (ed.) 2012. *Gagauzy v mire i mir gagauzov. Tom 1* [Gagauzs in the World and the World of Gagauzs. Volume 1]. Comrat: Tsentr po izucheniyu mezhetnicheskikh otnoshenii.

Guboglo, Mikhail N., and Ekaterina N. Kvilinkova. 2011. *Gagauzy* [Gagauzs]. Moscow: Nauka.

Kalchu, G. 1990. "Rezolyutsiya 1-ogo syezda predstavitelei avtonomnykh obrazovanii Soyuza SSR 'O priznanii Gagauzskoi respubliki' [Resolution of the First Congress of Representatives of Autonomous Units of the USSR 'On Recognition of the Gagauz Republic]." *Leninskoe slovo*, September 25.

Karakash, Ilia. 1990. "Realnye perspektivy resheniya gagauzskogo voprosa [Real Perspectives of the Solution of the Gagauz Question]." *Leninskoe slovo*, April 19.

Kelesh, F. 1994. "O gagauzskom byudzhete [On Gagauz Budget]." *Komratskie vesti*, January 29.

Kendigelyan, Mikhail V. 2009. *Gagauzskaya respublika. Borba gagauzov za natsionalnoe samoopredelenie. 1989–1995. Vospominaniya. Dokumenty* [The Gagauz Republic. A Fight of Gagauzs for National Self-Determination. Memories. Documents]. Comrat: Tsentr nauchnykh issledovanii i uchebno metodicheskoi raboty pri glavnom upravlenii obrazovaniya ATO Gagauziya.

King, Charles. 1997. Minorities Policy in the Post-Soviet Republics: The Case of the Gagauzi. *Ethnic a Racial Studies* 20 (4): 738–756.

Kolstø, Pål. 2006. The Sustainability and Future of Unrecognized Quasi-states. *Journal of Peace Research* 43 (6): 723–740.

Kolstø, Pål, and Helge Blakkisrud. 2008. Living with Non-recognition: State- and Nation-building in South Caucasian Quasi-states. *Europe-Asia Studies* 60 (3): 483–509.

Komratskie vesti. 1991. "Iz potoka novostei [From the News Feed]." *Komratskie vesti*, October 19.

Komratskie vesti. 1992a "Izdany ukazy [Decrees Issued]." *Komratskie vesti*, January 28.

Komratskie vesti. 1992b. "Zayavlenie Gagauzskoi narodnoi partii [Statement of the Gagauz National Party]." *Komratskie vesti*, November 21.

Komratskie vesti. 1993a. "Iz potoka novostei [From the News Feed]." *Komratskie vesti*, January 13.

Komratskie vesti. 1993b. "Kak srabotali v 1992 g [How Did We Work in 1992]." *Komratskie vesti*, March 20.

Komratskie vesti. 1993c. "Postanovlenie VII syezda narodnykh deputatov vsekh urovnei Gagauzii [Statement of the 7th Congress of National Deputies of Gagauzia at All Levels]." *Komratskie vesti*, June 12.

The Gagauz Republic 293

Komratskie vesti. 1993d. "Zhizn vse dorozhaet [Life is More Expensive]." 1993. *Komratskie vesti*, August 17.

Komratskie vesti. 1993e. "Iz potoka novostei [From the News Feed]." *Komratskie vesti*, November 20.

Komratskie vesti. 1995a. "Komrat stal stolitsei Gagauzii, no my eshche ne izbrali bashkana [Comrat Became the Capital of Gagauzia, But We Have Not Yet Elected Bashkan]." *Komratskie vesti*, June 3.

Komratskie vesti. 1995b. "Itogi golosovaniya v Gagauzii 28 maya 1995 goda [Results of Voting in Gagauzia May 28 1995]." *Komratskie vesti*, June 10.

Kosienkowski, Marcin. 2017a. "The Gagauz Republic: Internal Dynamics of De Facto Statehood." *Annales Universitatis Mariae Curie-Skłodowska. Section K: Politologia* 24 (1), 115–133.

Kosienkowski, Marcin. 2017b. "The Gagauz Republic: An Autonomism-Driven De Facto State." *The Soviet and Post-Soviet Review* 44 (3): 292–313.

Kretsu, V. 2008. "K nyneshnei avtonomii my prishli cherez Gagauzskuyu respubliku [The Way to Our Present Autonomy Led through the Gagauz Republic]." *Vesti Gagauzii*, December 5.

Leninskoe slovo. 1990. Fragmenty vystuplenii na sessii Verkhovnogo Soveta MSSR deputatov ot gagauzskogo naroda [Fragments of Speeches of the Gagauzian Deputies at the Session of the Supreme Soviet of the Moldavian SSR]." *Leninskoe slovo*, April 26.

Leninskoe slovo. 1991a. "Deklaratsiya chrezvychainogo syezda predstavitelei gagauzskogo naroda Gagauzskoi Avtonomnoi Sovetskoi Sotsialisticheskoi Respubliki v sostave Moldavskoi Sovetskoi Sotsialisticheskoi Respubliki [Declaration of the Emergency Congress of the Representatives of the Gagauz Nation of the Gagauz Autonomous SSR within the Moldavian SSR]." 1990. *Leninskoe slovo*. June 21.

Leninskoe slovo. 1991b. "Iz ofitsialnykh istochnikov [From Official Sources]." *Leninskoe slovo*, July 23.

Lynch, Dov. 2004. *Engaging Eurasia's Separatist States: Unresolved Conflicts and De Facto States*. Washington: United States Institute of Peace Press.

Marinov, D., 1990. "Avtonomiya – nashe pravoe delo [Autonomy – Our Right Thing]." *Leninskoe slovo*, July 21.

Marunevich, Mariya V. 1993. *Pravda o gagauzskom narode kak o samobytnom etnose i ego etnicheskoi territorii* [The True about the Gagauz Nation as a Distinct Ethnos and about Its Ethnic Territory]. Comrat: Aidynnyk.

Marunevich, Mariya V. 2003. *Istoriya gagauzskogo naroda (uchebnoe posobie)* [History of the Gagauz Nation (Study Materials)]. Comrat: Tsentr nauchnykh issledovanii i uchebno-metodicheskikh rabot Gagauzii.

Okunev, Igor, et al. 2016. "Geopoliticheskie kody postsovetskikh etnonatsionalnykh soobshchestv na primere gagauzov i bolgar v Moldavii [Geopolitical Codes of Post-Soviet Ethnonational Communities on the Examples of Gagauzs and Bulgarians in Moldova]." *Mezhdunarodnyie protsessy* 14 (1): 156–171.

Petku, V. 1993. "Napryazhenie ne spadaet [Tension is Not Going to Ease]." *Komratskie vesti*, February 5.

Popozoglo, D. 1990. "Skvoz gorech i obidu. Reportazh s mitinga v Komrate [Through Bitterness and Insult. A Report from Meeting in Comrat]." *Leninskoe slovo*, August 2.

Popozoglo, D. 1992a. "Novye tseny, novye problemy [New Prices, New Problems]." *Komratskie vesti*, January 18.

294 Slavomír Horák

Popozoglo, D. 1992b. "Rodilas novaya partiya [New Party Emerged]." *Komratsiie vesti*, October 17.

Popozoglo, D. 1994. "Prizrak 'Gagauz Khalky' brodit po Budzhaku [The Ghost of the 'Gagauz Halky' Roams in Budjak]." *Komratskie vesti*. July 23.

Protsyk, Oleh, and Valentina Rigamonti. 2007. "Real and 'Virtual' Elements of Power Sharing in the Post-Soviet Space: The Case of the Gagauz Autonomy." *Journal on Ethnopolitics and Minority Issues in Europe* 6 (1): 1–22.

Radova (Karantas), O. K. 2015. "Rol Gagauzskoi Avtonomii v sovremennoi Moldove [The Role of the Gagauz Autonomy in Contemporary Moldova]." In: *20 let ATO Gagauziia. Proshloe. Nastoyashchee. Budushchee* [20 Years of the Autonomous Territorial Unit Gagauzia. Past. Present. Future], edited by Petr M. Pašaly, 166–174. Comrat: Nauchno-issledovatelskii tsentr Gagauzii im. M. V. Marunevich.

Richards, Rebecca, and Smith, Robert. 2015. "Playing in the Sandbox: State Building in the Space of Non-recognition." *Third World Quarterly* 36 (9): 1717–1735.

Sato, Keiji. 2009. Mobilization of Non-titular Ethnicities during the Last Years of the Soviet Union: Gagauzia, Transnistria, and the Lithuanian Poles. *Acta Slavica Iaponica* 26: 141–157.

Shastalov, S. 1990. "Na sessii Verkhovnogo Soveta GR [In the Session of the Supreme Soviet of the Gagauz Republic]." *Leninskoe slovo*, November 24, 1.

Shastalov, S. 1991a. "Informatsionnye zametki s sessii Verkhovnogo Soveta GR [Information Notes from the Session of the Supreme Soviet of the Gagauz Republic]." *Leninskoe slovo*, May 25.

Shastalov, S. 1991b. "Sessiya raisoveta narodnykh deputatov [Session of the District Soviet of National Deputies]." *Leninskoe slovo*, June 4.

Shastalov, S. 1991c. "Ofitsialnaya khronika 1991 [Official Chronicle of 1991]." *Komratskie vesti*, November 5.

Shastalov, S. 1991d. "Zasedanie Vremennogo komiteta GR [Session of the Temporary Committee of the Gagauz Republic]." *Leninskoe slovo*, January 15.

Shastalov, S. 1992a. "Khvatit konfrontatsii, pora sest za stol peregovorov [Enough Confrontation, It is Time to Sit at the Negotiation Table]." *Komratskie vesti*, March 21.

Shastalov, S. 1992b. "Ilyuzii i realii. Intervyu s Prezidentom Gagauzii [Illusions and Realities. Interview with the President of Gagauzia]." *Komratskie vesti*, November 12.

Shastalov, S. 1992c. "Chto delat? Kak stabilizirovat ekonomiku? [What is to be Done? How to Stabilize the Economy?]." *Komratskie vesti*, December 5, 1992.

Shastalov, S. 1992d. "Na predele dopustimogo [On the Limits of Possible]." *Komratskie vesti*, March 7.

Shornikov, P. 2011. "Rumynizatsiya ili deportatsiya? Sudby slavyan i gagauzov v Bessarabii v planakh ofitsialnogo Bukharesta 1941–1944 [Romanianization or Deportation? Fates of Slavs and Gagauzs of Bessarabia in Official Plans of Bucharest 1941–1944]." *Rusin* 7 (4): 96–120.

Socor, Vladimir. 1994. "Gagauz Autonomy in Moldava: A Precedent for Eastern Europe?" *RFE/RL Research Report* 3 (33): 20–28.

Sovetskaya Moldaviya. 1990. "Postanovlenie Verkhovnogo Soveta SSR Moldova ot 27 iyunya 1990 goda 'O materialakh Komissii Prezidiuma Verkhovnogo Soveta SSR Moldova po izucheniyu zaprosov narodnykh deputatov SSSR i drugikh obrashchenii ob obrazovanii avtonomii gagauzskoi narodnosti' [Resolution of the Supreme Soviet of the Moldavian SSR on 27 June 1990 'On Materials of the

The Gagauz Republic 295

Commission of the Presidium of the Supreme Soviet of the Moldavian SSR on Hearing of the Inquires of the National Deputies of the USSR and other Representatives on the Formation of the Gagauz National Autonomy]." *Sovetskaya Moldaviya*, July 28.

Stoikov, I. 1990. "Tak li khorosho zhivut gagauzy [Do Gagauzs live well]?" *Leninskoe slovo*, September 6.

Taushanzhi, Konstantin. 1991. "Mnenie o 'Komratskoi estestvennoi ekonomicheskoi modeli'. Ekonomicheskaya reforma Gagauzii. Proshlo polgoda, chto sdelano? [Opinions on 'Comrat economic model'. Economic Reform of Gagauzia. Half of the Year is Gone, What is Done?]." *Leninskoe slovo*, January 29, 1–4.

Tishkov, Vladimir. 2013. "Ethnic Conflicts in the Former USSR: The Use and Misuse of Typologies and Data." *Journal of Peace Research* 36 (5): 571–591.

Topal, Stepan M. 1990. "Postanovlenie Vremennogo komiteta Gagauzskoi Respubliki 'O sozdanii respublikanskoi patrulno-postovoi sluzhby' [Resolution of the Temporary Committee of the Gagauz Republic 'On Formation of the Republican Patrol Service']." *Leninskoe slovo*, September 8.

Topal, Stepan M. 1991a. "Sessiya Verkhovnogo Soveta Gagauzskoi Respubliki [Session of the Supreme Soviet of the Gagauz Republic]." *Leninskoe slovo*, January 1991.

Topal, Stepan M. 1991b. "O kuponnoi sisteme v Gagauzskoi respublike [On the Coupon System in the Gagauz Republic]." *Leninskoe slovo*, April 11.

Topal, Stepan M. 2013. *Po zovu predkov* [At the Call of Ancestors]. Comrat: Tipografiya "Elena-V.I.".

Ukaz prezidenta... 1990. "Ukaz prezidenta SSSR o merakh po normalizatsii obstanovki v SSR Moldova [Decree of the President of the USSR on Measures to Normalize Situation in the Moldavian SSR]." No. UP-1215, December 22, 1990. Constitutions.ru. http://constitutions.ru/?p=3025.

Zabarah, Dareg A. 2012. "Opportunity Structures and Group Building Processes: An Institutional Analysis of the Secession Processes in Pridnestrovie and Gagauzia between 1989 and 1991." *Communist and Post-Communist Studies* 45 (1): 183–192.

Conclusion

Vincenc Kopeček and Tomáš Hoch

De facto states are not mere anomalies in the Westphalian system of states. On the contrary, they are its relatively permanent part, being produced by the system itself, by the international community, which grants recognition selectively. Instead of recognizing the facticity and viability of the breakaway entity, the international community aims to recognize the legality of the secession – which is often the subject of differing interpretations by major powers.

Whereas the very phenomenon of a de facto state is rather permanent, this is definitely not true for individual de facto states. Although four post-Soviet de facto states (Abkhazia, South Ossetia, Transnistria, and Nagorno-Karabakh) have survived for about a quarter of a century and the Mongolian People's Republic for almost a half century, some of Eurasia's de facto states were quickly re-integrated into their parent states. Thus, it is legitimate to claim that even the most longevous de facto states will either disappear (being re-integrated into their parent state as was the case of Gagauzia and Chechnya, or absorbed by their patron state, as was the case of Tuva) or they will finally gain international recognition (as was the case of Mongolia). De facto states thus emerge, exist for several years or even decades without international recognition (or with a limited recognition), and then disappear or transform. This is what we call the life cycle of de facto states and the logic of emergence, sustainability, and possible demise is the backbone of this whole book.

The fact of non-recognition brings a number of threats to de facto states – the most serious being the fact that their existence is not protected by international law and they have to seek protection from those states which are willing to provide it. Most post-Soviet de facto states in Eurasia are thus closely connected to their patron states, which provide de facto states with security guarantees on a unilateral basis. Naturally, this makes de facto states dependent on their patrons – and not only in the field of security but also of economics and foreign policy – and above all, it is Russia which attempts to use some de facto states as coercive tools against its neighbours. This fact leads many observers to the somewhat far-fetched conclusion that Eurasia's post-Soviet de facto states are mere puppets of their powerful

Conclusion 297

patron. We argue that although the influence of patron states, above all Russia, should not be disregarded, it should also not be overestimated.

On the one hand, most de facto states in Eurasia have been formed with either direct or indirect support from Russia. On the other hand, the very fact of their existence demonstrates a strong inner motivation for secession and for sustaining their de facto independence from their parent state. The key factors that enabled the emergence of de facto states in Eurasia at the beginning of the 1990s were identified as the legal and social chaos created by the disintegration of the USSR, the political and economic weakness of the newly independent states, the ethno-national ambitions of nations in present or former autonomous entities, a shared consciousness of historical grievances, and the patron state's direct or indirect support for separatists. The importance of individual factors, however, differs from case to case.

If the parent state is weak and is facing potential collapse, even a tiny de facto state can separate from a major power without external help (as was the case of the separation of Chechnya from Russia). However, the case of Chechnya also provided evidence that once Russia had recovered from its weakness, without a strong external patron, this de facto state was quickly reintegrated into its parent state. In other cases, however, it would not be possible for de facto states to secede from their parent states without military assistance from their patron state. The best examples were probably the wars over Karabakh, Abkhazia, and South Ossetia. Without Russian assistance Abkhazians and Ossetians would have had no chance against the Georgian army, and without Armenian assistance Karabakh Armenians would not have been able to defeat the Azerbaijani army. The war in the Donbass basically follows the same logic.

Notwithstanding the likely external support, each of the post-Soviet de facto states has had its own rationale for secession and this rationale was not imposed by an external power. Each of the conflicts which led to the emergence of a de facto state has its own internal logic and the external influence or instrumentalization of a de facto state is secondary, although it could have played a major role in the escalation of the conflict. The same is true regarding the sustainability of de facto states. Whereas the support of an external patron is of high importance, without internal legitimacy and support for nation-building, not a single post-Soviet de facto state would be a viable entity in the long run.

This brings us to the question of a de facto state's failure. Unlike de jure states, which can even completely collapse without being erased from the political map of the world, for de facto states internal failure represents the imminent threat of their demise. The cases of Chechnya and Gagauzia (the only two cases of de facto states that ceased to exist in the post-Soviet period) provided comprehensive empirical material; in none of the areas examined (internal policy, economics, and foreign policy) were these two de facto states viable. Internal failures, in both cases, resulted in reintegration into their parent state. The difference was that whereas Chechnya

298 *Vincenc Kopeček and Tomáš Hoch*

underwent a violent reintegration into Russia, Gagauzia was reintegrated into Moldova in a peaceful way. Our study of the historical cases of de facto state-like entities has basically brought similar findings. Internal weakness was one of the main factors which led to the demise of Bukharan statehood in the mid-1920s and Tuvan statehood two decades later. In these cases, however, they were incorporated into their powerful patron, the Soviet Union. Although we approach these cases with caution, and point out that the notion of sovereignty and state recognition in the early 20th century was somewhat different from how we understand these concepts today, the analysis of selected historical cases enables us to draw useful analogies with the present-day situation.

The state authorities in the Donetsk and Luhansk People's Republics, as well as in Transnistria and South Ossetia are failing in successful promotion of a viable independent and internationally recognized state among its population and most of their citizens prefer joining Russia. In these entities, the issue of independence largely overlaps with the idea of unification with Russia. This puzzled reality between independence and unification with a patron state also exists in the case of the Nagorno-Karabakh Republic, where the idea of joining Armenia is still present and is even supported by the new Armenian government. Thus, from all post-Soviet de facto states, it is only Abkhazia, where the narrative of independence is deeply rooted in the public space and the idea of joining the Russian Federation is marginal. We argue that whereas the Donetsk and Luhansk People's Republics, Transnistria, and South Ossetia will either most likely be reintegrated into its parent state or absorbed by their patron state, it is the Nagorno-Karabakh Republic and, above all, Abkhazia, which have a better chance to follow the example of Mongolia and become internationally recognized states. As the example of Mongolia shows us, international recognition can come even after decades of de facto statehood and can be connected with a major shift in the international system. In the case of Mongolia, this major shift was decolonization; Russia, Mongolia's patron state, exchanged the recognition of Mongolia for not blocking the UN membership of newly decolonized countries. The potential recognition of present-day de facto states would also most likely be connected with a major shift in the international system; however, it is beyond the scope of this book to speculate about what exactly this could be.

Index

Abkhazia 86–106, 159–79, 226–41
Abkhazians 89–93
absence of patron state 255–6,
  275–6, 287–9
Aghabeghyan, Artur 232, 234
Aitaira (political party, Abkhazia) 228
Akhalkalaki 114–29
Ajaria 33, 127
Alania and Alans 6, 87
Aliyev, Heydar 33, 125, 212–13
Amtsakhara (political party, Abkhazia)
  228, 233
Ankvab, Alexander 231, 233, 239
Ardzinba, Vladislav 226–8
Armenia-Azerbaijan land swap 212–13
Armenian diaspora and Nagorno-
  Karabakh 109, 119, 209, 213, 215
Armenian-Iranian relations 120–1, 213
Armenian-Turkish relations 120, 177–8,
  209, 213, 216
Armenian Velvet Revolution
  161, 210–12
Armenians in Abkhazia 236–40
Artsakh 6, 111
Association Agreement (with the EU)
  136, 178, 185–6
Azerbaijani-Turkish relations 209, 213
Autonomous republics and regions 31–4,
  82, 113, 116

Babayan, Samvel 227–9
Bagapsh, Sergei 228, 231, 233
Basaev, Shamil 265–70
Beria, Lavrenti 92, 102
Bishkek Protocol 210
Bogd Gegen 64–5, 72
Bukharan Communist Party 46, 51–2

Bukharan Emirate 47–50
Bukharan People's Soviet Republic
  46–60

Caucasian Albania 110–11
Ceadir-Lunga 283–4, 286–7
Chechen Republic of Ichkeria 262–71
civil war and de facto state 253, 255, 258,
  266, 270
civil society in de facto states 21, 114–15,
  229, 231–2, 241
clan politics in de facto states 211–12,
  228, 257–8, 263–5, 267
clientelism in de facto states 226–8, 236,
  238, 241
Cold War period 183–4, 190–1
Collective Security Treaty Organization
  (CSTO) 100, 126, 177, 214
Commonwealth of Independent States
  (CIS) 100, 125–6, 170, 268, 282
constitutions of de facto states 51, 73,
  97, 133, 145–6, 218, 230–2, 235–6,
  238, 281, 283
corruption in de facto states 56, 149,
  188, 225, 230, 236, 253
Crimea 31–5, 142–3

Dashnaks (political party, NKR) 226,
  234–5
de facto state, definition of 11–14, 20,
  27, 50, 81, 137–8, 252
declaration of independence 13, 33, 70,
  116, 142
decolonization and de facto states 11,
  28–9, 46, 298
Deep and Comprehensive Free Trade
  Area (DCFTA) 185, 187–8
Demirchyan, Karen 211, 214

300 Index

democracy in de facto states 17, 163, 228–35, 229, 232–6, 241
Democratic Party of Artsakh 234–5
democratization-for-recognition strategy 17, 163, 228–30, 235
disintegration of the USSR and emergence of de facto states 82–4, 93–9, 113–17, 124–5, 284–8, 297
Donbass 136–49, 186–9
Donetsk People's Republic (DPR) 136–51

East Bukhara 50–1, 58
economy of de facto states 55–6, 148, 162, 191, 194, 215, 256–7, 268–9, 281, 283–7
Elchibey, Abulfaz 125
elections in de facto states 140, 198, 226–35, 238–9, 277–9, 281, 283–4, 290
engagement without recognition 19
ethnicity 2, 147, 257, 276
ethnic cleansing 88, 112, 127, 176, 236
ethnic conflict 121, 127, 168
ethnic minorities in de facto states 237–40, 281–2, 286
Eurasia 5
Eurasian (Economic) Union (EAEU) 162, 185–6
Euro-Atlantic integration 169, 175, 178, 179, 185–8
Euromaidan 136, 143, 186
European Neighbourhood Policy 185

First Russian-Chechen War 100, 270–1
form of government in de facto states 218, 230–1, 235
Formation of de facto states 34, 50–3, 69–72, 81–103, 113–30, 148–9, 277–83
Four-day war (Nagorno-Krabakh) 131, 163, 214, 218, 235–6
Free Motherland Party (*Azat Hayrenik*, NKR) 234–5
FSB (Russian Federal Security Service) 160

Gagauz Halky (political movement, Gagauzia) 276–80
Gagauzia 31–2, 116, 250, 275–91
Gagauz-Turkish relations 288–91
Gali 90, 239
Gamsakhurdia, Zviad 93–7, 100, 113
Georgian civil war 100, 113, 116, 120, 130
Georgian enclaves in South Ossetia 171–2

Georgianization 91, 94
Georgian-Russian relations 99–100, 127, 172, 172–5
Ghukasyan, Arkadi 227, 239, 234
Gorbachev, Mikhail 96, 210

Hakobyan, Movses 214
hybrid political regime in de facto states 185, 230–1, 241

influence of de facto state on patron state 198–200, 210–15
instrumentalization of de facto states 124–7, 168–80
integration to patron state 34, 94–4, 112, 163, 209, 249
international recognition 27–9, 217, 229, 249, 254
internal legitimacy 21, 60, 163, 193, 297
Inner Mongolia 64–5
irredentism 33, 88, 94–5, 109–30, 143, 146, 208–10

Jadids 46–55
Javakheti 33, 109–32
Javakheti Armenians 110–30
Javakhk (organization, Georgia) 115–16

Karabakh clan 211–14, 218
Karabakh Khanate 111, 118, 130
Karabakh Committee 115, 119, 209
Karabakh Movement 114, 119, 128, 163, 206, 208–9
Karabakh war 112, 119, 209, 226–7
Karabakhi Armenians 110–12, 117–22, 161, 210, 236–7
Karabakhization of Armenian history 118, 213
Kendigelyan, Mikhail 281, 283–4, 286
kin-state involvement 128, 161, 164, 208, 218
Khachaturov, Yuri 214
Khajimba, Raul 163, 228, 233–4
Khiva 44
Khojayev, Faizullo 48–9, 52–3, 59–60
Kocharyan, Robert 117, 121, 209–13, 226–7
Kodori 33–4, 98, 160, 237
Kokand 48–9, 53, 58
Kosovo precedent 21, 28–9, 142, 229
Kozak Memorandum 188–9, 198
Kroytor, Dmitryi 283–4, 286
Krunk Committee 115, 117, 226–7
Kvitsiani, Emzar 23, 237
Kyakhta Conference 67–8

Index 301

Lachin 119, 213, 236
Law on Seccession (USSR) 31, 83, 113–16
Little Russia 145, 147, 149
Luhansk People's Republic (LPR) 34, 136–51

Manchuria 28, 63–6, 74–5
Manukyan, Vazgen 119, 214–15
Maskhadov, Aslan 264–8
Mayilyan, Masis 234–5
Medvedev, Dmitrii 176, 178
Megrelians 90, 237–40
military support of de facto states 48, 54–5, 119, 160–1, 169–73, 177–80, 209, 216, 279
Mkrtchyan, Artur 217, 226
Mongolian People's Republic 43–76, 249, 296, 298
Montevideo Convention on the Rights and Duties of States 13, 28
Mountainous Republic of the Northern Caucasus 30, 90
Movement-88 (*Sharzhum-88*, political party, NKR)) 234–5

Nagorno-Karabakh Republic (NKR) 82, 109–32, 208–41
Nagorno-Karabakh Autonomous Region (NKAR) 112–30, 208–9, 236
Nagorno-Karabakh Defence Army 119, 161, 209, 210, 216, 219, 227
Nakhchivan 30, 33, 36, 111, 120, 130, 213
nation-building 2, 17, 50, 71, 149, 192–4, 255, 257, 259
nationalism 82–3, 94, 101, 122, 129, 270, 277, 281
New Russia (Novorossiya), confederation of 137–46, 149
New Russian Governorate 144–5
North Ossetia 6, 89, 95, 97

occupied territories (Nagorno-Karabakh) 236–7
Ohanyan, Seyran 212
opposition in de facto states 53, 227–8, 232–5, 239–41
Outer Mongolia 64–6
Orthodox Church 146
Ossetians 86–9, 95–6, 101–4

Pan-Armenian National Movement 119, 209
Pankisi 33

Parent state 2, 19, 29, 50, 81–2, 121–4, 159, 190–1, 225, 250, 252–9
Pashinyan, Nikol 161, 163, 216–17
passportization 127, 141, 161–2, 173–5
patron-client relations 162, 173, 183–201
patron state 4, 18–19, 47, 50, 53–6, 59–60, 159–64, 208, 225, 249, 256
peacekeeping 98, 105, 152, 168
political parties in de facto states 231–2, 235, 283–4
pseudo-state 11–12
puppet state 4, 13, 30
Putin, Vladimir 143, 173–4, 179

quasi-state 11–12

referenda in de facto states 75, 116, 136, 143, 179, 190, 193, 197, 230, 235, 281–2
refugees 21, 33, 96, 138, 237
reintegration of a de facto state 159, 188–9, 191, 192, 196, 198, 201, 250, 254–6, 274–5, 282–3, 296–8
responsibility to protect (R2P) 175–6
Russian-Georgian War (August 2008) 32, 160, 239
Russian Civil War 44, 60, 67, 69
Russian military bases 120, 124, 126–7, 160, 177–8
Russian world (*russkii mir*) 139, 145–6

Saakashvili, Mikheil 33, 99, 121, 123–4, 172
Sahakyan, Bako 214, 234–6
Samachablo 87
Sargsyan, Vazgen 119, 211
Sargsyan, Serzh 210–18
Second Russian-Chechen War 32, 270–1
self-determination 17, 28, 69, 81, 101
Shahumyan District 112, 116–17, 226
Shevardnadze, Eduard 100, 122–3
Shevchuk, Yevgenii 197–8
Shusha 118
Smirnov, Igor 198, 279
Snegur, Mircea 278, 282
Sochi Agreement 97, 107
South Ossetia 86–106
Soviet constitution and right for secession 31, 83, 116
Stalin 72, 91–2
State Defence Committee (Nagorno-Karabakh) 210, 219, 226–7
state failure and de facto states 252–60, 262–71
Stimson doctrine 28

302 Index

sustainability of de facto states 159–65
Svans 90, 237

Tabunshchik, Georgiy 284, 290
Talibov, Vasif 33
Ter-Petrosyan, Levon 119, 210–11
Territorial integrity 18, 83
titular nationality 93, 113
Toka, Salchak 72–4
Topal, Stepan 278, 281, 283, 286
Transnistria 162, 183–201
Tskhinvali 86, 88, 96
Tuva 63–76
track II diplomacy 229–30

United Abkhazia Party (*Apsny Akzaara*) 233–4

United Nations Observer Mission in Georgia (UNOMIG) 170
Uriankhai 65–9

Vatan (political party, Gagauzia) 283–4
volunteers in secessionist war 119, 129, 144, 209, 279–80, 282

warlordism 33–4, 143, 225–32, 237, 258–9, 265–6, 270

Yanukovych, Viktor 136, 186
Yerkrapah 212, 227
Yesayan, Oleg 212, 226

Zakharchenko, Alexander 139, 145–6
Zangezur 111
Zviadists 126